Sacrifice, Scripture, and Substitution

CHRISTIANITY AND JUDAISM IN ANTIQUITY SERIES

Gregory E. Sterling, Series Editor

Volume 18

The University of Notre Dame Press gratefully acknowledges the generous support of Jack and Joan Conroy of Naples, Florida, in the publication of titles in this series.

Sacrifice, Scripture, and Substitution

Readings in Ancient Judaism and Christianity

edited by

Ann W. Astell *and* Sandor Goodhart

University of Notre Dame Press
Notre Dame, Indiana

Manufactured in the United States of America

Library of Congress Cataloging-in-Publication Data

Sacrifice, scripture, and substitution : readings in ancient Judaism and Christianity /
edited by Ann W. Astell and Sandor Goodhart.
     p.   cm. — (Christianity and Judaism in antiquity)
   "First delivered as papers in June 2002 at Purdue University in connection
with the annual meeting of the Colloquium on Violence and Religion" —
Acknowledgements.
   Includes bibliographical references and index.
   ISBN-13: 978-0-268-02038-5 (pbk. : alk. paper)
   ISBN-10: 0-268-02038-8 (pbk. : alk. paper)
   1. Sacrifice — Biblical teaching — Congresses.   2. Bible — Criticism,
interpretation, etc. — Congresses.   3. Sacrifice — Judaism — Congresses.
4. Sacrifice — Christianity — Congresses.   I. Astell, Ann W.
II. Goodhart, Sandor.   III. Colloquium on Violence and Religion.
Meeting (2002 : Purdue University)
   BS680.S2S23   2011
   203'.4 — dc22
                                                              2011009410

For René Girard and Martha Girard
In remembrance of things past

CONTENTS

ACKNOWLEDGEMENTS

In a letter addressed to "all those who had greeted him on his eighty-fifth birthday" (a group that included Emmanuel Levinas), Martin Buber once wrote of the difference between thanking in English and German and thanking in Hebrew. In the English and German languages, there is a close connection between thanking (*Danken*) and thinking (*Denken*), between having or holding in one's thoughts or memory, and practicing the activity of thanking. In the Hebrew, the word *hodot* means to come in support of someone, to rally on someone's behalf as their ally, and only later to thank. To thank is thus in this latter sense to move from the inside out, to "confirm [the other person] in his existence."[1] It is as if in the gesture of thanking, one confirms one's responsibility for the other. It is in that latter Hebraic sense that we extend our gratitude at the opening of this volume.

A number of the essays that follow were first delivered as papers in June 2002 at Purdue University in connection with the annual meeting of the Colloquium on Violence and Religion, a group formed in the early 1990s to examine, critique, and extend the "mimetic hypothesis" of René Girard. The topic of the year's colloquium was "Mimesis, Sacrifice, and Scripture: Judaism, Christianity, and the Ancient World." The themes of sacrifice, substitution, and scripture emerged as predominant and have inspired the present collection.

Two events occurred in the interval since 2002 to make the publication of this volume especially timely. In December of 2005, René Girard was inducted into the French Academy in the La Coupole, where, for four centuries, individuals of similar distinction and achievement have entered the highest levels of French intellectual life. And in 2005, Jews as well as Christians marked the fortieth anniversary of the landmark publication of *Nostra Aetate*, a document originating in the Second Vatican Council in 1965, which took up, among other topics, Jewish-Christian relations, and to all appearances changed their course. The editors of this volume share the hope that a better understanding of the ancient relationship between Judaism and Christianity, and of the dynamics of that relationship as René Girard's work illuminates it for us, will contribute positively to its modern evolution.

The editors would like to acknowledge the many individuals who have contributed to this volume in a wide variety of ways. First and foremost is René Girard, whose powerful and seminal reflections have remained a constant for all concerned. His ideas are altering the way we think about the world in which we live, and this book is a testimony to their enormous and enduring power. The seventeen other contributors to this collection have our admiration and gratitude, not only for the quality of their work, but also and especially for their patience and kind cooperation, as we have waited and worked together toward its publication through a long process from inspiration to appearance.

To Gregory Sterling at the University of Notre Dame we owe heartfelt thanks for his acceptance of this volume into the series. The two anonymous readers of the manuscript provided us with immensely helpful suggestions and guidance. We owe them a great deal. To Charles Van Hof and the expert staff of the University of Notre Dame Press we wish to express sincere thanks.

Thinking back to the origins of this book, we would like to thank the School of Liberal Arts at Purdue University, and in particular Margaret Rowe, Robert Ringel, David Santogrossi, the Finn Memorial Lecture Fund, Lillie Fisher, Adele Colella, Roberto Colella, Rabbi Gedalia Engel, and Don Mitchell. The officers of the Colloquium on Violence and Religion deserve our thanks for agreeing to convene the conference at Purdue, and we thank in particular Andrew McKenna, the editor of *Contagion*, who allowed us "first dibs" on publishing these fine pieces of work.

We thank James G. Williams, whose many writings and translations are often cited within these essays, for his thoughtful comments on early drafts of several of them. We also thank the editor of *Theological Studies* for kindly granting us permission to reprint the essay of Robert Daly, S.J., "Eucharistic Origins: From the New Testament to the Liturgies of the Golden Age," which first appeared in volume 66 (2005), 85–112, of that journal.

Finally, we would like to thank each other.

In a talk addressed to his students at the l'Enio (the École Normale Israelite Orientale, which trained Hebrew School teachers) on the occasion of his departure from the directorship, Emmanuel Levinas spoke of both his gratitude for his many years of service to the institution, and of his gratitude for the capacity to give thanks in the first place, a capacity he feels derives from the subject matter itself.

It is in that same double spirit of gratitude that we offer this volume.

Ann W. Astell and Sandor Goodhart

Note

1. See Emmanuel Levinas, *Proper Names*, trans. Michael B. Smith (Stanford, CA: Stanford University Press, 1996), 37–39.

Substitutive Reading

An Introduction to Girardian Thinking,
Its Reception in Biblical Studies, and This Volume

SANDOR GOODHART & ANN W. ASTELL

> *He looked up, saw a ram caught in the thicket, and took and sacrificed*
> *the ram instead of sacrificing his son.*
>
> — Genesis 22:13

Are cultures possible that are not founded upon the murder of one of their members? For as far back as we can construct historical memory, the violence of one member of a group against another in the same group seems to have been a resident feature of human community. Recent reports about the famous cave paintings—for example, those attested in Southern Turkey—suggest that the communities producing them may not have been engaging in funereal rites (as we have long surmised) but in sacrificial rituals.[1] Is it possible that the human species emerged, that it separated itself from the larger animal community, not on the basis of its propensity for violence (which is, with few exceptions, shared throughout the higher primates) but on the basis of its coordination of that violence against one member of the community uniquely? Is it possible that what is distinctive about "the human" is its channeling of that violence upon a victim arbitrarily chosen, one who, in that relative indifference to the motivating trigger of his or her isolation and removal, resolved conflict as a consequence? Could hominization itself be the product of coordinated, unidirectional shepherding

of otherwise disruptive communal energy against a substitute or surrogate victim, a one that may stand alone for many?

Perhaps the practice of exclusionary violence is so ancient, so pervasive, so looming that anthropologists have ignored it not in spite of
its enormity but because of it, somewhat in the same manner that children miscount the number of countries in a popular children's board
game not because the names of those regions are obscure or hidden but
because, like the evidence for a solution to a murder mystery in the
Edgar Allen Poe story, they are simply too blatant?[2] Something like
this question may have motivated Raymund Schwager when, in the
1970s, he wrote a book with the title *Must There Be Scapegoats?*[3] And
a similar question would appear to drive the extraordinary work of literary critic–turned–cultural anthropologist René Girard, who has taken
upon himself a systematic interrogation of the relation of sacrifice to
exclusionary violence — in all of its multifarious ramifications — as his
life's work.

Girard's theory unifies the best of the French and the Anglo-
German anthropological traditions. By temperament and conception,
Girard's work derives from Durkheim. It was Emil Durkheim who first
regarded the sacred (or the social) as something greater than the product of its individual parts, who first proposed that culture could be studied systematically. The work of his student and son-in-law, Marcel
Mauss (especially on the form and function of sacrifice and the gift
in this connection), and the work of his latter-day successor, Claude
Lévi-Strauss, the self-nominated father of structural anthropology,
form the soil in which Girard's insights germinate. And the insights
themselves — about the role of murder in founding ancient communities and about the role of the scapegoat victim in sustaining those
violent origins — are shaped by Sir James Frazer and Sigmund Freud:
on the one hand, by Frazer (for example, in *The Golden Bough* and the
writings of the so-called "Cambridge anthropologists") in his identification of violent scapegoat myths and rituals throughout known cultures; and, on the other, by Freud (for example, in the early *Totem and
Taboo* and the very late *Moses and Monotheism*), who envisioned the
explanatory power of such violent acts in engendering group and individual behavior in a manner that is scientifically observable.

Girard's thesis in a nutshell is that all culture is founded upon murder, upon the collective lynching of a surrogate victim or scapegoat whose removal restores peace and tranquility to a previously disrupted community. This insight gives specificity to what Girard calls "the mimetic hypothesis," which is that all culture is organized around the management of imitative desire and the control of its propensity for violent conflict. Human beings desire, Girard suggests, neither objects nor subjects but the desires of others, and that fact—that all desire is mediated through a model one has consciously or unconsciously appropriated—leads inevitably to conflict. In the primitive universe such conflictual potential is managed by a sacrificial mechanism that declares as sacred a violence that has been efficaciously removed from the community, and as violent a sacred that comes down from its segregated place outside of the city and is wreaking havoc upon the citizenry. The modern universe—in possession of the scriptures bequeathed to us by the revealed religions (and, for Girard, especially Judaism and Christianity)—remains the beneficiary of the exposure of this sacrificial system, an exposure that contributes to its disempowerment. But it is beset by its own dilemma, namely, how to continue in a world in which the sacrificial no longer works, in which scapegoating is no longer efficacious and reciprocal violence proliferates not only in spite of but now even because of such sacrificial gestures, and in which as a result the anti-sacrificial, the ethical, is of primary concern.

The volume that follows contributes to the elaboration of Girard's ideas by submitting his theses regarding scripture—and especially the idea that sacrifice is founded upon a logic of substitution and exposed in scripture as such—to the purview of a number of the leading scholars in the field of the study of ancient Judaism and nascent Christianity. The social sciences of sociology and anthropology and the humanistic endeavor of biblical studies have rarely benefited from each other's insights, and it is not overstating the case to say that both seem to have met the challenge posed by the thinking of René Girard with a modicum of caution, although biblical studies—for reasons that will be suggested below—seems to have embraced it somewhat more enthusiastically. In what follows, we have placed an interview with Girard side by side with contributions by Thomas Ryba, Michael Fishbane,

Bruce Chilton, Robert Daly, Alan Segal, and Louis Feldman on biblical sacrificial economies, postsacrificial views in Judaism of reading and prayer, the relation of the Eucharist and martyrdom to sacrifice, and historical assessments of exclusionary practices. We have followed that section with more attentive readings of individual passages from Jewish and Christian scripture. Our hope is that this collection may enhance all three disciplines: cultural anthropology, biblical study of the ancient Jewish and Christian scriptures, and Girardian thinking. To do that, let us turn more fully to Girard's ideas and to these two fields that have curiously (or perhaps not so curiously) resisted both each other and the insights of this maverick French intellectual.

Reading Girardian Thought

Girard's early work explores the relation of imitative desire to the great literary texts of our culture. The great writers of the European tradition—Cervantes, Stendhal, Flaubert, Dostoyevsky, and Proust (Girard would later add Shakespeare and Molière to this list)—would all appear to agree that desire is not object-based but mimetic, that we desire neither objects of our fantasies nor the subjects of our inspirations but what others desire. In the late 1960s and early 70s, Girard expanded this consideration with the introduction of Greek tragedy. Ancient Greek drama seemed to him to reveal a larger cultural orientation, one that allowed him to ask where mimetic desire originated.

The answer it gave is that older cultures manage mimetic desire as part of a larger system of sacralization, that the sacred and violence are one and the same. The sacred is violence that has been thrown out of the community, and violence is the sacred that formerly occupied a position outside of the city and currently circulates within it, wreaking havoc among its unfortunate participants. What sustains all of this activity is sacrifice, the collective substitution of a surrogate victim. A culture in this framework is understood as a system of differences, a set of distinctions for regulating every aspect of cultural life. And those distinctions may be understood in positive terms as sacrificial. Ritual behaviors govern all aspects of communal life: birth and death, initiation and marriage, and everything in between. Transitions through cultural life and one's status outside of (or within) the infinite variety of positions that make up cultural life are related by a system of statuses and ceremonies that operate everywhere and at all times—wall to wall, so to speak—in any given cultural community.

But things break down in culture as elsewhere, either through normal wear and tear, or through extraordinary accidental event (an earthquake or tidal wave, for example). And when that happens, the calculated anticipation of failure goes awry. The normal set of sacrificial distinctions that customarily insure the community's health and survival, now, paradoxically, become its greatest threat. In the midst of such a "sacrificial crisis," the very effort to secure a way out of the crisis (a way that inevitably worked in the past) now just as inevitably insures a way back in, compounding the difficulty, as it were, as difference goes wrong and sacrificial behavior turns to violence.

In such circumstances, substitution plays a critical role. The substitutive logic at the heart of the scapegoat mechanism becomes a little more visible than usual. Greek tragedy—in the hands of a Sophocles, Euripides, or Aeschylus—offers in Girard's view a window to such structurative social processes. Girard likes to cite *Oedipus Tyrannus*, for example. A malign plague is destroying the land. Oedipus declares he will do all he can to put an end to the plague and calls upon the local seer, Tiresias, for assistance. Although begun in viable distinction, the dialogue between the king and the blind prophet quickly turns sour. The king's counselor (and brother-in-law), Creon, has said (that the oracle has said) that they need to identify and remove the murderer of the former monarch. "I should not have come," the old seer declares, and Oedipus retorts, "What! You would withhold information you have for us! Then I say that you did the deed yourself." "What!" Tiresias replies. "Then I say that *you* are in fact the killer of the man whose killer you are seeking." Creon and Jocasta (Oedipus's wife) quickly enter the fray and very soon it is evident that if the discussion were allowed to proceed unabated, we would anon be beset by a community of doubles, a population of enemy twins locked in a confrontational exchange of (theoretically) endless reciprocal violence, in a veritable Hobbesean war of all against all.

Suddenly, the logic of substitution is determinative. As each approaches the condition of being enemy twin of each, any one approaches the condition of being the enemy twin of all, the surrogate victim each dreams of sacrificing. The smallest differences—differences of hair color, hair length, skin hue, physical stature—can in an instant suddenly become the absolute difference trumping all others. At any moment, the paroxysmic violence of all against all can suddenly unleash itself as the unanticipated violence of all against one in a sacrificial substitution. At that moment, the violence against the other is carried out, and the community is suddenly and inexplicably at peace. The violence of the "night before," the drunken Dionysiac revels turned hideously malevolent, seem like far off mountains as images of Apollonian calm and tranquility return. The first distinction after the storm is peace now, and horrific violence just a moment ago. Poetry, Wordsworth wrote perspicaciously, is violent emotion recollected in tranquility.

And once it does return, all else is organized around it. The sudden unexpected peaceful resolution of hostilities gives way to the second distinction: the genesis of the gods and ritual commemoration. Since the violence has ceased with the introduction of the small difference that made all the difference, the bearer of that distinction—its "vehicle" so to speak—must have been the god all along. And so every year at this time, we will repeat this performance up to a certain point to regain for ourselves its beneficial effects. We cannot of course sacrifice again the same victim or repeat the sacrifice in its entirety, for that would throw us once more into an entirely new paroxysm. But we can substitute someone or something else for the original victim: a relative (a twin, for example), or some livestock owned by the victim or that has been encouraged to act like the victim (a cow or a bull run rampant, for example). "Primitive culture," a term Girard borrows from Durkheimian ethnology, is made up in its entirety for Girard by such sacrificial substitutions: substitutions of one victim for another across every cultural boundary, but substitution more fundamentally of one potential victim for every other potential victim. Even more than a set of differences, the fabric of culture is for him at this level a series of such substitutions on which such differences are based.

How do we know? Is Girard not privileging one narrative structure over all others, the narrative of difference, of the violent assertion of difference in its inefficaciousness, of the sacrificial substitution of one of the doubles for all of the doubles, of the new order of differences that includes now a repetition of the former crisis up to a point (which now assumes the place of the new narrative of difference)? Is Girard not outdoing even Hegel in his postulation of a dialectical movement of history from thesis, to an opposition of thesis in contest with antithesis, to a new synthesis (which assumes the new thesis position)? In fact, Girard's description has the status of an Ur-logic. Like the morphology of the folktale described by Vladimir Propp, or like the complete score of a myth described by Claude Lévi-Strauss, the system in its entirety exists nowhere. No existent culture or community manifests all elements of the logic. But the logic nonetheless offers an account of the system as such, a hypothetical system, the *langue* after which Lévi-Strauss strives and for which every example is properly a *parole*.

There is another sense in which the question — "how do we know?" — remains to be answered and in relation to which the following volume assumes its rightful place in the discussion. For Girard, we know about sacrifice and its mechanism at the origin of culture because of Holy Scripture. In the primitive sacrificial situation, when the knowledge of the mechanism and the substitutive logic at its heart becomes known, that knowledge determines simply one more sacrificial position. A special status may be woven around it. The individual with that knowledge and the means of manipulating it may become known as the shaman. But the shaman remains a member of the community, always potentially of course substitutable himself for another — for another shaman, for example. But what happens when the sacrificial mechanism is no longer efficacious at all, when a sacrificial crisis breaks out that does more than just repeat the previous crises, when one breaks out that threatens to found a new system in its entirety, but yet one for which no more efficacious substitutions may be found?

Put in other terms, how is it possible, Girard asks, that we know about the sacrificial mechanism in its entirety and yet have survived to tell about it? If knowledge of the system undoes it (and the system functions only in so far as it remains unconscious — no one engaging in scapegoating or arbitrary victimage says, "I am engaging in scapegoating or arbitrary victimage"), then how is it that we are able to talk about it and not destroy ourselves?

The answer for Girard is first the Jewish and then the Christian scriptures. The Hebrew Bible reflects a history that is profoundly anti-sacrificial. Hebraic culture appears among cultures of the world that are as sacrificial as any other. The cultures of the Ancient Near East—Canaanite, Hittite, Syrian, Babylonian, Sumerian, Egyptian—suddenly give way to the appearance in their midst of the culture of Israel. Stories like those of Cain and Abel, the flood, the tower of Babel, the binding of Isaac, the thrusting into the pit and subsequent selling of Joseph by his brothers undoubtedly reflect counterparts in Egypt and elsewhere. But in the Hebrew Bible they are treated differently. Whether the Bible is understood to be uniquely a product of the Rabbinic period (from about 200 BCE to about 400 CE) or to reflect the previous four centuries of reflection, the consideration of these narratives in the Hebrew Bible remains dominated by the concept of Torah, which is to say, the law of anti-idolatry. If we regard idolatry as the name for the moment when the divine is mistaken for the human or, in Girardian terms, when the sacrificial and the violent become irrevocably confused, then the Hebrew Bible is a sustained meditation on the anti-idolatrous and its consequences, a meditation on a way to live when the primitive sacrificial mechanism no longer works, and as a consequence sacrifice and violence are one and the same.

And for Girard, Christianity is the record of the extension of that biblical Hebraic anti-sacrificial reading to the institution of sacrifice itself. Jesus offers himself as the last sacrifice, the sacrifice to end all sacrifices, the sacrifice intended to show us where our sacrifices must inevitably lead, which is to say, to violence and destruction. The writings of the synoptic Gospels, in Girard's view, say little else. And the Pauline letters and other writings extend that insight into the everyday world in which the practicing Christian continues to function. The apocalyptic book of Revelation, for example, extends that insight about the onset of reciprocal violence into our contemporary scene. For example, in his most recent book, *Achever Clausewitz*, Girard identifies in the uncompleted narrative of a nineteenth-century writer, the Prussian officer Hans von Clausewitz, the circumstances already predicted: the runaway reciprocal violence, the mounting to the extremes, that will offer us a choice between owning our own violence and giving it up entirely.[4]

The genius of the modern world—which is to say, for Girard, the world in possession of the Jewish and Christian revelation—is to have imagined for the first time in human history (as Girard understands it) the nature of sacrificial violence in all its dimensions: its origins, its strategies, and its consequences. How did we do that? Did we happen upon it? Did some group of breakaway members of one or another cultures of the Ancient Near East think it up on their own? Or was that knowledge handed to them from the outside, so to speak, through an intervention that can only be qualified as supernatural or divine? Girard insists repeatedly that he is not a theologian, that he is not offering a theory of revelation—Jewish or Christian—but that he is in fact a cultural anthropologist, and that he is offering the distinctly anthropological perspective that he finds the Hebraic and Christian scriptural texts are offering us. These are texts, he argues, that presuppose a sustained critical analysis of the cultural dynamics that have conditioned the context in which we find ourselves but that do not prescribe an ethical solution to their dilemmas, other than the anti-sacrificial itself, sometimes formulated as *refuser la violence,* to refuse (sacrificial) violence at those moments when the two (sacrifice and violence) have become irrevocably confused.

ONE WAY, THEN, OF DESCRIBING THE PROJECT THAT FOLLOWS is to say that we are assessing Girard's claim that scripture is anti-sacrificial and moreover in specifically the way Girard describes it: namely, as substitutive. Substitution here will mean four things. It will mean, in the first place, the logic of equivalency at the heart of the scapegoat mechanism, the very source of its efficacy, the equivalency or exchange that makes possible the instantaneous conversion of the war of all against all into the war of all against one. But secondly, it will mean the second order substitution of a commemorative experience for the original exchange. It will mean the repetition of the conversion—from a Hobbesean war of all against all into a unidirectional unleashing of the war of all against one—upon an independent secondary object or subject, one precisely that substitutes for the original victim.

Thirdly, it will mean the substitution of one sacrificial mechanism for another. If the system of the first two substitutions—the original victimage and its commemorative repetition—breaks down, another original victim may take its place. If, say, human victimage no longer works (for whatever reason), and even its commemorative repetition fails to engender the desired effects, a new "original" victim might emerge out of such a sacrificial crisis, one that would in turn require a new commemorative ritual duplication.

And, of course, there is a fourth sense in which substitution is used by Girard in this context. What if the entire mechanism goes bad, turns sour, "goes south," as they say? What if no victim any longer is able to be identified as viable? Then one begins to imagine the sacrifice of sacrifice itself, the sacrifice to end all sacrifices, the prophetic critique of sacrifice that declares "what good are all your sacrifices?" and begins to imagine an ethical system no longer based upon sacrificial substitution, or based upon sacrificial substitution in entirely new ways. Such a sense of the end of the sacrificial is, we have suggested, at the root of Girard's view of the modern. Tragedy would seem to have emerged from such "tragic prophetic" critique, and both the Hebrew Bible and the Christian scriptural canon would seem to be the product in significant part if not in its entirety of such prophetic interpretive reading.

Girard's thinking retains the idea of substitution in all four of these senses: as the logic of sacrifice, as the logic of ritual commemoration, as the logic of neosacrificial structuration, and as the logic of the end of sacrifice in the birth of the modern. No single contribution to the volume that follows, however—with the possible exception of Girard's conversation with Sandor Goodhart—displays all four, and several contributors introduce new understandings of both sacrifice and substitution, understandings that in turn confirm, critique, complement, or challenge Girard's own. Perhaps this mix of Girardian and non-Girardian approaches to these common themes will open a place for Girard's work in fields that to the present have largely eschewed it.

Reading the Reception of Girard in Biblical Studies

Anthropology and biblical studies in English, and American intellectual contexts would seem to have proven strange bedfellows to each other, and stranger still to the work of René Girard. We draw inspiration in this connection from the article of Gary Anderson (in the prestigious *Anchor Bible Dictionary*), who observes that "by and large, biblical scholarship has not kept up with the theoretical work of recent anthropology," and mentions Girard's work in particular.[5]

Although Girard has been writing on anthropological matters since the 1970s, and although a sizeable and increasing secondary literature has by now grown up around his work from within the community of his admiring readers, there has been no major anthropological endeavor to engage it. Robert Hamerton-Kelly attempted to foster one by inviting Walter Burkert and Jonathan Z. Smith to join Girard in a series of presentations and extended conversations in the 1980s.[6] And Mark Anspach, in a brilliantly insightful volume, has more recently attempted to explain the idea of gift exchange within the Durkheimian, Maussean, and Lévi-Straussian tradition in a way that makes room for the introduction of Girard's ideas.[7] In each case, however, these efforts have attracted little or no attention outside of the Girardian fold.[8] The little positive notice Girard's writing has received tends to link it with Burkert's as one more "universalist" approach that would reductively focus on one aspect of culture to the exclusion of all others.[9]

The situation in biblical studies is both better and worse. Since *Violence and the Sacred*, Girard has written three books primarily on biblical studies: *Things Hidden since the Foundation of the World*; *Job, the Victim of His People*; and *I See Satan Fall Like Lightning* (plus numerous essays on biblical topics and on the status of the Gospels vis-à-vis myth).[10] A book and an entire journal issue devoted to his biblical studies work have appeared.[11] And an international organization, the Colloquium on Violence and Religion (COV&R), was formed, an organization inspired less by literary critics or anthropologists than biblical studies scholars, who play a significant role in administering the organization and whose work remains by juridical decision one of its mainstays. Nonetheless, Girard's ideas have earned him, among his most negative critics, the familiar charges of supersessionism and triumphalism—even antiritualism.[12] How has the constitution of these fields contributed to the reception of his work?

Sacrifice, the Prophetic, and the Documentary Hypothesis

The primacy of sacrifice to the study of the Hebrew Bible has, in the eyes of biblical scholars, by no means proved self-evident. The issue of sacrifice, Anderson makes clear, for example, was a touchy one for scholars from the outset.[13] The detail with which the ancient institution exists is undeniable.[14] But the "Old Testament" is read precisely to the extent to which it prefigures the New, and so at best the presence of sacrifice in particular, and ritual in general, has been regarded by biblical studies scholars as a remnant of more ancient cultural styles.

Indeed, sacrifice was hardly dominant in the writings that served as foundational for the so-called "higher biblical criticism." Having freed itself from pre-Kantian dogmatism, biblical scholarship, under the tutelage of the Kantian historical-critical method, began to identify independent compositional units within the scriptural fabric. The acronym "JEPD" named biblical scripture as a series of distinct documents combining respectively Jahwist, Elohist, Priestly, and Deuteronomic compositional traditions (with the possible addition of an editorial or redactor tradition designated as R).[15]

Thus Julius Wellhausen's magisterial volume *Prolegomena to the History of Ancient Israel* is often credited with placing the so-called "documentary hypothesis" on a firm footing. In Wellhausen's view, the Hebrew Bible anticipates the New Testament, and the books of the prophets are prized more highly than those of Leviticus or Numbers, where much of the writing about sacrificial ritual is contained.[16]

The "documentary hypothesis" as a concept sustains multiple meanings, and other senses of "document" may be at play here. To these older readers of the "Old Testament," such compositional differences reflected (or "documented") multiple historical or cultural *realia*, all commonly lacking the moral progress, the evolutionary advantage, with which Christian European culture had been blessed. The anthropology upon which these writers relied supported their position, and it is not entirely surprising that an unabashed evolutionism, ethnocentrism, and antiprimitivism accompanied this thinking.

Thus was invoked the writing of Edward Tylor, who, in *Primitive Culture*, contrasts the modern with the primitive and elaborates sacrifice as a ritual gift within a highly opportunistic framework (*do ut das,* "I give in order that I may get"), a practice for him devoid of any significant moral or ethical content. Or these readers invoke the work of James G. Frazer, who in *The Golden Bough* saw the sacrificial death of the king, repeated annually, as a matter of primitive magical, pre-logical thought and superstition. Or they invoke the work of William Robertson-Smith, who in *Lectures on the Religion of the Semites* adopted a slightly more positive outlook but maintained the same premises. Robertson-Smith sought for ways in which such practices reflected a modicum of social bonding or unity among the people employing them. He embedded his observations within the nineteenth-century fascination with totemism in which Israel—though differing little from other cultures of the Ancient Near East, all of which were separated by a chasm from modern Christian European culture—continued to strive for a means of acquiring social "communion," a communion or union doomed necessarily to fail without the benefit of Christian understanding.

The view of sacrifice articulated by biblical scholars followed suit. George Buchanan Gray could write a book in 1929 on sacrifice in the "Old Testament" Priestly tradition in which such ritual material is thought to document historically the *realia* of a less sophisticated, more primitive mode of cultural understanding, citing in his defense among other writers Tylor, Frazer, and Robertson-Smith.[17] "I propose to examine," Gray writes, in this context, "the extent to which sacrifice was subsumed under the general class of sacred gifts."[18] Wellhausen's work on prophetic thinking and Gray's on sacrifice, though separated by some fifty years, are thus in important ways of a piece. And it is probably not insignificant that it is Robertson-Smith who served as editor for Wellhausen's book when it was reissued shortly after its original printing.[19]

Their view has sustained a remarkable vitality. In several long and detailed volumes published as late as 1961, the Dominican Father Roland de Vaux outlines the nature and function of sacrifice in the Israelite community in much the same terms as Gray. The same evolutionist writers are cited as support. And if Father de Vaux's conclusion is slightly different—sacrifice for him is not exclusively gift or social bond but the vehicle for a host of social functions in a way that Freud would no doubt characterize as "overdetermined"—his strategic alignments are familiar.

By 1970, much had changed in anthropology. Durkheim, Mauss, and Lévi-Strauss had gained prominence in French ethnology. But fifty years after Gray's original publication, biblical studies made use of virtually none of this new thinking, continuing to rely upon the insights of "anthropologists" from a hundred years earlier, writers who, having benefited from the historical-critical method and its critique of a dogmatic theology, in effect promptly reasserted the supersessionism and progressivism of their theological predecessors within their newly secularized context.[20] When Baruch Levine notes, in the prolegomena to the reissue of Gray's original volume in the early 1970s, that nothing has changed in fifty years, we understand his claim. On the other hand, the fact that Gray's book on sacrifice was reproduced at all is itself important. As if detecting a certain prescience, Levine notes that "something appears to be in the wind."[21]

Structuralism, Poststructuralism, and the Hypothesis of Textuality

What was in the wind has been called the "hypothesis of textuality" (Gary Anderson recently coined the word "scripturalization"), and this postwar phenomenon has occasioned a renewed interest in Durkheim. To understand his position (and Girard's in relation to it), we need to glance at Durkheim, Mauss, and Lévi-Strauss.

While Tylor, Fraser, and Robertson-Smith pursued anthropological research in one fashion, French theorists Durkheim and Mauss examined the sacred and gift in another. Durkheim, as noted, pursued the importance of the sacred beyond the sum of the individual parts comprising it. Mauss continued that pursuit, combining an interest in the intentional structure of the sacrificial gift that Tylor had noticed with the social bonding benefits Robertson-Smith observed.

Thus in *Sacrifice: Its Nature and Function*, Mauss and Hubert also saw sacrifice as a gift but one with precisely a unifying moral and ethical role in the community.[22] Later in the postwar period, Lévi-Strauss would continue to articulate this structuralist move. In his book on totemism, he exposed and undid nineteenth-century antiprimitivist and evolutionist presuppositions.[23] If he strategically eschewed consideration of the category of the sacred (the problem that started it all in France, and an exclusion for which Girard would later challenge him), he undertook this defense of Rousseau-ism from within a scientific perspective, one that grounded itself in concrete quotidian realities experienced by members of a primitive culture.[24] Borrowing models of structural linguistics from Roman Jakobson, Lévi-Strauss developed Saussure's distinction between *langue* and *parole* (or system and execution) and the study of culture as a system of signs (understood as the difference between *signifiant* and *signifié*—sometimes translated as "signifier" and "signified"—or between the sensible and the intelligible), and extended the work of Mauss to all of culture. He put anthropology on a firm new scientific footing, one that Girard among many others would utilize.

Thus Gary Anderson's neologism as a reference to textuality. For Anderson, scripturalization refers to the consideration of biblical phenomena neither as dogma nor as document but as text, and it is his contention that this new conception in biblical studies replaced the nineteenth-century interest in the Old Testament as a historical document to be examined within critical (which is to say nontheological) method. The interest of biblical scholars of the old school, he argues, was never really in *realia*. Although they spoke that way, when push came to shove, they relied upon texts, which is to say, upon narrative accounts in which the biblical tradition was necessarily passed to us.[25]

Thus, one way to understand sacrifice as an integral part of the Old Testament, Anderson suggests, is to regard it as writing. Just as Mauss suggested that social structure could be studied and Lévi-Strauss suggested that one way to do that was through its consideration as a system of signs (à la Saussure), so biblical sacrifice could be studied alongside prophetic thinking and the opposition between these two modes of thought could be overcome, much as Lévi-Strauss had overcome the objection that culture was either objective or subjective (and that one had to choose between two mutually exclusive alternatives) by studying it as language, and moreover language conceived as a system of signs. The "hypothesis of textuality" has replaced the "documentary hypothesis."

Where is René Girard in all of this? René Girard came along and globalized this analysis, extending it to all culture as the problem of the sacred.[26]

René Girard and the Mimetic Hypothesis

It is not often acknowledged that Girard fairly liberally adopts the structuralist postulates of these thinkers. Culture for them is a system of differences, and Girard often cites the account of difference he attributes to Emile Benveniste in his volumes on *Indo-European Vocabulary and Institutions* as walking away from the sacrificial altar.[27] The difference between these thinkers—Lévi-Strauss, Barthes, Lacan, and Derrida—is that, for Girard, difference is one moment of a diachronic process. Culture functions as a system of difference. Then a crisis of difference appears. Difference is asserted in its inefficacy, and the more it is asserted, the more inefficacious things become and the more it is asserted. Difference has now acquired the name of violence, and the process is described as one of "undifferentiation." Violence is difference asserted in the extreme, and difference is violence that is working, that is effective in generating separation. Violence is difference "gone wrong," and difference is violence "working well." It is with the absence of an account of the breakdown and recovery of differential systems that Girard challenges his structuralist and poststructuralist colleagues.

Although Girard rejects Lévi-Strauss's insistence on a kind of wall-to-wall structuring of social reality to the exclusion of the sacred (and turns instead to Freud for an instance of what he calls "the real referent" and to Frazer for a counterexample to the way he conceives of his own project—namely, as operating at the level of real human relations), he nevertheless remains curiously within the same Durkheimianism of his interlocutors. It is the same Durkheimianism from which Lévi-Strauss' and Mauss' work hail, insofar as he (like them) is interested in the sacred for its singularity within the social fabric, a singularity to which he assigns the origin of culture itself, an origin that he will identify as sacrificial substitution.

In this way, Girard's theory answers the problems posed by the two major traditions of understanding of the origin and function of

culture: the structuralist ethnological tradition in France (from Durkheim and Mauss to Lévi-Strauss), on the one hand, and the mythic or
psychological tradition in England and the Continent (from Frazer
to Freud), on the other. To the French structuralists for whom difference is all, Girard offers a theory of crisis and of the origin of difference. And to the Cambridge ritualists and Viennese psychoanalyst,
Girard offers an account of culture at the symbolic level of real human
relations, no longer the product simply (or uniquely) of either fear-
governed superstition or the imagination of primal hordes and their
libidinal desires. Girard finds a real referent for such behavior in sac-
rifical victimage, and a real origin for culture (and its conditions of
order and disorder) in the primitive and modern community. As such,
Girard's theories of social formation provide the basis for a theory of
hominization within the evolutionary biological sphere.[28] Girard's
insight is primarily and above all anthropological. It offers a hypothesis regarding the origin and function of human community within the
contexts in which other such proposals are made or fail to be made.

Girard and Biblical Scholarship

It is perhaps not without irony that Girard's poststructuralist position
should lead him back to an anti-sacrificial position that was already
there at the outset of the higher biblical criticism. Sacrifice for him is
readable as a text, even though the text for him is founded upon real
sacrificial gestures. In fact, his understanding is precisely that, to the
extent that it is readable, we progressively move away from the efficacy
of the sacrificial gesture.

Given this complexity of thought, it is perhaps not entirely surprising that biblical scholarship has for the most part not known what
to do with Girard's work.[29] The overt response for the most part has
been four stratagems of avoidance. His work has been excluded by silence, implicitly by mild reproach, or by inverse exaltation, or his work
has been forthrightly dismissed. And yet, one has the impression that in
a curious way, Girard's influence has been more pervasive than has been
customarily acknowledged. Few are willing to go on record as affirming his influence — hence, the strategies of avoidance — but even the

most negative of his critics (see the discussion of Klawans below) regard that influence to be "unmatched."[30]

The work of Roger Beckwith and Martin Selman reflects the first approach, ignoring Girard, even though COV&R had been meeting for five years and James Williams's book had already appeared.[31] David Janzen's book is an example of the second: mild praise. Janzen notes that "of all the more recent universal theories it is Girard's which has drawn the largest following within Biblical studies."[32] James Watts' approach is slightly more positive and promising.[33] Observing that "the view that human sacrifice is basic to society has circulated . . . widely in the form developed by René Girard," Watts also notes, "Girard's best evidence . . . comes from stories of executions, lynchings, and pogroms, including Jesus' crucifixion (which, for Girard, exposes scapegoating to criticism and resistance)." These are all "stories," he says, "only distantly associated with ritual acts, if at all. The application of [Girard's] theory to Temple rituals is strained" (177).

More respectful (if equally distant) are Christian Grappe and Alfred Marx.[34] "Does God agree to or require the putting to death of human beings?" these authors ask. "With regards to the Old Testament, the response is clearly negative. The God of the Old Testament resolutely refuses all human sacrifice. . . . What is at stake in these different narratives is the origin of violence" (83).

Girard, in their eyes, has clearly arrived. "According to the definition that is given in *le Robert*, the scapegoat is 'a person upon whom one causes to fall the wrongs of others.' As René Girard has magisterially shown, this function is of capital importance for society" (78). Girard's reflections in *The Scapegoat* are not far removed from these. The work of Grappe and Marx is entirely positive. They invoke the "magisterial" demonstrations of René Girard to talk about a topic they now take to be *de rigueur* in biblical scholarship: namely, the origins of violence.

But therein lies the difficulty. All of these writers—the silent, the negative, and the positive—exclude implicitly. Girard is no less distanced in Grappe and Marx than he is in Janzen, Watts, Beckwith, and Selman. The major engagement has not yet occurred in their work.

The case is different with the response of Jonathan Klawans, which is more directly negative.[35] "It is fair to say," Klawans notes, "especially with regard to [Mary] Douglas and Girard—that their impact on Biblical studies has been unmatched" (17). But then he quickly adds: "it is difficult to imagine two books more fundamentally different than *Purity and Danger* and *Violence and the Sacred.* . . . *Violence and the Sacred* is nothing short of an indictment of sacrificial rituals" (22). Girard's approach is "not unlike Robertson-Smith's approach to ritual impurity," or "like Frazer." And, for Klawans, the "supersessionist nature of Girard's project" is evident in the claim that the truth is revealed "only in Christian" texts and that Christianity is the "necessary completion of Judaism." Girard "blames Jewish authorities" for Jesus's death. Moreover, that "all sacrifice involves killing *innocent* victims which must mean guilty priests." Girard's "anti-ritualism" in Klawans' view, "drives his evolutionism."

Conflating Girard's view with that of Frazer and Freud, Klawans' position is understandable, if ill-spirited, and bound by an agenda linked to the promotion of the work of Mary Douglas to Girard's detriment. More interesting in the current context is a recent engagement of Girard's work by Bruce Chilton, whose essay on the Eucharist is included in this volume.[36] Chilton touches upon many of the same issues as Klawans but in a manner that is respectful and constructive, one that perhaps offers—despite its disagreements—the best chance for a future serious engagement on these matters.

What concerns Chilton is Girard's assertion that the sacrificial mechanism "was played out in *each and every* society that has ever existed, when there is no direct evidence to that effect" (35). Moreover, Chilton criticizes Girard for linking his analysis of sacrifice "with a full-fledged defense of Christianity as the *sole* religion that can get humanity past its violent origins. Having posited that all sacrifice originates in violence and perpetuates violence, Girard then announces that Christianity is the only cure for violence" (37).

This second point, according to Chilton, Girard derives from Jesus' innocence, the fact that "Jesus was executed without cause." "He was an innocent victim, and by asserting his innocence the New Testament reveals that human violence against scapegoats was unjustified. By stripping away the violent origins of humanity and all its religious institutions Girard claims that Christianity did what no other religion did or could do" (38). Moreover, the claim is brought up in contexts in the New Testament that "justify animosity toward the Jews," for example, Matthew 27:25 where "all the people" of the Jews are blamed. Such passages, Chilton argues, "provided a charter for violent Christian pogroms against the Jews in the Middle Ages" (39).

There is no place here to answer at length any of these charges. But perhaps in concluding this introduction it would be interesting to sketch the root (in our view) of their misunderstanding. Chilton's claim, that Girard sees the sacrificial mechanism as the motor force of all societies although no one society displays all the evidence for it, is accurate enough. But that is hardly an odd rhetorical strategy. Saussure uses it in distinguishing *langue* from *parole,* as does Propp in *Morphology of the Folktale,* and Lévi-Strauss in his discussion of Ur-mythology in the *Mythologiques.* It is the staple of a structuralist position. Perhaps Chilton's discomfort is more with structuralism than Girard.

And what if Girard's point is accurate? What if his theory *does* account for all instances of the ways in which cultures manage runaway mimetic behavior—across the board? What if it discloses the foundation of hominization? Should we cast it aside because it is too successful, because it works every time we invoke it? What if there is something distinctive about human communities and Girard has put his finger on it?

Chilton's second criticism—that Girard's position is supersessionist and triumphalist—is more complicated. Girard never claims "Christianity [is] the *sole* religion [to reveal culture's violent origins or] that can get humanity past its violent origins" but the sole religion for "us," for citizens of European history, which is to say, the history of the Holy Roman Empire. Girard's theoretical position is not normative but descriptive (whatever his personal adherence to a Christian ethical position). He is describing a reading, the anthropological interpretation that Christianity in his view makes of the cultures preceding it. We might appropriately argue that Judaism makes similar readings, or Hinduism or Buddhism or Islam, within the cultural contexts in which they speak. Girard never places himself outside of all culture, from some position (Christian or other) where he might make judgments about it. He always lodges himself squarely within it, commenting on the texts that speak to us in the most honest and most forthright manner about our own violence. In the Western universe, that position is necessarily (and exclusively for Girard) the one articulated by Greek tragedy, Hebrew scripture, and Christian scripture. And the innocence of the victim in all instances of these texts is the innocence of the charge for which the scapegoat is made uniquely culpable, although the scapegoat has often become a double, an enemy twin, of his persecutors. Jesus enacts the innocence of every scapegoat of the crime with which he is charged—namely, with being the source of all violence in the culture.

Nothing, moreover, prevents the revelation of the truth of our own sacrificial violence from slipping into neosacrificial behavior, even (or especially) among those closest to the revelation. Girard never tires of citing the ways in which the apostles themselves display mimetic behavior of the very kind under examination. The history of Western Christianity in Girard's view is not the history of a peaceful culture but of an intensely violent one struggling to free itself from mimetic entanglements that have become only more evident by virtue of its scriptural possessions. If historical Christianity becomes at times neosacrificial in its relation to Judaism in the Middle Ages, or to other groups during the Crusades, or to women during the witchcraft trials, that history for Girard is less reflective of any species of cultural arrogance endemic to the Christian revelation than of its efforts to eradicate behaviors that have plagued all cultures at all times in the history of the human community, abuses that we also know about because of that revelation and that a document like *Nostra Aetate* in the last century goes a long way toward acknowledging.[37]

What Girard requests (and in our view certainly deserves) is simply scholarly engagement. Here is where and why we agree. Here is where and why we disagree. This helps us to explain that. That other thing remains to be explained. Why has this kind of engagement been so difficult to generate? Why has his work either been ignored or invoked or indicted (mildly or forcefully)? Is the fate of Girard's work the fate of all important thinkers? Do we, for example, really engage Freud's work? It would seem to be appropriated or dismissed in accord with the dynamics Girard describes so well. Is it not our ethical responsibility as scholars to go beyond this kind of mimetic appropriation? Mindful of the difficulties of the task, that is what this book is attempting: to reserve a place for Girard's work in the ongoing scholarly discussion of sacrifice and scripture.

Reading This Volume

The collection is divided into two parts dealing with sacrifice and scripture, respectively. The first contains nine essays by the writers mentioned above. The second contains twelve essays on specific texts in each scripture (Genesis 22 and Job in the Jewish tradition, the Gospels and Epistles in the Christian tradition). The collection coheres around the notion of "substitution" in four ways: (1) as the logic of sacrifice or scapegoating at the heart of the victimary mechanism; (2) as the logic of its ritual repetition; (3) as the logic of the exchange in the "sacrificial crises" by which one system comes to be replaced by another; and (4) as the logic of scripture in the face of the crises from which Rabbinic Judaism and nascent Christianity have come and within the logic of critical reading of sacrifice and scripture since then.

The book opens with a conversation in which René Girard and Sandor Goodhart explore the relation between imitation and violence as a way of understanding sacrifice in primitive religion. In one way, we have always acknowledged the relation of imitation to conflict, Girard suggests, since both our great literary writers and our great religious texts—the Bible, for example—speak about little else (which is why the appearance of instances of unconscious scapegoating, for example, in medieval witchcraft trials or in certain political cases like the Dreyfus trial, trouble us in the first place). But at least since the ancient Greeks, in our more formal nonliterary writing, we have felt it necessary to separate them. We may understand religion more scientifically, Girard suggests, if we recognize in religion a way of managing this relation of imitation to conflict, with sacrifice (and sacrificial scapegoating) playing a decisive role. We may even be able to talk about the process of hominization in this fashion, since the appearance of human groups from among animal groups may derive from this capacity to control crisis with substitute victims.

The discussion with Girard opens up dialogically the topic of the origins and historical development of biblical sacrifice. In "Bloody Logic: The Biblical Economy of Sacrificial Substitution and Some of Its Eucharistic Implications," Thomas Ryba extends Marcel Mauss' anthropological theory of the gift and Michael Polanyi's definition of "economics" in order to identify "the form of exchange [sacrificial economies] imply, the form of substitution they allow, and the commensurable standard that makes both substitution and exchange possible." Assuming that "sacrifice did change from the form and significance it had in ancient Israelitic religion to the form and significance it had in ancient Christianity" and providing a formal, schematic description of those changes, Ryba nonetheless discovers in Eucharistic theology important continuities with the Judaic tradition of sacrifice. In particular, he argues that blood, as a symbol of the very gift of life, "signifies the commensurable standard behind biblical sacrificial practice."

Like Ryba, Michael Fishbane endeavors to trace and explain change and continuity in the historical forms of sacrifice. In "Aspects of the Transformation of Sacrifice in Judaism," Fishbane explores the logic of substitution within the Rabbinic tradition in the aftermath of the collapse of the Second Temple. He argues that sacrifice continues after the catastrophe in the form of study, prayer, and their attendant ascetic activities. The study of Torah for the rabbis, Fishbane notes, is equal in merit to doing all the commandments. Even in as late a work as the eighteenth-century writing of Hayyim of Voloshin, the *Nefesh Hayah,* the legitimacy of the substitution continues.

Bruce Chilton argues that, before the destruction of the Second Temple, Jesus of Nazareth also offered up forms of sacrifice that substituted for, and were perceived to rival, those offered in the Temple precincts. In "The Eucharist and the Mimesis of Sacrifice," Chilton turns to the question of the Eucharist as a premier instance of the treatment of sacrifice within the Christian text. Chilton proposes that there are not one but several traditions of Eucharistic sacrifice within Christianity. Outlining six types of Eucharist, he discerns their generative moment in an anti-sacrificial gesture on Jesus' part, a moment of mimetic substitution or surrogacy for Temple ritual practice.

Responding in different ways to Chilton's account of Eucharist are the following two essays, by Robert Daly, S.J., and Alan Segal.

In "Eucharistic Origins: From the New Testament to the Liturgies of the Golden Age," Daly reviews twentieth-century research into the origins of the Eucharist. He observes that many of the Church's theologians have yet to appropriate the significance of what is commonly accepted as historical fact by exegetes and liturgical theologians, namely, that there is no clear line of development from the Last Supper of Jesus to the theologically rich Eucharistic prayers of the patristic golden age. Daly discusses the implications of Chilton's account for methodology in systematic theology and ecclesiology, for liturgical and ecumenical theology, and for pastoral theology and homiletics.

Whereas Chilton underscores the Christian understanding of the Eucharist as a meal in preparation for the self-sacrifice of martyrs, Alan Segal notes that the death of martyrs has often been understood to be a sacrificial offering. In "Life after Death: Violence, Martyrdom, and Academic Life in Western Religions," Segal pursues the question of violence in connection with martyrdom and the afterlife. He argues that the modern idea of the importance of the immortality of the soul finds its counterpart in the ancient world in the Platonic tradition, and that resurrection was in fact imagined in more specifically bodily terms by ancient Jews, Christians, and Muslims alike. Although these two ideas of the afterlife—resurrection of the body and immortality of the soul—have often been combined in Western history, they do not, in Segal's view, form an easy synthesis. Taken together they have often been invoked by religious martyrs, and sometimes co-opted by the state itself to the furtherance of its own ends. Belief in a bodily resurrection has been used, Segal suggests, to justify both the self-sacrifice of martyrs and the state's sacrifice of its citizens.

Like Segal, Louis Feldman is interested in the relationship between the state and the religious community—in particular, the status of the Jewish people under Roman rule. Were they scapegoated (in the Girardian sense) by the empire? In "Anti-Judaism, Josephus, and the Hellenistic-Roman Period," Feldman examines the historical context (to the extent we can know it) with regard to the question of anti-Judaism during the ancient Hellenistic-Roman period, paying particular attention to the writings of Josephus. Feldman surveys the available ancient references to Jews within the Greco-Roman sphere and suggests that "it is time to revise the lachrymose view of [ancient] Jewish history." Jews in the ancient world were envied but also protected, accused of dual loyalty but also doing well. The pogroms that did occur (for example, in Alexandria) did so in communities where boundaries or structures of differences were unstable. The terrible anti-Semitism known to the medieval and modern world in Europe was, he concludes, for the most part absent from the ancient world.

In the essays that conclude the first part of this book, Feldman's position receives the endorsement of two other historians of the ancient world. Erich Gruen applauds Feldman's refusal to subscribe to "the lachrymose version" of Jewish history and suggests that Jews in the diaspora (which existed in his view since the time of Alexander) were singled out neither for special condemnation nor for special disdain but accepted—for good or for bad—among many other peoples in a pluralistic polytheistic economy. Perhaps because of their distance from the religious center in Jerusalem, he suggests, they lived within a community in which substitutions played a critical role, allowing them (in the eyes of the dominant culture) a variety of alternative civic practices, in keeping with their singular identity as Jews.

Stuart Robertson similarly approves Feldman's refusal to accept modern constructions of anti-Semitism as applicable as such to the ancient world, and compares Feldman's take on philo-Semitic attitudes with Girard's notions of the sacrificial consequences of runaway mimesis and conflict. Could supersessionism be founded upon obstructed admiration, he wonders? If the similarities between Feldman's view of emulation and Girard's of mimesis are not apparent, perhaps it is because of the differences of their epistemological models, he suggests: Feldman writing as a positivist empirical scholar, Girard as a theorist of cultural anthropology and crisis who understands the great literary and scriptural texts of our tradition as interpretive readings of these matters.

In the second part of the volume, a number of writers take up Girardian (and other than Girardian) ideas about sacrifice and the sacrificial as they are reflected within specific texts in the Jewish and Christian scriptures. Two writers examine the pivotal moment of Genesis 22 (a passage that Chilton has studied elsewhere from a Girardian perspective) when the question of the *Akedah*—the "binding" of Isaac to become an *olah* or burnt sacrificial offering upon Mount Moriah—is raised: Matthew Pattillo from within the context of blessing and creation, and Steven Stern in the context of Kierkegaard's questions about the potential for Abraham to engage in murderous violence.

In "Creation and *Akedah*: Blessing and Sacrifice in the Hebrew Scriptures," Matthew Pattillo explores the themes of creation and blessing. Refuting both of the charges often leveled against Girard—namely, that Girard ignores the biblical theme of blessing and that his thinking is supersessionist—Pattillo argues for a "relationship of interdependence for mutual blessing between Israel and the nations," one that is "ultimately intrinsic to God's revelation to the world." The anti-sacrificial thrust of the *Akedah* forms a new model for sacrifice, one that relies more upon obedience than upon the offerings of the victimary mechanism that Girard describes. "God's invitation," Pattillo notes, extends "from Israel to all the families of the earth to embrace the self-sacrificial character of the innocent victim and to join the family of God in submission and obedience to God. . . . The differentiated unity of the *Akedah* and the Gospel mirrors the divinely intended and enduring relationship between Israel and the nations."

Drawing upon Levinas's notion of our infinite responsibility for the other human being, and our access to that responsibility through the face of the other individual, Steven Stern argues that if the *Akedah* in Genesis 22 does not reject sacrifice entirely, it rejects killing Isaac as a demonstration of faithfulness. Qualifying Kierkegaard's radical individualism through the Jewish tradition of anti-idolatry, Stern argues that the Hebrew text remains profoundly anti-sacrificial. He examines the famous test in Genesis 22:1 "through an analysis of the three people directly affected by the test, [namely,] Abraham, Isaac, and Sarah," finding the passage to be "about Abraham's learning to take responsibility for the Other." His reading thus joins Pattillo's as a move away from the sacrificial postulates by which primitive culture would organize itself and looks forward to a world founded upon ethics and leading to justice.

The essays of Matthew Pattillo and Stephen Stern, Sandor Goodhart suggests, offer a fruitful basis for comparison and contrast. Pattillo examines the whole of Hebrew scripture in relation to Girard's reading of the Christian Gospel as an exposure of the scapegoat mechanism, while Stern focuses in upon one key moment of the Hebrew Bible from which all else in his view may be deduced. Although these two writers are diametrically opposed in their view of that one text, their views reflect divergent angles of approach to it that remain consonant, Goodhart argues, both with Hebrew scripture as the rabbis read it and with the thinking of René Girard.

In the next section, Chris Allen Carter, William Morrow, and Sandor Goodhart read the book of Job in light of Girard's analysis: Carter from within the wisdom tradition, Morrow from within the complaint tradition, and Goodhart from within the rabbinic tradition.[38] In "Mimesis, Sacrifice, and the Wisdom of Job," Chris Allen Carter argues that Girard tackles one of the more recalcitrant interpretive problems of the Bible. Surprisingly supportive of the documentary thesis, Girard develops his ethical critical position by comparing and contrasting the scriptural treatment of Job with the Greek tragedian treatment of Oedipus, thus positioning Job within a larger ethical and historical context than that engaged by other critics. Carter highlights Girard's position by contrasting it with three others, those of Moshe Greenberg, Robert Alter, and Stephen Mitchell, in which the documentary hypothesis is refuted in favor of new critical organic interpretations.

In "The Expulsion of Complaint from Early Jewish Worship," William Morrow also examines René Girard's thesis that the book of Job registers a sacrificial crisis in Israelite religion. Using an account of its literary history more accepted in biblical scholarship, Morrow notes that Job marks an important moment in the unveiling of the scapegoating mechanism, although he differs from Girard in his account of how this happens. The opposition between the God of the victim and the God of the persecutor, which Girard discovers in Job's speeches, Morrow derives from a preexisting tradition of lament. The opposition, he asserts, is not original to Job. In Morrow's view, however, Girard is correct to claim that the spirit of complaint is part of the larger cultural drift in the Judaism of the time. The book of Job attests to the emergence of social and theological dynamics that worked to suppress the complaint against God in Second Temple times. The expulsion of protest prayer from early Jewish worship took place, Morrow explains, under the aegis of what Karl Jaspers dubbed the "Axial Age."

In "The Book of Job and the Problem of Evil: Reading from Theodicy to the Ethical," Sandor Goodhart argues that René Girard's view of the book of Job is successful in unexpected ways. Girard's thesis— that apart from the remote or bullying God in which we usually frame the book, there is another drama afoot with more in common with the scapegoat dynamics of Greek tragedy than the scriptural dynamics of the Hebrew Bible—allows us to make sense of the rabbinic claim that Job is "not Jewish." The narrative, for Goodhart, traces the consequences of a perspective in which the law of anti-idolatry—the Jewish law—has been obscured: namely, that suffering and creation are irrevocably severed from each other. As a result, the four customary means of relating the realms of the divine and the human—myth, institutional ritual practice, the work of human justice, and cosmology— are now no more than free-standing explanations, arbitrary sacrificial theodicies moving independently amidst a sea of such sacrificial explanations, with no more contingent power than any other view in the ancient world. Girard's view helps us to understand the rabbinic advocacy that we move from such theodicies to an ethical perspective in which the law of anti-idolatry retains its province.

The next grouping of essays in part two features analyses of Gospel passages that sound themes important to Girard: mimesis, rivalry, and sacrifice. In "Luke and the Opportune Time: Reading the Temptation Story as Preface to Kingdom and Prologue to Passion," Martin Aiken calls attention to Luke's account of Jesus' temptation in the wilderness as uniquely dramatic in the way it stages the conflict between Jesus and the devil. Drawing upon N. T. Wright's summary of the three "identities that were available to a Jew of first-century Palestine"— that of the Essenes, the Herodians (inclusive of the Sadducees), and the Zealots (inclusive of the Pharisees)—Aiken argues that "the temptation story provides a Lukan synopsis of Jesus' encounters with these three identities . . . with an emphasis on the Essene-like community at Qumran." Driven out into the wilderness "as an outcast," a scapegoat belonging to none of the existing parties, Jesus is tempted to assume an identity defined through an earthly (and diabolic) mimesis, but chooses instead to derive his very self as God's Son from the Father, in obedience to his unique vocation.

In his account of the Gospel of Matthew as a "Gospel That Preaches Nonviolence and Yet Provokes Violence," Gérard Rossé also points to the singularity of the Matthean Jesus, who "explicitly distanced himself from movements advocating the use of violence, such as that of the Zealots," while proposing a "social revolution" that would begin "in the heart of the human being." "What particularly interests me," Rossé writes, "is the fact that, in Jesus' proclamation of the kingdom, the demand to love one's enemies is tightly bound up with the novelty of the *proximity* of the kingdom of God." Jesus' "solidarity . . . with the marginalized was certainly provocative in the eyes of both the political elite and other religious movements," Rossé asserts. At the time of the Gospel's composition, the expulsion of Christian Jews from the synagogues no doubt also intensified the Gospel's criticism of Jewish leaders. Characterizing the historical situation as a quarrel among brothers, Rossé argues that "the polemic against the leaders of Israel" is also and perhaps primarily intended as "a warning to the Christian community. . . . It is, above all, infidelity to the divine will that Matthew indicts, whether it be Jewish or Christian."

Complementing the essays by Aiken and Rossé, Ann W. Astell's "'Exilic' Identities, the Samaritans, and the 'Satan' of John" complicates the question of identities available to Jesus by calling attention to the Gospel according to John, where the Samaritans are featured alongside Jews as members of the house of Israel. Astell describes Jesus' encounter with the Samaritan woman at the well in John 4 as a Johannine substitution for the accounts of Jesus' temptation in the wilderness recorded in the synoptic Gospels. "While the Samaritan woman of John 4 is decidedly not the 'devil' of Luke 4 and Matthew 4 (or the 'Satan' of Mark 1:13)—indeed, she is emphatically human and ultimately becomes Jesus' disciple—she does have a shadowy, apparently promiscuous past (her five husbands perhaps representing Samaritan idol-worship)," Astell observes. She goes on to argue that "John uses the episode consciously to comment on the satanic nature of mimetic competition (the very theme to which Aiken has drawn attention in his masterful exposition of Luke 4)." She concludes that "the Johannine community, which almost certainly included Samaritan members, was struggling toward the realization of a more capacious, pluralistic understanding of Israel—an Israel composed of Jews and Samaritans united in Christ and welcoming to Gentile believers."

In the final section of this second part, in which the Christian Epistles are considered, Christopher Morrissey looks at a text from Colossians, and Poong-In Lee examines the famous sacrificial passages of Hebrews for the possibilities of an anti-sacrificial view. In "Aristotle's 'Natural Slaves' and Colossae's Unnatural 'Scythians': A Generative Exegesis of Colossians 3:11," Chris S. Morrissey unpacks a mimetic rivalry at work among Greek Christians, some of whom have adopted Jewish customs to the dismay of their fellow Greeks. He finds in this rivalry a generative possibility for the use for the derogatory word "Scythian" in a famous passage from St. Paul.

Noting René Girard's early response to the sacrificial theology expressed in the Epistle to the Hebrews, Poong-In Lee asks, "Is an Anti-sacrificial Reading of Hebrews Plausible?" He responds in the affirmative, first, by noting Girard's own revision of his earlier stance and Raymund Schwager's brilliant, Girardian interpretation of Hebrews and, second, by calling attention to the epistle's many exhortations addressed to a Christian community that has clearly suffered persecution. Investigating "the tension between anti-sacrificial and sacrificial stances in the epistle," Poong-In concludes that "new, anti-sacrificial notions of sacrifice and of covenant result from this creative tension," making Hebrews, in the end, "one of the New Testament books that is actually most supportive of Girard's evolutionary theory."

And finally, in "Hermeneutics, Exegesis, and René Girard: A Response to Christopher Morrissey and Poong-In Lee," Anthony Bartlett suggests there are two ways readers of biblical texts can go wrong: by applying Girardian theory either too strongly or too weakly. The goal he says is to let the apocalyptic nature of the Girardian insight speak for itself: "To be true to the dynamic of Girardian thought," he writes, so that "the [biblical] text is released in its authentic apocalyptic force," a force personified in Jesus. Citing Girard, Bartlett characterizes this apocalyptic force as "capable of undermining and overturning the whole cultural order of humanity and supplying the secret motive force of all subsequent history."[39] Morrissey and Poong-In offer us, in their respective Girardian analyses of Colossians and Hebrews, in Bartlett's view, the possibility for making significant headway into the release of these apocalyptic forces.

Reading, Substitution, and the Ethical

Taken together, the essays in this collection engage in what might appropriately be called "substitutive reading." They reflect directly or indirectly a reading, with Girard or in his context, of the cultural logic that allows one victim to substitute for others and culture to be generated (or regenerated) as a consequence. They reflect a reading, with Girard and the anthropologists, of sacrificial offerings as substitutive within specific historical, narrative, and religious contexts, a reading in some cases of cultural breakdown or sacrificial crisis, in which one sacrificial system comes to be substituted for another. But they also, finally, reflect a reading, in one other sense, a sense that occurs historically in two different versions, both relevant to biblical scholarship. On the one hand (following Fishbane's account of the rabbis' view of study and prayer), they reflect a reading of reading itself as a substitute for sacrifice and therefore as an anti-sacrificial means of sacrificial practice. And on the other, they reflect a reading (in the Christian sacramental context) of the Eucharist as a personally transformative sacrificial practice.

In the primitive religious community, in Girard's view, the substitutive economy of sacrifice is not readable. Those who begin to read it are quickly sequestered into shamanistic enclaves. If we in our own culture can read the sacrificial mechanism as its filigree, there must be a source for its legibility. The prophetic texts of the Jewish tradition and later the plays of the greatest of Greek tragic writers begin to formulate this move away from sacrificial origins, and the Christian Gospels, in Girard's view, complete this disclosure. But it is the entire complex of these texts—scriptural, anthropological, and literary in the widest possible sense—that opens the door to what we are calling substitutive reading.

Can we go further? Is there another sense of substitution that can take us beyond the senses we have enumerated (namely, the internal logic of sacrifice, the logic of ritual commemoration, the logic of sacrificial crisis whereby one system transforms itself into another, and the logic of the end to sacrifice and thus what we might call the scriptural anti-sacrificial)? Is there a sense of substitution that develops this anti-sacrificial further, into what could properly be called the ethical? Reading was already understood, among both the rabbis and the church fathers, as a continuation of the practice of sacrifice.[40] Would not an understanding of the anti-sacrificial or anti-idolatrous founded upon an unlimited non-indifference to the other individual (standing face-to-face before me) constitute an ethical continuation of substitution in an entirely new and fertile dimension? Would not the "take me for him" articulated by Yaakov's son, Yehuda, at the conclusion of Genesis, or the "I am guilty—responsible—before all, for everyone and everything, and me more than all the others" articulated by one of Dostoyevsky's characters (and cited repeatedly by René Girard and Emmanuel Levinas), serve such a purpose?

Such an infinite "one for the other" or substitutive reading would of necessity be descriptive before it was prescriptive. It would found itself upon persecution rather than reason, suffering rather than sacrificial structure (which is to say, radical abiding, passivity rather than distinctive action, a passivity more passive than the opposite of active), and it would confer upon us, upon me, the status of a hostage rather than that of an independent observer (within a consciousness newly understood as a heteronomy rather than an autonomy).

Such a constitution of an ethical would thus answer, if Girard is right, the oldest demands made upon our species: that we sacrifice another in order that human community become possible. It would provide a responsible foundation for interhuman groups by refusing violence in an especially egregious fashion: by reversing sacrifice, by acknowledging in its place an infinite responsibility for the other human being, and by abiding an obligation or election that has been available to us in the West for some two thousand years now and that continues, in both the Jewish and the Christian traditions, to go by the unlikely name of love.

Notes

1. René Girard delivered a talk, "Scapegoating at Çatalhöyük," at the annual meeting of the Colloquium on Violence and Religion, "Catastrophe and Conversion: Political Thinking for the New Millennium," on June 20, 2009, at the University of California, Riverside, on this topic.

2. Cf. Edgar Allen Poe's "The Purloined Letter," one of his Auguste Dupin mystery stories, which refers to this game.

3. Raymund Schwager, S.J., *Must There Be Scapegoats? Violence and Redemption in the Bible*, trans. Maria L. Assad (San Francisco: Harper and Row, 1987).

4. For an English translation of this book, see *Battling to the End: Conversations with Benoît Chantre*, trans. Mary Baker (East Lansing: Michigan State University Press, 2009).

5. See Gary A. Anderson, "Sacrifice and Sacrificial Offerings (OT)," *The Anchor Bible Dictionary*, edited by David Noel Friedman, 6 vols. (New York: Doubleday, 1992), 5:872.

6. See Robert G. Hamerton-Kelly, ed., *Violent Origins: Walter Burkert, René Girard, and Jonathan Z. Smith on Ritual Killing and Cultural Formation* (Stanford, CA: Stanford University Press, 1987).

7. Mark Rogin Anspach, *À Charge de Revanche: Figures Élémentaires de la réciprocité* [*On Condition that You Allow Me to Do the Same: Elementary Forms of Reciprocity*] (Paris: Éditions du Seuil, 2002).

8. Hamerton-Kelly's book has been largely ignored, and Anspach's book has not been translated.

9. See David Janzen, *The Social Meanings of Sacrifice in the Hebrew Bible: A Study of Four Writings* (Berlin: Walter de Gruyter, 2004).

10. *Things Hidden since the Foundation of the World* appeared in English in 1987, *Job* in 1987, and *I See Satan Fall Like Lightning* in 2001. An essay on Salome, "Scandal and the Dance: Salome in the Gospel of Mark," appeared in *New Literary History* 15 in 1983. And an essay on the mythical status of the Gospels, "Are the Gospels Mythical?" appeared in *First Things* 62 in 1996.

11. See James G. Williams, *The Bible, Violence, and the Sacred: Liberation from the Myth of Sanctioned Violence* (San Francisco: HarperSanFrancisco, 1992), and Andrew McKenna's "René Girard and Biblical Studies," *Semeia* 33 (1985).

12. Jonathan Klawans makes those charges in *Purity, Sacrifice, and the Temple: Symbolism and Supersessionism in the Study of Ancient Judaism* (New York: Oxford, 2005).

13. See Anderson, "Sacrifice and Sacrificial Offerings (OT)," 5:870–76.

14. Consider, for example, Roland de Vaux's work on the intricacy of sacrificial ritual: *Ancient Israel: Its Life and Institutions*, trans. John McHugh (New York: McGraw Hill, 1961).

15. For a contemporary survival of this "documentary hypothesis," see Richard Elliot Friedman's *Who Wrote the Bible?* (New York: Summit Books, 1987), and later, his *Commentary on the Torah* (San Francisco: HarperSanFrancisco, 2001).

16. See Julius Wellhausen, *Prolegomena zur Geschichte Israels* (Berlin: Reimer, 1883), trans. J. Sutherland Black and Allan Menzies, and with a preface by W. Robertson Smith, as *Prolegomena to the History of Ancient Israel* (Edinburgh: Adam and Charles Black, 1985). For an exposition of the differences between this Wellhausenian tradition of the prophetic and the more properly sacrificial traditions of blessing, see Hans Jensen, "Nature, Bible, Priestly Theology: A Reply to Sandor Goodhart and Charles Mabee," American Academy of Religion / Society of Biblical Literature, Chicago, November 18, 1994. For an account of this talk, see http://www.uibk.ac.at/theol/cover/bulletin/xtexte/bulletin08-4.html. Jensen sees sacrifice in this context as a kind of kitchen and the activities associated with it a kind of food preparation. On that idea, see also Anderson, "Sacrifice and Sacrificial Offerings (OT)."

17. Sir Edward Burnett Tylor, *Primitive Culture: Researches in the Development of Mythology, Philosophy, Religion, Language, Arts, and Custom* (London: J. Murray, 1871); Sir James George Frazer, *The Golden Bough: A Study in Magic and Religion*, 3rd ed., 12 vols. (London: Macmillan, 1906–15); and William Robertson Smith, *Lectures on the Religion of the Semites: The Fundamental Institutions* (London: Adam and Charles Black, 1889).

18. See George Buchanan Gray, *Sacrifice in the Old Testament: Its Theory and Practice* (1925); reissued in 1971 with a "Prolegomenon" by Baruch A. Levine, from Ktav Publishing House. The quote is from Levine, "Prolegomenon," 2.

19. Wellhausen, *Prolegomena to the History of Ancient Israel.*

20. Gary Anderson's comment, at the outset of his article on sacrifice in biblical studies, that biblical scholarship to date has not benefited significantly from anthropological research, would seem trenchant.

21. Levine, "Prolegomenon," 2.

22. See Henri Hubert and Marcel Mauss, *Sacrifice: Its Nature and Function* (Chicago: University of Chicago Press, 1964).

23. See Claude Lévi-Strauss, *Totemism*, trans. Rodney Needham (New York: Beacon Press, 1963).

24. On Lévi-Strauss' anti-Durkheimianism, see *Tristes Tropiques* (New York: Penguin, 1992). On his articulation of his method as a "science of the concrete," see *The Savage Mind* (Chicago: University of Chicago Press, 1966), 1–34. It is significant that he wrote one of the longest and one of his best texts as an *Introduction to the Work of Marcel Mauss* (London: Routledge, 1987).

25. In a conversation with Norbert Lohfink that followed my presentation in 1983 at Cerisy on the Joseph story, Sandor Goodhart made that point. What about those texts in Deuteronomy that call for Israel to take possession of the lands of Canaan? The same principle of textualization applies there, I argued, and the fol-

lowing day over lunch he agreed. Historical reality and ritual practice are important in so far as the biblical scripture perceives them as textual phenomena.

26. See Andrew McKenna's *Violence and Difference: Girard, Derrida, and Deconstruction* (Urbana: University of Illinois Press, 1992) on this point. For more discussion of Girard's role in upsetting the traditional boundary between criticism and literature, see Sandor Goodhart, *Sacrificing Commentary* (Baltimore: Johns Hopkins University Press, 1996), and, more recently, Robert Doran's introduction to René Girard, *Mimesis and Theory: Essays on Literature and Criticism, 1953–2005* (Stanford, CA: Stanford University Press, 2008), i–xxvi.

27. See, for example, Émile Benveniste, *Le Vocabulaire des institutions Indo-Européennes, Tome I: Économie, parenté, société*; vol. 2: *Pouvoir, droit, religion* (Paris: Edition de Minuit, 1969 and 1980).

28. A posthumous English translation of a work by the Jesuit Father Raymund Schwager attempts to discern a parallel between a Girardian account of hominization and theological discussion of "original sin." See *Banished From Eden: Original Sin and Evolutionary Theory in the Drama of Salvation*, trans. James Williams (Leominster: Gracewing, 2006).

29. This observation, of course, does not take into account the hundreds of books and articles written on Girard's work in general (on a yearly basis) by his devotees in (or around) the Colloquium on Violence and Religion and other groups taking Girard as their focus, writings that are not part of the mainstream disciplines.

30. Girard's general reputation has had some odd turns. He started as a historian of medieval marriage conventions. Upon writing *Mensonge romantique et vérité romanèsque*, he was hailed as the premier thinker of "triangular desire"; see Lucien Goldman's commentary, for example, in *Pour une sociologie du roman* (Paris: Gallimard, 1964). When Girard started writing about sacrifice and violence, his literary critical audience diminished somewhat, but his importance as a cultural anthropologist, religious studies thinker, and general essayist was affirmed in his admission to the French Academy and echoed in Michel Serres's introductory presentation at the l'Académie française (December 15, 2005), writing that Girard "invented the most fruitful hypothesis of the age"; see "Receiving René Girard into the l'Academie francaise," in *For René Girard: Essays in Friendship and Truth*, ed. Sandor Goodhart, Jörgen Jörgensen, Thomas Ryba, and James Williams, 1–17 (East Lansing: Michigan State University Press, 2009), at 15.

31. Roger Beckwith and Martin Selman, *Sacrifice in the Bible* (Grand Rapids, MI: Baker Book House, 1995).

32. David Janzen, *The Social Meanings of Sacrifice in the Hebrew Bible* (Berlin: Walter de Gruyter, 2004), 79.

33. James W. Watts, *Ritual and Rhetoric in Leviticus: From Sacrifice to Scripture* (Cambridge: Cambridge University Press, 2007), 177.

34. Christian Grappe and Alfred Marx, *Sacrifices scandaleux? Sacrifices humains, martyre et mort du Christ* (Paris: Editions du Cerf, 2008).

35. Klawans, *Purity, Sacrifice, and the Temple.*

36. See Bruce Chilton, *Abraham's Curse: The Roots of Violence in Judaism, Christianity, and Islam* (New York: Random House, 2008).

37. *Nostra Aetate* is one of the central documents of Vatican II. See *Declaration on the Relation of the Church to Non-Christian Religions, Nostra Aetate, Proclaimed by his Holiness, Pope Paul VI, October 28, 1965.*

38. For Girard's analysis, see *Job, the Victim of His People,* trans. Yvonne Freccero (Stanford, CA: Stanford University Press, 1987).

39. Girard, *Things Hidden since the Foundation of the World* (Stanford, CA: Stanford University Press, 1987), 209.

40. Origen is cited in this context within the Christian fold, and Hugh of St. Victor might be added to that group. See Henri de Lubac, *Medieval Exegesis: The Four Senses of Scripture,* vols. 1–2 (Grand Rapids, MI: Eerdmans, 1998–2009), on this idea.

PART I

Sacrifice

ONE

Mimesis, Sacrifice, and the Bible
A Conversation with Sandor Goodhart

RENÉ GIRARD

> *If each is the double of another, if all doubles are the same, all equally*
> *and identically monstrous, it is clear this time that any one at almost any*
> *moment can become the double of all others. One victim alone can substitute*
> *for all potential victims for all those that each dreams of sacrificing, that is,*
> *for everyone without exception.*
>
> —René Girard

SANDOR GOODHART: René, in a sense you are not really discovering anything new with the mimetic hypothesis, are you? You are just taking seriously—perhaps more seriously than ever before—what we have known for a long time: namely, that imitation and violence are linked.

RENÉ GIRARD: That's right. The main thing about mimetic theory is that imitation has always played an important role in the thinking of mankind. It's extremely important in the Bible and in the Gospels. The imitation of Jesus, for example, is absolutely essential. But imitation is so unpopular today that in many churches they don't say "imitating" Jesus, they say "following." What does following mean if not imitating? Imitation is everywhere. Imitation is essential in the greatest of all philosophers—Plato.[1] Aristotle defined mankind as the most mimetic of all animals—which remains for me the most profound definition, one that is still valid today.[2]

At the same time, we have for the most part separated imitation from violence. At the end of the nineteenth century there was a period when imitation explained everything, and all the theoreticians talked about it. In France, Gabriel Tarde is revived a little bit from time to time.[3] But theorists like Tarde remove the drama from imitation. How could there be drama in imitation, they ask? They fail to see that imitation is the main source of violence in mankind. When we say imitation, we think of being sheepish, gregarious, following people. That is true in many instances, of course. But what is equally true is that imitation affects not merely your gestures — your words, your ideas, which you borrow, no doubt, from other people — but also your desires. You imitate the desires of other people.

SG: The great writers on the other hand understood all that.

RG: Yes. The people who really know that are the great writers. Shakespeare talks about little else. That's why I fell in love with Shakespeare when I was teaching in Buffalo. Most of the first comedies of Shakespeare begin with two young friends, sometimes four, as in *A Midsummer Night's Dream*. And they have been friends since early infancy. They are friends (they say to themselves) because they like everything alike — the same books, the same everything. Then suddenly, what happens? Because they like everything alike, they fall in love with the same girl, and all hell breaks loose. It's so important in Shakespeare that he comes back to it at the end of his life in the greatest of his plays, *The Winter's Tale*, which is very mysterious, and an even greater play on jealousy in my view than *Othello*. But it comes after *Othello*, and it's about the insane jealousy of a man for his best friend. There are only two great writers who understand that to the same extent as Shakespeare; one is Dostoyevsky, and the other, in my view, is Dante. But if you love the same thing as your best friend, he becomes your worst enemy, of course. In Shakespeare the number of lines that express this mystery of the conflation of the greatest affection for your friend with the greatest jealousy for the man who is in love with the same thing — is quite large.

SG: One would think that the human sciences, which after all present themselves as the study of the human, would take account of this phenomenon.

RG: The theory of mankind should be able to assimilate this insight. It does not, and that for me is very sad. Take, for instance, evolutionary theory. The theory of evolution is very important today, and I am a Darwinist; I believe in natural selection.[4] Richard Dawkins has said that we have to explain culture by evolutionary theory. He invented what he calls "memes," which he described as "units of imitation."[5] Dawkins did not develop the project himself. But following Dawkins, many evolutionist theoreticians today discuss culture in terms of *memetics*.[6] They write many books, but seem to have missed the fact that *mimesis*—the Greek word for imitation—is potentially conflictual, and obviously the greatest source of conflict between nations.

SG: The idea of nations would seem to be a particularly good place to turn in order to understand the relations between imitation and conflict.

RG: Two nations become rivals for the area that belongs to both, and that process fuels nationalism. National conflict is about the territory you crave that the next country possesses. If it does not exist, then you need to invent it. But we do not like knowing that. We cover up the fact that we desire the same thing for the same reason under a pretense of different ideas. Most conflicts of ideas—and they can be important—are like this. When people have real ideas and believe in them, they usually argue quite peacefully. But very often conflicts of ideas are a cover for a rivalry of desire, because it's very humiliating for all of us to understand when we are rivals that we owe our desire, which is supposed to be mostly ours, to other people.

SG: The advertising industry would also seem to be an especially good arena in which to study this.

RG: Yes, of course, advertisers know that very well, and they are never trying to show you that one product is really better than the next product. They are trying to show you always that a product is desired by the most desirable people. They show you beautiful people playing on the sand on a beautiful beach and using their soft drink, or whatever the product is, and because you want to be like these people, you are going to drink that soft drink, you are going to use that soft drink as a kind of sacrament. And you say, "Maybe if I drink that soft drink, I will look a little more like these people on the beach than I really do" (because, deep down, I know that I do not look at all the way they do).

SG: So what would you say then is the origin of their linkage? How did imitation get linked to conflict? Where does it all begin?

RG: I think that mimetic theory really does have to be inscribed in evolutionary theory. We know that animals already have mimetic rivalry, and that mimetic rivalry in animals is the source of what biologists today call their culture. When two animals that do not know each other desire the same female, the same territory, the same food, they fight as we do. But they never fight to the finish. They fight moderately, we might say. When the weaker animal knows his weakness, he gives up. And the stronger animal always spares his life. From then on, the stronger becomes the dominant animal, and the other the dominated animal, which is a little bit like an animal slavery. It is not completely slavery, of course, because mankind, in enslaving his fellow human being, learns how to use the working capacity of it. I do not think animals can do that, but maybe we'll find some examples someday. Anyway, the solution to this rivalry among animals is called "dominance patterns." When biologists talk about animal culture, they always talk about these patterns; and they may be hierarchical, they may be complicated.[7]

But we know, on the other hand, that human beings fight to the finish. They even fight beyond the finish because if you fight to the death with someone in an archaic culture, that is not the end of it. The victim's brother will pick up the fight and kill the murderer, and then the brother of the second victim will keep up the fight, and so forth. That's what we call the blood feud. In a way, the blood feud is already a religion of violence: it transcends individuals, it transcends time, it may transcend space, because if your relatives go on endlessly picking up the fight with the last murderer, its society is sure to end right then and there. That is why revenge is not a cultural institution; it's the opposite, in a way, of a cultural institution. It's really very interesting, because revenge is pretty much universal if you start looking at archaic culture. But all cultures have to prohibit it. If they did not, they would be doomed from the start. They would kill themselves. So there you have a contradiction in mankind.

The question is how can the human community form societies, long-term associations on the basis of that form of rivalry that is endless, that goes on forever. And what does it mean? Should we speak here of evil? I don't think so. I think we need to use a scientific language. It just means that that you cannot stop imitating the violence of your opponent any more than you can stop imitating the kindness of your friend. Kindness escalates and turns into what we call love, which obviously animals don't have. But it escalates the other way too, and it turns into deadly violence, which animals don't have either. There you have two characteristics of mankind that you can define practically and empirically. And I think it is very important to do that.

Take, for example, the notion of reciprocity. Have you noticed that all human relations are absolutely reciprocal, the worst as well as the best? What is that? It's imitation. If someone does something kind to you, you do the same. You are compelled to do the same, because if you do not, something is wrong. Therefore, what do you do? You imitate them. But if they start being mean or turning their back on you, what do you do? You turn your back too. Most of the time they don't see it, since their back is already turned, but usually you manage to make it known to them that you understand how they feel about you and that you feel the same—which means you add a tiny bit of disagreeableness to the existing disagreeableness as you see it. But this little something added is going to look to your partner as an enormous provocation, as a declaration of war; then your relations are going to go from bad to worse. But whether you exchange compliments, niceties, greetings, or insinuations, indifference, meanness, bullets, atom bombs, it's always an exchange. You always give to the other guy what he's giving to you, or you try to do so.

But what is reciprocity? No one ever talks about it. Even the word reciprocity is a little bit mysterious, because it probably refers to the back and forth movement of the tide, which is a strange way of referring to human relations. But if you look at animals, they are not having reciprocal relations. As a matter of fact, they never look at each other. Rudyard Kipling wrote about animals, of course, in his *Jungle Book,* which is not very popular today because it is not politically correct; it is imperialistic, and all sorts of things that are bad, so people don't read it anymore.[8] Well, he has an anthropocentric myth that animals cannot sustain the look of human beings. Mowgli in the *Jungle Book,* for example, looks at the wolves, and they have to move away. And it is true empirically. If you look at an animal in the eyes, you will see that very quickly his eyes will wander away. But I don't think it's for the reason Kipling gives. For Kipling, it meant that mankind is so superior that animals cannot stand the look of human beings. I think this is pure myth, of course. But to an animal the look of a human being means absolutely nothing. He's not going to eat your eyes. He is looking away because it does not interest him in the slightest. The real explanation in a way is the opposite to that of Kipling, even though Kipling's observation is accurate.

SG: How far can we take this idea that imitation and violence are linked? Could we distinguish between human culture and animal culture on its basis, for example? Could we think of human culture as a way of dealing, perhaps, with a runaway crisis of reciprocity, or of reciprocal violence?

RG: You can show that you cannot deal with human culture as you deal with animal culture, because human culture begins with a crisis. We know that there are many crises in human culture. All communities have crises, and maybe crisis is a special human feature that tells us something about what it means to be human. Mankind, we may say, is a crisis animal. I think that the real problem with our social sciences is that they have never learned that truth.

In other words, social sciences confuse the science of man with what human beings say about the order of their community. If you are a sociologist, you study the order according to the people who talk about their own culture. If you are a psychologist, you talk about the self according to what the self is telling you. But when a society gets into a serious crisis, who is in charge? Very often the government is no longer in charge, and so none of the rules apply.

SG: So, the notion of crisis is absent from scientific talk about social reality?

RG: Social science cannot, in a way, define a crisis. A great political scientist—Carl Schmitt—first said that. He is fairly unpopular today because he behaved like a Nazi for quite a while, although he

was not really a Nazi.⁹ He said a social science should first be the science of crisis.¹⁰ It's often very easy to define who the government is.
But in most societies the government is not the most important authority, and you have to study a crisis in order to see who is in charge
there, who's fighting whom, what's really going on. If you listen to the
government, you listen to their propaganda. In a way, the mimetic
theory would like to do that, to move beyond propaganda, because the
mimetic theory necessarily starts with crisis.

SG: So, it seems Aristotle was right all along: we just left crisis
out of the definition of the mimetic.

RG: Aristotle is right in saying that mankind is the most mimetic
of animals, because we know very well that the great apes are next to us;
they are more mimetic than other animals. They are so mimetic that
we laugh at them, just as we laugh at ourselves. But we are obviously
much more mimetic than they are. Therefore it must be out of that
crisis that we emerged. What must have happened at the time of hominization, over the course of hundreds of thousands of years perhaps, is
that dominance patterns disappeared. Since animals have a culture
now, to talk about the process of hominization, the beginning of the
human community, it is not enough to talk about biological changes.
You have to talk about cultural changes, because we know that the last
stages of the evolution of mankind are both cultural and physical.

For example, the infant. The human infant needs so much care for
so many years that it is impossible to think humanity could develop
without any culture, in other words, without any taboos on violence,
on violence inside the family. We know that the male would not tolerate being separated from the female for as long as it is necessary in a
human family for the education of the young children. Therefore, there
must be a mix between the two. We have to find mechanisms that are
at the same time part of culture and also quite mechanical and happen
spontaneously, because no human being was capable of inventing them.

I think that religion goes back that far, that the incredible power
that religion has over us must be there already at the beginning of
human community, that we have to find a way to talk about religion in
a scientific way that will not be either antireligious, as it is today, nor
proreligious in a spiritualist way—which is completely out of order

at that time. Therefore, the discussion between creationists and evolutionists, and even between spiritualists and materialists—all these things today are becoming outmoded. The question is to find ways to talk about what happens when these dominance patterns disappear and when a human culture, a human type of culture, is beginning to take over.

SG: How do we do that, since, in this realm, we have very few "records" to speak of?

RG: I think we have to look at the structure of religion. Today again, when people discuss religion (or talk against religion), they tell you that religion is a view of the world, and most scientists are stuck with an idea that religion is an especially outdated view of the world, a kind of fanciful view, invented because these people did not know how to explain better the mysteries of the universe.

But if you look at an archaic society, they could not care less for the mysteries of the universe. They never talk about them. They do not suspect that there are mysteries of the universe. You have to be remarkably sophisticated, you know, really closer to someone like Matthew Arnold than an individual within an archaic society, to look at the starry night and do that. And yet that is how the nineteenth century saw the beginning of religion. We are asked to believe that you look at the stars, and then you invent God. It's not true at all. These archaic cultures had more serious problems to contend with, problems that not only derived from the outside world, from the forces of nature, from disease—animals cope with that—but from intraspecies fighting, fighting that must get worse and worse as people get closer and closer to each other. At the very moment when mankind needs the most protection against his own violence, suddenly it is not there anymore (if the dominance patterns have disappeared), and so a new mode of survival must be found.

SG: Religion in your view would function then as a protection against our own violence.

RG: That conclusion, I think, is inevitable if you observe the most ancient religions we know, which are the archaic religions. These religions do not care at all for the mysteries of the universe. And they are divided into two or three different parts. The first one is prohibitions—

what you shouldn't do, ever (although sometimes there are exceptions). The second part is sacrifice—which is very strange, because in some ways sacrifice is the opposite of the prohibitions. Prohibitions forbid violence, and sacrifice requires of you one certain violent action, which is the killing of a victim. Many theologians, and people who are politically correct, try to say that the sacrifice, the violent part, may not be the essential part, that it is only incidental. If you're sending an animal to the god, what can you do after that? You cannot keep this animal in the flock. You have to get rid of it, somehow, discreetly, and what else can you do but kill the animal. It's not true. Violence is essential in sacrifice, and wherever you have very important texts on sacrifice they tell you about this essential nature of violence. In particular in India where we have texts going back very far and we can see that violence is essential.

So, you have that mystery of religious institutions, which are at the same time against violence and for prohibitions. Prohibition has only one object if you look at it carefully. It's the prohibition of violence inside the community. Violence outside the community is not really violence; you can do anything you like there, it doesn't matter. But inside the community you must not touch anyone. Many people feel it's very smart, very chic, to denigrate the prohibitions of others in order to promote their own, which are thought to be completely rational. But if you look at archaic prohibitions, they are rational too; the only thing is that sometimes archaic people had a conception of violence that is just empirically false. They are aware that the more people are alike, the more they fight.

SG: You are thinking, for example, of the appearance and treatment of twins.

RG: Yes. This is the reason why so many archaic cultures are against twins. There is no objective truth in their belief. There are many archaic cultures that understand very well that twins have nothing to do with violence and they pay no attention to twins any more than we do. But there are many other archaic cultures that will not tolerate twins to stay within the community; they feel that if they allow that, violence will spread like wildfire and destroy the whole community. Therefore, they don't kill twins out of some meanness of spirit or some absurdity like that; they feel that twins, as soon as they are born, have something to do with violence. That is why they often think that the mother has been misbehaving, that she has been, in other words, transgressing prohibitions against violence. And if you transgress prohibitions against violence, you will have twins. In other words, you will produce violence. Many communities, I repeat, understand that it is not true in the case of biological twins. But many do not. As a result, sometimes they will get rid of only one twin, which really shows that it's the similarity of twins that bothers them.

SG: How does the second part of religion—sacrifice—function in this context?

RG: In order to know what sacrifice is, I think you must go to the third branch of primitive religion, which is myth. Some people will say that myths have something to do with mysteries of the universe, no doubt because we are thinking of Greek myth. But we did not receive Greek myths as religious myth; they were already philosophized. They come to us through the philosophers, and they are contaminated with philosophical thinking, which is fine and very interesting, but which has little to do with archaic religion. If you look at an archaic myth, it does only one thing: it tells you how a religion was born—a sacrificial cult and prohibitions. That's all. It was born, of course, in violence, in a type of crisis that looks very much like the one I said must have happened when dominance patterns disappeared. People get into a cycle of violence; more and more violence occurs, and the whole community goes haywire.

Many myths tried to disguise that crisis behind natural disasters, and one very common theme at the beginning of myth is the plague. But we know very well that in archaic societies they do not distinguish the plague as a disease. (This happened only in the sixteenth century.) The plague is primarily violence, people killing each other. Therefore, an epidemic of plague was conceived as people killing each other. If you look at the description in *Oedipus the King*, you will see that it's really that. I think that the plague, or the flood, or other phenomena of that type, are very often sacrifice gone wild; that there's a monster in the community, so to speak, and he wants more and more victims. As he gets more and more victims, of course, sacrifice disappears as a source of peace; it becomes violence itself. It joins up with the violence of the community, which normally the community would fight. And the whole community then goes haywire; you have a crisis that seems to be impossible to cure, because the more you turn to prohibitions and sacrifice, the more violence you have.

SG: And then, of course, scapegoating begins. How does an individual member of the community come to play the role of a scapegoat victim here?

RG: If you look at the myth in its entirety, you will see that after this crisis is described, the focus shifts from the community to a single character, and this single character is always ultimately accused of being responsible for the whole crisis. Here again, if you know *Oedipus* (which I always mention at this point, because it's a great play, and the foundation of the myth people know best), you can see that this is true. Oedipus was looking for the solution to the plague, and people decided he himself was the problem, not the solution; he is the plague, because he is their king, which is legitimate. To me, that's why there are so many interpretations of the *Oedipus* tragedy in political terms. No doubt they are tired of their king, just as the people in Job's village are tired of Job, and they are about to get rid of Oedipus. But in the case of Oedipus, we are in an archaic community, and so we find a reason for it. There is a god who is mad at him, and who has decided that he's responsible for the plague epidemic; in other words, that he has brought the violence to the community, and he must be killed or cast out. We are in a very polite myth, so we don't really kill Oedipus, but we expel him, and he blinds himself; therefore, he punishes himself. But in any case, as in all myth, you have a crisis in the beginning that gets worse and worse until suddenly it comes to a head, so to speak, in a single victim. And that single victim ultimately is killed, very often by the whole people together. Which is pretty strange, no doubt.

Sophocles, of course, wrote a second Oedipus play, and in some ways you can see what I am saying by comparing the two. The thing that is fascinating about the second Oedipus play, *Oedipus at Colonis,* is that it describes the arrival of Oedipus in the suburb of Athens, which is the place of birth of the author, Sophocles. Sophocles likes to think that Colonis in a way adopted Oedipus. But the second play is very different from the first because instead of seeing the culprit, the man guilty of parricide and incest, we see the god.

In other words, we see the transformation of the guilty victim into a good god, because Oedipus was a minor divinity in Greece. What kind of divinity? An archaic god is always the god of the law he transgresses, before it exists in principle. He is a god of marriage. But many scholars say, "Well, the second *Oedipus* is very different from the first; it's not a real tragedy because Oedipus was very old and just couldn't be as tragic." I really think that Sophocles follows his own religion, and it is the divinized Oedipus who is the hero of *Oedipus at Colonis,* whereas it is the mean scapegoat who is the hero of *Oedipus the King.* So, in a way, in the two plays you have the whole evolution of a normal archaic religion—in a tragic context, of course, which changes many things, makes many things more civilized. Oedipus seems to be the object of a real investigation, of a real trial. But it is a form of lynching, you can be sure, because behind the play is sacred violence. The archaic sacred must always contain that element of violence that makes it potent, that can turn into peace.

In the Oedipus myth, which is highly civilized, there's the pretense of a trial. But if you look at really archaic myth, you will see that the myths where you have that crisis—it's always there at the beginning— end up with actual lynching. In Australian myths, for instance, you have examples of that. It's not described explicitly, of course, but it is a whole community that rushes against the culprit and kills him. Very often it's animals that are capable of charging collectively. The Blackfoot Indians have a lynching myth that involves buffaloes, who lynch either some kind of a man or another buffalo. But in Australia, which could not be influenced by the Blackfoot Indians, it's the kangaroos who kill another kangaroo, who becomes the god kangaroo. And all over Africa, you have lynching myths. The scholars don't want to talk about these lynching myths, or to wonder why there are so many of them. And even in Greece—our dear civilized Greece, the most civilized country in the world, according to the West—and moreover in the most famous mythological cycle, that of Dionysus, there are many such episodes, and they all end with a lynching. Have you seen a classical scholar wonder why there's always a lynching? That would not be a decent question. You don't ask questions about violence; you push them under the rug. That's what western society has done, especially since the Enlightenment, because the Greeks cannot do any wrong. And today we believe that texts are violent, but only texts, not people. Of course, our contemporaries are violent, but there's no violence before our contemporaries, and, especially, among the Greeks. If you look at the texts, however, you see that some of our great Western thinkers have reacted against that.

SG: You are thinking no doubt of Nietzsche.

RG: One of them was Nietzsche. But Nietzsche in a way embraced this violence. He made it his own. He said it's better than the peace that was in his own world at the time, and he went mad. But any average Greek who would have seen Dionysius embraced by Nietzsche could have foreseen that Nietzsche was going to go mad.[11] Because if you look at this lynching mania, this lynching mania that takes the form of the Dionysiac cult (the word *mania*, of course, comes from the Greeks, and from the Dionysiac cult where it means homicidal mania, and refers to that moment in the myth and in the sacrifice), if you consider this lynching mania, it looks exactly like the myth. They have to take very small animals, so that the faithful will be able to tear the animal apart and eat it alive. That's called homophasia, and originally it is cannibalism. But the Dionysiac religion remains shaped by it; it's really quite remarkable. It's most popular with our modern thinkers, who do not seem to realize what they are talking about. But I think it is very important to maintain that connection.

SG: Why should lynching be regarded as something on the one hand capable of bringing peace and on the other linked to the prohibitions?

RG: You have a community that is in a serious crisis, which is mimetically mad, so to speak, where people are imitating each other's violence to a great extent and are fighting about objects. When you are fighting mimetically for the same object of desire, you cannot be reconciled. Sooner or later, this object will be destroyed, and only the antagonists will be left. When you are fighting the same antagonist mimetically, you immediately reconcile; you form an alliance against other people. People cannot desire together the same object, but they can hate together. As a matter of fact, if you read the trilogy of Aeschylus, who may be the greatest Greek tragic writer, in the last play, the *Eumenides,* the goddess Athene and Eumenides say, "We must give up vengeance; and we can do it anyway because now we have an outside enemy, the Persians." Aeschylus himself was a soldier in the first Persian wars of Athens, when Athens repelled Persia, and more or less Aeschylus says that the Athenian empire will be great because, instead of resorting to vengeance (which was some sort of tribal vengeance, in the days before classical Greece), we chose to move against the enemy from outside. From now on, we are a nation, and we have only enemies from the outside. In the conclusion of the *Eumenides,* this insight is very clear. It should be read, in a way, as a foundation of the Athenian empire.

So, what do we see there? Why that single victim? How could a crisis be reduced to a single victim? Because ultimately if you have that imitation, that contagion or antagonism, there will only be a few victims left, and finally (in theory) only one, and the entire community will fight that one. When they kill that singular enemy, of course, no enemy will be left in the community, and peace will return. That is the reason, I believe, that the victim becomes the god. The victim is regarded not only as very bad, very dangerous because he made us fight, but also very good because he reconciled us. So ultimately, I think, that single victim is the origin of the archaic gods, who are always very violent and very peaceful when they want to be, but they are always both at the same time. What we have here is the origin of archaic religion.

SG: Weren't the so-called "Cambridge anthropologists" in their own way close to discovering this origin?

RG: I think that the anthropologists of the period 1850–1950 were *very* close to discovering that origin. I think they just didn't dare say that violence conquered by sacrifice might be the origin of religion and of culture as a whole. Because what is sacrifice, ritual sacrifice? If human communities have in their past an experience like the one I have just described, at first they are very happy, they are all reconciled, they kiss each other, they love each other; but human beings are human beings, and they will become rivals again. And then what happens? They remember that there was in the past that single victim who reconciled them, and they try to do it again with substitute victims. Ritual sacrifice, in my view, is nothing else.[12] If you talk to people today, they say, "Well, we cannot do that anymore." But the anthropologists in 1895, who talked to archaic people, found that they all talk in the same way about their sacrifices: "They were given to us by a god, and this god gave them to us in order to keep peace among us." Peace and the gods are always mentioned together. And it is true. The proof that they want to repeat a phenomenon of that type, which is a crowd phenomenon, is what happens at the beginning of sacrifice, which is the problem that the old anthropology could never solve. In many communities, especially in Africa but also in other areas, when people have trouble among themselves, what do they do: they sacrifice! If you look at the places where sacrifice is located in archaic communities, you will see that it is always where there is the most trouble — rites of passage, for example, in the youth, dangerous youth, male youth. Rites of passages are a group of sacrifices and ordeals that come from the crisis I was talking about.

SG: How about the institution of sacred kingship? Does kingship play a role in this discussion?

RG: Who are the sacred kings?[13] A sacred king is an individual who is selected as king and is in power for a while and after a certain number of years (which varies, and as a matter of fact we don't know anything about it), the king is sacrificed, is killed. Then we know there is an evolution, and later on the king is no longer sacrificed. A substitute for the king is sacrificed. Or an animal. Or there are other substitutes. But what does it mean that the king is sacrificed? I really think that at the beginning you have the phenomenon that I talked about. You have the killing of a victim, and the killing reconciles the community, as any crowd will be reconciled by its own violence. The tendency of the crowd is to worship the victim, the victim that at the same time it also greatly fears, and that is what an archaic god is. But then, when you have trouble, you are going to have a new victim, and you know that you are going to sacrifice that victim, so if you believe in the thing again, that victim becomes sacred even before he is killed. And if the victim is very smart (and let's suppose so), this victim will become very powerful inside the community before dying.

What is the monarchy in this connection? It's just reliving the original phenomenon with the victim in charge until his death. So the sacred monarchy is a very strange institution. You have a king, and one fine day you kill the king. We know it was really done because we have documents. As a matter of fact, behind the Oedipus myth there might very well be a very old myth of a sacred monarchy, because Oedipus is king, after all. Why is he king? Ultimately, because he committed parricide and incest. Therefore, he's a sacred king. So, if you kill the victim immediately after selecting your victim, you have what we call sacrifice. If you wait, and worship the victim alive, and put the victim in charge of your community, you have invented the monarchy. I don't think human cultures invent anything *ex nihilo*. They always invent by copying sacrifice. As a matter of fact, if you start looking at institutions from that point of view, you become convinced that it has to be true, because sacrifice is present at the heart of all archaic institutions.

This even happens historically. Behind the institution of the French kings there is a little whiff of sacred monarchy. If you look at Louis XIV, Louis XV, you find no hint of sacred monarchy. But go and look at the trial of the king and of the queen at the time of the French Revolution. The queen was accused of incest with her son. If you look at the trial of Louis XVI and Marie Antoinette, you find all the archaic accusations (and some historians are interested in this), and suddenly the king is killed, and for the same reasons or nonreasons as you find in archaic religious communities. It was a crowd phenomenon ultimately, a huge one. You can read the French Revolution in terms that are not the same, of course, but then you see aspects of this archaic reality that reappear quite suddenly.

It's very weird, I admit. But read the anthropological literature. We are very lucky, you know. It's true. We don't have archaic societies any more. But between 1860 or thereabout (or even a little before and the end of archaic religions), we have anthropologists (most of them English, and who are accused of imperialism at present) who recorded religious institutions of the last archaic people in a manner which is incomparable.[14] And when people were tired of accusing religion of this and that, and really interested again in the facts, they would go back to these records. As a result, we know much more about the Greek

world from these archaic religions than through the historians Herodotus and Thucydides, although they were much closer to it. My theory
is really the result of the reading of these English anthropologists. I
think you can unify the whole thing, make sense of it literally, and find
behind it the same phenomenon, which is always interpreted a little
bit differently but always turned into a religion. This victim is not really dead, since he saved us. After destroying us halfway, he saved us.
He brought us peace, and peace becomes so important in that crisis
that you worship whoever brings it to you. It is the creature that is
supposedly the most violent that we worship.

SG: So, rites of passage are sacrifices, and ordeals come from the
sacrificial crisis. How does the scapegoat enter this discussion?

RG: Sacrifice is really nothing but the most accurate repetition
of the spontaneous phenomenon I have described before. This phenomenon—we still know about it. We have a name for it. We call it the
scapegoat phenomenon. The word "scapegoat" comes from a ritual in
the Bible,[15] but when we say scapegoat phenomenon, we don't think
about that ritual at all; we think about an entire group, maybe a small
group like a family, maybe a big group, that unites against an innocent
victim. But when the people do that, they believe the victim is guilty.
They persuade each other that the victim is guilty. There would be no
scapegoat phenomenon if there were no conviction that the victim is
guilty. The most essential thing, when you look at myth, and at the
parricide and incest of Oedipus, is that Oedipus is supposed to be
guilty. He himself doesn't know about it, but he's guilty nonetheless.
Freud, you know, thought that the invention of parricide and incest in
the Oedipus myth was something unique, marvelous, a stroke of genius. But it's not true at all.[16] You have parricide and incest everywhere
in mythology. Even today when a crowd—perhaps a crowd that is
agitated—gets in serious trouble, they always find parricide and incest around, and they kill in that name.

SG: Do we still have myths today?

RG: Today we would still have a myth if we were not the society
we are. As a matter of fact, in the Middle Ages they still had half-
formed myth, which we call a witch hunt. What is a witch hunt? You
sometimes call a woman (but sometimes also a man) a witch. You are

in trouble, you have a crisis, and you are looking for a culprit. And you usually find a lonely woman, or something, and you accuse them of all sorts of crimes. In other words, it's the scapegoat phenomenon. In this sense, the Oedipus myth is nothing else. If we started to compare seriously the witch hunt—in countries where you still find it very commonly, and what we call the witch hunt—with mythology, we would see that it's exactly the same thing. But in mythology they crystallize into something coherent, into a cult, a sacrificial cult. So the question is whether it's true or not true. Well, in my view a more interesting question is: Why don't we have these things anymore? Why in the Middle Ages were they already only half-formed, and then later they were completely gone? The amazing thing about the witch hunt epidemics of the Middle Ages is not that they happened; it's that they were the last ones. We are the only society in the world that has done away completely with that sort of thing. That's why it's become unthinkable to us. But the Middle Ages are very important for this—not because they were bad, or because Christianity is bad—but because it was a period where the influence of the Bible was becoming so important, and as the Bible was becoming important, this sort of thing was becoming more and more impossible in our society.

SG: Nonetheless, it still happens.

RG: Yes, it's true, it still happens. But we understand it. We never believe it's an epiphany of a god. So what is the difference between Judaism and Christianity in this regard? It's very paradoxical, because if you look at Judaism and Christianity, or rather at the Hebrew Bible and at the New Testament, what do you find? You find, and here's the most important thing, in my view, that there you have exactly the same sort of thing that I have been describing. The death of Jesus is obviously a "scapegoat death." As a matter of fact, the Gospels themselves use a word which is practically the same as scapegoat, which is the "Lamb of God." But the lamb is a sacrificial victim, which says that Jesus has been killed by people for reasons that have nothing to do with him ultimately, and that he was an innocent victim, that he was a kind of scapegoat. The "Lamb of God" is a much nicer expression for exactly the same significance.

SG: What about the Hebrew Bible?

RG: I gave a lecture at Purdue on the Joseph story.[17] Who is Joseph? He's not a son like Oedipus, he's a brother, but unfortunately for him he has eleven brothers, and they are all jealous of him. And what do they do? They sell him into slavery. At first, they want to kill him. They dip his tunic in blood to show his father, and to say he has been devoured, and so forth. But what they do? They scapegoat poor Joseph. This is so true that Joseph ultimately threatens to commit them to a scapegoat trial before forgiving all of them.

Now look at the Psalms. You know, some people will tell you that the Psalms are very violent. You have a victim there who curses his fellow citizens and so forth. But what is the situation? In probably half of the Psalms, you have the narrator who is surrounded by a crowd, and the crowd is moving in to close the circle. The crowd is becoming more and more threatening. And the crowd is compared to bulls, to dogs, or to other lynching animals. The narrator is the mythical hero on the point of being lynched, complaining about the lynching that is going to take place, and calling to God to stop it. It's the same thing as in myth.

Or take Job.[18] Job presents himself in the dialogues (the prologue, you know, is something different) as the darling of his community. He was in charge completely, he was a kind of dictator. And suddenly the entire community turned against him; now they hate him, and they find him guilty of all sorts of things, and they delegate the three friends, who are not friends at all, in order to force him to confess, as if he were a Soviet leader in the 1930s, you know, and that's a difference with Oedipus. Job protests. He's not very happy with that. Then if you go to the prophets, they tell some pretty serious news to the people. They tell them that if they continue in their ways, they are going to disappear. And they are very unpopular, and they are terribly mistreated. The most autobiographical of the prophets is Jeremiah, who really shows himself as a "scapegoat" of his community. Then ultimately you have these two incredible chapters of Second Isaiah, 52–53, where you have a description of the lynching of the Suffering Servant. The Suffering Servant is lynched for reasons that have nothing to do with anything he has done. As a matter of fact, the texts tell us he was the sort of man that the people don't like, that crowds don't like; they want to get rid of him, they want to destroy him. The Gospels are absolutely centered on a phenomenon of this type.

SG: So how do we distinguish biblical writing from myth in this connection?

RG: This was a concern of the anthropologists of the end of the nineteenth and the early twentieth century about whom I was speaking a moment ago. One of their main goals, their open goals—it was the great anticlerical period in Europe, and they were mostly English and French at the time—was to do the equivalent of Darwin's enterprise. They felt that Darwin was marvelous because it was a great blow against religion. They said, "We are going to find, to explain, the origin of religion; we are going to show that religion is only a bunch of myths, that the Bible is only a bunch of myths, and therefore we are going to deal religion the last blow after Darwin." They were all racing toward that end, thinking that each one of them was going to write the final theory of religion.[19] I think they were very close to it. They were far from being like people today. You know, today it's fashionable to say that systems methods are impossible, that if you are systematic you are necessarily wrong. But in fact, there is no great scientific discovery that is not systematic. Only systematic thinking works. Maybe it's impossible at some points, but we are always aiming at systematic theories. I'm aiming at a systematic theory too, of course.

So, were they right—these anthropologists—to think that the Bible and mythology are the same? They were right in the sense that they saw the structure—that big crisis moving toward a single victim, who is seen as responsible for the whole thing. But the difference is so plain, so evident, that no one has seen it yet. In a way, religious people are as guilty as the scientists. The scientists were naïve in thinking they were going to reduce the Bible to a bunch of myths. They were completely wrong. But the Christians were fools not to trust the Bible enough, and be scientific themselves and say, "Yeah, let's push that comparison to the end, and see what there is behind it." And if you do that, you discover the truth, of course.

SG: The truth of all mythology.

RG: Yes. That all mythical heroes are guilty. Why are they all guilty? Because of the point of view on the event that the myths describe. The event they describe is a crisis plus its resolution, which means the return of peace. They anticipate the return of peace, but they also believe in the scapegoating. When you have a scapegoat, you don't call him a scapegoat. You say he has committed parricide and incest. No scapegoating outfit will talk about scapegoating. In order to be able to talk about scapegoating the way we do, we have to understand it. And how do we understand it? Because of the Bible, because the Bible tells us that these same victims are innocent. Joseph is innocent. The Bible tells you that his brothers are jealous. Job is innocent. Unlike the Oedipus of the myth who submits immediately, there are a few sentences in *Oedipus the King* that show that Sophocles already had doubts about his own myth.[20] But if he had changed the myth *in situ,* he would have been lynched by the crowd because it was a play given in the theater, in front of the whole population. It was like a religious function.

This is true of the Suffering Servant, and it is true of the Gospels. The Gospels show it in a way more completely than any other text. Why? Because the thing that is so marvelous about the Gospels is that they show you completely the creation of mythology and the fact that the death of Jesus is a crowd phenomenon. The most important text in my view is Peter's denial.[21] It's really foolish, in my view, to say, "Oh, Peter, if I had been in Peter's place, I would have resisted better." No, Peter is the best of the apostles. The Gospels want to show you something decisive in his denial, and the truth is that as soon as Peter gets into a crowd that believes that Jesus is guilty, he believes it too. For a few seconds, he has to join the crowd. We are crowd-joiners, because we are terribly mimetic. That is why we had scapegoat religions. But the Gospels show you Peter in order to teach you not to do the same thing. That is why the very fact of Peter's denial is so important. Think what it means to have this idea coming from the apostles! All the scholars today tell you that the Gospels are a bunch of crooked texts that are trying to deceive you. But if they were crooked texts, the first thing they would have done away with was Peter's denial, since he was the head of the Church. They did not do that. Why? Because it is absolutely essential. It tells you about human beings, which is the essential thing. Most of the time, they fight together, but when a crowd forms, they will all join the crowd. That's why there can be a society.

SG: Is it possible to resist a crowd mentality? To resist the mob?

RG: I think the time has come to try to do something else. In the Gospels and the Bible, you have the same victims as in mythology, but they are seen from the point of view of the victim him- or herself, or the people who join with the victim. In the Gospels you can see that it happens because at the time of Jesus' death all the disciples scatter; no one is left on his side. In other words, what do the Gospels tell you? That it is a light from God that taught them the truth, that they never learned by themselves. They are unable to learn by themselves. The Gospels are built exactly like a myth with one exception, that a few people secede from the crowd to say: "It's not true! Stop everything! It's not too late. Stop everything! The victim is innocent!"

Which of course never happens in a myth. A myth is based, the divinity of the god is based, on the capacity of the god to inflict good and evil at the same time. And so the Gospels and the Bible are totally different. Conceptually, we have never been able to reach that truth. It's the simplest truth in the world, and we don't see it. I think the one single thinker who did was Nietzsche. But Nietzsche was so perverse that he said: "It is better to be with the violent than with the peaceful." He said that Christianity was against sacrifice, against the necessary victims that a society should have in order to be healthy. That is the whole theory of the extreme Right, even today. But Nietzsche, in a way, is better than all the nineteenth-century theologians because he understood. He said, "The death of Dionysus is justified, the victim is guilty; the death of Christ, unjustified. Therefore, it destroys the peace of humanity." And it's true, in a sense.

SG: Have we made much progress in the past two thousand years on that score?

RG: We've not been very peaceful in the past two thousand years, but perhaps we've been fighting about more serious things. Because probably now we talk better, or we are in a position to talk about the essence of human community where there is always some kind of violence in the background, about which we would prefer to keep silent. But the fact that the Gospels are active among us is significant. When I say what I'm saying now, many people say, "And so what?" So what! Everything is at stake there. I'm going to show you an example of a modern scapegoat.

SG: You are thinking, no doubt, of the Dreyfus case.

RG: Yes. We all know about the Dreyfus case in France at the end of the nineteenth century. It's not very good to have a Dreyfus case, of course, but if you have people who are treated like Dreyfus was by the judicial system, it's better to have a Dreyfus case than no Dreyfus case at all, because it means that the judicial error will be shown.

Who was Dreyfus? He was a French officer; he was Jewish, a favorite scapegoat of the culture, and he was accused very specifically of having written a document that was a classified secret and had been sent to the Germans.[22] Moreover, France was in a crisis. France knew that the war of 1870 was not the end of it, that the Germans were stronger. France was worried about itself and about its army especially. So it was nice — the idea of having a good traitor there whose punishment would comfort the people. So the majority of the nation believed in the guilt of Dreyfus, who, as you know, was sent to forced labor on *l'Ile du Diable.*

Then, after a while, some people began to have doubts, and these people were no revolutionists, no Leftists. One of them was the vice-president of the senate, a very conservative man and a very well-known politician. Another was a colonel who knew Dreyfus. And they said, "It's not true." Colonel Picquart, who was the first to denounce specifically the situation, had to go to jail.

But look at the Dreyfus case. What does it mean? Who are the scapegoaters? They are the people who believed in Dreyfus's guilt. Therefore, they would not call Dreyfus a scapegoat. In their mind, he was a justly condemned spy. The people who started to use the word scapegoat were the few people who rebelled against the situation,[23] and who said, "Dreyfus is a scapegoat," because the word has been in the French language with its modern meaning since the seventeenth century.[24] If you go to another language, you will find the same thing. I have a Japanese friend, an anthropologist, who says, in effect, when we want to talk about scapegoats in Japanese, we have to use the Western words, because we don't have them in our own language, not in that demystifying sense. We have many words for the ritual action comparable to scapegoating, but no word that would mean the revelation of the truth behind the ritual, the demystification of the violent religion. And yet we do have it. Why? Because we have the Lamb of God.

People should not say "scapegoat"; it would be much nicer and better to say all these victims are "lambs of God" because they are other Christs. They are Christ-figures, as we sometimes say, because in a way they suffer from the fact that the crowd is not taking responsibility for it, which to me is the absolutely fascinating thing.

SG: The scapegoat seems to be a particularly popular conception right now.

RG: Everyone is interested in scapegoats today, except the scientific researchers. You would think they'd jump on it, to study it. But in fact they don't. One individual may be the scapegoat of some people, but he is the hero of other people. Inevitably, we live in a world that, from the point of view of this phenomenon I'm talking about, is completely imperfect. We live in a globalized world.[25] Many different communities with many different interests interpenetrate each other. If you go back to archaic communities, you go back to communities that, we can assume, were fairly isolated and that were experiencing certain things all by themselves. Today, there are constant interferences from the outside. Therefore, you cannot entirely theorize it. You know that you are dealing with the same phenomena that have evolved in a certain way, but that are not "perfect" in the sense that you can see them operating in certain myths. You can say that there are mythical aspects to everything. But usually, if you start talking about them, you will want to use them for one side against the other, which means that you are necessarily going to distort them. You are going to interpret them according to your own views. We don't have any more tests of objectivity. We can have judgments, for lots of reasons, because not all violence is the same. But I don't feel we are able to analyze the case of a contemporary individual branded as a scapegoat successfully or even significantly.

SG: If not an individual, then can we examine contemporary group phenomena? Does the scapegoat mechanism function for example when we speak of minority groups?

RG: Well, it's a very interesting subject, because it's an additional clue. In most archaic communities there were probably no minorities. But there may have been in larger societies. You won't find a trace of a religious minority in a myth, even if there is one. But you find something else that is a proof of scapegoating. Mythical heroes or witches in other religions very often had physical defects. Oedipus limps. Witches may be represented as truly, very ugly. And if you look at Greek gods, for instance, Hephaestos limps too, but some are hunchbacked, some are one-eyed. Think of Wotan, the great Germanic god![26]

At any rate, the number of gods who have a physical defect is enormous. And this fact offers one more argument in support of my thesis. Why? Because if you take a very primitive crowd—and I do not hesitate to use the word primitive, uneducated, and so forth—it will tend to move against victims who are easy to spot, who have some physical defect or something that makes them noticeable.

Probably in terms of evolutionary theory, it links up with predation. We know that in the case of great predators, for example, people say, "Oh, they go after in the flock the animal who is the slowest." But it's not really true. They end up picking out the animal who doesn't run as well as the others, but it's because there is a physical defect, because he's smaller than the other one, because he limps sometimes. In a mass of zebras, you cannot isolate anything, but if some one zebra is different, the lion will rush to attack this one. Nine times out of ten, it will be a good choice because there is a physical defect.

So it's true whether you look at Greek heroes or at primitive heroes all over the world. The amazing thing about myth is that you have features that are universal, worldwide. The hero who limps is everywhere. We cannot say it is something ethnic, something cultural; it's universal. And that makes me think that it's an objective thing.

I'm a realist, you know. I think that texts talk about reality and real events. If a text tells you that so many people limp, there must be a reason. Or many mythical heroes are twins. Why? Because twins fight all the time, or are supposed to do so, and they kill each other. Cain and Abel are not far from that.[27] Romulus and Remus are twin brothers.[28] No Roman would dream of regarding Remus as the good guy. The good man is Romulus, who is the first priest, the first king, the first law-giver of Rome. If we accept that, all of us, and we look at Remus as the bad trespasser, who crossed the line, meaning a line in the sand that his brother had drawn, then you understand what I mean. But the Bible chooses Abel against Cain. Already there, the victim is right.

So the story of Cain and Abel is significant. If people tell you that it's the same thing as Romulus and Remus, you can tell them, "Not true at all!" The Bible is for the victim right there, and it tells you the murderer is wrong. "What did you do with your brother?" No myth would ever ask you that. It's absolutely essential. It's all the difference in the world. All our civil rights come from there.

SG: How would you answer people who say you are privileging the Greeks, the Hebrews, the Christians, these various peoples of Western cultural heritage, over other groups?

RG: I would say that is a misunderstanding. I don't want to privilege the Bible absolutely. Because if you take the evolution of Indian religion, the Indians have the most incredible scriptural texts. Everything I say about sacrifice, they say. Because they don't have myth only; they have commentaries and explanations of myth, which are still within the orbit, of course, of mythic thinking, but they tell you about the rivalry before. They tell you about the victim as a solution to the violence. They tell you everything. When you get to the period of the great Jewish prophets, you have the *Vedanta,* and these great texts that are the *Upanishads.* There are so many we haven't translated them all. In the *Upanishads* you have an anti-sacrificial thrust, where sacrifice is regarded as murder and rejected. Later, Hinduism went back to sacrifice. But you have a period that is analogous to that of the Hebrew prophets. And they are great texts; they don't give up the word sacrifice, but they say that sacrifice should be purely interior.[29] Very often they have funny stories about the demons being behind sacrifice, and the gods trying to stop it, the demons exploiting men, and so forth. So this anti-sacrificial theme is present in the classical Indian texts. Buddhism is the same thing, in the sense that Buddhism comes entirely from within the Indian tradition. But it separated itself, whereas the *Upanishads* are in continuity with the great Indian tradition.

We know that Buddhism is against sacrifice. We know that for sure. At the same time, one has to recognize that Buddhism, in the territory where it dominates, has not eliminated earlier forms of sacrifice to the same extent that Christianity has. Neither has Islam. Islam remains compatible with certain forms of animal sacrifice, which are acknowledged. Is that true of Christianity? No. In Judaism, of course, the sacrifices ended with the end of the Second Temple.

SG: How does our knowing about these things change the situation? What happens when a society has exposed this mythological core and must deal with the violence that comes with that exposure?

RG: It's often very difficult for us to do that. I talked about witchcraft trials a moment ago, and I said that witchcraft trials are not the same thing as myth, since we don't believe in them. We manage to turn it against Christianity. We say, "Oh, Christianity was so primitive and savage," and that it favored witchcraft trials — which is absolutely untrue. There were some popular orders, you know, like the Franciscans in certain places, that had certain complicities. But the church as a whole in the Middle Ages was against these things. As a matter of fact, it's a very funny thing. We have a letter of the Grand Inquisitor of Spain in the year 1600 against witch-hunting in the name of rationalism. It's not often quoted. But it shows the complexity of these matters, in contrast with our simplistic attitudes.

Why don't we believe in witchcraft trials? For the same reason we don't believe in the Dreyfus case. Even though we are not able to conceptualize what I've been talking about, that fact is fairly insignificant. What is important is the deep emotional attitude toward victims. We have a unique attitude toward victims. We don't realize that, of course. We tell ourselves we are so bad, so violent. We are the only society in the world that has ever been worried about its own violence. You can go back to any society in the past. There is no society that ever worried about violence, especially its own, the way we do. It was regarded as one of these facts of life about which you cannot do anything. We are constantly accusing ourselves, as if there were better societies before that we could give as examples of nonviolence compared to us.

Someone like Voltaire wanted to believe that so much that, when he wrote *Candide*, he decided to have a counterexample.[30] There is no doubt that he looked for some place that he could use, and he decided finally there was none. So he invented a false one, his Eldorado, which is of course a myth, as the place without violence. Because Voltaire was the first one to have that attitude toward violence that we now maintain, which is that everyone is responsible for violence except me, except us. People before talked in terms of evil but not about some kind of objective violence. What does violence mean objectively? I don't think we can define it. I don't even think we should try. It's always a relationship, a relationship with sacrifice that no longer works, with difference that is no longer efficacious. But the modern world has a very special attitude: someone owes us absolute peace, plus comfort, money, computers, and everything else. It doesn't seem to be working quite right at this present moment, and people are having second thoughts about Enlightenment optimism. And all I want to do is to increase a little bit these doubts.

Notes

1. See, for example, *The Republic,* especially Books II and III, and the *Ion.*
2. See, for example, *The Poetics.*
3. Gabriel Tarde, *Laws of Imitation,* 2nd ed., trans. Elsie Clews Parsons (New York: H. Holt, 1903).
4. Darwin's book, *On the Origin of Species by Means of Natural Selection,* which was first published in 1859, defined the classic theory of human evolution through the idea of "the survival of the fittest."
5. Richard Dawkins coined the word "memes" in *The Selfish Gene* (Oxford: Oxford University Press, 1976). See also his *The Extended Phenotype* (Oxford: W. H. Freeman, 1982).
6. See, for example, Stephen Shennan, *Genes, Memes, and Human History: Darwinian Archeology and Cultural Evolution* (New York: Thames and Hudson, 2003); and Robert Aunger, ed., *Darwinizing Culture: The Status of Memetics as a Science* (Oxford: Oxford University Press, 2000).
7. The literature on this topic is vast. Among the classic studies are Adolf Portmann, *Animals as Social Beings,* trans. Oliver Coburn (New York: Viking, 1961); Konrad Lorenz, *On Aggression,* trans. Marjorie Kerr Wilson (New York: Harcourt, Brace, and World, 1966) and *Studies in Animal and Human Behavior,* trans. Robert Martin (Cambridge, MA: Harvard University Press, 1970). These comparative approaches to animal and human behavior helped to define the field of ethology. See Klaus Immelmann, *Introduction to Ethology,* trans. Erich Klinghammer (New York: Plenum Press, 1980). See also Edward O. Wilson, *Sociobiology: The New Synthesis* (Cambridge, MA: Harvard University Press, 1975).
8. Rudyard Kipling was born in Bombay, India. He is noted for *The Jungle Book* (1894), *The Second Jungle Book* (1895), and perhaps most notoriously his poem "The White Man's Burden" (1899).
9. For intellectual biographies of Carl Schmitt, see Joseph W. Bendersky, *Carl Schmitt, Theorist for the Reich* (Princeton, NJ: Princeton University Press, 1983),

and Gopal Balakrishnan, *The Enemy: An Intellectual Portrait of Carl Schmitt* (London: Verso, 2000). A professor at the University of Berlin, Schmitt joined the National Socialists in 1933, refusing after the war to accept de-Nazification. See Heinrich Meier, *Carl Schmitt and Leo Strauss: The Hidden Dialogue*, trans. J. Harvey Lomax (Chicago: University of Chicago Press, 1995).

10. See Carl Schmitt, *Crisis of Parliamentary Democracy*, trans. Ellen Kennedy (Cambridge, MA: MIT Press, 1985) and *The Concept of the Political*, trans. George Schwab, with commentary by Leo Strauss (New Brunswick, NJ: Rutgers University Press, 1976). Leo Strauss's letter to Schmitt, dated September 4, 1932, summarizes Schmitt's view as follows: "There is a *primary* tendency in human nature to form *exclusive groups.* . . . Because man is by nature evil, he therefore needs *dominion.* But dominion can only be established, that is, men can be united, only in a unity *against*—against other men. Every association of men is *necessarily* a separation from other men" (Meier, *Carl Schmitt and Leo Strauss*, 124–25).

11. In his classic essay, "The Birth of Tragedy Out of Music" (1872), Nietzsche opposes the plastic art of the Apollonian to the Bacchic drunkenness of the Dionysian. See Friedrich Nietzsche, *The Birth of Tragedy and the Genealogy of Morals*, trans. Francis Golffing (Garden City, NY: Doubleday, 1956), 19.

12. Cf. Girard's analysis of Euripides' *The Bacchae* (cited in the epigraph to this chapter), in which he makes a similar point. See René Girard, "Dionsyius and the Violent Genesis of the Sacred," trans. Sandor Goodhart, *Boundary 2*, vol. 5, no. 2 (1977): 493.

13. On the topic of sacred monarchies, see Girard, *Things Hidden since the Foundation of the World*, trans. Stephen Bann and Michael Metteer (Stanford, CA: Stanford University Press, 1987), 51–58; *Violence and the Sacred*, trans. Patrick Gregory (Baltimore: Johns Hopkins Press, 1977), 104–16, 302–6. See also Simon Simonse, *Kings of Disaster* (Leiden: E. J. Brill, 1992).

14. Elsewhere René Girard writes concerning the famous anthropologist Sir James Frazer, author of *The Golden Bough* (1911–1915): "In the work of writers like Frazer one sometimes comes across descriptions that correspond well enough to what our theory requires" (*Things Hidden since the Foundation of the World*, 58). See also Robert G. Hamerton-Kelly, ed., *Violent Origins: Walter Burkert, René Girard, and Jonathan Z. Smith on Ritual Killing and Cultural Formation* (Stanford, CA: Stanford University Press, 1987).

15. See Lv 16.

16. The notion of the Oedipus complex, which takes its inspiration from the play *Oedipus Rex* by Sophocles, is of fundamental importance to psychoanalysis, as Sigmund Freud himself bears witness in the 1920 edition of *Three Essays on Sexuality* (1905). See Peter L. Rudnytsky, *Freud and Oedipus* (New York: Columbia University Press, 1987).

17. See Gn 37–50. At the invitation of the Program in Jewish Studies, Girard spoke on "Joseph and Oedipus" in the spring of 1999 at Purdue University, in the

Distinguished Ben and Louise Klatch Family lecture series. He has since published on this topic. See René Girard, *I See Satan Fall Like Lightning,* trans. James G. Williams (Maryknoll, NY: Orbis, 2001), 107–15, 118–20.

18. See René Girard, *Job, the Victim of His People,* trans. Yvonne Freccero (Stanford, CA: Stanford University Press, 1987).

19. For statements by the major modern theorists of myth, see the 113 essays collected in *Theories of Myth,* 6 vols., ed. Robert A. Segal (New York: Garland, 1996).

20. See Sandor Goodhart, "*Leistas Ephaske*: Oedipus and Laius's Many Murderers," chap. 1 of *Sacrificing Commentary: Reading the End of Literature* (Baltimore: The Johns Hopkins Press, 1996), 13–41.

21. See Mt 26:69–75; Mk 14:66–72; Lk 22:54–62.

22. Alfred Dreyfus (1859–1935) was accused of treason and arrested in late October 1894. He was publicly degraded in January 1895 and sentenced to life imprisonment. It was subsequently determined that the charges were false and the evidence fabricated. He was finally exonerated in full on July 12, 1906, after a turbulent decade during which the "Dreyfus Affair" polarized the nation.

23. Among the outspoken defenders of Dreyfus's innocence were the Jewish journalist Bernard Lazare; the socialist, Catholic poet Charles Péguy; and the novelist Émile Zola.

24. The French expression is *le bouc émissaire.* According to the *Oxford English Dictionary,* the word scapegoat was first used in its modern, psychosocial sense in the nineteenth century.

25. See Zygmunt Bauman, *Globalization: The Human Consequences* (New York: Columbia University Press, 1998).

26. Wotan (Wodin, or Odin) was one of the principal Teutonic and Scandinavian gods, whose worship the Roman historian Tacitus associated with that of Mercury and thus with Wednesday ("Wodin's day"). Thor, the Zeus-like god of thunder, is variously named as Odin's father or his son. According to Andy Orchard, "Among the main physical attributes of Odin are the hat and cloak of his wandering, his spear, . . . and his single eye" (*Dictionary of Norse Myth and Legend* [London: Cassell, 1997], 123).

27. See Gn 4:1–17.

28. According to legend, Romulus and Remus were the twin offspring of the god Mars and Rhea Silvia, a Vestal Virgin, who was the daughter of Numitor, one of the Alban kings. Thrown into the Tiber by Amulius, the king who had deposed Numitor, the twins, washed ashore, were nursed by a she-wolf and then sheltered by a royal servant, who recognized them for the princes they were. After restoring Numitor to the throne, the brothers set out to found Rome. They quarreled, and Remus was killed by Romulus and his followers. See the entry for "Rome" in *The Oxford Companion to Classical Literature,* ed. Sir Paul Harvey (Oxford: Clarendon Press, 1940, repr. 1962).

29. Compare on this point the debate that Aeschylus stages between Athena and the Furies in the third play of the *Oresteia* trilogy, the *Eumenides*, to which Girard refers above.

30. Voltaire wrote *Candide* (1759) as a refutation of Leibniz's "metaphysical optimism." The text recounts in a hyperbolic fashion the terrible trials and misfortunes of a young idealistic hero, Candide, who comes to doubt that this world is indeed the best of all possible ones. On Voltaire's aversion to metaphysics, see Patrick Henry, "Voltaire as Moralist," *Journal of the History of Ideas* 38 (1977): 141–46.

T W O

Bloody Logic

*The Biblical Economy of Sacrificial Substitution and
Some of Its Eucharistic Implications*

THOMAS RYBA

In this chapter I propose to sketch a theory of Israelitic sacrifice as a
key to unlocking the meaning of eucharistic sacrifice as understood in
the Roman Catholic tradition. It is my intention to explain Israelitic
sacrifice on the basis of an extension of Marcel Mauss' anthropological
theory of the gift, an anthropological theory that interprets exchange
as a fundamental operation in one of the earliest examples of economy.
It seems to me that Mauss' discovery provides particularly fruitful basis
for disentangling some of the more intriguing symbolic features of
eucharistic ritual. But my appropriation of Mauss will be more than a
simple application: I propose to extend Mauss' conclusions in a way
that provides a more precise formulation of how sacrificial economies
are in fact *economic*. I hope to identify the form of exchange they imply,
the form of substitution they allow, and the commensurable standard
that makes both substitution and exchange possible.

One of the issues that inevitably arises in discussions of this sort
is the question of what sacrifice meant in its original form, on the assumption that its original meaning sheds light on its subsequent development. To think that this question is important is not automati-
cally to fall prey to the genetic fallacy. I am not claiming the original
meaning determines later meanings, although I admit that sacrifice's
original meaning may provide a clue both to the change in subsequent
meanings and to the logic that is operative in the establishment of later
meanings without being fully expressed. It is a background assump-

tion to my argument that sacrifice did change from the form and significance it had in ancient Israelitic religion to the form and significance it had in ancient Christianity. But the discontinuity was neither complete nor essential, at least with respect to how sacrifice came to be interpreted in post–first century CE Christianity and Judaism.

An important, related question is how the varieties of sacrifice can plausibly be understood as having been simplified, reinterpreted, and fused in the Eucharist. But that is not an explanation that any scholar has yet been capable of providing. And neither do I claim to provide it. Instead, I will simply assume this evolution as a fact—even with the gaps in our understanding of it—and instead settle for a more manageable accomplishment. My hope is to show how the continuities between the Jewish and Christian understandings of sacrifice help to clarify eucharistic theology.

A second issue that I will address is whether and how blood signifies the commensurable standard behind biblical sacrificial practice. The notion that the spilling of Jesus' blood had some metaphysical effect in the salvation of humankind is an idea that is hardly alien to the New Testament. Most Christian theologians are at a loss, however, to explain what kind of logic operates behind these assertions. Often, theologians attempt to relate the significance of the blood of the Atonement to ancient Israelitic sacrificial practices, but without explaining how there can have been a continuity between a tradition (Judaism) that, in its ancient past, superseded both human and animal sacrifice and one (Christianity) that saw a theandric sacrifice as both the completing feature and supersession of sacrifice. Especially since the Enlightenment, theologians tend to pass over the *metaphysical* significance of Jesus' bloody crucifixion as an atavism, or they pass over it in relative silence.

Sacrifice as a Theoretically Contested Idea and Practice in the Academic Study of Religion

Sacrifice as a religious phenomenon has been the object of an extensive body of writings in the fields of both theology and religious studies.

In the West, theology was the academic discipline in which the ground-work for theories of sacrifice was laid, the interest in understanding sacrifice growing out of Christian theological reflection on Christology and soteriology, that is, on the meaning of the bloody sacrificial death of Jesus and the attendant meaning of a cluster of related terms such as atonement, propitiation, justification, sanctification, and so on. Much of the interest of Christian theologians about sacrifice in the Hebrew scriptures was driven by the attempt to understand how Jesus' death could be construed in continuity *with* or in opposition *to* the more an-cient Jewish understanding.

As theology became secularized in the nineteenth-century Euro-pean university system—and particularly the German system—its re-searches into the historical origins of sacrifice provided the data for the emergent anthropological, sociological, and historical approaches to the study of religion. Initially, the influence was chiefly unidirectional—from theology to the academic study of religion. But as the academic study of religion came into its own, its researchers distanced themselves from the original theological purpose, realizing these early theologi-cal studies were far too parochial, focused as they were on the Judeo-Christian phenomena.

With the hubris typical of practitioners of relatively young and promising approaches, the late nineteenth- and early twentieth-century scientists of religion sought a theory of sacrifice that would unite and explain sacrificial phenomena across all religious traditions and across all times, a quest that has proven futile even through the present. The com-plexity and variety of internal interpretations of sacrifice have eluded unification in an enduring explanatory theory.[1]

It is not my purpose, here, to propose any new universal theory of sacrifice, but to use the insights of some of the secular researchers in the academic study of religion to venture a solution to the riddle of the significance of blood in Jesus' sacrificial death. I shall thus "bracket" the question of the origin of sacrificial practice to consider how sacri-fice functioned in the practice of ancient Jews and Christians. Anyone who lets one's theory of sacrifice be driven by the way it came into being may be prey to the genetic fallacy.[2] To allow one's theory to be driven thusly is also to suggest that the sacrificial structure is inseparable from its earliest meaning and is thus incapable of representing a development out of or a rupture with that earliest practice. This means that the elemental features of sacrifice act upon the psychology of each generation in exactly the same way throughout history. The latter is demonstrably false with respect to the *conscious* theoretical formulations of sacrifice that come from within a religious tradition but may be true with respect to its subconscious effects, as Girard has shown.

Even if Girard is right in interpreting mimetic rivalry as a subconscious cause of the emergence of sacrificial practice, that does not establish it as the only cause. One need not judge all other reasons for ritual sacrifice (besides mimetic rivalry) to be legitimations which occlude its real function. It may be that the reasons for sacrifice are polytonic instead of monotonic, in which case Girardian explanation of sacrifice would be correct but incomplete. It may be that part of the psychology of sacrifice is explicable in terms of mimetic rivalry but that there are also additional conscious and unconscious reasons for sacrifice that *synergistically* cooperate with mimetic rivalry. In that case, the compatibility of reasons for sacrifice is what contributes to its historical durability. It should be made clear that the synergism of the Girardian theory of mimesis and exchange theory is, in fact, presupposed in what follows.

Sacrificial Economies, Gods, and Archaic Humans

The pathfinder who provided the anthropological background for the theological solution that I tentatively propose is Marcel Mauss. In his work *The Gift: The Form and Reason for Exchange in Archaic Societies,* Mauss used the method of exact comparison to show that exchange and contract are closely linked in an economy even in societies that had been previously claimed to be "devoid of economic markers."[3] It is merely the system of exchange that is different.[4] Even so, Mauss believed he had discovered that some constants of morality and organization in archaic societies still functioned "hidden, below the surface" of modern societies as one of the "human foundations on which societies are built."[5] He calls the form of exchange typical of archaic societies "systems of total services" because their exchanges extend far beyond modern economy.[6] His specific discoveries can be grouped according to the most general features of all systems of total services, and those that characterize its various subspecies.

These systems have four general characteristics. First, natural economies have never existed either in archaic times or in ages of close temporal proximity to our own.[7] Second, the economies that do exist are never characterized by the "simple exchange of goods, wealth, and products" among individuals, but it is "collectivities that impose obligations of exchange and contract upon each other." Third, these archaic systems of exchange not only include wealth and property but also acts of politeness and honor. Fourth, and finally, on the surface these exchanges are apparently partly voluntary, though upon closer examination they are "strictly compulsory, on pain of private or public welfare."[8]

The economies that fit into this general classification form a scale from systems of "total services of an agonistic type" to systems—if we may introduce a neologism not employed by Mauss—of "total services of a magnanimous type."[9] The former are based upon elaborate social hierarchies and hostile rivalry between leaders where competition knows few restraints. It can result in acts of violence ranging from the "sumptuary destruction of wealth" to the killing of rivals.[10] In these agonistic types, "the whole clan . . . contracts on the behalf of all, for all that it possesses and . . . does through the person of its chief," who acts usuriously and sumptuously to gain advantage for his clan at a later date.[11] Because sumptuary sacrifice is most often connected to aggressive competition among tribes (and managed by their tribal chieftains), the potential for resentment and scarcity caused by their excessive waste threatens the equilibrium of the social unit. Identified by Mauss is, perhaps, a possibility left unrealized in the Girardian theory of sacrifice— that sacrifice, itself, might become the object of desire as well as the occasion for the kind of competition for the object of desire, instead of being its "solution."

In the magnanimous variety, on the other hand, the "emulation is more moderate," and the rival groups "entering into contracts seek to outdo one another in their gifts."[12] Especially in the gratuitous variety of economic systems of total services, the legal obligation between the receiver of the gift and the giver of the gift, namely, that the giver must be reciprocated, is based in a metaphysical understanding of the giving as giving what constitutes an extension of one's self. The gift is thought to be a metaphysical *part* of the self—one's spirit (the *hau* according to Maori informants)—and its possession by the recipient makes the recipient the possessor of the power over the other. In this case, the magnanimous gift also becomes a kenotic gift because the gift becomes, in some sense, a gift of self in a real metaphysical sense. It is a literal pouring out of self.[13] Retention of the gift without equal or excessive reciprocation is viewed as dangerous, immoral, and illegal. The spirit of the gift—among the Maoris—is said to seek to return to its place of origin.[14]

Now, Mauss interprets the demand for reciprocity here as a returning of the spirit in the form of the original gift or its equivalent. It seems to me that it is equally possible to interpret the intention behind this reciprocal action by construing the gift of the reciprocating party as the gift of an equivalent part of him- or herself, the exchange really being about reciprocity in giving a part of oneself to another in whom it is held in trust. In this way, the original part of the self that is surrendered is ransomed or hostaged by the return of an equally valued or better gift of self to the other.

Ownership is conceived among many archaic peoples as a "spiritual bond," according to Mauss.[15] Thus, the relations connected with ownership establish rules for exchange. There is an obligation to give, but also to receive, invite, and accept. To refuse any of these is "to declare war; it is to reject the bond of alliance and commonality."[16] It is also to lose one's stature.[17] But even if one does receive, reception carries with it its own burdens. A gift received is always received "with a burden attached."[18] That burden is the challenge to reciprocate, to return honor, or to prove that one is equal to the gift. Very often this takes the form of besting one's donor in the return of gifts.[19] Driving the reciprocity of exchange is the human tendency toward mimesis, but it is a mimesis in the service of a primitive conception of justice. Here, the human mimetic impulse follows the necessity of the equitable distribution of goods, services, and sociality. In some archaic societies, the exchange of the various media is tantamount to the constant circulation of "spiritual matter."[20] The spiritualization of exchange means that occult powers are thought to be present in the circulation of media.

Within this system of the circulation of spirit, sacrifice has a distinctive place. Because the gods "are the true owners of the things and possessions of the world," exchange with them is most necessary: "With them it was most dangerous not to exchange," but also "with them it was the easiest and safest to exchange."[21] "The purpose of destruction by sacrifice is precisely that it is an act of giving that is necessarily reciprocated."[22] Moreover, it is a most ancient belief that "purchases must be made from the gods," and it is they who set the prices for this commerce.[23] Mauss places the theory of contract sacrifice in this context because the gods set the terms for the exchange of gifts, terms that generally reward modest giving with extraordinary largesse.[24] Finally, gifts made to humans and gods "serve the purpose of buying peace."[25]

According to Mauss, almsgiving to the poor represents a later development of the archaic notions of fortune and sacrifice. Rather than engagement in destructive sacrifices of sumptuary waste, almsgiving means the magnanimous distribution of blessings among those who have little.[26] Although he does not say it precisely, what Mauss has hit upon in the practice of alms is a widening of the circuit of the distribution of blessings that is productive of many reciprocal relations outside of sumptuary sacrificial circulation. The engendering of reciprocity at all levels of a society through almsgiving means the proliferation of mutual obligations that, though often carried as burdensome, also serve, positively, to reduce the resentment and conflict between the haves and have-nots. The *blessed* thus become the instruments by which abundant gifts are shared and distributed further afield. The largesse of the rich in the horizontal distribution of goods, services, and sociality functions *sacrificially* for them. Even so, their gifts and honor return to them the form of obligatory exchanges between the poor and the rich, and the poor and the gods.

What Mauss does not also explicitly note is that among some religions the status of the gods is fixed; they cannot be shamed by a non-symmetrical response. Their gifts are so extraordinarily profligate as to mean neither the individual nor the society can return them reciprocally. In these religions, the gods' honor cannot be tarnished in any meaningful sense nor can their life be diminished. Therefore, the expectation that the creature reciprocate the gift of the gods is an obligation connected with his status within an economy whose rules of exchange are established by the gods. Its stakes are not those of life or honor as it exists among humans but rectitude or righteousness within a preestablished divine order.[27] Thus the obligation to return the gift—to sacrifice—rests upon the side of creature in relation to the creator.[28] The giving of the gift, in the first place, is at the good pleasure of the gods.

Redefining Sacrifice

In their monograph *Sacrifice: Its Nature and Function,* Marcel Mauss and Henri Hubert attempt a definition of sacrifice that stands in contradiction to Mauss' later analysis of the economy of the gift. In the earlier work, Mauss and Hubert inadequately relate sacrifice to the moral state of the person.[29] Against this earlier formulation, as we have seen above, Mauss in *The Gift* implies that sacrifice may be related to an economy in the circulation of a social debt—even metaphysically hypostatized—as a better way of generalizing its features. I take the later work of Mauss as more useful for making sense of sacrifice in the Semitic context and suggest that the umbrella category for interpreting the central structural features of sacrifice is not personal guilt or immorality but *indebtedness* in a broader social-metaphysical sense. Extending—and thus reframing—the later Mauss, and joining with his earlier definition of sacrifice, I would argue that the universal features of sacrifice might be better expressed in the following two definitions:

> Sacrifices are religious acts that, through the offering of victims, discharge debts that humans have incurred in their relations with the gods. Those kinds of debt that humans incur establish a system of exchanges that may be called sacrificial economies between humans and the gods. The debts thus incurred may also define the moral and ontological status of the individual.

Specifically, among the most general kinds of debts related to sacrifice are the following: (a) the debt of existence, (b) the debt of thanksgiving/honoring, (c) the debt of sin, (d) the debt of indiscretion/impurity. It is my thesis that at the root of sacrifice is human communal eating, which since time immemorial has been used to cement relations between members of society, to discharge social debt by defusing affronts, and to include the less fortunate in the celebration of success, among other things. For each function, something is killed, cooked, shared, and eaten with the participation of all the conviviants. Thus, I would argue, at the basis of Jewish religious sacrifice lies the sumptuary banquet (in Mauss' sense) whose purpose is the discharging of social debt and the cementing of relations between the parties attending.

> Sacrifice is the formalized ritual of communal participation that heals rifts or shores up relations by discharging the implicit debts that are perceived to exist between the parties present. These debts are attached to the circulation of spiritual goods whose value is measured by a commensurable standard established by a covenant contracted by Hashem and his people.[30]

Note that explicit in the two definitions is a challenge to the Girardian interpretation of sacrifice, which shifts the intention of the *sacrificium,* "the making of something holy," from the victim to those participating in the rite.[31]

Sacrifice as a Spectrum of Ideal Types

The varieties of sacrifice can be idealized as a sequence of forms representing the possible kinds of substitution.[32] The descriptions and arrangement of what follows are what Max Weber has called an ideal type.[33] The varieties of sacrifice form a purely ideal sequence defined at one end by a sacrificial form having the least utility (greatest disutility) and ending with a sacrifice possessing the greatest utility (least disutility). In their historical emergence, these sacrificial forms supersede one another in a sequence that generally demonstrates increasing utility, but this is not always necessarily so. A priori, there is nothing to prevent historical sacrificial practice from jumping steps to move from a form with greater disutility to a step with greater utility without passing historically through the intervening forms. Just as there is nothing a priori that prohibits a religion to regress to a sacrificial form that possesses greater disutility from an earlier form with greater utility.

Total or Nonsubstitutionary Sacrifice

The logical structure of substitutionary sacrifice must begin at the null point of sacrifice, at sacrifice that is exactly sacrifice without substitution, or that may also be called the sacrifice in which the whole self is reflexive, that is, a sacrifice of the self for the self. Here, the death is the death of the individual seeking propitiation, expressing thanksgiving, and so forth. It presupposes that anything short of self-destruction is not adequate to the exchange. It represents the sacrificial act in which the offering is total, at least with respect to the life of the victim. Whether or not there is an afterlife conditions the totality of what is sacrificed because those traditions that postulate an afterlife make the sacrifice less absolute than those which do not. Nevertheless, there are even exceptions to this rule. For example, Martin Luther distinguishes the saints as those who are so obedient to God that in their teleological suspension of the ethical would go so far as to sacrifice an eternity of fellowship with God to be obedient to him.[34] This variety of sacrifice may extend over a class of victims as long as the sacrificial demand is understood as claiming each individual must stand as sacrifice for itself. We can represent this first variety of sacrificial substitution symbolically as follows:

(S1) The sacrifice of the total self for self:

$$\exists (a) \ni \cup S(a) \supset \cup SACfor(a),$$

where this equation is read as: "There is a class of a's such that a is a substitute for itself and a is a sacrifice for itself." Here, the notation $\cup$ represents the reflexivity of substitution and sacrifice.

Historically, this form of sacrifice is represented by the practice of the Donatists in fourth-century North Africa, Buddhist self-immolators, and Christian martyrs.[35] All have given up their lives for various causes, seeing the only fit or total sacrifice is one that results in the annihilation of their lives in the here and now. The explicit psychology of this act is one that sees the sacrifice of the total self as the only legitimate exchange for the expiation of sins, the achievement of paradise (or release), or both. Note that this sacrifice is not quite total in that an aspect of the individual is thought to survive. Its ultimate form would be a self-sacrifice in which the hope for reward or expiation in a next life would not be a consideration.

With awareness of the total debt owed to God, the ideal limit to sacrificial practice is the sacrifice of self, which constitutes the return of life for the gift of life. This variety of sacrifice is that of total sacrifice (or S1 above). It is not really substitutionary but a sacrifice of parity. What has been given is given back. This is the sacrifice of self for the gift of self, a sacrifice that historically has been connected with sin and not thanksgiving. For obvious reasons, this practice has always been associated with a profound disutility because if a religion obligates its members to its universal practice, it ultimately ends the lives of its adherents. If ever universally practiced in any religious tradition, it would have rapidly faded from practice because it prevented generational succession. It constituted an adaptation that had a negative survival value.[36]

The Sacrifice of One Individual for Another within the Same Species

The second variety of sacrificial exchange is the sacrifice of a single individual having approximately the same attributes as that for which it is substituted. This variety can range all the way from a sacrifice of a nearly identical victim to the sacrifice of a victim who possesses only the most general species characteristics. Moreover, the kind of substitution associated with this variety of sacrifice may not only be isomorphic — or one-for-one — but it may also be one-for-many as long as the victim possesses *specific* (that is, species) identity with the group. One variety of sacrifice may be defined as the sacrifice of one individual for another belonging to the same species, symbolized as follows:

(S2¹) The sacrifice of one individual for another of the same species:

$$\exists(a, b) \ni ([(a \neq b) \cdot ((a \cdot b) \in C_s)] \supset [\vec{S}(a, b) \cdot \overrightarrow{SACfor}(a, b)]),$$

where this equation is read as "If there is an *a* and a *b* such that *a* is not identical to *b* and *a* and *b* are members of some class *C* then *a* is a substitute for *b* and *a* is a sacrificial victim for *b*."

One can, therefore, imagine that the substitutionary sacrifice of parity (one-to-one sacrifice) must be superseded by an adaptive mutation of the original total sacrifice that diminishes its extreme disutility. This is a variety of sacrifice involving a substitutionary victim drawn from the same species but not identical with the debtor. I know of no human community in which this kind of one-for-one substitutionary sacrifice was practiced. The reasons for this are probably related to limits on power and enforcement.[37] What would a society look like that demanded the dyadic pairing of victim and debtor and then enforced it? The disutility of such an arrangement would be only slightly better than the first form.[38]

The form that this transitions structure mutates into is rather the following:

$$(S2^2) \quad \exists(\hat{a}, b) \ni ([(b \in \hat{a}) \cdot C(\hat{a}) \supset [\vec{S}(b, \hat{a}) \cdot \overrightarrow{SACfor}(b, \hat{a})]).$$

This new equation is read as "If there is a set *â* and a member *b* such that *b* is a member of set *â* and set *â* constitutes a community *C*, then *b* is a substitute for *â* and *b* is a sacrificial victim for the set *â*."

This sacrifice has measurably greater utility because it allows the members of a community to return the requisite life demanded by the affront of the deity (or the squandering of life) by offering a single life to cover the debt of the community for a duration determined within the religious tradition. Whereas there is a perfect symmetry between debt and payment in the practice of total sacrifice, the substitution of a human victim for the community means that the majority will live while only some of its members will die. Here, the disutility of the sacrifice is measured in terms of the pain, disaffection, broken emotional ties, and lost love caused by the wrenching of the victim from the place she or he has in the community.

This variety of sacrifice is most notoriously represented by human sacrifice as practiced in Carthaginian Africa and the complex of cultures associated with what may be loosely called Caananite. As in variety S1 the key to sacrifice is the propitiatory spilling of blood.

If the disutility of sacrifice is connected with members of the in-group, a further mutation is eventually encouraged in which the victim is drawn from *outside* of the closed community. These victims are typically sought among the different, despised, destitute, or alien. Because the same nest of social relations does not connect the community with the victim, the disutility is lessened but not entirely removed. This sacrifice is symbolized as:

$$(S2^3) \quad \exists(\hat{a}, b) \ni ([(b \notin \hat{a}) \cdot C(\hat{a}) \supset [\vec{S}(b, \hat{a}) \cdot \overrightarrow{SACfor}(b, \hat{a})]).$$

This new equation is read as "If there is a set *â* and a member *b* such that *b* is not a member of *â* and *â* is a community *C*, then *b* is a substitute for *â* and *b* is a sacrificial victim for the set *â*."

When with the increasing cosmopolitanism of the surrounding environment the religious tradition develops an awareness that the sacrifice of outsiders is morally problematic—or when it proves its disutility because they begin to be known as a particularly inhospitable or cruel people—a more well-known form of sacrificial substitution supplants this form. This is the substitutionary sacrifice of an animal.

Generic Sacrifice

The third variety of sacrifice is what might be referred to as *generic sacrifice,* or the sacrificial substitution of one living being for another. It operates within generic orders of greater or lesser specific distance.[39] Animate life seems to be the highest genus within which the substitution is accomplished, though sometimes the inanimate serves as an acceptable sacrificial substitute for the animate. For example, in this variety of sacrifice, individual animals or vegetables may be substituted for individual humans. The sacrifice of one individual for another individual across different species but within the same genus or super-genus can be symbolized as:

(S3¹) $\exists(a, b) \cdot \exists(C_1, C_2) \ni ([(a \neq b) \cdot (C_1 \neq C_2) \cdot (C_1 \not\subset C_2)$
$\cdot (C_2 \not\subset C_1)] \cdot [((a \in C_1) \cdot (b \in C_2)) \cdot ((C_1, C_2) \subset G)]$
$\supset [\vec{S}(a, b) \cdot \overrightarrow{SACfor}(a, b)]),$

where this equation is read as "If there is an a and b and a C_1 and C_2 such that *a* is not identical with *b* and C_1 is not identical to C_2, and C_1 is not a subset of C_2 nor is C_2 a subset of C_1, and a is an element of C_1 and b is an element of C_2, and C_1 and C_2 are subsets of some genus G, then a is a substitute for *b* and a is a sacrificial victim for *b*."

Likewise, on an analogy of S2², increasing utility would demand that generic sacrifice allow a single victim from one species for a class from another.

(S3²) The sacrifice of one individual for another species but within the same genus or super-genus can be symbolized as:

$\exists(\hat{a}, b, C_1, C_2) \ni ([(b \not\in \hat{a}) \cdot [(C_1 \neq C_2) \cdot (C_1 \not\subset C_2) \cdot (C_2 \not\subset C_1)]$
$\cdot [C_1(\hat{a}) \cdot C_2(b)] \cdot [((C_1, C_2) \subset G)]] \supset [\vec{S}(b, \hat{a}) \cdot \overrightarrow{SACfor}(b, \hat{a})]),$

where this equation is read as "If there is a set *â* and individual *b* and a C_1 and C_2 such that *b* is not an element of *â* and C_1 is not identical to C_2, and C_1 is not a subset of C_2 nor is C_2 a subset of C_1, and *â* is an element of C_1 and b is an element of C_2, and C_1 and C_2 are subsets of some genus G, then *b* is a substitute for *â* and b is a sacrificial victim for *â*." This expresses the substitionary nature of sacrifices like the holocausts which are for a tribe or people—as in ancient Judaism—or the horse sacrifice in Hinduism, which can be offered for the entire human race.

Analogical Sacrifice

The fourth variety of sacrifice—which, perhaps, represents the outer limits of sacrificial substitution—is what I would call analogical substitution. It operates according to a perceived resemblance or analogy between the victim and that for which it is substituted. Here, what is minimally necessary is that some structural resemblance exist between the two objects. The appropriateness of the substitution is based upon a set of features each object possesses in itself or relative to some context.

Typically, the context is some mandate in culture that certifies the acceptability of the substitution. Such mandates can be works of great mercy. Symbolically, this variety can be defined as:

(S4¹) The analogical substitute of one individual for another:

$$\exists (a, b) \ni ([s_1 \subset a] \cdot [s_2 \subset b] \cdot [s_1 \propto s_2]) \supset [\vec{S}(a, b) \cdot \overrightarrow{SACfor}(a, b)]),$$

where this equation is read as: "If there is an *a* and a *b* such that s_1 is a structure (or feature) of *a* and s_2 is a structure (or feature) of *b*, and s_1 resembles s_2, then *a* is a substitute for *b* and *a* is a sacrificial victim for *b*."

Or, if the relation of resemblance is contextual and not simply a matter of similar features, then it can be symbolized as:

(S4²) $\exists (a, b) \ni ([(f_1(a) \text{ in } CNTXT_1) \cdot (f_2(b) \text{ in } CNTXT_2)$
    $\cdot (f_1(a) \propto f_2(b))] \supset [\vec{S}(a, b) \cdot \overrightarrow{SACfor}(a, b)]),$

where this equation is read as: "If *a* has *function 1* in *context 1* and *b* has *function 2* in *context 2* and if *function 1* resembles *function 2*, then *a* is a substitute for *b* and *a* is a sacrifice for *b*."

Analogical substitution based upon shared features can be connected with what Frazer called sympathetic magic. It is dependent upon the principle that like can be substituted for like. A burning in effigy would be an example of this variety of substitution. In the case of functional substitution, the ability to substitute one victim for the other is not based on an immediately perceived similarity but on the context—often cultural—in which each object functions. Thus, in a culture that didn't know wine or bread it might be legitimate to substitute banana beer and yam pies in the eucharistic sacrifice.

Metonymic Sacrifice

Finally, one of the most widespread notions of sacrifice is that of the sacrifice of self that is not total or suicidal but metonymic. Thus, we can talk about a sacrifice of time, money, effort, the development of virtue, and so forth. In this case, some part of the psyche or resources of the individual stands in the place of the individual as a sufficient offering, the understanding being that the difficulty of dedicating the portion is a measure of the sincerity of the sacrifice. The metonymic sacrifice can be symbolized as follows:

$$(S5) \quad \exists(a) \ni ((a \subset b) \supset [\vec{S}(a, b) \cdot \overrightarrow{SACfor}(a, b)]),$$

where this equation can be read as: "If there is an *a* such that if *a* is a part of *b* then *a* is a substitute for *b* and *a* is a sacrifice for *b*."

An example of this variety of sacrifice would be the Jewish practice of circumcision. If one believes in an afterlife, then one could make a cogent argument that the metonymic sacrifice is one of the forms of the sacrifice of life. But it has not been historically taken as simplistically equivalent. Metonymic sacrifice may require repetition to be equivalent to total sacrifice. It is clear, for example, that Jesus distinguishes between death to self (*psuchê*) and the sacrifice of one's life for one's friends. The latter is the ultimate sacrifice, but the former requires durative or diachronic repetition for it to be equivalent. For this reason, the martyr's death within Christianity has always been viewed as a fast track to beatitude, while the life of the ascetic is its protracted approximation.[40] Since the first century CE, metonymic sacrifice has been the chief variety recommended within both the rabbinic tradition of Judaism and Christianity, though for different reasons.

HAVING ELABORATED THE LOGICAL STRUCTURE OF SACRIFICIAL victimhood, the following observation remains. Note that, in all of the above logical types, a precondition for the possibility of sacrifice has been overlooked: the condition under which substitution is warranted. In other words, what constitutes the authorization of such a substitution remains unspecified.

A priori, whatever warrants sacrifice must have the following features. First, obviously, whatever counts as a substitute in a sacrifice must be valued; it must be difficult or expensive to offer up. This observation is especially relevant to the first variety of sacrifice. Anything worthy of being exchanged for the very existence of the self would seem to have great value, particularly from the side of the victim. Second, for sacrifice to retain a common meaning—in its historical development within a specific religious context—it must be premised upon a commensurable standard. Without a commensurable standard, the transition between two historical versions of sacrifice would mean a radical change in its stakes. It would mean that the two kinds of sacrifices operated according to different logics. that such a metamorphosis can take place is unquestionable, but for the historical transition periods in which one variety of sacrifice displaces a preceding variety, the acceptance of the new formulation requires that it operate according to the older rationale, at least for a while.

The Importance of Commensurable Standards

The notion of *commensurable standard* (general equivalent or symmetric measure, *metron summetra*) is a notion that explains the possibility of exchanges. Aristotle places his discussion of the commensurable standard in the heart of his discussion of justice.[41] Recognizing that simple reciprocity is at variance with some forms of justice, it has only *proportional* application to human association; it is not a matter of perfect equality. As Aristotle puts it,

> [P]roportionate requital is effected by diagonal conjunction. For example, let A be a builder, B a shoemaker, C a house, and D a shoe. It is required that a builder shall receive from the shoemaker a portion of the product of his labor, and give him a portion of his own product. Now if a proportionate equality between the products be first established, and then reciprocation take place, the requirement indicated will be achieved; but if this is not done, the bargain is not equal, and intercourse does not continue. Hence all commodities exchanged must be able to be compared in some way. It is to meet this requirement that men have introduced money; money constitutes in a manner a middle term, for it is a measure of all things . . . ; for without this reciprocal proportion, there can be no association; and it cannot be secured unless the commodities in question be equal in a sense. There must therefore be some one standard, and this is accepted by

agreement; for such a standard makes all things commensurable, since all things can be measured by money.[42]

Without "exchange there would be no association, and there can be no exchange without equality, and no equality without commensurability."[43] A commensurable standard is a middle term that makes all things proportionate or measurable against one another. Key to Aristotle's definition is the recognition that all human association is based upon exchange. But I would go further, following Mauss, to suggest that, in primitive societies, this observation can be extended to include association between gods and men, as well. Though currency has been the most common example of a commensurable standard, its applications in transactions involving material commodities among humans has blinded us to the relevance of commensurable standards in understanding the transactions between gods and humans.

More recently, Jean-Joseph Goux has expanded this notion beyond its Aristotelian and Marxian limitations to apply to all exchange systems, whether consisting of commodities or symbols.[44] His summary of this expansion bears citing.

> Thus the notion of *general equivalent*—a standard measure [commensurable standard] . . . was methodologically extended in what constituted the original core of my analysis. While the notion of the general equivalent has its source in theories concerning economic exchange-value, it may acquire outside of its native field a heretofore unspecified significance that contributes to the illumination of our cultural institution as a whole. The general equivalence pertains first of all to money: what is in the beginning simply one commodity among many is placed in an exclusive position, set apart to serve as a unique measure of the values of all other commodities. Comparison (essential to equitable exchange) and the recognition of abstract value despite perceptible difference institute not simply an equivalence but a privileged, exclusive place, that of the measuring object—either as ideal standard external to exchange or currency proper, which takes part in circulation. A fresh reading of the genesis of the money form elaborated by Marx allows us to discern a structural logic of the formation of the

general equivalent, a logic that leads to my methodological extension of this notion to other domains, where values are no longer economic, where the play of substitutions defined the quantitative values.[45]

In what follows, I accept the genius of Goux's expansion, *mutatis mutandis*. However, in contrast to Goux's application, my hunt for the commensurable standard that lies behind sacrifice in ancient Israel is focused on one of the *general equivalents* ("ideal standards") used to establish a homogeneous basis for the spiritual exchange expressed in the Hebrew scriptures and the New Testament and not on the phallus or *jouissance* as the general equivalents of sexual difference.

Life Was the Commensurable Standard Operative in Jewish Temple Practice in the First Century CE

Following Goux, I would like to argue that *life* represents the commensurable standard used to establish a homogeneous basis for the spiritual exchange expressed in the Hebrew scriptures and the New Testament. That it always functioned as such from the time of the emergence of sacrificial practices in Israel, I will not argue, but simply that it is the standard that allows us to bridge the meaning of Temple sacrifice and the sacrifice of Jesus in the first century.

The book of Leviticus provides the instructions for sacrifice, but they are given there with very little explanation. The origin of these rites and their most primitive surviving meaning do not exist before the Priestly period or later.[46] What we have in Leviticus is probably a compilation of practices and rituals that were first put into writing in the post-exilic period, but they are certainly older than the Babylonian exile. Though they are at the very heart of what is definitive of pre-diaspora Judaism, they are likely to be what Pareto describes as residues.[47] Although the Sages of the Second Temple period may have stated that "the world rested on three things: the Torah, Temple worship, and charitable deeds," and even though preexilic prophets condemn "those who substituted the offerings of sacrifice for true penitence, . . . [they] nevertheless never objected to sacrifices as such and denounced those who spoiled sacrifices by choosing flawed animals."[48] Later, post-diaspora Judaism moved to an interpretation of sacrifice that associated it with the actions and intentions of humans, though the *Shemoneh Esreh, Musaf* prayers are addressed to God for the "rebuilding of the Temple, restoration of worship and sacrifice."[49]

In particular, sacrifice follows a logic that is not obvious and requires reconstruction because its originary and subsequent preexilic meanings have been in part lost. This means that all reconstructions of the earliest period of sacrifice in Israel must be speculative, at best. The nature of sacrifice is not illuminated much when we turn to the commentaries (*midrashim*), the oral Torah (*Mishnah*), or the discussions that take *Mishnah* as object (the *Talmud*). Even a recent rabbinic commentator like Steinsaltz has admitted that there is "no systematic attempt . . . to explain the ideological basis of the injunction on sacrifice, and the issue can only be understood through the hints dispersed throughout the text and from the various commentaries written over the ages."[50]

An interpretation especially useful for bridging the Christian understanding of Jesus' sacrifice and Temple sacrifice comes from a medieval commentary by Nachmanides. Nachmanides provides an explanation for what the commensurable standard for sacrifice is, and the strength of this explanation is that it clarifies the relationship between Jewish Temple sacrifice as well as the sacrifice of Jesus and the Mass.

However, straightaway a problem is apparent in the temporal distance that separates Nachmanides' explanation and first-century sacrificial practice. We must ask what justifies the use of this late commentary to bridge two first-century meanings? My justification for this employment follows along three lines: first, as Steinsaltz has argued, within the Jewish tradition there is no universally accepted theology of sacrifice that brings the historical data into coherence; second, Nachmanides' explanation represents a scholastic tradition that is considerably older than his commentary and may have had its rabbinic theoreticians at the time of Jesus; and, third, that the first two possibilities remove most of the barriers to a speculative interpolation of the Nachmanidean explanation. I would argue that on the basis of the coherence of meaning that the Nachmanidean commentary restores to the data, on the basis of

the way it brings intelligibility of the sacrificial practices of Jews and
Christians, it provides some of the missing elements for a theory of
sacrifice that establishes a continuity between the two traditions.

Nachmanides on the Blood of Sacrifice

The text that supplies the missing link for a possible economic interpretation of Jesus' blood sacrifice is found in Nachmanides' commentary on Leviticus. There he provides an explanation of blood sacrifice
that brings it squarely into the camp of those notions of exchange that
Mauss describes as the circulation of spirit. Moreover, Nachmanides'
explanation also provides a description of the commensurable standard that allows the convertibility of Temple sacrifice and the sacrifice
of Jesus.

Treating the notion of atonement, Nachmanides is clear that animals are substitutes for the life to which God has a right because of sin.
The point of animal sacrifice as sin offering, according to Ramban, is
that the participants realize it is they who should be slain.

> All these acts [laying on sacrifice of hands, confession of sins, burn-
> ing of the innards and kidneys, burning of limbs, and sprinkling of
> blood corresponding to the sinful deed, evil speech, organs of desire,
> and the guilty blood] are performed in order that when they are done,
> a person should realize that he has sinned against G-d with his body
> and his soul, and that "his" blood should really be spilled and "his" body
> be burned, were it not for the loving-kindness of the Creator, Who
> took from him a substitute and a ransom, namely this offering, so that
> its blood should be in place of his blood, its life in place of his life, and
> that the chief limbs of the offering should be in place of the chief parts
> of his body. The portions [given from the sin offering to the priests],
> are in order to support the teachers of the Torah, so that they pray on
> his behalf.[51]

The blood of the sacrifice is thus linked symbolically with the
blood of the sinner(s) for whom it stands. But there is a second, metaphysical aspect to the significance of blood, one that defines the great

circulation of spirit or life that the economy of salvation generates. When he glosses the passage in Leviticus where the prohibition of eating blood occurs, Nachmanides observes that animals stand for humans in sacrifice (and may be eaten) because they were redeemed by Noah from the flood. But, though their flesh may be consumed, the blood of the animals is excluded from consumption because it is charged with special properties.

> Thus He permitted man to use their bodies for his benefit because their life was on account of man's sake, and that their soul [that is, blood] should be used for man's atonement when offering them up before Him, blessed be He, but not to eat it, since one creature possessed of a soul is not to eat a creature with a soul, for all souls belong to G-d. The life of man just as the life of the animals are all His, *even one thing befallen them; as the one dieth, so dieth the other; yea they have one breath.* [Ecclesiastes 3:19][52]

The blood of living beings is thus identified with the spirit that God breathed into the first human in Genesis, not in the materialist sense of corpuscular oxygenation but according to an implicit biblical metaphysics.[53] For Nachmanides, all animals have souls "in a certain sense."[54] As he explains, "[An animal] has sufficient understanding to avoid harm, and to seek its welfare, and a sense of recognition towards those with whom it is familiar, and love towards them, just as dogs love their masters, and they have a wonderful sense of recognition of the people of their households, and similarly pigeons have a sense of knowledge and recognition."[55]

The eating of blood is prohibited because of the danger that the blood of humans would fuse with that of animals and make the life of its recipient coarser.[56] This devolution happens because — according to Nachmanides' primitive understanding of physiology — blood is not digested but immediately moves to the bloody parts of the body to be mixed with the blood of the human host. He describes the process of this mixing as follows:

> [T]he blood is the life, and the life is in the blood, as both are mixed together, similarly to wine when diluted with water, in which case the

water is in the wine and the wine is in the water, and each one is "in" the other. . . . [T]he blood is the very life, meaning to say that both have become one inseparable substance, so that you can never find blood without life nor life without blood. . . . [Air, originating in the heart, is the *hulê* from which all dispositions proceed] supplying the substance which gives nutrition and makes blood, and it is the blood which in turn creates it and sustains it. [The relationship between *blood and life*[57] is] like that of matter and form in all physical creatures, where one cannot be found without the other.[58]

The relation between blood and life is *perichoretic:* blood and life interpenetrate one another so as to become, as it were, a single substance.[59] Nachmanides finds it impossible to think of blood in isolation from animal life and to think of life in isolation from animal blood. He concludes that "it is not fitting to mix the soul that is destined to destruction with that which is to live [on] in the [hereafter]. Rather it is to be as an atonement upon the altar to be acceptable before G-d."[60]

Given these preceding expositions, it is now possible to express a positive thesis about how blood functions in the Christian economy of salvation. Blood is the currency with which Jewish and Christian sacrificial practice trades, but blood stands to its commensurable standard as the greenback once stood to the gold standard. In the first-century sacrificial economy of Christian and Jews, the gold standard of sacrificial exchange was life.

The Sacrificial Economy in Ancient Israel Had Life as Its Commensurable Standard

All sacrifices in the Hebrew scriptures can be represented in terms of a system of exchanges, but that system is defined by a single commensurable standard.[61] That commensurable standard is life—as contained within blood; it is the general equivalent on the basis of which sacrifice must be understood. But the kind of reciprocity it establishes—like the Anselmian notion of honor—cannot be one of perfect equality, for God cannot expect to receive precisely what he gives to humans. By covenant, the responsibilities of God and the people of the covenant are different. The relation between the two sets is one of proportionate requital. Even so, the apparent disproportion between the things exchanged can be expressed by means of a commensurable standard, and that standard is life.

Life circulates in the system of exchanges. God gives humankind life and expects life in return. The life given by God requires—by covenant—that thanksgiving sacrifice be offered. In the same way, when humans negate the life given by God, God requires that that negation must be remediated. Gratitude and repentance are two possible responses to two kinds of exchanges: one (gratitude) is the response to having received the gift of life; the other (repentance) is the response to having squandered (sinned against or negated) the gift of life. Life is associated with order, death with disorder, virtue and obedience with life and order, sin and disobedience with death and disorder. All varieties of sacrifice in the Hebrew scriptures may be interpreted in terms of these two responses. Thus, sacrifice exists as a system of exchanges in which gratitude and repentance are valorized by the exchange of life. Gratitude is expressed in sacrifice—the shedding of blood to offer it or transmute it and return it to God. Repentance is expressed in sacrifice, and the shedding of blood as an offering of transmutation make it recompense. There is a parallel, here, between Mauss' magnanimous variety of exchange and its attendant sumptuary banquets and Israelitic sacrificial ritual.

In ancient Israelitic sacrifice, blood as convertible with life is really the tangible medium that "contains" life. Thus blood is the currency of life that makes its commensurable magnitude (life) tangible. Like paper bills or metallic coins, blood is the tangible signifier of the hidden reality. Even the digitized data of banking transactions requires the reality of electronic coding in electromagnetic units interpreted as binary digits. As intangible as they may seem, they are material. Likewise the blood is the tangible sign of life, and it is its tangibility that allows it to have effect and to be exchanged.

The commensurable standard of sacrifice—life—stands not as an abstract representation of value—like a greenback—but as a commensurable standard (life) that is continuous with the sacrificial substitute as well as the substituted-for and that, at the same time, has use value. The blood of an animal is not identical with the blood of a human, but the blood of an animal is a sacrificial equivalent for human blood, first, by the rule of substitution that allows the locus of life for another animate being to stand for the locus of life for another but also by analogous substitution by which a similar continuous part of one being can be substituted for a similar continuous part of another being. Finally, sacrificial substitution of the victim for the other entails that the blood—the physical shroud or form of the commensurable standard, life—itself is charged with a function or use value. That function or use value is proportionate to the ontological level from which the victim is drawn. The commensurable standard connected with sacrificial exchange in the Hebrew scriptures is not an arbitrarily assumed standard—as may be in Aristotle or according to other economic theoreticians.[62]

Sacrifice is not practiced as a ritual divorced from its antecedent human analogues. Its meaning would be lost were this so. It is, quite the contrary, a ritualization of those analogues that are the banquets of celebration and reconciliation, banquets in which the sacrificial victim is consumed either to celebrate the good fortune of the tribal factions or to heal the rift between them. The logic of the meal sacrifice is that of a sharing of a common corpus with God and the community. Unity is achieved in the consumption of the common meal shared. In banquets in which all the celebrants are humans, the choicest foods are put before the most honored human guests, and the honored guest may even eat first with the leavings going to the others, but usually everyone participates in the banquet feast. In the case of the sacrificial meal with God, however, the mode of his existence prohibits the consumption of the banquet offering according to any crude interpretation that makes it literal, physical mastication.

The sacrificial substance, therefore, requires transformation or conversion before it may actually be returned to God. According to one view, the transmutation of the victim is the immolation of the victim. The required transmutation follows a primitive logic: airy spirit requires a similarly rarefied consumable. The transmuted form of the sacrifice returns to its source—God—in the rising smoke of the holocaust. Return of the sacrificial victim in gratitude and return of the sacrificial victim by substitution for atonement are both accomplished through the transformation by immolation.

In sacrifices to God in which the immolation is complete, the blood too is returned to God. In sacrifices in which the sacrifice is consumed by the offerers (or the priests), the blood is separated from the flesh. The separated blood becomes the means for topical purification through anointing of sacred objects (the altar) or participants, but it must not be consumed. In a real sense, the blood is meant for external use only. This may seem odd, but it suggests that different effects issue from its different possible applications. God graciously apportions the blood for topical sanctification or purification.

Applied apotropaically, this means that one is marked by the blood of the sacrificial victim as one who has made atonement or as one who has been justified. It is presumably in this sense that the blood of the atonement sacrifice is used to mark the persons of the Israelites and the blood of the Pascal lamb is used to mark their doorways. Externally, the blood effects substitution or healing and is the mark of atonement. But its internal consumption—which is forbidden—follows a different logic. To take blood internally—by the Nachmanidean logic—means more intimately to become one with the being from whom it issued. *We are what we eat.* Things taken internally become part of the subject consuming them.

But to be distinguished is a physical becoming from a spiritual becoming. Here, the logic has acquired a new scope. It has become the logic of transformation not the logic of simple substitution. Eating the flesh of a sacrificial victim means that I assimilate its substance to my own. It is I that it becomes. But eating the blood of a sacrificial victim means that my soul is assimilated to it. It is I that become it.[63]

This explains the biblical prohibitions against the eating of the blood. Even so, both logics issue from the sacrificial blood. The logic of Judaic sacrificial substitution is essentially a masking of the proper object of death by the substituted sign of the victim, its blood, whereas the consumption of the blood means the inner transformation into the being of the victim.

We are finally in a position to pull all of the above features together and to describe sacrificial practice in the Hebrew Scriptures as having the following features:

1. It is a sharing of a meal with God.
2. It is a part of a *substantive economy* of the *magnanimous kind.*
3. It is an *appropriational exchange* according to a *commensurate standard,* life.
4. It is an exchange of life for life (both for atonement and thanksgiving).
5. It is a *substitutionary sacrifice* of type *S3* (generic sacrifice).

The Sacrificial Economy of Early Christianity Was a Sacramental Economy with Life as Its Commensurable Standard

The Eucharist is a celebration of the sacrificial death of Jesus; it is a ritual that commemorates and makes that sacrifice present without its repetition. As such, it is a simplification and confluence of all other sacrifices described in the Hebrew scriptures. According to the Christian tradition, it displaces the ancient forms of Israelitic sacrifice because is a sacrifice of a God-man, a sacrifice whose virtue is so great as to supplant the successive repetitions of animal sacrifice.[64] It also displaces these sacrifices because it gives its participants access to the very life force of God.

Theories of exchange that ignore the notion of commensurable standard or that ignore the possibility that the standard can be mediated by the currency that represents it, are not of adequate complexity to describe sacramental sacrificial exchange. For example, the Baudrillardian formulation of economy is not sufficient in its description of the varieties of exchange to capture the kind of sacrifice described in the New Testament. Baudrillardian exchange always entails the substitution of the value of one thing for the other, according to binary pairings of four possibilities.[65]

Sacramental exchange introduces a new possibility that breaks outside of this schema; it is about transformative or metamorphic exchange. It is about an exchange that allows a common middle term that can effect, transmit, or participate in a reality. As such, it remains the substitution of one victim for another according to a commensurable standard, but a commensurable standard of a special sort.

God's new covenant is not a covenant of the arbitrary choice of blood as though many other substances might just as well be chosen. Blood is redolent with a seriousness that is connected with its primacy to human life. It may be that the choice of blood was not in any sense necessitated as the commensurable standard, but it is—to use the terms of the patristic authors—a part of God's economy for God to have so chosen this symbol because of its association with the life-force. The wine in the eucharistic sacrifice signifies the blood as the substance of transformation. It is the medium by which those participating come to possess life and are conformed to divinity. This represents a special kind of commensurable standard. It is neither nominalistic nor binary but capable of ingressing into the very being of the participant.[66]

Just as ancient Israelitic sacrifice is an exchange whereby "life" (the absolute commensurate standard) is accessed through the blood of the sacrificed animal, the blood—in a very direct way—makes those participating in the sacrifice healthy, whole, or complete. Likewise, the Eucharist is the medium by which direct access is given to Christ, who is life and love. The Christian command to eat the bread and wine—and more transgressively to eat the body and blood of Jesus—and the Israelitic prohibition from consuming the blood of the sacrificial victim presuppose the same logic. To drink the blood, the life force of another is, in a sense, to become the thing that one consumes. The literal consumption of the blood of sacrifice (or the consumption of the transubstantiated bread and wine in eucharistic feast) may be instructively contrasted with the consumption of economic goods. The latter are generally about an extrinsic or accidental change to the subject that is made possible by exchange, while the former is about an intrinsic habitual or dispositional change in the subject made by an exchange.[67]

In sacramental meals of sacrifice, the meal is the mediating instrumentality of the union, eating being one of the primordial forms of unifying fellowship. In those religions where the victim is thought to be the god then the meal becomes not only a symbol of the fellowship between the community and the god, but the community is also really transformed into that god. The sacrifice results in a real transformative virtue that is imparted via the blood and flesh.

In ancient Israelitic sacrifice the animal stands in for the human, but the standing in precludes the humans communing with the very life-force of the animal. To be sure, humans eat the flesh of animals, but they are forbidden the drinking of the blood. In the Eucharist, the bread that represents the flesh and the wine that represents the blood are both consumed. In that very consumption, communion with body and soul is established. The logic of the flesh is a logic of causation, metamorphosis, and participation that transforms animal into human, but the logic of the blood is one that transforms human into animal. To eat the flesh of an other is for the other to become you. To eat the soul, the life force, of an other is to become like that other. Bread and wine in the Eucharist thus signify a *perichoresis,* which is hinted at in the words of Jesus in his post-supper discourse in John's gospel (Jn 17). In the Eucharist, Jesus becomes us in the flesh as we become him in the spirit. The sacramental exchange necessarily involves this participatory dimension. Its various relations can be described with the help of a diagram (figure 1).[68]

Half of what the Eucharist represents is recognized in ancient Judaism: those who participate in the sacrificial banquet are one in the consumption and transmutation of a common victim. In the Eucharist, they are one in this sense, too, but they are also participants in one soul/life/spirit by the communicant's ingestion of the body and blood.

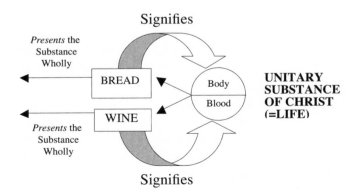

FIGURE I. Eucharistic Sacramental Exchange

Though disallowed and otherwise considered transgressive, the drinking of blood is allowed when it is in the form of wine and the eating of flesh is allowed when it is in the form of bread. In both cases it is not the reality of the flesh and blood under all its accidental aspects that is ingested; it is the substance that stands behind both that is the source of life. But, in Christianity, as the commensurable standard is extended from flesh and blood to bread and wine, a new exchange structure is introduced.

What we have in the Christian Eucharist is a *sacramental economy* emergent from a *sacrificial economy*. A sacramental economy is an economy where (1) the commensurate standard is an absolute (and not a relative) standard and (2) the medium of exchange mediates the presence or effect of the absolute standard. If the greenback bill were sacramental then its commensurate standard—gold—would be an absolute value instead of a conventional value. Moreover, the greenback would be—*through its own material presence*—an instrument of access to the substance of gold. It is not a question of the greenback *representing* a conventional commensurate standard—which it historically has—but of the greenback *giving direct access* to the reality of an absolute commensurate standard. This constitutes a form of exchange that Baudrillard has not anticipated except—perhaps—under the form of symbolic exchange. It is operative primarily within the realm of religious belief and practice. The difference is between the kind of exchange that can be formulated in terms of representational signs versus the kind of exchange that can be formulated in terms of presentational signs.

We are finally in a position to pull all of the above features together and to describe the sacrifice of Jesus in the New Testament (which is ingressive in the Eucharist) as having the following features:

1. It is a sharing of a meal with God.
2. It is a part of a *substantive economy* of the *magnanimous kind.*
3. It is an *appropriational exchange* according to a *commensurate standard,* life, but it is an appropriational exchange of a special kind. It is a sacramental exchange whereby the commensurate standard, life, is equivalent to the substance of the God-man Christ but is mediated by this standard's tangible media, bread and wine.

4. It is an exchange of life for life (both for atonement and thanksgiving).
5. It is a *unique substitutionary sacrifice* that combines features of types
   $S2^2$ and $S3^2$. Moreover, it is a unique sacrifice in that it is so efficacious
   that it perpetually satisfies the requirement of victim sacrifice and thus
   ends the necessity of its repetition, except in the form of the celebration of the Mass.

In terms of the preceding formulations defining sacrificial exchange, it is possible to describe how $S2^2$ and $S3^1$ are combined:

(SE) $\exists$ (â, b, c, *C*, *G*, *H*, *B*, *W*) $\ni$ ([(((b $\in$ â) • (b ≠ c)
       • *G*(b) • *H*(â) • *C*(â) • *B*(c$_1$) • *W*(c$_2$)) • ([*G* ≠ *H* ≠ *B* ≠ *W*]
       • $\not\subset$ [*G*: *H*, *B*, *W*] • $\not\subset$ [*H*: *G*, *B*, *W*] • $\not\subset$ [*B*: *H*, *G*, *W*]
       • $\not\subset$ [*W*: *B*, *H*, *G*])] $\supset$ [$\vec{S}$(b, â) • $\overrightarrow{SACfor}$(b, â)]
       • BECOMES(<c$_1$ • c$_2$>, b)
       $\supset$ $\overrightarrow{SACfor}$(BECOME (<c$_1$ • c$_2$>, b), â)]).

This can be read as "If there is a set *â* and a member *b* such that *b* is a
member of set *â* and set *â* constitutes a community *C* (of humans), and
b is God (G), and if there are members *c₁* and *c₂* such that *c₁* is bread
and *c₂* is wine and God and humans (H) and bread (B) and wine (W)
are different species of things, then if *b* is a substitute for the class of
humans *â* and *b* is a sacrificial victim for the class of humans *â*, and if
this bread and wine *become b*, then *bread-and-wine-become-b* is a sacrifice for the class of humans." This description conflates the description of human sacrifice, one for the group, with that of generic sacrifice,
one member of one species (bread) and one member of one species
(wine) substituted for all members of the human species. But it also
requires a *transubstantiation* of bread and wine for the substitution to
be effected.

Of course, this formulation is merely a tease, because it leaves
"BECOMES" and "*bread-and-wine-become-b*" metaphysically unde-
fined. Because of this, it also neglects the relation between the singularity of the God-man, Jesus Christ, as well as the singularity of the
human sacrifice that is made present across space and time at different
Masses. To attempt a logical description of this, or to bring all five fea-

tures of eucharistic sacrifice together in a logical formulation would require another paper.

Therefore, I come to the end of my argument. The importance of the preceding is to show that the main features of eucharistic sacrifice are roughly expressed both in their continuity and discontinuity with sacrificial practice in Ancient Israel. With this formulation, we have also come closer to unpacking the significance of Christian sacrifice against both the background of sacrificial practice among the ancient Jews and also against the background of anthropological data such as those presented by Mauss. Finally, this formulation helps explain the cultural and theological significance of the shedding of Christ's blood, significance that can be expressed under the categories of substantive economics, a significance whose elaboration is just in its beginning phases.

Notes

1. Among the theological theoreticians of Judeo-Christian sacrifice are Tertullian, Porphyry, Anselm, Thomas Aquinas, Luther, Calvin, De Maistre, Keil, Neumann, Baehr, Oehler, Delitzsch, Hofmann, Wellhausen, Bushnell, Gray, De Vaux, Daly, Hamerton-Kelly, Milgrom, Finlan, et al. Among the anthropological or historian-of-religions theoreticians of sacrifice among world religions are Tylor, Frazer, Robertson-Smith, Jensen, Hubert, Mauss, Durkheim, Bloch, Malina, Douglas, Burkert, Girard, et al. This is a list of some of the most famous theoreticians; I do not mean it to be comprehensive.

2. The genetic fallacy is an argument that reduces the significance of an idea to its origin, either to approve it or to damn it. It is a fallacy not because one who is guilty of it maintains that the origin is relevant to understanding the idea but because its proponent maintains the origin of an idea necessarily makes it true or false. It confuses the circumstances for an idea's emergence with its logical status as true or false.

3. See Marcel Mauss, *The Gift: The Form and Reason for Exchange in Archaic Societies* (New York: W. W. Norton, 1990 [1950]), 4. Although Mauss gives a general definition of economy as a "system of total services" imposed by collectivities and characterized by exchanges of "property and wealth, movable and immovable goods, and things economically useful" but also by acts of respect and spiritual reciprocation, it is possible to make the notion of economy more precise without negating his arguments in such a way that these arguments will be made more persuasive in light of the biblical data (5–7).

Following (but expanding) Michael Polanyi's definition, we may distinguish two separate meanings of the word "economics": a *substantive meaning* and a *formal meaning*. The substantive meaning includes human dependence on nature, on fellow humans, and on gods for existence. It refers to the exchanges that take place between these sectors of reality insofar as they provide the satisfaction of material and spiritual needs. See Michael Polanyi, "The Economy as an Instituted Process" in *Trade and Market in the Early Empires*, ed. K. Polanyi, C. M. Arensberg, and H. W. Pearson (Chicago: Henry Regnery, 1971), 243. In contrast, the formal meaning of "economics" refers to the logic of the ends-means relationship in a situation of choice between means, no one of which secures the end without some cost. Here, the rules governing the choice of means as *economical* or *economizing* constitute the rationality of the economic process, a rationality that can be expressed by logical or mathematical formulae (243).

Only the substantive meaning yields the means for the social-scientific study of "all the empirical economies of past and present" (244). At base, the two definitions have little in common. The formal meaning is a definition of the rationalization of economic exchange of a specific type; it is an idealization of the way rational actors have behaved (at least since the Enlightenment) in a free market. The former refers to the historically variable systems of exchange that may or may not follow this logic. It includes market and nonmarket phenomena that are premodern, and that, exactly because they are premodern, include exchanges that are not susceptible to precise analysis by the formal means developed to study the rationality of the free market (244).

4. Ibid., 244. Inseparable from the notion of economy is the notion of exchange. In simplest terms, exchange is an interchange of two things from one person to another. But the simplest variety of exchange—*operational exchange*, reckoned as the mere physical interchange of things from one set of hands to another—is most uninteresting because its description does not include the reason that the exchange is made. Most relevant, for the purposes of this paper, is *decisional exchange*, which is reckoned as an appropriational exchange at a set rate or according to a set rule or standard. Decisional exchange may be defined as a reciprocity between two actors each of whom gives *to* and receives *from* the other something according to an established rule, price, or standard. The reciprocity may be immediate, so that in the moment one gives something, one also receives something, or it may be delayed, so that one gives something with the hope and expectation of receiving something in the future. But for an exchange to be a decisional exchange there must be an interchange: something must be given and something must be received according to some standard, whatever the temporal duration between the giving and receiving is (254). Irrelevant here is the third variety of exchange designated by Polanyi as *integrative exchange*. The latter is an appropriational exchange at a bargained rate and is typical of free markets. It is not treated here because religious economies generally do not function like free markets (254). I would argue that religious economies presuppose a standard that is absolute.

5. Mauss, *The Gift*, 5–7.

6. Ibid.

7. By "natural economies" Mauss is referring to the German notion of *Naturalwirtschaft*: speculative, ideal-typical economies based on a state of nature unblemished by culture and existing before the emergence of money and credit. Two idealizations that were dominant at the time Mauss was writing seem to be the objects against which this denial is pitched. The first is Adam Smith's notion of a simple, primitive system of free exchange, without artificial restraints. Guided by the "invisible hand," it tends toward a state of equilibrium in the relation between supply and demand, and it is rational and predictable. The second is Karl Marx's notion represented by the first stage of human economic development in which the economic actors are functionally undifferentiated—everyone makes everything for him- or herself—and exchange is by barter. In the context of this paper, a third ideal-type of a natural economy might also be proposed, a theological model of Edenic, prelapsarian existence and modeled on the perichoretic exchange of being in the Trinity, but this is certainly outside of the scope of what Mauss intended.

8. Mauss, *The Gift*, 5.

9. Ibid., 7.

10. Ibid., 6.

11. Ibid.

12. Ibid., 7.

13. For those conversant with the subtleties of Trinitarian theology, these notions of pouring out and reciprocation find analogues in the intra-Trinitarian economy in which each person of the Trinity is said to give his being to the other and to have that act of giving reciprocated. Whether one thinks that human practice is the means for understanding these metaphysical relations, or that the Trinitarian relations ground the human practice, or both, they seem to form a particularly fruitful analogy for theological speculation.

14. Mauss, *The Gift*, 11–12.

15. Ibid., 13.

16. Ibid.

17. Ibid., 41.

18. Ibid.

19. Ibid., 42.

20. Ibid., 14.

21. Ibid., 16.

22. Ibid.

23. Ibid. The "setting" of the price by the gods presupposes an objective— and one would presume absolute—standard that defines the equity of the exchanges. See the discussion of commensurable standard below.

24. Mauss, *The Gift*, 17.

25. Ibid.

26. Ibid., 18.

27. A superficial reading of Anselm's *Cur Deus Homo* leads to the conclusion that it is God's honor that the sacrifice of Jesus restores, but a careful reading makes it clear that God is immune to human disrespect; see Anselm of Canterbury, *The Major Works,* ed. Brian Davies and E. R. Evans (Oxford: Oxford University Press, 1998), book 1, chap. 15, 288–89, and book 2, chap. 19, 352–54. As Anselm puts it: "Nothing can be added to, or subtracted from, the honour of God, in so far as it related to God himself. For this same honor is, in relation to him, inherently incorruptible and in no way capable of change" (book 1, chap. 15, 288). The real problem is that the sacrifice of Jesus is demanded by the original sin that destroys an established order: the *economy* (in the patristic sense) of human-divine relations. "But when a rational being does not wish for what is right, he dishonours God, with regard to himself, since he is not willingly subordinating himself to God's governance, and is disturbing, as far as he is able, the order and beauty of the universe" (288). It is at this point that the juristic argument for Jesus' death is called into service as the means by which the original order is reestablished. "[T]he supreme Wisdom changes . . . wrong desire or action into the order and beauty of the universal scheme of things . . . [for] voluntary recompense for wrongdoing, or the exaction of punishment from someone who does not give recompense, retain their own proper place in this same universal order and their same regulatory beauty. If the divine Wisdom did not impose these forms of recompense . . . , there would be in the universe, which God ought to be regulating, a certain ugliness, resulting from the violation of the beauty of order, and God would appear to be failing in his governance" (289).

28. It is a sense of the utter incongruity between the status of God and the status of man that makes it impossible for the nineteenth-century theologian Ritschl to understand how an exchange can take place in Anselm's conception of the Atonement; and it is exactly this problem that Christians believe is solved in the Incarnation. There is a theological point to be made here about one of the classical interpretations of the sacrifice of Jesus, that of Anselm. Against the background of what Mauss has said, it is easy to see that, under one interpretation, Anselm's thinking is continuous with archaic notions of law (the *lex talionis*) and archaic notions of economy, especially in light of the blood feuds that break out among the agonistic societies of exchange. With respect to the issue of justice, Anselm's argument describes one of the major circuits in the Christian economy of salvation as it is interpreted within the West. (Moreover, in Anselm's recognition that the dishonored has a right to demand more than equal payment, we are thrown back to an atavism, to a regressive historical moment prior to awareness of the *lex talionis*.) Mauss has not provided a model for the second moment, that of purification or sanctification. It is my thesis that this second moment may be discovered in the idea of blood propitiation with which Anselm's juristic interpretation is complementary.

29. For purposes of comparison, let me cite the definition with which Mauss and Hubert begin their famous monograph: "Thus we finally arrive at the following definition: *Sacrifice is a religious act which, through the consecration of a victim, modifies the condition of the moral person who accomplishes it or that of certain objects with which he is concerned.* For brevity of expression we call those sacrifices in which the personality of the sacrificer is directly affected by the sacrifice *personal sacrifices,* and those in which objects, real or ideal, received directly the sacrificial action *objective sacrifices.*" This definition, for reasons I shall soon make clear, narrows the real structure of sacrifice according to some specific features of the Semitic model, while it neglects others. The definition provided above, the one that sees sacrifice as a category of economic behavior, I think is the broader—and hence stronger—generalization of sacrifice, wherever we see it in religious practice. See Henri Hubert and Marcel Mauss, *Sacrifice: Its Nature and Function,* trans. W. D. Halls (Chicago: University of Chicago Press, 1981 [1898]), 13.

30. I do not believe this undermines the Girardian interpretation of sacrifice in any overt way but instead provides a supplementary explanation for sacrifice connected with thanksgiving, a category that does not, to my mind, receive adequate treatment in his discussion of mimesis. Thanksgiving sacrifice—as Mauss has shown—is susceptible to a Girardian interpretation when the potential discord ameliorated is not a preexisting discord or societal malady or disorder but a potential one triggered by the resentment of one segment of the population who envy the good fortune of another. A Thanksgiving feast thus becomes the means by which the good fortune of one group is shared with the other, thus being an anticipatory defusing of potential strife. Here, the mimetic desire is the desire of what the other has but will not share. The Thanksgiving banquet thus becomes the sharing and group consumption of a real but representative victim that stands in symbolically for the boon of the fortunate. It is clearly not the democratic distribution of that boon but a common *fête* that substitutes for it. This way the fortunate—at small expense to their actual reserves—offset the desire of the have-nots by offering a substitute for the actual distribution of their boon *in extenso.*

31. Whatever the value of Girard's etymological excursus on *sacrificium* as applied to religions outside of the Judeo-Christian tradition, when viewed in the context of the latter, the meaning of this word would seem more accurately to be connected with the righteousness and sanctification of those who are party to the sacrifice. Girard's etymological interpretation—because of the word's inherent ambiguity—does, however, apply well to scapegoat sacrifice *as he has defined it.* But this interpretation does not provide a complete enough meaning to cover all the ways sacrifice is construed in the Bible.

32. Also omitted in Mauss' discussion is a specification of the notion of substitution. Most exchanges of goods (whether sacrificial or otherwise) are not precisely reciprocal, such as a loaf of bread for a loaf of bread, an eye for an eye, etc. The earliest form of nonsymmetric exchange was probably barter exchange. When

the earliest economies based upon common economic standards emerged, they (like the barter economies) were only possible because they were based on the possibility of *substitution*. Otherwise, there would have been no reason for exchange. In the case of barter economies, the varieties of substitution were of one kind of good for the other or the substitution of one collection of different kinds of goods for another good or collection. This implied, though it may have been done quite unconsciously, a reckoning that the items exchanged were in some sense equally valued, although this notion of equality possessed a certain elasticity from one exchange to another and according to the desires and needs of each party to it. Even so, the conditions behind the decision for barter established that the exchange could be made because the goods could be substituted for one another. Substituting one for the other was the operation that allowed the exchange to take place no matter how that substitution was reckoned. When economic standards were devised, they provided a common criterion in terms of which disparate goods might be reckoned.

In the broadest sense, substitution is an operation that allows one to replace one thing with another according to a rule-governing equivalence. In mathematics, the substitution of the value of one variable by another value is judged correct if the equation continues to be balanced. For example, in the equation $x + y = 5$ correct substitutions are those which for x and y according to the operation of addition result in the equivalent of 5. The rules that govern this substitution are implicit in the structure that this equation denotes. Equations presuppose respective strings of variables and functors and syntactic conventions as to how these are to be construed. But even the functors in a mathematical equation may be the terms for substitution depending upon purpose. The substitution of functors results in a taxonomy of elements united under specific mathematical relations, a taxonomy whose objects are called groups. What is required in all cases is that a consistent interpretation of fundamental operations be preserved even in metamathematical and metalogical substitutions.

As rough correlates to the two kinds of substitutions described in a mathematical (or formal) economy, we find that substitutions of goods and tangible symbols also take place in the exchange of things and services in a substantial economy. What preserves the possibility for such substitutions—whether mathematical, material, or symbolic—is precision in the definition of both the value and rules that define commensurability or equivalence.

33. Weber describes an ideal type as follows: "To understand means . . . interpretive understanding of (a.) concrete cases, as for example in historical analysis; (b.) average cases, that is approximate estimates, as in sociological mass analysis; or (c.) a pure type of a frequently occurring scientifically formulated construct. Such ideally typical constructs are, for example, the concepts and axioms of pure economic experience. They show how a given type of human behavior would occur, on a strictly rational basis, unaffected by errors or emotional factors, and if, further, it

were directed only to a single goal. Actual behavior takes this course only rarely and then only approximately so as to correspond to the ideal type. To be sure, every interpretation strives to achieve utmost verifiability. But even the most verifiable interpretation cannot claim the character of being causally valid. It will remain only a particularly plausible hypothesis." See Max Weber, *Basic Concepts in Sociology,* trans. H. P. Secher (Secaucus, NJ: Citadel Press, 1972 [1925]), 36–37.

34. Luther says this explicitly in his *Lectures on Romans,* when he distinguishes the three kinds of the elect: "Now there are three ranks in the company of the elect. To the *first* one belong those who are content with the will of God, whatever it is; they do not grumble against it, but trust, rather that they are elected, and they do not want to be damned. To the *second* one, which is higher, belong those who have resigned themselves to God's will. They feel content in it or at least they yearn for such a feeling, in case God should not want to save them but place them among the rejected. To the *third* and the best and the highest rank belong those who in actual reality resign themselves to hell if God wills this, as it happens perhaps with many in the hour of death. These are perfectly cleansed of their own will and of 'the prudence of the flesh.' They know what it means that 'love is strong as death and jealousy hard as hell' (Song of Solomon, 8:6)." See Martin Luther, *Luther: Lectures on Romans,* trans. and ed. Wilhelm Pauck (Philadelphia: Westminster Press, 1961 [1515–1516]), 8:255. There are similar passages in the *Theologia Germanica* (chaps. 11, 23, and 27), which Luther discovered and published in 1516, and similar themes are expressed throughout the Weimar edition of Luther's works: 2:126; 10:345; 11:468f.; 18:694; 44:180; etc. See *Theologia Germanica,* trans. Susanna Winkworth (London: Stuart & Watkins, 1966 [1874]), 50–52; 68–69; 77–78; and Martin Luther, *D. Martin Luthers Werke,* 127 vols. (Weimar: Heidelberger Akademie der Wissenschaften, 1883–2009 [1501–1546]).

35. Muslim suicide murderers and Christian crusaders would not fit into this category because their forfeiture of life comes at a price: that of taking other lives with them. The notion of *jihad as leading to salvation* and the notion of plenary indulgence possess a symmetry in what they warrant and how they warrant it. What they warrant is the self-sacrificial killing of others. How they warrant it is as an exchange, a payment, for the self sacrificed in the killing of others. Understood in this way, religiously sanctioned self-sacrifice as the instrument of killing others is an infernal inversion of Jesus' sacrificial death, which was to save others.

36. In some traditions—the Roman Catholic, for example—this variety of sacrifice is discouraged precisely on opposite grounds, namely, that the subject undervalues the self in light of the gift that has been given it. Life itself exceeds the estimate that the subject simplistically associates with it, and consequently the sacrifice of the self is not sufficient to pay for the gift of life. In those traditions that resist the logic of total sacrifice, the durative nature of life is emphasized on an exact parallel with the durative nature of work within capitalist economics. Because the potential fruits of a life are the measure of its total value, the sacrifice of

the instrumentality that produces those fruits—the self—does not measure up as equivalent. Thus it may be a greater sacrifice to live and continue to produce the fruits of faith than to offer oneself up to a cavalier martyrdom. Consequently, many are the circumstances under which the religions that emphasize a life lived as sacrifice may view the total self-sacrifice of self-annihilation as frivolous self-sacrifice. The monastic rules of the desert fathers that prohibit excessive acts of supererogation may be interpreted, in part, according to this calculation, even though the call to monasticism—particularly after the great persecutions were over—was simultaneously considered an act of martyrdom (in both of the original senses of the word as "witness" and "sacrifice").

37. As communal sacrifice, the extreme limit would be half of a society being sacrificed for the other half. At this limit, it is difficult to see how such a sacrificial practice could be secured, unless all the power lay in the hands of the faction of the sacrificers and none in the hands of the sacrificial victims. Some of the issues suggested by a society organized along these lines are given fictional treatment in the Jesuit mission to the planet *Rakhat* and its discovery of the *Jana'ata* and the *Runa* in the science fiction of novels of Mary Doria Russell, *The Sparrow* (New York: Ballantine Books, 1996) and *Children of God* (New York: Fawcett, 1998).

38. Girard views this variety of sacrifice as a "decadent" later stage in the evolution of sacrifice that is contrary to the communal spirit, but that assumes that all sacrifice is, in fact, communal. Abraham's substitution of the ram would seem to be an example that complicates Girard's interpretation, unless one views it as a "decadent" later development. In any event, examples of one-for-one sacrifice do occur. See René Girard, *Violence and the Sacred,* trans. Patrick Gregory (Baltimore: Johns Hopkins Press, 1989), 101–2.

39. Girard stipulates that all sacrificial victims must bear a certain resemblance to what they are substituted for but not so close a resemblance as to be confused (ibid., 10–12).

40. One could make the case that in the absence of imperial persecutions, after the time of Constantine, the monastic life becomes the durative approximation of the martyr's death.

41. Aristotle, *Nicomachean Ethics,* trans. H. Rackham, Loeb Classical Library 19 (Cambridge, MA: Harvard University Press, 1982), 5.5.14, 287.

42. Ibid., 5.5.8–15, 280–83.

43. Ibid., 5.5.14, 283.

44. Jean-Joseph Goux, *Symbolic Economies: After Marx and Freud* (Ithaca, NY: Cornell University Press, 1990), 3.

45. Ibid.

46. See Robert J. Daly, S.J., *The Origins of the Christian Doctrine of Sacrifice* (Philadelphia: Fortress Press, 1979), 11–12, and Stephen Finlan, *The Background and Content of Paul's Cultic Atonement Metaphors* (Atlanta: Society of Biblical Literature, 2004), 29–44.

47. Pareto distinguishes between logical (rational) and nonlogical (irrational) human behavior. The tendency toward rationality means that humans tend to rationalize or legitimate the irrational. The theories that legitimate an irrational sentiment have the patina of rationality but are fundamentally irrational. In irrational theories, there is a constant and a variable element. The variable element is called the "derivation" and constitutes the various ways different cultures or religions attempt to legitimate the irrational component, the common "residue." Although the actions taken in conjunction with the residue may be as reasonable as those taken on the basis of scientific premises, Pareto counts the former as fundamentally irrational. A residue, as common, consists of (or is driven by) human sentiments or states of mind. Thus a common practice — sacrifice, for example — across cultures, religions, or even within the same religions across different historical periods, may be driven by common sentiments or mental states, but its rationalizations across cultures, religions, or times will be quite different. See Vilfredo Pareto, *A Treatise on General Sociology*, 4 vols., trans. Andrew Bongiorno and Arthur Livingston (New York: Dover Publications), 1:2:145–248; 1:3:249–367; 2:842–88.

48. Adin Steinsaltz, *The Essential Talmud* (New York: Basic Books, 1976), 175.

49. Ibid. In these commentaries, the ubiquitous challenge for the historian of the antiquity of Jewish sacrifice is to separate later rationalization from earlier intention, but since my concern is to posit its logic at the time of Jesus, my task is easier.

50. Ibid., 176.

51. Nachmanides, *Commentary on the Torah: Leviticus* (New York: Shilo Publishing House, 1974), 1:9, 21. Ramban's intention, here, is made clear in his sermon titled *Torah Hashem Temimah*: "Now the opinion of Rabbi Abraham ibn Ezra on the matter of the offerings is that they are an atonement for the soul" (*Kithvei Haramban* 1, 164). This is Ramban's interpretation of what he found in Ezra, but it is not found verbatim. Ibid., 1:9, 21n120.

52. Nachmanides has it that, prior to the flood, men and women were vegetarians. Noah's ransoming animals during the flood meant that humans could use them for human purposes, including substituting their blood for human blood in sacrificial atonement. See Nachmanides, *Commentary on Torah: Leviticus*, 17:11, 239.

53. Here, Ramban introduces a theoretical gloss presumably borrowed from Aristotle (or, more probably, the Neoplatonists). He argues that Aristotle thought that the active intellect "emitted a very fine and bright flash and glitter of light, from which came forth the spark which is the soul of the animal" (ibid.). Aristotle, to my knowledge, does not associate the soul with the blood. Aristotle's thought functions here not as the driving insight of Nachmanides' interpretation but as a thin metaphysical veneer that is laid over the text to support the biblically based arguments. The Aristotelian attribution is clearly directed to the theologians and philosophers of the time. It is collateral support for the biblical argument. However, Nachmanides' recourse to the Aristotelian tripartite division of the soul (vegetable, animal, and rational) may also signal that he imagines there are levels to the process

of substantial assimilation. Nachmanides is also implying that, while ingestion of animal flesh only sustains the biological life of humans, the ingestion of the soul-substance (blood) is soul altering. See ibid., 240.

54. Ibid.

55. Ibid.

56. Ibid.: "Now it is also known that the food one eats is taken into the body of the eater *and they become one flesh.* If one were to eat the *life of all flesh,* it would then attach itself to one's own blood and they would become united in one's heart, and the result would be a thickening and coarseness of the human soul so that it would closely approach the nature of the animal soul which resided in that which he ate, . . . which thereby become changed, and thus man's soul will become combined with the blood of the animal!"

57. Correcting Chavel who has the reverse interpolation, "life and blood," not grasping that life is the formality of blood, life and blood together constituting one substance. To have it Chavel's way would be to make Nachmanides a materialist. This is more consistent with Yehuda Halevi in his *Al Khazari,* which Chavel cites as saying that the animal soul originates out of the sphere of the active intellect just below that of the moon. In other words, the sphere of the air — air supplying the substance "which gives nutrition and makes blood" — provides the celestial formality that animates living beings. This is supported in the adjacent text, cited above in note 53.

58. And further: "*No soul of you shall eat blood,* meaning: 'Because the blood is identical with the soul, and it is not proper that one soul devour another, therefore I had compassion upon man's life and gave it [the animal's soul] to him upon the altar, so that the soul of the animal should effect atonement for his soul'" (Nachmanides, *Commentary on Torah: Leviticus,* 17:11, 242).

59. Nachmanides may be expressing his familiarity with ancient chemistry here or one kind of mixture according to Aristotelian and Stoic natural philosophies. According to Aristotle, a mixture is either a *sunthesis* (an aggregate composite), a *mixis/krasis* (or resolvable *tertium quid*), a *sugchusis* (an irresolvable *tertium quid*), or an *eis to kratoun* (a combination in which one element predominates by power). Nachmanides' discussion makes it clear that he views the ingestion of animal blood as resulting in the latter. See Harry Wolfson, "Philosophical Implications of Arianism and Apollinarianism," in *Religious Philosophy: A Group of Essays* (New York: Athenaeum, 1965), 154–55.

60. Nachmanides, *Commentary on Torah: Leviticus,* 17:11, 242.

61. Polanyi's substantive notion of economy and Mauss' notion of economy as a system of total services are compatible with *economia* as a gathering concept in the patristic period. The patristic notion of economy (*oikonomia* or *dispositio, dipensatio*) can mean, alternately (or conjointly, in some cases): (1) any system of distribution and reception of goods, services, powers, or qualities (in the broadest sense); (2) God's dispensation of actions and graces for the salvation of human-

kind, that is, God's ordering of the cosmos, including his covenants; (3) the distribution of essential powers over the Trinitarian persons (*perichôrêsis*); and (4) the Incarnation (*enanthrôpêsis*), specifically. See Catherine LaCugna, *God for Us* (San Francisco: HarperSanFrancisco, 1991), 24–28.

In my argument, here, I am concerned especially with the *substantive* meaning of economics or economy and Mauss' understanding of economy as a total system of services. The primary focus is on Polanyi's and Mauss' meanings as they intersect with the patristic senses 1 and 2 but in a way that allusively includes senses 3 and 4, as well. Economy is a notion of order into which the economy of salvation, covenant, and sacrifice are all enfolded. Thus, I am claiming that there is a specific relation between the patristic notion of economy and the biblical understanding of covenant (*diathêkê*). The patristic notion possesses a wider semantic horizon that allows it to function as an expansion of what occurs in the scriptural understanding of the economy of the covenant. In other words, that broad notion—which possesses wider cosmic implications (and which includes the patristic cosmic and Trinitarian economies)—is grounded in a narrower set of historical data (the biblical covenantal economy). Also see G. L. Prestige, *God in Patristic Thought* (London: S. P. C. K., 1952), 57–67, 98–102, and J. H. Newman, *The Arians of the Fourth Century* (Westminster, MD: Christian Classics, 1968), 64–99.

62. See Polanyi, "The Economy as an Instituted Process."

63. Curiously, this follows a sort of Aristotelian logic. If we allow a distinction between the physical body and the soul that is mirrored by the distinction between the flesh and the blood of the sacrificial victim, then the consumption of the flesh means the building up of the body—as long as the food is healthy—while the consumption of the blood means the tearing down of the soul, if that being is at a lower ontological level than the consumer of the blood. One might surmise that the powerful prohibitions against cannibalism are directed to deflect the logical inference to which this understanding of physical/spiritual assimilation leads. That cannibalism is practiced in some cultures based upon something like this logic is well known.

64. Nachmanides admits that Israelitic sacrifice to be effective had to be repeated: "The reason for the Daily public Offering is that it is impossible for the public [as a whole] to continually avoid sin. Now these are the words which are worthy to be accepted, appealing to the heart as do words of Aggadah" (*Commentary on Torah: Leviticus*, 1:9, 21). Nachmanides rests his case, here, on the Aggadic Midrashim.

65. In Baudrillardian axiology, there is use value, exchange value, sign value, and symbolic value, which are related dyadically one to the other by a functor that may be an equivalence sign, a proportionality sign, etc. The relationship between what has pairwise comparison is drawn diremptively by Baudrillard according to his interpretation of the Sassurian distinction between the signifier and signified. To my mind, the weakness of the Baudrillardian economy of signs is that it neglects

the triadic notion of signification proposed by Peirce. For Peirce, signification—
in the broad sense—may also have a causal component, as is the case with a class
of signs he terms "indexic" or "indices." Sacraments are presumably presentational
signs that belong to this category. If Peircean triadic signification were admitted
into the Baudrillardian economy of signs, this would mean that the signified and
signifier were—at least in some instances—constitutive of one another. In axio-
logical terms, this would entail some order of foundedness or ingression between
use-value, exchange-value, sign-value, and symbolic-value. See Jean Baudrillard,
For a Critique of the Political Economy of the Sign, trans. Charles Levin (St. Louis:
Telos Press, 1981), 123–63.

   66. I use the terms "ingress," "ingression," "ingressing" in a sense close to
that of Whitehead. When Whitehead uses the verb "ingress" or the noun "ingression" he means to designate an actuality's definiteness in coming into existence or
in being changed because it is "informed" or "determined" by an eternal object.
For Whitehead, there is no separate realm of self-subsistent forms, so that an eternal object may ingress only because it is a part of a previous noneternal actuality.
For Whitehead, God (as one) is an actuality that is both nontemporal and temporal and thus not eternal. But I use the term 'ingress' to designate (a) determinations
from eternal objects (God in his oneness) to nontemporal actualities and to temporal actualities, as well as (b) determinations from nontemporal actualities to temporal actualities or simply (c) between temporal actualities. Ivor Leclerc, *Whitehead's
Metaphysics: An Introductory Exposition* (Bloomington: Indiana University Press,
1975), 95–99, 196–202.

   67. In the scholastic understanding, virtue or habits are a sort of second nature. If we understand human nature as an entelechy rather than as a fixed collection of properties, then the development of habits or virtues is the actualization of
human possibility, a process that is pitched toward the fulfillment of human po-
tentiality. The consumption of the sacramental flesh and blood is tantamount to
the consumption of a substance that energizes this fulfillment. The flesh builds
the body; the blood transmutes the spirit.

   68. This should not be understood as undermining the traditional model of
transubstantiation in Roman Catholic eucharistic theology—far from it. Here we
must keep the order of signification separate from the metaphysical order. According to the semiotic order, the accidents of the bread and wine signify the body and
blood—not inasmuch as the wine and the bread individuate the body and blood
because, metaphysically, the substance is wholly present under either species—but
inasmuch as bread signifies flesh or body and wine signifies blood, a separation that
does not occur in a living (metaphysical) substance but whose distinction at the
level of signification preserves the sense of the operations of flesh and blood as
they are understood in the sacrificial practice of the Old Testament. Thus, transubstantiated bread signifies that aspect of Christ's indivisible substance that nour-
ishes, and the transubstantiated wine blood signifies that aspect of Christ's indi-

visible substance that spiritually transforms. If the Eucharist only consisted of bread—standing for body—and wine was absent or applied apotropaically, then wine could not signify transformation of the recipient's spirit. Here, the qualities of the bread and wine are the accidents to which the substance of Christ is joined, but the bread and wine also *notionally* signify a distinction between body and blood that is not *real* in the organic union that is the indivisible, unitary substance. The analogue here is the way we form separate predicates in order to understand God's perfections. The only difference is that in the case of Christ the body and blood are distinct organic features that cannot be really separated in that immortal being. We name them with the bread and wine, understanding that the bread is not simply the flesh/body and the wine is not simply the blood of Christ. Though either bread or wine presents Christ wholly, bread and wine also serve to distinguish the symbolic significance of sacrificial flesh and blood. We can put this realization as follows: The substance of Christ is wholly contained under the accidents of the bread and is wholly contained under the accidents of wine, so that either bread or wine *present* the whole substance of Christ while bread and wine also *signify* the blood and body of Christ in their sacrificial import. This is represented in the diagram in the main text.

THREE

Aspects of the Transformation of Sacrifice in Judaism

MICHAEL FISHBANE

Judaism is a great and complex historical phenomenon, with many diverse perspectives on any given subject—as even the merest peek at the vastness of its forms and traditions will confirm. The textual record and foundation document upon which it all stands, the Hebrew Bible, is equally a great and complex phenomenon, and modern scholarship has rightly begun to appreciate its own proper vastness and variety—eschewing any generalization of its teachings through such character-izations as "the Bible says." Surely both the canonical compendia of classical Judaism and the sacred canon of scripture contain a panoply of religious and cultural information, and reveal transformations of topics at every turn.[1]

As we begin to consider some aspects of the transformation of sacrifice in Judaism, it would be well to bear the forgoing considera-tions in mind, and even to narrow the angle of vision so that some-thing manageable and instructive can be brought into view. Let me therefore begin by recalling three topics within the Hebrew Bible that will set us thematically on our way.

The first topic I wish to stress is *the omnipresence and importance of sacrifice and ritual gifts in ancient Israel.* Indeed, sacrifice and ritual gifts occur at every turn and every cultural stage. The scriptural record seeks to emphasize the primordial nature of these actions, beginning with the gifts of Cain and Abel from their economic produce (be it the growth of the earth or the animals of the flock and herd), and the need and

114

desire to win the favor of the divine source of life and fertility (Gn 4:3–4). And it is a notable event that Noah offers a sacrifice soon after the flood, and this entreats the divine to its sweet savor and leads to a covenant and pact (8:20–21). Abraham, also, is said to have offered a sacrifice upon his entry into the land of Canaan, as he invoked the divine as a patron (12:7–8) — and his action is repeated by the other patriarchs in the course of generations, as they mark their connection to the land and the god of the fathers. Thus the sacrificial act marks a basic connection between the person and the divine for the sake of religious life and basic survival. And the fundamental aspects of sacrifice as marks of celebration and connection (involving the grains of the earth and the flesh of the flock) mark the rituals prescribed to commemorate the exodus from Egypt, from the first textual formulations in Exodus 12 on down through the various other pentateuchal rules and formulations. Indeed, these latter sources provide enormous detail from diverse times and places concerning the offerings that are appropriate (as well as how and where and by whom they are appropriate) in order to celebrate the cycles of life (for persons, animals, and the earth) and mark the key seasons and events (in nature and history). Such acts have a cyclical character, being done on a recurrent basis.[2]

But there were also offerings designed to heal ruptures between persons and the divine, with different modes prescribed at different times for different degrees of sin and inadvertence. In this way sacrifices and offerings not only mark and maintain the cycles of life, but also restore and repair breaks in the bond between heaven and earth (Lv 1–7). Cultic practices and institutions are thus of primary importance, and they dominate all the strata of scripture, from first to last. Indeed, the appropriateness of such practices is never doubted, though one always had to be vigilant concerning their propriety under certain circumstances and the purity of their performance. This attempt at vigilance led to rivalries among various ritual groups and to critiques by purists and prophets. For some it was inconceivable that God would destroy his sullied shrine, while for others this act was just the sign of utter divine disfavor (1 Kgs 21; Is 1; Jer 7 and 26). When the great shrines of the north and south were destroyed, this destruction meant not only severe rebuke and punishment, but a crisis of ritual life. A basic religious concern, inevitably, became how sin could be atoned for in the absence of the Temple and its sacrifices. Certain solutions were notable, if deemed temporary. For example, Psalm 50 makes it clear that, in the absence of the old cultic rites of atonement, the most proper substitute was spiritual abnegation and abasement, along with confession and inner purgation (although it is also clear from the conclusion appended to this source that it was believed that once the shrine were rebuilt, the primary modality of sacrifices would again supervene). No wonder, then, that the first act the returnees performed upon return from the exile in Babylon was to build a shrine and prepare for the rebuilding of the Temple (Ezr 3). No wonder, too, that visionaries of various types promised a new Temple, and that some even provided a precise architectural blueprint (Ez 40–48). A suspension of the sacrifices was thus variously deemed necessary. But it was hardly conceived to be final, even by the severest critics, who doubted the appropriateness and conceivability of building a temple to the God of heaven and earth, or who rebuked the people for permitting certain Levitical groups to perform sacrifices in the old shrine, or who actually envisioned a more universal ritual service that even included foreigners and nonpriests (Ez 47; Is 56 and 66).

Let me turn to a second topic of importance for the religious history of ancient Israel, and for the theme we are to consider below. That topic is *the transformation and expansion of the use and meaning of Torah*. In priestly sources, the word "torah" means a concrete ritual instruction concerning proper procedure or practice. It is this sense that recurs, for example, in the summary lines that follow each of the rules in the priestly collection found in Leviticus 11–16—rules dealing with the proper distinction between pure and impure animals and other creatures, with postpartum purity, with the detection and variations of skin lesions and scabs, and with the fact and consequences of seminal emissions and gonorrhea, as well as of menstrual or other blood flows. By contrast, designations such as "the Torah," "this Torah," "the Torah of Moses," or even "the scroll of this Torah" found in the book of Deuteronomy refer to that source and the range of material found therein: historical narrative, rules for rites and institutions, as well as civil and cultic norms. It is surely this comprehensive sense that is meant at the beginning of the book, when we are told that "Moses began to explicate this Torah" (Dt 1:5), and at the conclusion, in the proclamation incorporated into the final blessing, which says that "Moses commanded us Torah, an inheritance for the congregation of Jacob" (33:4). And it is surely just such a comprehensive notion of Torah, perhaps comprising something of what became the Pentatuech, that Ezra investigates and recites upon the return from Babylon. The late record of these events refers to the work as "the Torah of YHWH" (Ezr 7:10) and "the scroll of the Torah of Moses" (Neh 8:1). The "Torah of YHWH" is the designation of choice by the psalmists who variously celebrate the delights and transformative perfection of Torah and its study in Psalms 1, 19, and 119. In these late, latter three texts especially, the reader will easily perceive the sense of Torah as a sacred divine wisdom. It is not just the comprehensive quantity of instructions of this divine source, transmitted and taught by Moses, but its very special quality as a revealed teaching of God.[3]

This last point leads us directly to the third topic, *the diverse and increasingly expansive character of Torah instruction and study in ancient Israel.* In some very notable ways, this topic runs parallel with the previous one. And that is how I shall epitomize it here. Let us deal with the cultic teachings first. Notably, just prior to the anthology of ritual rules in Leviticus 11–16 mentioned earlier, there occurs an instruction to Aaron and his sons to beware of being intoxicated when entering the shrine, that they not die; and they are also told "to distinguish between the sacred and the profane, between the impure and the pure, and to instruct the people of Israel concerning all the statutes which YHWH spoke to them through Moses" (Lv 10:8–11). One must therefore note that the priests had the special authority and knowledge to administer the ritual rules called "torah" in the subsequent list. Significantly, we are even privy to just such inquiries made with respect to dubious or questionable cases of ritual "torah" in the late, postexilic prophet Haggai (2:10–14). A celebration and exaltation of this function is put in the mouth of an even later contemporary, Malachi, when he delivers a divine oracle concerning the privileges of the priestly Levites to prevent people from falling into iniquity: "since the lips of the priest preserve wisdom, and [the people] seek torah from his mouth—for he is a messenger of YHWH" (Mal 2:4–8). This role as instructor may also be observed among Ezra and his Levitical assistants when the people returned from the exile. On the one hand, Ezra himself, a priest and scribe, is referred to as one who "prepared his heart to inquire of the Torah of YHWH, and to observe and teach statute and law in Israel" (Ezr 7:10); and we may presume that this reference indicates a somewhat comprehensive role for investigation and application of the old instructions. Such a presumption is confirmed from the account of his public recitation of the Torah to the people and from the role of a class of Levitical teachers who explicate and clarify the teachings read to the people (in this instance, the rules pertaining to the festival of booths at the harvest season; Neh 8:5–18). There is no doubt, however, that this class of interpreters (whose precise function is called *mebinim 'et ha-'am la-torah*, "instructing the people in the Torah") was involved in a more comprehensive role of providing sense and meaning to what was read (see v. 8).[4]

In the book of Deuteronomy, Moses is still cast as the principal explicator of the teachings (1:5), and it is partially in this sense that some of the differences between Deuteronomy and other priestly traditions may be accounted for. In any case, with the expansion of the notion of Torah fostered by this corpus, and with the presentation by Ezra of the Torah as a received instruction to the people from God, there developed an ideal of study as a task and goal of the religious life. Such an ideal is celebrated in Psalms 1 and 19, as I have noted; and its exaltation in Psalm 119 goes so far as to suggest that study and interpretation had begun to emerge as a mode of receiving the ongoing will of God. And not only this. In at least some circles, the ideal of study became a means of attaching oneself to God and His living presence; indeed, one not only seeks the Lord and hopes to cleave to Him, but now seeks the Torah and hopes to cleave to it. All this betokens a transformation of the most remarkable sort, not only of the role of the Torah, but also of study as a public religious ideal not limited to guilds of specialists.[5]

Ancient Judaism is built upon these three foundations: (1) the ideal of the Temple as the sacred site par excellence, the site for the harmony of the cycles of life and fertility, and the site for the celebration of divine beneficence and the reparation of sins and impurities; (2) the ideal of the Torah of Moses as the sacred text par excellence, the site of the teachings of God and His messengers, and the site of national meaning and memory and hope; and (3) the ideal of Torah study as the sacred task par excellence, the situation by which God's instructions can be learned and transmitted, and the means by which that primary revelation could be expanded through interpretation and instruction. This three-fold knot of temple, text, and teacher entered the complex fabric of life and was taken up by all the groups vying for validity. These were the ideals of the community at Qumran, as reflected in all their literature—one thinks especially of *The Rule Scroll, The Damascus Document,* and *The Temple Scroll.* These were equally the ideals of the Pharisees and their heirs among the sages of rabbinic Judaism—one thinks especially of such works as the *Mishnah,* the *Tosefta,* and the various ancient collections of legal and theological *Midrash.* Put differently, it was not the nature of the ideals that separated these and other related groups, but rather the substance of the matter. What was the true nature of the Second Temple, and who was permitted to serve as its legitimate priests? What was the nature of the sacred Torah, and who were its legitimate guardians? And what was the true meaning of the divine revelation, and who were its proper interpreters (not least, this question included the meaning of the rules of purity and the role of the priests and the dimensions of the Temple—though it comprised, of course, much more). The three ideals were thus not only principles for implementation but the grounds of contestation over authority and authenticity. All incumbents to the mantle of Judaism had to take a stand on these points.

Here we arrive at the task at hand, for the heirs of Judaism had inevitably to deal with the destruction of the Temple and its principal role as the means of purity and reparation. Thus the end of sacrifices had to be dealt with, and to fill the breach rabbinic Judaism had to reach into its innermost and most authentic resources. Central to those resources were its ethical ideals and especially the greatly transformed position of Torah and Torah study (and interpretation) in postexilic culture. It is to some aspects of this remarkable reconstitution of ancient ideals that we now turn.

Teachings of the Amoraim

The classical sources of Judaism provide a striking conspectus of examples whereby the transformation of sacrifice can be appreciated. Perhaps the most famous is the remark made by R. Yohanan ben Zakkai to a distraught colleague right after the destruction of the Temple. With bold economy, he dismissed the despair of this person (and those like him) who lamented that "the place where the sins of Israel are atoned for is destroyed" when he said: "We have an atonement equivalent to it, and that is acts of loving-kindness." As scripture says: "For I [God] desire loving-kindness, not sacrifice" (Hos 6:6).[6] That is, the sage elevated acts of ethical devotion and care into the primary position, utterly transforming the intent of the prophetic passage, even as he turned the rebuke into a consolation.

Surely this transformation of offerings into ethical deeds is a remarkable teaching, but it is not the only instance of exegetical transformation in the sources. As against the social character of R. Yohanan's statement from the first century, I shall present in what follows a selection of teachings from the initial generations of the sages known as Amoraim from the third and fourth centuries CE, and shall focus on other spiritual and cultural modalities. Three principle types will focus the discussion.

Spiritual and Physical Mimesis

We noted earlier that sacrificial service provided an offering from one's own substance, principally from the animals of the flock and herd, and then also from the crops and grains of the field. These donations were in effect substitutes for the self, provided from the self's own resources. Accordingly, we find attempts to provide substitutes for these substitutes, now from the self itself, a somewhat paradoxical return to the core of sacrifice. Most notable among these is the call for the individual to donate one's will to God, to submit one's self to God through humility and lowliness of spirit. Note the following striking passage taught by R. Joshua b. Levi, a third-century Amora from the land of Israel. According to a tradition preserved in the *Babylonian Talmud*, *Sota* 5b, he taught:

Come and see how great are the lowly of spirit in the esteem of the Holy One, blessed be He, since when the Temple stood a person brought the burnt-offering and received the reward of a burnt-offering, a meal-offering and received the reward of a meal-offering; but as for him whose mind is lowly (*she-da'ato shefela*), Scripture ascribes it to him as if (*ke-'ilu*) he had offered every one of the sacrifices, as it is said: "The sacrifices of God are a broken spirit" (Psalm 51:19). More than that, his prayer is not despised, as [the verse] continues, "A broken and contrite heart, O God, Thou wilt not despise."[7]

For all the homiletical rhetoric, which builds its teaching about the comprehensive rewards of humility on the plural "sacrifices," there is no doubt that the teacher is promoting a spiritual ideal of great power. He is quite aware of the constructed nature of this substitute for a substitute, as we can see by the formulary "as if." But we would be wrong, I think, to see in this phrase a mere sense of the hypothetical quality of the exchange. Rather, the power of the teaching lies precisely in the substitutive nature of the exchange, that one thing is like the other. In fact, the substitute serves to activate the original benefit—and more! The rabbinic ideal is contrition presented in rabbinic terms, alongside the original biblical formulation. The self is exhorted to offer one's pride to God as the ritual mimesis for the offering of burnt- and meal-offerings. The spiritual act is thus a totalizing ideal that will effect the benefits believed to result from these gifts, these being the gifts of donation in thanks and hope, and the gifts of donation to effectuate atonement and reparation. Hereby, during a time of the absence of the Temple, the issue is not merely a ritual offering with the proper attitude and intention, as the rabbis prescribe in various sources, but the effacement of human will and pride, a transformation of self through a transformation of attitude and intent. This is the gift that God will accept, and it transcends in its comprehensive power the animals and grains offered in days of yore.

There are other similar examples whereby the phenomenon of sacrifice is transformed through rabbinic exhortations concerning the moral-religious self, and these also build upon the language of scripture and stress the element of mimesis. Particularly noteworthy is the following teaching on Psalm 51:19, taught here by a sage named

R. Yose b. Parta (an Amora from the land of Israel) and recorded in
Midrash Leviticus Rabba 7.2.[8] He said,

> From where can we learn that with respect to one who does repen-
> tance Scripture accounts it for him as if (*ke-'ilu*) he went up to Jeru-
> salem and built the Temple and the altar, and sacrificed upon it all the
> sacrifices in the Torah?—from this passage. "The sacrifices of God
> are a broken spirit" (Ps. 51:19).

In this teaching, we have further confirmation of rabbinical proc-
lamations of the power of contrition to effect divine forgiveness in the
absence of the Temple. In a manner similar to the teaching of R. Joshua
noted above, R. Yose also taught about the effectiveness of humility,
though his emphasis is on an act of repentance (since he bases himself
on the historical context of David's words in this psalm, which are spoken to God after his sinful affair with Bathsheba, mentioned in the
superscription, v. 2). Also like R. Joshua, R. Yose finds the textual basis
for his homily in the plural noun "sacrifices" and the equivalence articulated by the speaker that "the sacrifices of God *are* a broken spirit,"
meaning that a broken spirit *is like* the sacrifices of God. And finally,
here too the "as if " formulary has a strong force and serves to impress
upon the audience the effectiveness of this act of exchange. Thus
the only difference of note between this passage and the earlier one is
the particular list of effects it invokes; for a contrite spirit is not only
deemed to be like the sacrifices, but it is also functionally equivalent to
a pilgrimage to Jerusalem and building the Temple and its altar. The
inner act of repentance is thus portrayed to have the religious efficacy
of these external actions.

But perhaps a further dimension was involved. From the perspective of religious psychology, it would seem that for R. Yose the act of
contrition was something like an interiorization of religious action;
namely, that the process of repentance was deemed to be something
like a pilgrimage to a sacred site, and the act of contrition to be like the
building of an inner temple, in which the heart is the altar upon which
one offers the self. Hence the rebuilding of the Temple and its benefits need not remain a messianic longing directed toward the future,
but can become very much a spiritual possibility *hic et nunc,* in the here

and now of one's religious life. Surely one cannot doubt that R. Yose remained hopeful for the fulfillment of the physical ideal and prayed for the restoration of the ancient Temple. But he does not emphasize the element of future hope and expectation; rather, he shows how the language of scripture preserves a trace of a present possibility, whereby a sinful person could nevertheless function as a priest through acts of inner purgation and humility. Through a striking series of substitutions, a new self is thus envisioned and exhorted. The Temple may not be standing, but we are told that God will not even now reject the truest of offerings—namely, the sacrifice of one's inner spirit. To have perceived this possibility and to have taught it as a truth of scripture is a measure of the great wisdom and spiritual leadership of the sages.

An even more striking act of physical mimesis is attested in a teaching attributed to Rav Sheshet (a Babylonian Amora from the late third century), as preserved in the *Babylonian Talmud, Berachot* 17a. It is reported that when this sage kept a fast, in days after the destruction of the Temple, and without its official powers of atonement, he used to add the following prayer:

> Sovereign of the universe, it is revealed and known to You that in the Time when the Temple was standing, if a person sinned he would bring a sacrifice, and although all that was offered of it was its fat and blood, he received atonement therewith (*u-mitkapper lo*). And now, I have kept a fast and my fat and blood have diminished. May it be Thy will to account my fat and blood which have been diminished as if (*ke-'ilu*) I had offered them to You upon the altar, and do Thou favor me.

For all the formulaic language involved, the religious pathos of Rav Sheshet is deeply felt in this prayer. He juxtaposes a past time "when the Temple was standing" and sacrifices were efficacious, with a present time, "now," when all he has is his body to give. He appeals to God to accept his personal gift as like the official sacrifices of yore, and he relies upon the words of his prayer (as well as the fact of fasting) to demonstrate the purity of will and intention. Apparently, the language of divine reckoning and accounting had become traditional in diverse circles, as had the language of "as if," though it is notable that here it is not the scriptural record that is appealed to, but God's will, and the strong assurance of equivalence sensed in the exemplars of this formulary considered above is somewhat weakened. Here the worshiper is acutely aware of dependence upon the divine will, which may or may not favor him, and he cannot lean upon a scriptural passage for support. Nevertheless, let us not too quickly dismiss the power of this passage. Surely, the sage had confidence that a fast rightly wrought would be deemed favorable, and therefore the very fact of a perceived correspondence between the old sacrifices and present mortification of the flesh should be stressed. Had fasting not been perceived as a potentially efficacious mimetic act, the prayer itself would not have been uttered. Certainly, the redactors of the Talmud have preserved this prayer as an exemplar for the community of worshipers, who, like Rav Sheshet, were bereft of the Temple. And once his prayer entered the body of tradition, and was studied as part of the curriculum, its efficacy was enhanced. Rav Sheshet's prayer, in fact, served as a model for various prayers and liturgical poems in the Middle Ages, whereby the faithful appeal to God's mercy through the diminished fat and blood of their fast.

Once again, and most remarkably, the human body is restored to the center of religious activity as the self seeks divine atonement, despite the fact that the fast is a substitute for a substitute, and the words of prayer are a substitute for the language of scripture. The violence done to the self through an act of self-mortification is proclaimed in prayer, this now being the account of the gift. If other sages trusted in scripture that God would not reject the sacrifice of one's will, Rav Sheshet (and those who took up his mimesis) prayed that the sovereign of the universe would turn His will towards the self-sacrifice of the penitent, and grant him favor. The pathos of his prayer is riven with anxiety; there is no hope here in a hermeneutical revision of scripture, only in the physical fact of suffering as the trace of an older offering of flesh and blood.

The Mimesis of Study and Recitation

We earlier considered the great change that took place in ancient Israel with the importance of study and interpretation; and in the previous section we saw something of the power of exegesis to proclaim new religious ideals. Let us now see how the ideal of the study of scripture could itself be proclaimed as a substitute for sacrifices and their efficacious transformation. As remarkable as it is, such a change is something that arises out of the deepest resources of Judaism as it tries to deal with the historical and religious crisis of the Temple's destruction. Here are two striking examples of the phenomenon.

At the beginning of this section on transformations, I referred to the R. Yohanan b. Zakkai's celebrated ethical reinterpretation of Hosea 6:6, "I desire loving-kindness, not sacrifice." The same textual source preserves a striking teaching bearing on the topic of study and sacrifices, and it uses the theme of "fat and blood" as the metonym for fleshly offerings upon the altar. We encountered this idiom above, and thus the following teaching provides a good segue between the previous discussion and the one at hand. After citing and discussing Hosea 6:6, we are then told:

> Torah study is dearer to God than burnt-offerings. For if one studies Torah he comes to know the will of God, as Scripture says, "Then you will understand the fear of the Lord, and find the will of God" (Prov. 2:4). Hence, when a sage sits and expounds to the congregation, Scripture accounts it to him as if (*ke-'ilu*) he had sacrificed fat and blood upon the altar.[9]

Once again the rhetorical components we have been noting recur: the issue of sacrifices, the issue of a scriptural accounting, and the issue of the "as if" formulary. Now however we are told that the study and exegesis of a passage dealing with burnt-offerings is functionally equivalent to the offerings themselves. This is remarkable. Equally striking is that the text makes no reference to the fact that the Temple is not standing and that the recitation of scripture and its exposition by the sages is a substitute for sacrifices. Rather, here the text stresses study as superior to sacrifices because by this means one can come to know God and His will—the new and vaunted ideal of the sages. Study is the sacred act par excellence, and knowledge the superior value. But could such activity serve the religious concerns of the worshiper as well?

A striking cluster of teachings on the subject of sacrifice and study is transmitted in the *Babylonian Talmud, Menachot* 110a. The teachings are from several notable third-century CE Amoras, who lived in the land of Israel and in Babylon. I shall cite this ensemble at length, both for the power of the teachings (singly and together) and their use of the customary formulary of equivalence, but also to show how such teachings are based upon scriptural exegesis. It is not, in other words, merely the recitation of the biblical passage and its exposition for the sake of knowledge, but also its study and exposition as a virtual substitute for these very offerings.

> Resh Lakish (R. Simeon b. Lakish) said: "What is the significance of the verse, 'This is the law (torah) for the burnt-offering, for the meal-offering, for the sin-offering, and for the guilt-offering' (Lev. 7:37)? It teaches that whoever is occupied (*'oseq*) with [study of] the torah is as if (*ke-'ilu*) he were offering a burnt-offering, a meal-offering, a sin-offering, and a guilt-offering." Rabba asked, "Why then does the verse say '*for* the burnt-offering, *for* the meal-offering'? It should rather have [simply] said '*a* burnt-offering, *a* meal-offering'! Rather," said Rabba, "[the formulation of scripture therefore] means that whoever is occupied with the [study of] the Torah needs neither burnt-offering, nor meal-offering, nor sin-offering, nor guilt-offering." Rabbi Isaac said, "What is the significance of the verses 'This is the torah of the sin-offering' (Lev. 6:18) and 'This is the torah of the guilt-offering' (Lev. 7:1)? They teach that whoever is occupied with the law of the sin-offering is as if (*ke-'ilu*) he were offering a sin-offering, and whoever is occupied with the law of the guilt-offering is as if (*ke-'ilu*) he were offering a guilt-offering."

This passage is a very valuable collection of interpretations, and teaches us much about how our subject was taught, studied, and justified in early Amoraic circles, both as a teaching based on different verses and readings of scripture, and as a matter passed down and discussed within the study-tradition itself. How so?

As is evident, this collection is a collation of three separate teachings. The first, by R. Simeon b. Lakish, a third-century Amora from

Tiberias, saw a special significance in the particular Hebrew formulation of the sacrifices used in Leviticus 7:37 (*zo't ha-torah la-*x, "this is the torah [law or instruction] *for* the x-offering"). In his understanding, it comes to teach that whoever studies the law or instruction of the particular offering accrues the same merit as if he actually offered such an offering. Presumably, this sage construed the Hebrew phrase to mean something like the following: "this is the torah (to be studied that is equivalent to) the x-offering." But Rabba, a fourth-century Babylonian Amora (and head of the academy of Pumpeditha), debated the Palestinian tradition that had been passed down to him. Clearly, it is R. Simeon's exposition that is under discussion in the academy, for Rabba begins by referring to R. Simeon's own reference to *a* specific offering. He then contends that if that reference had been the point, scripture would have been formulated differently and would not have used the preposition *la-* (viz., "*for the* [offering]"). Hence he offers a variant of the teaching he had received by making explicit use of the received language of scripture. He presumably understands the preposition involved to mean something like "in exchange for" or as "a substitute for." Hence his teaching goes beyond that of R. Simeon. It will be recalled that the latter taught his generation that study of the offerings was functionally equivalent to their performance; that is, it was "as if" one performed the sacrifice. By contrast, Rabba does not use the "as if" formulary, for his point is that study of the sacrifices is in fact a substitute for them (and not simply like them). In this way, he subtly but quite significantly changes the performative mimesis of study. The merit of Torah study for him is not equal to the type of sacrifice being studied, but has its own independent merit! Torah study for Rabba has thoroughly replaced the old sacrifices and is its own reward—presumably providing the reparations and atonements desired.

One may certainly suspect here that there had been an ideological shift in Babylon a century later. In Rabba's circles, the power of exegesis was meritorious on its own terms and became its own rite of redemption. Hence I would regard the third teaching, by R. Isaac (presumably R. Isaac Napaha, an important third-century Amora from Tiberias), as a variant of the one offered by R. Simeon from roughly the same time and place. The main difference between the two is the specific formulation of scripture that is used to make the point, for R. Isaac sees significance in the phrase *zo't torat ha-x* ("this is the torah/ law *of* the x-offering"). In his view, this formulation best serves to make the exegetical point that study of a specific torah teaching about an offering is functionally equivalent to its performance. Note that he, like his Tiberian contemporary, also uses the established "as if" formulary. Hence we should assume that the two teachings from the land of Israel were transmitted to Babylon as a unit, making the same point (though in different terms), but that when they were studied there, Rabba offered an exegetical and theological revision of R. Simeon's interpretation. This latter was subsequently incorporated into the formulation of the two traditions and passed on together with them to students and tradents in the Babylonian schools, and thereby (in its final redaction) to later Judaism (which studied these traditions and received them as authentic teachings of the ancient masters). Thus although Rabba's point is now bracketed within the interpretations of R. Simeon and R. Isaac, we should not miss its more powerful and different claim, the powerful claim of a culture for which study was the great ritual act par excellence. Indeed, in Rabba's mind, it would seem, the role of actual sacrifices was thoroughly transcended: one who studies them has no need of sacrificial offerings—for Torah-study is efficacious in its own right.

Memory and Memorialization

Up to this point, I have adduced examples from the classical tradition of Judaism that emphasize living rites that are the equivalent of or substitute for the sacrifices in the Temple. One final type of some note may now be added, and that is the way ritual references to Abraham's near-sacrifice of Isaac, as well as the various ritual substitutes for it, all serve in later generations as the means for entreating God for mercy. It is thus that the memory of a sacrificial act (variously actualized) is recalled to serve as an abiding mode of intercession and influence—one whose power has not abated over the millennia. The benefits of this old act are paradigmatic for the nation, and even in vastly displaced forms it reminds us of the efficacious power of sacrifices. There are many examples of this phenomenon is the midrashic sources (early and late), and there are numerous ways in which these matters entered religious poetry and ritual recitations over the past two thousand years. These must be bypassed in the present context, for all their significance, and only several traditions will be cited. I choose as exemplary three sets of teachings on three successive verses from Genesis 22 that were reported in *Midrash Genesis Rabba* (an important Amoraic collection) and through it had a decisive impact on later generations and the sense of the efficacy of Abraham's act and its replacements.

Let us begin with a comment on Genesis 22:12, "And he [the angel of YHWH] said: 'Do not set you hand against the lad,'" found in *Genesis Rabba* 56.7.[10] The biblical passage has the divine voice acknowledge Abraham's merit in proving his faithful love to God, insofar as "you [Abraham] did not withhold your son, [your special one, etc.]." An anonymous teacher provides the following remark at this point, presumably as the continuation of the words of the intervening angelic being: "And do not say that all wounds external to the body are not wounds, for I account [your act] as if (*ke-'ilu*) I said to you that you should offer Me yourself and you did not hold back." The comment focuses on the efficacy of Abraham's near-act, for though the sacrifice of Isaac was not completed, Abraham's readiness to offer himself was completely enacted. How so? Here we must assume that the teacher understood the phrase "your special one" (*yechidekha*) to refer not to Isaac (who had just been specified by the phrase "your son") but rather to Abraham's own soul (*yachid* being one of the old rabbinic terms for the soul). In fact, precisely this interpretation is explicitly spelled out in the traditional printed edition of this Midrash (and also in later collections, like the *Tanhuma*). Hence, although Isaac was unharmed, Abraham's total devotion of himself was deemed an interior sacrifice that was accounted as efficacious. This act of faithfulness serves as the primary reason the episode was said to evoke God's beneficent mercy in subsequent generations. But it is not the only reason, as we shall see.

In the next verse, scripture goes on to say that Abraham raised his eyes "and saw a ram [there]after (*'achar*) caught (*ne'echaz*) in the thicket (*ba-sebakh*) by its horns" (v. 13). At this point a cluster of teachings follow in *Genesis Rabba* 56.9.[11] Among them we find the following: "R. Judah bar Simon said, 'After (*'achar*) all the generations Israel will be caught (*ne'echazim*) in sins and trapped (*mistabbekhim*) in sorrows, and their end is to be redeemed [by the merit] of the horns of the ram, as Scripture says, "and the Lord God will blast a shofar" (Zech. 9:14).'" A similar teaching, following the same stylistic form, is given by R. Hinena b. Isaac, but now the issue is not redemption by the merit of the horn in the end of days, but redemption every Rosh Hashanah from the sins of "all the days of the [past] year"—by virtue of the trumpet blasts blown with the ram's horn. Presumably here too the adverb *'achar* is also the key factor in the interpretation, now meaning that "after" the accumulation of sins each year the people will get benefits from the horn. Hence a substitute for the substitute for the sacrifice itself serves later generations: through blasts on a ritual replica of the ancient ram's horn, events of the past are evoked, and the people are redeemed. The Temple may no longer stand, and the sacrifices no longer brought, but nevertheless redemptive forgiveness may be achieved for subsequent generations through a mimetic substitute. In this way, the powers of sacrifice remain efficacious, though in vastly transformed ways. Remarkably, warrant for this transformation was found in Scripture itself, through a deft and provocative exegesis of the verse.

In the continuity to v. 13, we are told that "Abraham went and took the ram, and offered it up as a burnt-offering in place of (*tachat*) his son." The following comment occurs in *Genesis Rabba* 56.9:

> Rabbi Yudan in the name of Rabbi Benayah [taught]: "[Abraham] said before Him: 'Master of the entire universe: Regard the blood of this ram as if (*ke-'ilu*) it was the blood of Isaac my son, and the fats of this ram as if it they were the fats of Isaac my son'; as we have learned [in the Mishnah]: '[If one said:] Let this be in place (*tachat*) of this, [or] the substitute for this, [or] in exchange for this—it is a [valid] substitute.'"[12]

In this passage, an Amoraic sage (probably R. Yudan II, or Yudan Nesia, of the early third century) reported an earlier tradition (from

R. Benayah, a last generation Tanna) that perceived in the biblical narrative not just a stylistic reference to a sacrificial substitution, but a reference to a specific legal act performed and articulated by the patriarch Abraham. As we now have it, this legal act is bolstered by an explicit reference to the valid formulary for such acts, as specified in the Mishnah (*M. Temurah* V.5). In this way, the teaching was able to suggest that the replacement was valid, and thus the cultural effects of this substitute were valid as well. However, one may also surmise that the citation formulary is not that of this Tanna himself but of his tradent, or the editor of the Midrash. This possibility may be proposed, first, because the citation formulary of the Mishnah is in Aramaic, and this would not have been the original formulation of a Tanna; second, because the statement attributed to Abraham does not follow the legal formulary of the Mishnah, which might have been expected if the patriarch's statement had been formulated with the Mishnah in mind; and finally, the words of Abraham follow the standard "as if" type, whereas the Mishnaic formulary is in an "x for y" style. This being so, what led to this supplement? It is most likely explained by the concern of the ongoing tradition that the act of Abraham be formulated as the model for all valid acts of substitution in the Temple. In this way, the substitution of the ram could serve as the prototypical form of animal sacrifice, and the altar on Mount Moriah, upon which the offering was made, could correspondingly be the prototype for the slaughter-site of the Temple itself.

Two later midrashic traditions echo just this point with exegetical precision and help us see the deep reverberations of our theme in Jewish thought. In the one case, we are told:

> The very day the patriarch Abraham put up his son Isaac on the top of the altar, the Holy One, blessed be He, instituted [the *Tamid* or Perpetual-offering] of the two lambs, the one for the morning and the one for twilight. For what purpose? So that at the time when Israel offers up the *Tamid* on the altar and recites the verse "*tzafonah* (to the north side) before the Lord" (Lev. 1:11; this refers to the biblical passage prescribing the place of this offering), the Holy One, blessed be He, might recall the "Binding of Isaac" son of Abraham.

And just this point is then dramatically confirmed by the personal testimony of the prophet Elijah, a testimony that also makes clear that in later days the divine recollection was solely for the recitation of the passage dealing with this offering in study and prayer (as is still the practice): "I summon heaven and earth as my witness! When Gentile or Jew, man or woman, male or female slave, recite this verse '*tzafonah* before the Lord,' the Holy One, blessed be He, recalls the 'Binding of Isaac' son of Abraham."[13] And what, further, is remembered? The merits due for that ancient deed. For on the basis of a powerful and evocative wordplay, this Midrash goes on to cite Songs 7:14, "New and old which I have stored-up (*tzafanti*) for you, O my beloved," thereby indicating that the benefits of yore and those to come were laid-up for generations to come as a result of the patriarch's faithful obedience.

One may also suppose that knowledgeable readers of this teaching would perceive here a deeper resonance of and allusion to this entire matter in the old Mishnaic reference to the *Tamid*-offering. For that source not only spoke of the animals "bound" on the northern side of the altar in precisely the terms used for the binding of Isaac (*M. Tamid* IV.1), but it also referred to the persons who had not yet made offerings and those who had done so as "new" and "old" officiants (*M. Tamid* V.2). For ancient readers, such a concordance between scripture and Mishnah was highly evocative and theologically instructive. Indeed, in just this way Midrash could provide deep consolation and confirmation of divine merits in a world without physical sacrifices.

As for the second tradition alluded to just above, let me simply note the midrashic etymology given to Mount Moriah in *Pesikta Rabbati* 40,[14] whereby that place is so called because it refers to the *Temurah* or substitute offering that was performed there. Such a supplement to the etymology found in scripture testifies like one-hundred witnesses to the rabbinic ideology about the institutionalization of animal sacrifices in the patriarchal period. But as for the etymology found in the Bible itself, one should hardly assume that it was simply cited and accepted on its own terms. It too was transformed by the exegetical imagination of the sages. It is to this that I now turn.

A comment on the next verse in the scriptural account (v. 14) picks up on Abraham's naming of the place where the offering was made:

YHWH yir'eh, "The Lord will see." The comment that follows in *Genesis Rabba* 56.10 stresses the future intercessory effect of Abraham's act, and in doing so it brings us back to the theme of the patriarch's devotion noted earlier; but it does so not with reference to the angel seeing his submission to God's will, but rather with his own assertion to that effect.

> R. Bibi Rabba said in the name of R. Yohanan, "[Abraham] said: 'Master of the entire universe, from the time You said to me "Take now your son, your special one" (Gen. 22:2) I could have said, Yesterday You said to me "For your seed will be called in Isaac's name" (*ib.* 21:12), and now You say to me "Take now"?! Heaven forfend that I did so, but rather I suppressed my mercy in order to do Your will. Thus, May it be Your will, Lord our God, that when the children of Isaac come to grief You will remember on the behalf this "binding" and be filled with mercy for their sake.'"[15]

Thus the divine "seeing" mentioned in the toponym is understood as a kind of attentive regard, and the future tense (will see) is understood as a prayerful optative (May the Lord see), presumably because R. Yohanan (the head of the academy of Tiberias, early third century) could not believe that Abraham would have issued an ultimatum or command to God. He therefore implies that it is a request for permanent divine mercy through the way he formulates Abraham's prayer (May it be Your will). Hereby it is the devoted suppression of the father's mercy that is supposed to evoke divine mercy and the suppression of wrath; and hereby it is the father's act of binding with the intent of sacrifice that is stressed — not the act of substitution itself or the metonymic reminder of it (the ram's horn) that is mentioned. The suppression of will is the sacrificial correlate in the father that is vaunted by the Midrash; it is itself a kind of ritual substitute. In this respect it provides an interesting and significant variant for the previously mentioned instance of Abraham's readiness to offer himself, as well as an interesting correlate to the types of humility and self-abnegation noted at the outset of this part, which were regarded by other contemporary sages as equivalent to performing the sacrifices.

In all these and many other ways, the sages of classical Judaism acknowledged the powers of human sacrifice to effect divine mercy and atonement, even as they found ways to capitalize on these benefits in new cultural ways. By attending to these changes and transformations, we as much later receivers of the tradition are nonetheless still able to perceive something of the inner-spiritual dimensions of Jewish piety and praxis in its formative age.

The *Nefesh Ha-Hayyim* of R. Hayyim of Volozhin

Judaism built upon these texts in the course of the next millennium and a half, and reformulated them in many and diverse ways. Sometimes the imagery and also the language of "as if" were taken concretely and directly, while at other times the language was read more metaphorically and indirectly—all according to the spirit of the age and the mind of the interpreter. We can hardly follow this trail here, but it would be wrong, I think, to ignore it entirely. As a compromise, I propose to cite a section of an important text from the eighteenth century. It is called *Nefesh Ha-Hayyim*, by R. Hayyim of Volozhin (1749–1821; the title of the book means "The Soul of Life," and plays on the author's name). The work is deemed one of the great spiritual handbooks of the time and was composed by a person who praised the study of the rabbinic, and especially Talmudic, tradition. In that spirit he founded the most celebrated of Lithuanian rabbinic academies, the Yeshiva of Volozhin.

R. Hayyim's book stresses the religious and spiritual power of study, as was befitting the foremost disciple of the greatest Lithuanian Talmudist of the age, R. Elijah b. Solomon—known as the "Vilner Gaon" (the exalted genius of Vilna). But as a compendium of spiritual matters, it is also most noteworthy that the *Nefesh Ha-Hayim* transmits teachings of various sorts, particularly from the greatest of all works of Jewish mysticism, the *Zohar*. The importance of this fact should not be overlooked or underestimated, of course, despite modern ignorance and misconceptions (for there were celebrated masters of the old mystical sources in Lithuania, and the Vilner Gaon himself composed kabbalistic tracts as well as commentaries on one of the

most recondite portions of the *Zohar*). But the value of citing from
this work is particularly justified by the way it can shed light on how
the body of tradition (on our themes) was selected, arranged, and presented by this master at a most pivotal time in Jewish religious and
cultural history. But there is more. Citing from this work will also
allow us to adduce some of those sections from the *Zohar* and related
literature that bear on our topic and that were singled out by this author. We may not therefore be able to present the whole complex of this
literature, but we can nevertheless receive a special insight into particular paradigmatic exemplars of it. I begin with a passage taken from
chapter 31.

> Study of the Torah atones for all the sins of the sinful soul, as (the
> sages) of blessed memory (have said in) their teaching (at the end of
> tractate *Menachot*, in the *Babylonian Talmud*): "Why (does Scripture)
> say 'This is the Torah for the burnt-offering, for the meal-offering,
> for the sin-offering, etc.'?—and concludes that whoever studies Torah
> has no need of the burnt-, meal-, sin-, or guilt-offerings." And (this
> teaching is) similarly (found) in (*Midrash*) *Tanhuma parashat Tzav*,
> and in *Exodus Rabba*, chapter 38—(where we read): "'Take words
> and return to the Lord' (Hosea 14), insofar as Israel says . . . 'We are
> poor and cannot bring sacrifices' and God responds 'It is words that
> I want, and I shall forgive all your sins'—and the meaning of 'words'
> is Torah." In *Tanhuma Va-yaqhel*, in connection with the ark, (the
> sages) said that "It bears (or: carries off) Israel's sins" because the
> Torah within it "bears Israel's sins." . . . And in the book of *Zohar*
> (*Shelah* 159a), "R. Judah began [his discourse thus] . . . 'How im-
> portant it is for human beings to contemplate the (sacrificial) service
> of God; how important it is for them to contemplate the words of
> Torah—for whoever labors in the Torah it is as if he sacrifices all the
> sacrifices of the world before God. And not only that, but God for-
> gives him all his sins and prepares for him several thrones for the
> world to come. Moreover, even for those severe sins that sacrifices
> cannot atone for the study of Torah provides atonement; as the rabbis
> of blessed memory said concerning the sons of Eli (*Babylonian Tal-
> mud, Rosh Hashanah* 18a): "Neither sacrifice nor meal-offerings pro-
> vide atonement, but the words of Torah do." And they also said (in

tractate *Megillah* 3b): "The study of Torah is greater than offering the daily sacrifice (the *Tamid*)." And in the *Zohar* (*Tzav* 35a) [it says]: "Come and see . . . Whoever labors in Torah-study has no need of sacrifices or offerings; for Torah is preferable to all. . . . [For indeed,] a person is only purified through words of Torah. . . . For the Torah is called holy, as it says, 'For I, the Lord, am holy', and the Torah, which is God's Name is of supernal holiness. Hence, whoever labors in Torah-study is purified and then made holy."'"

This is a remarkable compendium of traditions dealing with our theme of sacrifice and its substitutes, taken from classical rabbinic and medieval mystical sources. But it is a very decisive and selective compendium, as one can see from the outset, when R. Hayyim begins by citing from the Talmudic teaching found in tractate *Menachot* 110a of the Babylonian Talmud, but only draws his point from the teaching of Rabba—which, as noted earlier, is the only one given there that stresses that study actually replaces sacrifices (and recall, as well, that it appears to be a Babylonian deliberation on a tradition received from the land of Israel). However, the point made by Rabba serves R. Hayyim's purposes quite well, as this ancient opinion expresses the value that he valorizes most and that he brings to the fore among the various traditions adduced on the subject. Certainly, it is the chief point he wants to stress to his students and audience. Indeed, in R. Hayyim's world of values, study of Torah was the premier religious act and the supreme means of religious perfection and purification. Thus the particular funneling of midrashic and other streams of tradition into this chapter helps us see the kind of person this master wanted to cultivate and how he viewed the spirituality of study. On this basis, one can therefore anticipate that for him the study hall or rabbinic academy would therefore be something of a substitute for the ancient Temple. And in this R. Hayyim does not disappoint, insofar as he chooses passages from the older sources that make this very point, and one more besides: that the service of study is an act of priestly piety, which delights God and sustains the sacred divine dimensions of the universe, a virtual and actual transumption of the old sacrifices and their powers. The following brief excerpts from chapter 34 of his work will provide a glimpse of his striking theme.

And from the time that our sacred Temple was destroyed and the sons were exiled from the table of their father, the Presence (*Shekhinah*) of [God's] blessed Glory wept and wandered, as it were, without rest; and there is no remnant left [of the Temple]—save for this Torah. And when Israel, the sacred people, chant and study it properly, they provide a "small sanctuary" for it, to establish it and sustain it. And [then] she [the *Shekhinah*] dwells among them and stretches her wings over them, as it were; and thus there is a little rest [or solace], as in the saying of [our sages] of blessed memory in the first chapter of [the Talmudic tractate] *Berachot* (8a), "From the day the Temple was destroyed, the Holy One, Blessed be He, was only left with the four ells of the *halakhah*"; and they also said there: "From where [in Scripture] can we deduce that even if one person sits and studies Torah the *Shekhinah* dwell with him?—from what is said, 'Every place where I [God] shall have My Name mentioned, [I shall come to you and bless you'; Exod. 20:21]" . . . and in [the book of] *Zohar, Balak,* 202a [we learn] . . . "And from the day that the Temple was destroyed, and the sacrifices ceased, the Holy One, blessed be He, has only those words of Torah and the Torah that is renewed in the mouth [of the sage]."

In this passage we come to a striking transformation of our theme. Beyond the teachings that study is a substitute for sacrifices, and thus a consolation and benefit for the sage, we now see two teachings— one from the ancient rabbinic period, the second from medieval mystical sources—that present study as nothing less than a divine consolation and gift. The student (and the place of study) serves as a sanctuary of sorts (the term "small sanctuary" derives from the prophet Ezekiel, and came to refer to synagogues or any substitute for the ancient Temple), where the divine Presence may dwell and be sustained. Study is a place that draws God to it (the biblical word "place," *maqom*, refers to an ancient site of sacrifice), and the words of study are something of the transformed substance that once ascended from the shrine to God in heaven. Remarkably, the passage in the *Zohar* has somehow retrieved or reactivated the most ancient sense of the sustenance of sacrifices for the gods. In the Hebrew Bible, only traces of this notion are retained in such idioms as "sweet-smelling savor" or "my meat sacrifice," but it is often difficult to discern how concretely to understand these terms, both how they were intended by the priestly authors and how they were perceived in antiquity. The rabbinic evidence is also quite diverse, and the idioms and various imagery reflect a complex picture.

This is not the place to resolve the point, save to note that the medieval passage (like others cited here, and more besides) derives its literary force from the lost concreteness implied (and images of the sustaining power of the sacrifices is a component of the *Zohar* and other works). Just how concretely this citation was understood by R. Hayyim is not indicated. But we should beware of being too modern and too metaphorical. These passages form the conclusion to the tract *Nefesh Ha-Hayyim*, and thus bring the whole program of study and spirituality it advocates to a climax. At the very least, we can say that we have in this eighteenth century classic a presentation of the priestly dimension of Torah study and its role in divine service in the exile. The words of study sustain the student and God, and temporarily alleviate the wandering of exile. The sacred divine Presence is hereby given a Temple in which to dwell, however momentarily, among the students of scripture; and indeed the words of study provide that Presence some solace and sustenance. Study of Torah (taken here in the most comprehensive sense, as meaning the entirety of the rabbinic sacred canon) is thus not solely an act for the sake of the doer (and, specifically, through the study of the sacrifices), but it now truly approximates the old order of sacrifices as a divine gift and beneficence.

In a manner hardly to have been expected, older traces and actualities of the myth and ritual of sacrifice have been spiritualized and reactualized here. Indeed, in the final pages of *Nefesh Ha-Hayim*, Torah study is presented as the culminating substitute for sacrifices: the words of sacred scripture and its library of explanations are transformed through recitation and interpretation, and uttered as a votary offering to God—and nothing less than the violence of exile and the sorrows of divine absence are said to be healed somewhat by this act. Might it seem too bold to suggest that we may have here a striking attempt to reformulate and renew a core myth and ritual of (early and medieval) rabbinic Judaism since the time of the destruction of the Second Temple?[16] I think not.

Notes

1. For a consideration of interpreted teachings and traditions in the Hebrew Bible itself, see my *Biblical Interpretation in Ancient Israel* (Oxford: The Clarendon Press, 1985).

2. For a wealth of detail and bibliography, see the materials and analyses in Jacob Milgrom, *Leviticus 1–16*, Anchor Bible 3 (New York: Doubleday, 1991), and *Leviticus 17–22*, Anchor Bible 3a (New York: Doubleday, 2000); and also Israel Knohl, *Temple of Silence* (Minneapolis: Fortress, 1994).

3. See my discussion in *The Garments of Torah* (Bloomington: Indiana University Press, 1989), chap. 6, "From Scribalism to Rabbinism: Perspectives on the Emergence of Classical Judaism."

4. I have discussed many of these texts at length in my *Biblical Interpretation in Ancient Israel.*

5. For details, see the discussion referred to in n. 3.

6. See the report in Solomon Schechter, ed., *Aboth de-Rabbi Nathan* A IV (repr., New York: Feldheim, 1967), 21.

7. This quote is from the *Soncino Babylonia Talmud, Tractate Sotah*, trans. Rabbi Dr. I. Epstein (London: The Soncino Press, 1935–48); I have made minor emendations to this translation.

8. See in the edition of Mordechai Margoliot, *Midrash Vayiqra Rabbah* (Jerusalem: Wahrmann Books, 1962), 150–51.

9. Schecter, *Aboth de-Rabbi Nathan* A IV, 18.

10. Juda Theodor and Hanokh Albeck, eds., *Midrash Bereshit Rabba* (Jerusalem: Wahrmann Books, 1965), 603.

11. Ibid., 605–6.

12. Ibid., 606.

13. See Meir Ish Shalom (Friedmann), ed., *Seder Eliyahu Rabba* 7 (repr., Jerusalem: Wahrmann Books, 1969), 36.

14. Meir Ish Shalom Friedmann, ed. *Pesikta Rabbati* (Vienna: Selbstverlag, 1880), 170a.

15. Theodor and Albeck, *Midrash Bereshit Rabba*, 607.

16. It goes without saying that we must absent from this generalization all those Jewish scholars who argued that the biblical and rabbinic sources must be read in the key of philosophical allegory. But these individuals always constituted a fairly elite minority.

FOUR

The Eucharist and the Mimesis of Sacrifice

BRUCE CHILTON

Each act of Eucharist is a mimetic moment, involving ritual gestures, a defined liturgical group, and an agreed field of the meaning of what is done. By conceiving of the Eucharist within the New Testament in mimetic terms, we can overcome two impediments to understanding that have emerged repeatedly in the critical literature. The first of these has been the tendency to reduce all eucharistic acts to a single origin—usually a heroic, mythologized account of "the Last Supper." The desire to distance criticism from that mythology has produced the second impediment: efforts to locate the genesis of Eucharist apart from Jesus (in the influence of Paul, for example) prevent us from accounting for the generality of the practice within earliest Christianity. Mimesis is sufficiently varied *and* sufficiently general to steer us between Charybdis and Scylla, provided that we both absolve Jesus from having to explain *all* Christian practices and allow for the mimetic recollection of Jesus as a unifying element within the varieties of that practice.

Over the past fifteen years, I have developed an account of the development of eucharistic practice within Christianity, beginning with the contributions of Jesus as a conscious practitioner of Judaism. The first book that explored this issue engaged explicitly with the work of anthropologists of sacrifice, including René Girard, in order to assess Jesus' position in relation to the sacrificial cult in Jerusalem.[1] Eucharist at the time I initially researched the book was not foremost on my mind. My principal concern had been to evaluate Jesus' attitudes toward and his actions within the Temple in Jerusalem. But in the course of that work I saw the direct connection between Jesus' last meals with his followers and his action in the Temple. The Eucharist emerged as a mimetic surrogate of sacrifice. Encouraged by several scholars, notably Bernhard Lang, I then undertook a strictly exegetical study in order to detail the evolution of the texts within the typical practices of the first Christians.[2]

Here I wish briefly to explain the six types of Eucharist attested within the New Testament that I have identified on exegetical grounds. These types are mimetic moments that characterize the particular groups that produced them. In the way of mimesis, the types attest fluidity in their ritual acts, their constituent communities, and their accounts of meaning. Even Jesus, in my reading, developed not one but two types of Eucharist during his life. At the end of this paper I wish to return to a theoretical question in order to be more precise about the moment Eucharist emerged as a mimetic surrogate of sacrifice within Jesus' practice, because that appears to have been the moment generative of the subsequent types and therefore of Christianity's emergence as a religion separate from Judaism. In the sense of recent, sociological discussion, I will suggest that at this generative moment Jesus' practice may usefully be said to have been magical.

Six Types of Eucharist in the New Testament

The Mishnah, in an effort to conceive of a heinous defect on the part of a priest involved in slaughtering the red heifer, pictures him as intending to eat the flesh or drink the blood (*m. Parah* 4:3**). Because people had no share of blood, which belonged uniquely to God, even the thought of drinking it was blasphemous. To imagine drinking human blood, consumed with human flesh, could only make the blasphemy worse. So if Jesus' words are taken with their traditional, autobiographical meaning, his last supper can only be understood as a deliberate break from Judaism. Either Jesus himself promulgated a new religion, or his followers did so in his name and invented "the Last Supper" themselves. Both those alternatives find adherents today among scholars, and the debate between those who see the Gospels as literally true reports and those who see them as literary fictions shows little sign of making progress. But in either case, the nagging question remains: if the generative act was indeed anti-sacrificial (whether that act was literal or literary), how did the cycles of traditions and the texts as they stand come to their present, sacrificial constructions?

There is another, more critical way of understanding how Eucharist emerged in earliest Christianity, an approach that takes account of the cultural changes that the development of the movement involved and that allows for the consistent concern for effective sacrifice across the cultures involved. Interest in the social world of early Judaism, and in how Christianity as a social movement emerged within Judaism and then became distinct from it within the Hellenistic world, has been growing for more than a century.

We are no longer limited to the old dichotomy, between the "conservative" position that the Gospels are literal reports and the "liberal" position that they are literary fictions. Critical study has revealed that the Gospels are composite products of the various social groups that were part of Jesus' movement from its days within Judaism to the emergence of Christianity as a distinct religion. When we place eucharistic practices within the social constituencies that made the Gospels into the texts we can read today, we can understand the original meaning Jesus gave to the last supper, and how his meaning generated others.

The Last Supper was not the only supper, just the last one. In fact, "the Last Supper" would have had no meaning apart from Jesus' well-established custom of eating with people socially. There was nothing unusual about a rabbi making social eating an instrument of his instruction, and it was part of Jesus' method from the first days of his movement in Galilee.

Meals within Judaism were regular expressions of social solidarity and of common identity as the people of God. Many sorts of meals are attested in the literature of early Judaism. From Qumran we learn of banquets at which the community convened in order of hierarchy; from the Pharisees we learn of collegial meals shared within fellowships (*chaburoth*) at which like-minded fellows would share the foods and the company they considered pure. Ordinary households might welcome the coming of the Sabbath with a prayer of sanctification (*kiddush*) over a cup of wine, or open a family occasion with a blessing (*berakhah*) over bread and wine.

Jesus' meals were similar in some ways to several of these meals, but they were also distinctive. He had a characteristic understanding of what the meals meant and of who should participate in them. For him, eating socially with others in Israel was an enacted parable of the feast in the kingdom that was to come. The idea that God would offer festivity for all peoples on his holy mountain (see Is 2:2–4) was a key feature in the fervent expectations of Judaism during the first century, and Jesus shared that hope, as may be seen in a saying from the source of his teaching conventionally known as Q (see Mt 8:11 = Lk 13:28, 29):

> Many shall come from east and west,
> and feast with Abraham, Isaac, and Jacob
> in the kingdom of God.[3]

Eating was a way of enacting the kingdom of God, of practicing the generous rule of the divine king. As a result, Jesus adamantly accepted as companions people such as tax agents and others of suspect purity and received notorious sinners at table. The meal for him was a sign of the kingdom of God, and all the people of God, assuming they sought forgiveness, were to have access to it.

Jesus' practice of fellowship at meals caused opposition from those whose understanding of Israel was exclusive. To them, he seemed profligate, willing to eat and drink with anyone, as Jesus himself was pictured as observing in a famous saying also from Q (Mt 11:19 = Lk 7:34):

> A man came eating and drinking, and they complain:
> Look, a glutton and drunkard,
> a fellow of tax agents and sinners.[4]

Some of Jesus' opponents saw the purity of Israel as something that could only be guarded by separating from others, as in the meals of their fellowships (*chaburoth*). Jesus' view of purity was different. He held that a son or daughter of Israel, by virtue of being *of Israel*, could approach his table, or even worship in the Temple. Where necessary, repentance beforehand could be demanded, and Jesus taught his followers to pray for forgiveness daily, but his understanding was that Israelites as such were pure and were fit to offer purely of their own within the sacrificial worship of Israel.

As long as Jesus' activity was limited to Galilee, he was involved in active disputes but essentially inconsequential ones. (Deviant rabbis in Galilee were far from uncommon.) Jesus' practice coincided to some extent with that of a *chaburah*, although his construal of purity was unusual. Given the prominence accorded wine in his meals,[5] we might describe the first type of his meals — the practice of purity in anticipation of the kingdom — as a *kiddush* of the kingdom. Indeed, there is practically no meal of Judaism with which Jesus' meals do not offer some sort of analogy, because the meal was a seal and an occasion of purity, and Jesus was concerned with what was pure. But both the nature of his concern and the character of his meals were distinctive in their inclusiveness: Israel as forgiven and willing to provide of its own produce was for him the occasion of the kingdom. That was the first type in the development of the Eucharist.

Jesus also brought his teaching into the Temple, where he insisted on his own teaching (or *halakhah*) of purity. The incident that reflects the resulting dispute is usually called the "Cleansing of the Temple" (Mt 21:12–13 = Mk 11:15–17 = Lk 19:45–46 = Jn 2:13–17). From the point of view of the authorities there, what Jesus was after was the opposite of cleansing. He objected to the presence of merchants who had been given permission to sell sacrificial animals in the vast, outer court of the Temple. His objection was based on his own, peasant's view of purity: Israel should offer, not priests' produce for which they handed over money, but their own sacrifices that they brought into the Temple.[6] He believed so vehemently what he taught that he and his followers drove the animals and the sellers out of the great court, no doubt with the use of force.

Jesus' interference in the ordinary worship of the Temple might have been sufficient by itself to bring about his execution. After all, the Temple was the center of Judaism for as long as it stood. Roman officials were so interested in its smooth functioning at the hands of the priests whom they appointed that they were known to sanction the penalty of death for sacrilege. Yet there is no indication that Jesus was arrested immediately. Instead, he remained at liberty for some time, and was finally taken into custody just after one of his meals, "the Last Supper." The decision of the authorities of the Temple to move against Jesus when they did is what made this supper last.

Why did the authorities wait, and why did they act when they did? The Gospels portray them as fearful of the popular backing that Jesus enjoyed, and his simultaneously inclusive and apocalyptic teaching of purity probably did bring enthusiastic followers into the Temple with him. But in addition, there was another factor: Jesus could not simply be dispatched as a cultic criminal. He was not attempting an onslaught upon the Temple as such; his dispute with the authorities concerned purity within the Temple. Other rabbis of his period also engaged in physical demonstrations of the purity they required in the conduct of worship. One of them, for example, is said once to have driven thousands of sheep into the Temple, so that people could offer sacrifice in the manner he approved of (see *Besah* 20a–b in the Babylonian Talmud). Jesus' action was extreme but not totally without precedent, even in the use of force.

The delay of the authorities, then, was understandable. We may also say it was commendable, reflecting continued controversy over the merits of Jesus' teaching and whether his occupation of the great court should be condemned out of hand. But why did they finally arrest Jesus? The texts of the Last Supper provide the key; something about Jesus' meals after his occupation of the Temple caused Judas to inform on Jesus. Of course, "Judas" is the only name that the traditions of the New Testament have left us. We cannot say who or how many of the disciples became disaffected by Jesus' behavior after his occupation of the Temple.

However they learned of Jesus' new interpretation of his meals of fellowship, the authorities arrested him just after the supper we call last. Jesus continued to celebrate fellowship at table as a foretaste of the kingdom, just as he had before. But he also added a new and scandalous dimension of meaning. His occupation of the Temple having failed, Jesus said of the wine, "This is my blood," and of the bread, "This is my flesh" (Mt 26:26, 28 = Mk 14:22, 24 = Lk 22:19–20 = 1 Cor 11:24–25 = Justin, *1 Apology* 66.3).

In Jesus' context, the context of his confrontation with the authorities of the Temple, his words had one predominant meaning. He did not mean to say, "Here are my personal body and blood"; that is an interpretation that only makes sense at a later stage. Jesus' principal point was rather that, in the absence of a Temple that permitted his view of purity to be practiced, wine was his blood of sacrifice and bread was his flesh of sacrifice. In Aramaic, "blood" and "flesh" (which may also be rendered as "body") can carry such a sacrificial meaning, and in Jesus' context, that is the most natural meaning. The meaning of "the Last Supper," then, actually evolved over a series of meals after Jesus' occupation of the Temple. During that period, Jesus claimed that wine and bread were a better sacrifice than what was offered in the Temple: at least wine and bread were Israel's own, not tokens of priestly dominance.

No wonder the opposition to him, even among the Twelve (in the shape of Judas, according to the Gospels), became deadly. In essence, Jesus made his meals into a rival altar, and we may call such a reading of his words a ritual or cultic interpretation. This second type of Eucharist offered wine and bread as a mimetic surrogate of sacrifice.

The cultic interpretation has two advantages over the traditional, autobiographical interpretation as the primary meaning Jesus attributed to his own final meals. The first advantage is contextual: the cultic interpretation places Jesus firmly with the Judaism of his period and the final dispute of his life, and at the same time accounts for the opposition of the authorities to him. The second advantage is the explanatory power of this reading: the cultic interpretation enables us to explain sequentially four subsequent developments in the understanding of Eucharist within early Christianity.

The third type of Eucharist is that of Petrine Christianity, in which the blessing of bread at home, the *berakhah* of Judaism, became a principal model of Eucharist. A practical result of that development was that bread came to have precedence over wine, and Acts refers to the ritual as the "breaking" of bread (see Acts 2:42–47). More profoundly, the circle of Peter conceived of Jesus as a new Moses, who gave commands concerning purity as Moses did on Sinai and who expected his followers to worship on Mount Zion. As compared to Jesus' practice (in both its first and second stages), Petrine practice represents a double domestication. First, adherents of the movement congregated in the homes of their colleagues rather than seeking the hospitality of others. Second, the validity of sacrifice in the Temple, rather than its replacement, was acknowledged. Both forms of domestication grew out of the new circumstances of the movement in Jerusalem and fresh opportunities for worship in the Temple; they changed the nature of the meal and the memory of what Jesus had said at "the Last Supper." The application of the model of a *berakhah* to Eucharist was a self-conscious metaphor, because the careful identification of those gathered in Jesus' name with a household was emphatically metaphorical (cf. Mk 3:31–35).

The fourth type of Eucharist, the contribution of the circle of James (Jesus' brother), pursued the tendency of domestication further. The Eucharist was seen as a seder in terms of its meaning and its chronology (see Mk 14:12–16, and the contradictory, more historical timing explicitly indicated in 14:1–2). So understood, only Jews in a state of purity could participate fully in Eucharist, which could be truly recollected only once a year, at Passover in Jerusalem among the circumcised (so Ex 12:48). The Quartodeciman controversy (concerning the timing of Easter) of a later period, fierce though it appears, was but a shadow cast by much a more serious contention concerning the nature of Christianity. The Jacobean program intended to integrate Jesus' movement fully within the liturgical institutions of Judaism, and to insist upon the Judaic identity of the movement and upon Jerusalem as its governing center. Nonetheless, there is never any doubt but that Eucharist is not portrayed as a literal replacement of all the seders of Israel, and the Jacobean "Last Supper" does not supplant the other types of Eucharist in the New Testament. For those reasons the language of metaphor is appropriate here, as well as at the Petrine stage, in order to convey the type of mimetic activity involved.

Paul and the synoptic Gospels represent the fifth type of Eucharist. Paul vehemently resists Jacobean claims, by insisting Jesus' last meal occurred on the night in which he was betrayed (1 Cor 11:23), not on Passover. Paul emphasizes the link between Jesus' death and the Eucharist, and he accepts the Hellenistic refinement of the Petrine type that presented the Eucharist as a sacrifice for sin associated with the Temple (see, for example, Rom 3:25).

In the synoptic Gospels the heroism of Jesus is such that the meal is an occasion to join in the solidarity of martyrdom.[7] The synoptics insist by various wordings that Jesus' blood is shed in the interests of the communities for which those Gospels were composed, for the "many" in Damascus (Mt 26:28) and Rome (Mk 14:24), on behalf of "you" in Antioch (Lk 22:20). The synoptic strategy is not to oppose the Jacobean program directly; in fact, the Passover chronology is incorporated (producing internal contradictions). But any limitation of the benefits of Eucharist to circumcised Israelites is superseded by the mimetic imperative to join Jesus' martyrdom and its sacrificial benefits.

The synoptic tradition also provided two stories of miraculous feeding—of five thousand and of four thousand—which symbolized the inclusion of Jews and non-Jews within Eucharist, understood as in the nature of a philosophical symposium (see Mk 6:32–44; 8:1–10; and parallels). This willingness to explore differing meanings with eucharistic action attests that any such meaning, taken individually, was understood metaphorically, and that it was reproduced mimetically.

The feeding of the five thousand—understood as occurring at Passover—is taken up in John 6 in a fully Paschal sense. Jesus himself identified as the *manna*, miraculous food bestowed by God upon his people. The motif was already articulated by Paul (1 Cor 10:1–4), but John develops it to construe the Eucharist as a mystery, in which Jesus offers his own flesh and blood (carefully defined to avoid a crude misunderstanding; Jn 6:30–58). That autobiographical reading of Jesus' words—as giving his personal body and blood in Eucharist—had no doubt already occurred to Hellenistic Christians who followed synoptic practice and appreciated its sacrificial overtones.

The Johannine practice made that meaning as explicit as the break with Judaism is in the fourth Gospel. Both that departure and the identification of Jesus himself (rather than his supper) as the Paschal lamb are pursued in the Revelation (5:6–14; 7:13–17). The sixth type of Eucharist can only be understood as a consciously non-Judaic and Hellenistic development. It involves participants in joining by oath (*sacramentum* in Latin, corresponding to *musterion* within the Greek vocabulary of primitive Christianity;[8] Jn 6:60–71) in the sacrifice of the mysterious hero himself, separating themselves from others. Eucharist has become sacrament, and involves a knowing conflict with the ordinary understanding of what Judaism might and might not include.[9]

"The Last Supper" is neither simply Jesus' "real" seder nor simply a symposium of Hellenists to which the name of Jesus happens to have been attached. Such reductionist regimens, which will have the Gospels be only historical or only fictive, starve the reader of the meanings that generated the texts to hand. The engines of those meanings were diverse practices, whose discovery permits us to feast on the richness of tradition. A generative exegesis of eucharistic texts may not conclude with a single meaning that is alleged to have occasioned all the others. One of the principal findings of such an approach is rather that meaning itself is to some extent epiphenomenal, a consequence of a definable practice with its own initial sense being introduced into a fresh environment of people who in turn take up the practice as they understand it and produce their own meanings. The sense with which a practice is mediated to a community is therefore one measure of what that community will finally produce as its practice, but the initial meaning does not entirely determine the final meaning.

The meanings conveyed by words must be the point of departure for a generative exegesis because those meanings are our only access to what produced the texts to hand. But having gained that access, it becomes evident that Eucharist is not a matter of the development of a single, basic meaning within several different environments. Those environments have themselves produced various meanings under the influence of definable practices. Eucharist was not simply handed on as a tradition. Eucharistic traditions were rather the catalyst that permitted communities to crystallize their own practice in oral or textual form. What they crystallized was a function of the practice that had been learned, palpable gestures with specified objects and previous meanings, along with the meanings and the emotional responses that the community discovered in Eucharist. There is no history of the tradition apart from a history of meaning, a history of emotional response, a history of practice: the practical result of a generative exegesis of eucharistic texts is that practice itself is an appropriate focus in understanding the New Testament.

The Moment of Magical Surrogacy

The cultic sense of Jesus' last meals with his disciples is the generative moment that permits us to explain its later meanings as eucharistic covenant, Passover, heroic symposium, and mystery. Those four last types of Eucharist, developed within distinct circles of practice and belief within the primitive church, evolved from the initial two types, eschatological banquet and surrogate of sacrifice, which Jesus developed. In that evolution, Jesus' insistence on the mimetic surrogacy of his meals is evidently the key element. If Jesus is seen as generating Eucharist as a surrogate of sacrifice, the question emerges: why did he undertake such an action with such an understanding? In terms of circumstances at the time, his failed occupation of the Temple provides an adequate occasion but not a sufficient cause from the point of view of later developments. How did the framing of a meal as a mimetic surrogate of sacrifice lead to the emergence of a new sacrament in a religious system distinct from Judaism?

Since the work of Morton Smith, the identification of Jesus as a magician has featured in the critical literature.[10] Ralph Schroeder has made an especially productive contribution from this point of view by actively criticizing the work of Max Weber.[11] Schroeder explains:

> The most undifferentiated form of magic, in Weber's view, is where magical power is thought to be embodied in a person who can bring about supernatural events by virtue of an innate capacity. This belief is the original source of charisma. "The oldest of all 'callings' or professions," Weber points out, "is that of the magician" (1981a:8). From this point, charisma develops by a process of abstraction towards the notion that certain forces are "behind" this extraordinary power— although they remain within the world (1968:401).[12]

Schroeder complains that Weber's perspective leads to an analysis of magic as static, while from a sociological perspective religion is notable for its capacity to change and to cause change.[13] What Schroeder does not say, and yet may easily be inferred from his study, is that magic should not be seen as the changeless foundation of religion but as a specific manifestation of religion, when the entire system is held to be concentrated in an individual or individuals. Magic expresses more the crisis of a system than the presupposition of systems.

Such a description accords well with some of the figures whom Josephus calls false prophets. There has been a tendency to class John the Baptist with these leaders, who were presumably called prophets by their followers. In fact, Josephus simply calls John a good man (*Antiquities* 18.117), and describes Bannus' similar commitment to sanctification by bathing in approving terms (*Life* 11). Nothing they did (as related by Josephus) can be compared with what Josephus said the false prophets did: one scaled Mount Gerizim to find the vessels deposited by Moses (*Antiquities* 18.85–87); Theudas waited at the Jordan for the waters to part for him, as they had for Joshua (*Antiquities* 20.97–98);[14] the Egyptian marched from the Mount of Olives in the hope the walls of Jerusalem might fall at his command (*Antiquities* 20.169–72), so that he might conquer Jerusalem (*War* 2.261–63). If there is an act in the Gospels that approximates to such fanaticism, it is Jesus' entry into Jerusalem and his occupation of the Temple; apparently he expected to prevail against all the odds in insisting upon his own understanding of what true purity was, in opposition to Caiaphas and the imposing authority of a high priest sanctioned by Rome. When Jesus is styled a prophet in Matthew 21:11, 46, that may have something to do with the usage of Josephus, but to portray John the Baptist in such terms is incautious.

These acts of "magic" are not spontaneous or heroic foundations of new religions by means of Weberian charisma. Rather, each instantiates a response to a sense of crisis, the conviction that the entire religious system has gone wrong and may only be retrieved by a magician who takes that system on to himself. Finding Moses' vessels, parting the Jordan, taking Jerusalem, and occupying the Temple are all examples of the attempt to right the system by seizing and manipulating its most central symbols. They are instances of magic as theurgy, the access of divine power in order to change and mold the ordinary structures of authority, whether social or natural.

Seen in this light, Jesus' mimetic surrogacy of sacrifice, as well as his occupation of the Temple, represents a distillation of principal elements of his own religious system into his actions and his person. Raw materials of Christology, as well as of eucharistic theology, were generated by this deliberate—and in Schroeder's terms magical—concentration. But the directions of those streams were no more determined by their source than a thunderstorm can be thought to guide a river in the twists and turns of its environment. In the manner of a magician, Jesus concentrated the sacrificial ideology of Israel in his own meals with his disciples—and released forces whose results he could scarcely have calculated.

Notes

1. Bruce Chilton, *The Temple of Jesus: His Sacrificial Program Within a Cultural History of Sacrifice* (University Park: Pennsylvania State University Press, 1992). In this essay, as in my earlier work, I deploy Aristotle's definition of mimesis, rather than Girard's. For that reason, I do not identify mimesis or sacrifice with violence, although I agree that sacrificial mimesis might justify or occasion violence (see the analysis of the Johannine Eucharist below).

2. Bruce Chilton, *A Feast of Meanings: Eucharistic Theologies from Jesus through Johannine Circles,* Supplements to Novum Testamentum 72 (Leiden: Brill, 1994).

3. Because my interest here is in the traditional form of the saying, prior to changes introduced in Matthew and Luke, I give a reconstructed form; see Bruce Chilton, *God in Strength: Jesus' Announcement of the Kingdom,* Supplements to Novum Testamentum 1 (Freistadt: Plöchl, 1979; repr. Biblical Seminar 8, Sheffield: JSOT Press, 1987), 179–201. More recently, see *Pure Kingdom: Jesus' Vision of God,* Studying the Historical Jesus 1 (Grand Rapids, MI: Eerdmans and London: SPCK, 1996) 12–14.

4. When I participated in the Jesus Seminar, I noticed that the enthusiasm of the fellows for the authenticity of this saying was surpassed only by their refusal to see its implications for Jesus' conception of purity. See Robert W. Funk, Roy W. Hoover, and the Jesus Seminar, *The Five Gospels: The Search for the Authentic Words of Jesus* (San Francisco: HarperSanFrancisco, 1997).

5. See the order of wine followed by bread in 1 Cor 10:16; Lk 22:19–20; and *Didache* 9:1–5; and the particular significance accorded the wine in Mk 14:25; Mt 26:29; Lk 22:18.

6. Professor Albert Baumgarten has pointed out to me that a Rabbinic tradition in the name of R. Nehemiah supports this analysis. In the Tosefta (Chagigah 3.19), as Baumgarten says in a personal letter dated March 8, 1998, Nehemiah "explains the willingness of temple authorities to be flexible, understanding and willing to trust all Jews at the time of pilgrimage festivals as motivated by the fear

lest someone set up his own altar or offer his own red heifers. Erecting one's own altar or offering one's own red heifers were intolerable assaults on the legitimacy of the Jerusalem temple. Accordingly the law was to be stretched as much as possible to avoid that outcome."

7. I would not deny for a moment that a sense of impending martyrdom might well have suffused Jesus' last meals with his disciples; see Bruce Chilton, *Rabbi Jesus: An Intimate Biography* (New York: Doubleday, 2000), 253–68. The elevation of that sense to the predominant meaning, however, seems to me a later development. I treat that later development extensively in my *Abraham's Curse: Child Sacrifice in the Legacies of the West* (New York: Doubleday, 2008), where I trace the association of Abraham's sacrifice of (a cooperative) Isaac on Mount Moriah with the willing sacrifice of Jesus on the cross and thus with the Eucharist as a food of martyrs. See especially 78–79, 83, 116–17, 177, 186.

8. See Günther Bornkamm, "*musterion, mueo*," in *Theological Dictionary of the New Testament*, ed. G. Kittel, trans. G. W. Bromiley (Grand Rapids, MI: Eerdmans, 1978), 802–28. More recently, see Marvin W. Meyer, ed., *The Ancient Mysteries: A Sourcebook; Sacred Texts of the Mystery Religions of the Ancient Mediterranean World* (San Francisco: HarperSanFrancisco, 1987); Walter Burkert, *Ancient Mystery Cults* (Cambridge, MA: Harvard University Press, 1987); and David Ulansey, *The Origins of the Mithraic Mysteries: Cosmology and Salvation in the Ancient World* (New York: Oxford University Press, 1989).

9. In this regard, see Reimund Bieringer, Didier Pollefeyt, Frederique Vandecasteele-Vanneuville, eds., *Anti-Judaism and the Fourth Gospel* (Louisville, KY: Westminster John Knox, 2001).

10. See Morton Smith, *The Secret Gospel* (New York: Harper and Row, 1973) and *Jesus the Magician* (New York: Harper and Row, 1977). Throughout, the influence of Hans Lewy, *Chaldean Oracles and Theurgy* (Cairo: Institut français d'archéologie orientale, 1956), is apparent. It may be that some of Smith's other assertions about Jesus have obscured this well-documented and incisive aspect of his contributions. Recently, for example, I have come to the reluctant conclusion that Smith perpetrated a fraud when he claimed he had discovered a "secret Gospel of Mark"; see Bruce Chilton, "Unmasking a False Gospel," *New York Sun*, October 25, 2006: 16.

11. See Ralph Schroeder, *Max Weber and the Sociology of Culture* (London: Sage, 1992) 33–71, a chapter entitled "The Uniqueness of the East." For further discussion, see Bruce Chilton, "Eucharist: Surrogate, Metaphor, Sacrament of Sacrifice," in *Sacrifice in Religious Experience*, ed. Albert I. Baumgarten, 175–88, Numen Book Series 93 (Leiden: Brill, 2002).

12. Schroeder, *Max Weber and the Sociology of Culture*, 37, citing *Wirtschaftgeschichte* (Berlin: Duncker and Humblot, 1981) and *Economy and Society* (New York: Bedminster, 1968).

13. Schroeder, *Max Weber and the Sociology of Culture*, 40.

14. According to Colin Brown, Theudas was inspired by John the Baptist, whose program was not purification but a recrossing of the Jordan; see his "What Was John the Baptist Doing?" *Bulletin for Biblical Research* 7 (1997): 37–49, at 48. That seems a desperate expedient to avoid the obvious connection with purification. In this avoidance, many conservative evangelical scholars are at one with the Jesus Seminar. The equally obvious obstacles are that crossing the Jordan is not a part of any characterization of John's message in the primary sources and that Josephus does not associate John with the "false prophets." For the context of John's immersion (and Jesus'), see Bruce Chilton, *Jesus' Baptism and Jesus' Healing: His Personal Practice of Spirituality* (Harrisburg, PA: Trinity Press International, 1998).

FIVE

Eucharistic Origins

From the New Testament to the Liturgies of the Golden Age

ROBERT DALY, S.J.

Many a liturgical theologian has groaned inwardly on Holy Thursday upon hearing the assembly sing "At that first Eucharist . . ." or upon hearing the homilist proclaim that we are "doing what the Lord did at the Last Supper."[1] It is, of course, a theological commonplace that the Eucharist, in the full sense of the word, is the high point of both the expression and the inchoative realization of the church's marital covenant relationship with God. The center of this Eucharist is the church's ritual action and prayer in which the assembly, led by its duly appointed minister, addresses God the Father, through the Son, and in the Holy Spirit, praising and thanking God for the salvation-historical gifts of creation, covenant, and redemption, especially redemption in Jesus Christ, and asking God to send the Holy Spirit in order, by means of the transformation of the eucharistic gifts, to continue the transformation of the community and its individuals toward their eschatological destiny as the true Body of Christ. The ritual celebration culminates in the assembly coming forward to receive, as Augustine put it, "what you are," the Body of Christ. But this, of course, is still just the beginning. The full realization of the ritual celebration continues beyond what takes place in church. It continues as the assembly is sent forth to live out this eucharistic mystery in the world of everyday life. And it will finally be completed only at the eschaton when the universalistic hope expressed in the prophetic proclamation has been fulfilled: "Blessed are those who are invited to the marriage supper of the Lamb" (cf. Rev 19:9).

Is this what Christ did at the Last Supper? Was the Last Supper a Eucharist in this full sense of the word? Obviously not. This does not deny that Jesus instituted the Eucharist. What Jesus did at the Last Supper is obviously at least the generative moment of the institution of the Eucharist. But Eucharist in the full sense we have just described? No, that was still to come. The Holy Spirit had not yet been given to the church, nor had the trinitarian theology yet been developed that is at the heart of the classical eucharistic prayers. Thus the church, the assembly of those who address the Father through the Son and in the Holy Spirit, was not yet constituted at the Last Supper. The Eucharist that Christians now celebrate is what the church, under the guidance of the Holy Spirit of the risen Jesus, and over the course of generations and centuries, learned to do as it celebrated table fellowship with its risen Lord.

John Meier brings precision to this issue when he asks two questions: "Is it historically true that Jesus held a last Supper with his disciples?" "Is it historically true that, during that supper, Jesus did and said certain things regarding bread and wine that form the basis of the later Christian celebration of the eucharist?"[2] To both of these historical questions, Meier answers with an unequivocal "yes." But one needs to note that there is considerable nuance contained in the way he phrases these questions. For he adds something with which most students of eucharistic origins will agree: "We must appreciate that the Last Supper and eucharist are not the same thing pure and simple."[3]

If that is the case, how does one move from the dominical instituting moment with Jesus at the Last Supper to the full-fledged eucharistic celebration that one can find, for example, in the anaphoras associated with the names of Chrysostom and Basil that were developing by the end of the fourth century in the "golden age" of patristic theology? That story has not been fully told, nor is it within the purpose and competence of my essay to try to tell it. Actually, unless a lot more data from the first few Christian centuries can be recovered than is presently available, that full story may never be told.[4] The available evidence indicates that it is a misconception, although a common one, to assume that there is *one* story, one relatively unified line of development from the Last Supper to the fully developed Eucharist. "Eucharist" is, of course, not an equivocal concept, but neither is it unqualifiedly univocal. For as one looks back and looks around, one sees that there have been and still are many different ways of celebrating the Eucharist. The exegetical and historical data indicate that this seems to be true *right from the beginning.* The starting point of this article is the apparent fact that the New Testament gives witness to a number of different Eucharists, or, more precisely perhaps, different practices of religious table fellowship that can be called Eucharists.

The first main part of my article will outline some of the major developments over the last century in the history and theology of eucharistic origins. This is done primarily, but not exclusively, from a Roman Catholic or high-church sacramental point of view. In a second section, using as a foil the exegetical research and interpretations of Bruce Chilton, I sketch out what one can know and what one can surmise about the different "Eucharists" in the New Testament. The third and concluding section begins to explore the significance and consequences of this for theology, ecclesiology, liturgical theology, and ecumenical theology.

Before beginning, let me be open about the fact that one of the purposes of this essay, as I have come to realize in the course of writing it, is apologetic. I mean apologetics not in the sense of defending Christianity against attacks from without, but defending Christianity from that internal undermining that takes place when Christian theologians do not deal adequately with facts that are generally accessible to serious scholars. For example, Elizabeth Johnson, reviewing John Haught's recent *Deeper Than Darwin,* a book that she describes as "an apologetics without rancor," writes: "One reason why scientifically educated people today have little interest in formal religion is the failure of theology to integrate the revelatory experience of a personal God into an expansive cosmological setting."[5] Analogously, one reason why people educated with a historical awareness have difficulty today taking the church seriously is its failure, and the failure of pastoral liturgical theology, to integrate into its official forms of worship both the insights of modernity—let alone postmodernity—and the generally accessible facts of history and culture.

Major Twentieth-Century Developments
in Eucharistic Theology

The twentieth century saw several paradigm shifts in the interpretation of the eucharistic texts of the New Testament.[6] At the beginning of
the century, Protestant-Catholic polemical positions dominated. Each
side tended to read the texts as supporting its own particular position.
Catholics saw them as supporting its understanding both of the transubstantiated real presence and of the eucharistic celebration itself as
a sacrifice. Protestants generally claimed the opposite. However, even
then, the development of liturgical studies and the inexorable advance
of the historical-critical method indicated that the days of respect-
ability for such polemically driven exegesis and interpretation were
numbered. The work of Dom Gregory Dix in 1945 was a singular sign
of this move away from the polemical. His particular findings, however adopted or modified by others, remain a striking example of liturgical research that is acclaimed for its value to a broad range of scholars
and theologians across the ecumenical spectrum.[7] But the first significant breakthrough might well have been what was taking place from
the mid 1930s in the work of Joachim Jeremias on *The Eucharistic Words
of Jesus.*[8] Jeremias expertly drew on the resources of modern philology
in the effort to recover, at least conjecturally, the *ipsissima verba Jesu.*
Even critics who questioned the validity of the venture had to respect
the enormous scholarship at work.[9]

On the other hand, more conservative scholars, among them
Catholic exegetes still struggling under the restrictive instructions of
the Pontifical Biblical Commission, found the method and results con-
genial.[10] Jeremias argued that behind the four extant accounts of the institution of the Eucharist (Mk 14:22–25, Mt 26:26–29, Lk 22:19–20,
and 1 Cor 11:23–26, as well as Jn 6:51b–57), there can be discerned
a "primitive Semitic tradition . . . traceable back into the first decade
after the death of Jesus with the assistance of exact philological observation."[11] However, the meaning of the reconstituted *verba* could still
be debated. For, as Chilton put it, "the debate between those who see
the Gospels as literally true reports and those who see them as literary
fictions shows little sign of making progress."[12] Sometimes this debate
circles around the category of "cult legend." In terms of literary genre,

it is unproblematic to read such narratives in the Gospels as cult legends, as long as one understands cult legend in the neutral sense. But if one understands a cult legend as necessarily having no historical basis, the debate is on.[13] Jeremias provided strong support for those who favored the historical side of the debate. The available evidence, however, embedded as it is in faith documents, does not, as exegetes now more readily admit, allow for definitive scientific conclusions. In addition, as indicated above, and as the body of my essay demonstrates, the idea that there is just one line of development in the early history of the Eucharist seems to be a misconception.

Another significant breakthrough in this trajectory of development took place in the 1950s in the work of exegetes like Heinz Schürmann and theologians like Johannes Betz.[14] These scholars and others like them brought to bear all the resources of the increasingly sophisticated methods of historical criticism and historical liturgical studies in order to work from the New Testament texts back towards the probable shape and meaning of the words of institution in a very early Christian Eucharist. Rather than a major paradigm shift, however, this effort was more of a continuation of the attempt, à la Jeremias, to work back towards an (i.e., "the") original form of the Eucharist. The result was what Betz called the "Antioch-Palestinian account," a reconstruction of the probable wording of the eucharistic celebration in Antioch within ten or fifteen years of the original Last Supper. This reconstruction reads (with the more conjectural elements in parentheses):

The Lord Jesus, on the night he was betrayed
took (taking?) bread, and, having said a prayer of thanks,
he broke [it] (and gave [it] to them) and said:
this is my body which is given for many;
(do this in memory of me.)
In the same way also the cup, after supper, saying:
this cup [is] the (new?) covenant in my blood;
(do this in memory of me).[15]

This reconstruction, it was claimed, even with the removal of its more conjectural elements, contains, at least virtually, a remarkably well-developed theology of the Eucharist. It also lies chronologically so close to the historical Jesus that it cannot easily be written off as due primarily to the process of community formation. Finally, it allows one to sketch out both a reliable picture of the at least implicit eucharistic theology of the first generation and some clear indications of what Jesus probably had in mind in instituting the Eucharist.[16] But all this still suffered under major limitations. Left unresolved was the debate between "literally true reports" and "literary fictions," as can be seen in Betz's debate with Willi Marxsen and with the more radical form critics.[17] It also continued to assume, what is now challenged by more recent liturgical scholars like Paul Bradshaw, that there was something like a linear development in the earliest Eucharists. The work of Rudolf Pesch,[18] who took the Last Supper account of Mark as, in effect, a preferred historical source, has not been widely accepted, and in any case it fails to break out of the methodological history-versus-fiction impasse.

The Six "Eucharists" in the New Testament

In this ongoing search for eucharistic origins, the work of Bruce Chilton suggests that we have come to a significant paradigmatic breakthrough.[19] This breakthrough has been prepared by a half century of New Testament redaction criticism and the continual refinement of critical methods that have made scholars more sensitive to the sometimes irreducible particularities of the biblical texts. To be able to "find"[20] in the New Testament six different ways of celebrating what Christians came to call the Eucharist, and to locate each of these in its own specific socio-religio-political setting, each with its own theological implications and thus, cumulatively, with massive theological implications, brings one paradigmatically into a whole new situation. If Chilton's exegetical findings are accurate, indeed even if they should be only approximately accurate, leaving details to be argued about, this would seem to make irrelevant, or at least to sublate, a number of time-honored scholarly approaches of the kind I have been describing. Fundamental to these traditional scholarly approaches (to which I myself have also adhered) was, first, the importance given to the already-mentioned "literally true" vs. "literary fictions" debate, and, second, the assumption that there was a somewhat unified line of development that one could trace from the established Eucharist of later centuries back close to the time of the historical Jesus. History and exegesis now seriously question the hegemony of such assumptions.

Jesus' Practice of Table Fellowship

Jesus joined with his followers in Galilee and Judea, both disciples and sympathizers, in meals that were designed to anticipate the coming of God's kingdom. The meals were characterized by a readiness to accept the hospitality and the produce of Israel at large. A willingness to provide for the meals, to join in the fellowship, to forgive and to be forgiven, was seen by Jesus as a sufficient condition for eating in his company and for entry into the kingdom.[21]

Jesus' view of purity was doubtlessly quite lax in the estimation of the rabbis of his time, for the carefully guarded purity rules defined who could share in meals, the primary marker of social grouping in first-century Palestine. Jesus' "rules" were distinctive in that they did not seem to restrict purity—access to meals with him, which seemed to imply anticipatory access to the kingdom he was proclaiming—to any already existing religious, family, or social group. It is not that he was unconcerned with purity, but his approach to it was distinctive in its inclusiveness. For Jesus, the primary markers of purity, the primary requirements for table fellowship in the kingdom were: Israel as forgiven and willing to provide of its own produce. Chilton sees this practice of table fellowship as the first type in the development of the Eucharist. Thus far, few, if any, would disagree with at least the major thrust of such findings.[22]

The "Last" Supper

Despite the controversy involved, Jesus might have continued this practice indefinitely. But, in the incident referred to as the Cleansing of the Temple, he also sought to influence or reform purity practices associated with the Temple. Given the importance of the Temple, this attempt to occupy it—that is, to change its purity rules—might have been enough to bring about his execution. But the authorities did not act immediately, and Jesus, apparently realizing that he had not succeeded, took a significant further step. In his meals, as he shared wine, he started referring to it as the equivalent of the blood of an animal shed in sacrifice, and, in sharing bread, claimed that its value was that of sacrificial flesh. Here was a sacrifice of sharings that the authorities could not control and that the nature of Jesus' movement made it impossible for them to ignore. "In essence," Chilton writes, "Jesus made his meals into a rival altar, and we may call . . . this second type of Eucharist [which] offered wine and bread . . . a mimetic surrogate of sacrifice."[23]

Against the many voices that will protest that this massively over-interprets the exegetical and historical evidence—and I do agree that there is over-interpretation here—let me make two immediate observations and a request. First, I will come back later to some of the exegetical data and arguments that can support Chilton's position on this point. Second, the theological implications of there being a number of different "Eucharists" in the New Testament (that is, at least types of religious table fellowship) that constitute the main purpose of this essay do not stand or fall with one's agreement or nonagreement with any particular detail, or with this particular interpretation of Jesus' Last Supper. Thus, I ask readers to suspend temporarily their possible skepticism on this point while I work out the rest of the exposition.

Petrine Christianity: The Blessing and Breaking of Bread at Home

In this stage of eucharistic development, the *berakhah* prayer of Judaism seems to have become a principal model of Eucharist. Bread took precedence over wine, and, as Acts 1:12–26, 2:46, and 3:1–4:37 clearly describe, a double domestication took place. Instead of seeking the hospitality of others, as the itinerant Jesus seemed to do, adherents of the movement, under the leadership of Peter or the Twelve, gathered in the homes of colleagues where they "broke bread at home and ate their food with glad and generous hearts, praising God and having the goodwill of all the people" (Acts 2:46–47). In addition, apparently they also acknowledged the validity of sacrifice in the Temple. In doing this they seemed—if the Gospel accounts of the Last Supper and this account of primitive Christian worship have significant historical content—to be changing the nature of the meal and the memory of what Jesus had said at that meal. For example, there is no mention of wine nor does there seem, in this account of the earliest Christian gatherings, to be any sense of being in tension with the officials or the religious practices of Judaism.[24]

These are facts and inconsistencies that cry out for an explanation. Chilton's hypothesis, actually supported by what meager historical evidence is available, offers such an explanation, namely, that in the years immediately following Jesus' death, the cultic regulations of the Temple had temporarily shifted to something much closer to what Jesus was agitating for. At the very least, whatever hypothesis is followed, this Eucharist (or pre-Eucharist) of the primitive church described in Acts seems to have been quite different from the synoptic accounts of the Last Supper and the reflection of those found in John 6. However, in terms of eucharistic origins, this practice as described in Acts was anything but a phase to be passed through and then forgotten. For from this phase of the development came two additional constitutive features of the Christian Eucharist: the construal of the supper as a sacrifice of sharings with specifically covenantal meaning and the repetitive, ritual character of the Christian meal.[25]

The Passover, the Circle of James

The tendency toward domestication is here pursued further, for the Eucharist is now seen as a seder, open only to Jews in a state of purity, and to be celebrated only once a year, at Passover, in Jerusalem, as prescribed in Exodus 12:48. The effect of this Jacobean program (a possible antecedent to the later Quartodeciman practice?), Chilton writes, was "to integrate Jesus' movement fully within the liturgical institutions of Judaism, and to insist upon the Judaic identity of the movement and upon Jerusalem as its governing center," but without actually replacing Israel's seder.[26]

Paul and the Synoptic Gospels

Locating the Last Supper on the night on which Jesus was betrayed (1 Cor 11:23), Paul vehemently resisted Jacobean claims. He also emphasized the link between Jesus' death and the Eucharist, and he accepts what Chilton calls the Hellenistic refinement of the Petrine type that presented the Eucharist as a sacrifice for sin.[27] This Pauline type is also what we find in the synoptic Gospels, which use words to suggest that Jesus' blood is shed in the interests of the communities for which those Gospels were composed: for the "many" in Damascus (Mt 26:28) and in Rome (Mk 14:24); and on behalf of "you," in Antioch (Lk 22:20). The synoptic Gospels also emphasize the heroism of Jesus so as to make the meal an occasion to join in the solidarity of martyrdom. In addition, the synoptics have two miraculous feeding stories that symbolize the inclusion even of non-Jews within Eucharist understood as a sort of philosophical symposium (see Mk 6:32–44, 8:1–10, and parallels).[28]

The Gospel of John

Jesus identifies himself in John 6 as the *manna*, a motif already in Paul (1 Cor 10:1–4), but now developed to construe the Eucharist as a mystery in which Jesus, not literally but sacramentally, offers/gives his own personal body and blood in Eucharist. This construal would probably not be a totally new idea to Hellenistic Christians who followed synoptic practice. But Johannine practice now makes this meaning explicit. It was, as is characteristic of the fourth Gospel, an unambiguous, clear break with Judaism as understood by Chilton. For with this development, Eucharist has become a "sacrament" understandable only in Hellenistic terms, and involving "a knowing conflict with the ordinary understanding of what Judaism might and might not include."[29]

To sum up, Chilton's purpose in laying out the evidence for these different Eucharists in the New Testament is to free us from such "reductionist regimens, which will have the Gospels be only historical or only fictive, [and thus] starve the reader of the meanings that generated the texts to hand." The generative exegesis of eucharistic texts that he proposes does not allow one to conclude "a single meaning that is alleged to have occasioned all the others," nor, in this approach, does the initial meaning determine the final meaning.[30]

Theological Implications

As I noted earlier, the theological implications or consequences of these findings do not depend on full agreement regarding all the exegetical details and interpretive reconstructions that Chilton lays out. There is significant debate, and in some cases significant disagreement about certain details of Chilton's interpretations. Despite this debate, it is my assumption that there is a consensus among critical exegetes and liturgical historians that what Chilton attempts to do is what they attempt to do. I argue that his findings, even if reduced by many grains of salt, are sufficiently similar to findings common among exegetes and historians so as to require serious attention. There is enough there to oblige theologians across a wide spectrum of subdisciplines—theology, ecclesiology, liturgy, ecumenism, and pastoral theology—to sit up and take notice. But allow me now to formulate some further remarks about Chilton's methodology.

Methodology

When one stands back and looks at the large picture, one can see that over the past century there has been a series of ever more sophisticated refinements in the historical-critical method. For the purposes of this essay, one of the most significant of these developments has been the general acceptance of *Redaktionsgeschichte* and the now broadly recognized need to attend to the specific context and purposes of each biblical author. These refinements are now increasingly being applied to the study of patristics, church history, liturgical history, and, as here, the history of eucharistic origins. Fifty or sixty years ago, Chilton's whole approach could easily have been dismissed as reductionism by mainstream theologians. Now, only a fundamentalist or biblical literalist could so dismiss them. However, though not rejected, findings like those of Chilton have not yet been appropriated and seriously dealt with by the common body of mainstream Christian theologians (as distinct from exegetes and historians). It is by theologians, especially by church theologians, that Chilton's views are likely to be seen as new and upsetting. I single out two points where Chilton's findings and exegetical reconstructions are especially likely, for theological reasons, to encounter strong resistance.

The first is his reconstruction of what Jesus did at the Last Supper.[31] Few exegetes would contest the general thrust of Chilton's characterization of Jesus' practice of inclusive table fellowship. Nor would they seriously contest that at the meal of Jesus commonly called "last,"— or, by extension, in his final few meals with his disciples—something special, something new, took place, after which he was immediately arrested and executed.[32] What one can obviously contest are the details of Chilton's interpretive reconstruction to the effect that Jesus was probably saying something like: "this bread [that is available to any and all] is what serves for me—for you, for us—as the flesh of sacrifice"; and "this wine [that is available to any and all] is what serves for me— for you, for all—as the blood of sacrifice." Many will obviously find this to be an overly conjectural and minimalist reconstruction. For those committed to viewing the Eucharist that is now celebrated as "doing what the Lord did the night before he died," it is an unacceptably minimalist reconstruction.

But in defense of such a reconstruction one can point out that it has great explanatory power. It, or something like this, helps to explain why the authorities, who apparently did not act immediately after Jesus' action in the Temple,[33] now act quickly. It also helps set up the context of the Eucharist in the circle of Peter (see Acts 2:43–47) that apparently, at least as Chilton interprets it, "changed the nature of the meal and the memory of what Jesus had said at 'the Last Supper.'"[34] Breaking bread "in their homes" and going "to the Temple area together every day" (Acts 2:46) is not the kind of challenging, or revolutionary activity that even our minimalist reconstruction suggests, let alone a maximalist reconstruction. If the community of Acts 2:43–47, even according to a minimalist reconstruction, was doing what Jesus did the night before he died, it would hardly have been "having the good will of all the people" (Acts 2:47).

Notice the methodological shift that is taking place here. In contrast to traditional theologies of eucharistic origins, this approach is not an attempt to find in the various words of the New Testament a line of development (at times awkwardly harmonized) that would enable one to explain the more developed theology and praxis of the church's Eucharist. Instead of that, this approach tries to identify and reconstruct the praxis that explains the words that have come down to us in the New Testament. There is, of course, some circularity here, as there necessarily is in any such interpretation of limited data. For one first has to use the words that have been handed down to us in order to reconstruct the praxis that explains the words. The result is that reconstructing in this way, a way that makes better use of modern historical-critical tools, reveals a pluriform eucharistic practice in the New Testament church and, in our case, the six types of "Eucharist" (or of the practice of table fellowship that might be called "Eucharist") that Chilton finds there.

A second (but related) point where Chilton's findings and reconstructions are likely to meet theological resistance is the place where he locates what theologians, especially in the Western church, tend to see as the heart of eucharistic theology: the autobiographical identification of the meal elements of bread and wine with the body and blood of Jesus. Chilton locates this explicitly only in the sixth (Johannine) type of the Eucharist, and only implicitly or inchoatively in the fifth (Pauline and synoptic) type. Historical criticism does not allow one to trace this identification all the way back to the historical Last Supper. But traditional theological approaches still use that criticism in an attempt — à la Jeremias, Schürmann, Betz, and, more recently, Meier — to trace it back as far as possible. But careful attention to the exegetical evidence *in its own right and in its own context,* suggests that this approach, especially the use to which it is put by much traditional theology and preaching, may owe more to Procrustes than to the Holy Spirit.

Theology

The Eucharist, the central sacrament of the church, was instituted by Christ. It is not the "that" but the "how" of this affirmation that is in question here. For it is clear that the Eucharist was not instituted by Jesus in the historicizing manner that has been taken for granted as the basic position of Christian orthodoxy. We do not know and cannot reconstruct in precise detail what Jesus did at his "Last Supper." The New Testament itself remembered and interpreted what Jesus did in quite different ways. Attending to these differences undermines the assumption that there is a single line of development that runs from Jesus to the later Eucharist of the church, and that can be traced back by us towards Jesus. And indeed, if by Eucharist is meant what is now done in the church, the farther back one goes, for example, to the "Eucharists" of James, Peter, and Jesus, the farther one gets from the Eucharist of the present. Indeed, if an exact reconstruction of what Jesus did at the Last Supper were possible, it would probably look quite different from what Christians now celebrate.

Where then, does that leave us? How should one react to this loss of what was formerly thought to be the sure foundation of eucharistic theology? One way would be to succumb to the temptation to react the way so many did over Galileo's hypotheses, thinking that the Bible really does teach us how the heavens go instead of how to go to heaven. That is why so many want to read the New Testament as teaching them how to celebrate the Eucharist, instead of reading it as revealing something about the different ways in which Jesus and some of his earliest followers celebrated table fellowship, ways that have grown (with the Holy Spirit guiding) into the somewhat different ways in which today's Christian churches celebrate the Eucharist. But if these are the alternatives, the Christian theologian is left with the unsettling question: Is there any anchor, any port of refuge from the Scylla of an uncritical dogmatic fideism and the Charybdis of a reductionist relativism? Let me suggest two.

First, theologians must renew both their faith in Jesus' promise to be with his church and their faith in the presence and activity of the Holy Spirit in the church and world. The Eucharists that we now celebrate are what the church, under the guidance of the Holy Spirit of Jesus, learned to do over the course of the first few centuries as it celebrated table fellowship in memory of Jesus. I have consciously used the plural, Eucharists, not to undercut the affirmation of the Eucharist as the sacrament of unity (at least in hope), but simply to point out that Christians have significantly different ways of celebrating Eucharist, as the recent Roman Catholic recognition of the Chaldaean Anaphora of Addai and Mari reminds us.[35] In other words, one does not need to be able to trace eucharistic praxis back to the historical Jesus or even to the New Testament in order to legitimate it.

A second suggestion is to rephrase or relocate the question that is being asked. Instead of asking only how the earliest Eucharists can teach us anything at all — if we have so little data with which to reconstruct them, and if the reconstructions are so different and at times so contradictory to each other — perhaps it is a very different question that needs to be asked. Where, for example, do Christians now meet God? Where and how do Christians, as living stones in God's Temple (see 1 Pt 2:5–10) offer sacrifice? How do they enter into, become ritually, sacramentally, and really present to, the Christ-event? They do this by both celebrating Eucharist together and, in an extension of that liturgical act, making that Eucharist real by living it out in their daily lives. In the eucharistic celebration, a Christian assembly with its duly appointed presider prays to the Father through the Son, asking the Father to send the Holy Spirit to transform the eucharistic gifts and, through that transformation, to continue to transform the eucharistic assembly into the Body of Christ. This is a marital covenant event in which is actualized the closest relation that is possible between the church and the church's divine partner.[36] On the part of the members of the eucharistic assembly, their participation in the offering of Christian sacrifice is a dynamic, interpersonal reality that begins with the self-offering of the Father in the gift of the Son, continues with the totally free and loving self-offering response of the Son in his humanity to the Father and for us, and then, finally, becomes "Christian sacrifice" when the Christians themselves, in the power of the same Spirit that was in Jesus, are transformatively (at least inchoatively) taken up into that trinitarian reality.[37]

This, in the full theological sense, is what is happening when one celebrates Eucharist. If it is not happening, both liturgically and in one's everyday life, one must challenge, as Paul did in his context (1 Cor 11:17–30, especially v. 20), whether it is indeed the Lord's Supper that is being celebrated. It is critically important to realize that the theological developments that make possible this theological sketch of the Eucharist were spread out over the first four Christian centuries. This was the time it took for the theology of the Trinity to reach some maturity, and for that theology to become embedded in the classical eucharistic prayers that are associated with the names of Chrysostom and Basil. In other words, for a true understanding of the Eucharist, one must look primarily to what has developed in the church rather than to fragile reconstructions of the earliest Christian Eucharists.

Ecclesiology

My exposition has already located the Eucharist as a church event, indeed *the* church event par excellence. So, what does ecclesiology have to say? There is a curious irony here. Many of the implications and consequences of what I have been developing challenge the adequacy of a number of aspects, even recently emphasized aspects, of official Roman Catholic magisterial teaching. But on the other hand, this same development powerfully elevates the centrality and role of the church, in the development of eucharistic praxis and theology. This tension is palpable in the very title of the Holy Thursday Encyclical of John Paul II: *Ecclesia de Eucharistia* (April 17, 2003). The dynamic line of development that the Pope presumably has in mind is the traditional Catholic way of conceiving that Christ/God ordains the priest to act *in persona Christi* in confecting the Eucharist, and from that comes the church: *Ecclesia de Eucharistia*. However, the dynamic line of development that lies behind this essay, and which corresponds to the conceptions of most contemporary liturgical theologians, is that Christ and the church are in a dynamic (covenantal/marital) relationship out of which comes the Eucharist. In this conception, the priest is perceived as being more *in persona Christi capitis ecclesiae* (in the person of Christ, head of the church), and indeed not as a kind of mediator between Christ and the church but as embedded in the Christ–church relationship.[38]

There are very significant differences between these two conceptions and their various theoretical and practical consequences. If these are to be worked out peacefully, the official magisterium and the theologians of the church will have to call much more earnestly upon the

Holy Spirit of wisdom, understanding, forebearance, and charity than perhaps they have in the past. In that Spirit, I suggest that the approach of this essay with its powerful emphasis on the role of the church in the patristic development of the classical eucharistic prayers should find some positive resonance with the official magisterium. It should enable the magisterium to think complementarily not only in terms of *Ecclesia de Eucharistia*, but also in terms of *Eucharistia de Ecclesia*.

Liturgical and Ecumenical Theology

"Liturgical" and "ecumenical" are consciously placed together in this section, reflecting the reality that the academic study of liturgy has long since become ecumenical, and that this ecumenical richness is already having its effect on the liturgical worship and practices of the different Christian churches.[39] But the main focus of my essay has been, first, on the fact that variety and even divergence have been characteristics of the Eucharist right from the beginning, and, second, on the implication that such variety has apparently always been integral to the Spirit-guided history of Christian liturgy and therefore should be integral to efforts to reform the liturgy.

This is by no means a plea for liturgical anarchy. We may at times chafe under it, but we cannot get along without church order. Paul's various practical instructions about who should speak, and in what tongues, and so forth, show that the concern for liturgical order goes back right to the first few decades of Christian table fellowship. And in the early third century, Origen's charming *Dialogue with Heraclides* suggests that the need for "conventions" in the celebration of the liturgy, in the public prayer of the church, has been a constant.[40] But the incontestable evidence of great variety and diversity suggests that the greater tolerance of liturgical diversity in the Protestant churches, in contrast to the Catholic Church, is more in line with the overall Christian tradition, including, as I indicated earlier, what one can reconstruct of Jesus' practice of table fellowship.

Here, however, as in most human situations, there are few absolutes. There is, on the one hand, the general right and need of Christian assemblies to have "conventions" of public praying and worship with which they can become reasonably comfortable and within which they can grow spiritually. A primary purpose of liturgical rules and regulations is to take care of this need for convention. But overemphasis on rules can lead to atrophy. Christian assemblies not only need to be made "comfortable," they also need to be challenged. How can the right balance, the right tension, between these two needs be achieved? One way, while meeting the basic need for liturgical communities to have conventions with which they can be comfortable, might be to put much more emphasis on ecumenical and interreligious relationships in worship. Another way, increasingly available to people living in the global village, is to become familiar with the way different cultures worship differently, even within the same communion. Observe, for example, how an appropriate veneration of ancestors is becoming a natural part of Christian worship, often in advance of official approval, in many Asian and African cultures. In other words, there is need to recognize and validate the experience of the sacred, the holy, the transcendent that can take place when Christians share in — or even just come close to — the worship of people who "do it differently."[41]

Pastoral and Homiletic Implications

This may be the most delicate and, in practical terms, most important part of my study. Most of what has gone before could be categorized as theory and thus left for a relatively few theologians to argue about. Guardians of magisterial orthodoxy, if they become aware of it, might see it as the kind of annoying thing theological journals sometimes publish, but not something to get deeply concerned about, since so few people read such journals. Still, if it is improper to sing "At that first Eucharist . . ." and misleading to preach simplistically about "doing what Jesus did the night before he died," one needs then to teach and communicate responsibly the more complex development of the Eucharist to the Christian faithful.

First, and my enumeration is not intended to suggest priority, one must be sensitively aware that this new paradigm for studying eucharistic origins and their implications will seem, to some, to be directly threatening the basis of their belief in the Eucharist. Therefore, in homiletic and catechetical situations one should first of all avoid anything that seems to be a frontal attack on traditional theological and religious assumptions. Rather than trying to pull people through one's own door—for example, by explaining more or less directly, as my essay tries to do, what a more adequate theory of eucharistic origins might be—one should explore the possibilities of "entering through their door." For example, analogous to what I have suggested as pastoral strategy for "unveiling" Christian sacrifice,[42] by not using the easily misunderstood terminology of "sacrifice" until people have been alerted to the authentic experience of Christian sacrificial living in their own lives, one should attempt, *mutatis mutandis,* to do the same here.

Second, teachers and preachers should work to reconceive and rephrase their teaching and preaching about the eucharistic mystery in order to avoid doing and saying those things that seem to support—or worse, seem to absolutize—the old paradigm. For example, while not challenging traditional belief in the transformation of the eucharistic gifts, one can find ways to emphasize that the most important transformation is the one that is taking place in the Christian faithful as they celebrate and go forth to live the Eucharist. In other words, one needs to find helpful ways to stress that the most important transformation is not the one that takes place "without," on the altar, in the physical realm, however important that transformation really is, but the one that takes place "within," in the spiritual realm of grace.

Third, teachers and preachers must constantly be attentive to how people react to new emphases and be ready to comfort them in their disorientation. It can help to point out that Peter, James, and Paul had quite different ideas about Eucharist, not all of which could be harmonized. There are things that they did that have not become part of our eucharistic praxis, and there are things in our eucharistic praxis that were not part of theirs. One needs to remind people that it took the Holy Spirit about three centuries to bring the church—or, more accurately, perhaps, some of the Christian churches—to an understanding of the Eucharist that approximates our understanding of the Eucharist. And also one needs to remind the faithful that, as the whole Christian tradition teaches, and as Vatican II showed and taught, Jesus is still present to the church and the Holy Spirit is still at work in the church.

Finally, while the church has and must have a major concern for order, and in this case for appropriate liturgical "conventions," this church is also, and apparently going right back to Jesus himself, the Body in which developments, and sometimes conflicting and apparently irreconcilable developments, have taken place. Some of these conflicts are abuses and scandals that one must, in charity, learn to move beyond, as is now finally being done with many of our traditional Protestant-Catholic conflicts. Other conflicts are more internal. We must deal with the conflicts in fidelity, wisdom, patience, and—above all—charity, so that they may be a source of learning as well.

Notes

1. This essay was first published in *Theological Studies* 66 (2005): 85–112. It is reprinted here with a grateful acknowledgement of the editor's kindness.

2. John Meier, "The Eucharist and the Last Supper: Did It Happen?" *Theology Digest* 42 (Winter, 1995), 347.

3. Ibid., 348.

4. Paul Bradshaw, *The Search for the Origins of Christian Worship: Sources and Methods for the Study of Early Liturgy,* 2nd ed. (New York: Oxford University Press, 2002), points out that the presently available historical information about liturgy in the first few centuries is but a fraction of what would be needed to sketch out a reliable history of it.

5. Elizabeth Johnson, C.S.J., *America* 189, November 17, 2003, 18. See John Haught, *Deeper Than Darwin: The Prospect for Religion in the Age of Evolution* (Boulder, CO: Westview Press, 2003).

6. Much of what follows in the next few pages is a summarizing update—and also correction—of what I wrote in "The Eucharist and Redemption: The Last Supper and Jesus' Understanding of His Death," *Biblical Theology Bulletin* 9 (1981): 21–27.

7. Dom Gregory Dix, O.S.B., *The Shape of the Liturgy* (London: Dacre, 1945).

8. Joachim Jeremias, *Die Abendmahlsworte Jesu* (Göttingen: Vandenhoeck & Ruprecht, 1960; first ed. 1935); English trans., *The Eucharistic Words of Jesus,* with the author's revisions (London: SCM, 1966; repr., Philadelphia: Westminster, 1977).

9. Critical scholarship recognizes that the New Testament eucharistic words of institution are already the result of community formation. Working back to their likely formulation in Aramaic does not necessarily bring us back to the *ipsissima verba Jesu.*

10. In those early years, before the "Magna Carta" of Catholic biblical scholarship, the 1947 encyclical, *Divino afflante Spiritu,* Catholic exegetes found it safer to focus more on philological exegesis than on the more "radical" aspects of the historical-critical method, such as source criticism and form criticism.

11. Jeremias, *The Eucharistic Words of Jesus* (1964), 196.

12. Bruce Chilton, "The Eucharist and the Mimesis of Sacrifice," an essay included in the present volume, 141–42. His essay recounts many of the findings of his earlier works: *The Temple of Jesus: His Sacrificial Program Within a Cultural History of Sacrifice* (University Park: Pennsylvania State University Press, 1992) and *A Feast of Meanings: Eucharistic Theologies from Jesus through Johannine Circles* (New York: E. J. Brill, 1994).

13. See Meier, "The Eucharist and the Last Supper," 336.

14. Johannes Betz, *Die Eucharistie in der Zeit der griechischen Väter. I/1: Die Aktualpräsenz der Person und des Heilswerkes Jesu im Abendmahl nach der vorephesinischen griechischen Patristik* (Freiburg: Herder, 1955); *II/1: Die Realprasenz des Leibes und Blutes Jesu im Abendmahl nach dem Neuen Testament* (1961; 2nd ed., 1964); "Eucharist (I. Theological)," *Sacramentum Mundi 2* (New York: Herder and Herder, 1968), 257–67. Heinz Schürmann, "Die Semitismen im Einsetzungsbericht bei Markus und bei Lukas (Mk 14, 22–24; Lk 22, 19b–20)," *Zeitschrift für katholische Theologie* 73 (1951): 72–77; "Lk 22, 19b–20 als ursprüngliche Textüberlieferung," *Biblica* 32 (1951): 364–92; 522–41; *Der Paschamahlbericht Lk 22, (7–14) 15–18,* Neutestamentliche Abhandlungen 19/5 (Münster: Aschendorff, 1955); *Der Einsetzungsbericht Lk 22, 19–20,* Neutestamentliche Abhandlungen 20/4 (Münster: Aschendorff, 1955); "Die Gestalt der urchristliche Eucharistiefeier," *Münchener theologische Zeitschrift* 6 (1959): 107–31; "Eucharistiefeier (urchristliche)," *Lexikon für Theologie und Kirche* (2nd ed., 1959), 1159–162.

15. Betz, *Die Eucharistie,* II/1, 18. Meier, some thirty-five years later makes basically the same move, a bit more reserved in his reconstruction of the *verba,* but also a bit more bold in his openness to see them as *ipsissima verba Jesu:* He writes: "The closest we can get to the earliest form of the narrative is this: 'He [i.e., Jesus] took bread, and giving thanks [or: pronouncing a blessing], broke [it] and said: "This is my body." Likewise also the cup, after supper, saying: "This cup is the covenant in my blood."' Obviously, the words spoken by Jesus would be older than the narrative surrounding them. At least the very 'words of institution,' as we call them, may well go back to Jesus himself" (Meier, "The Eucharist and the Last Supper," 347).

16. See Daly, "The Eucharist and Redemption," 22–23.

17. See Johannes Betz, *Die Eucharistie,* II/1, 215–18. Betz is challenging Willi Marxsen, *Das Abendmahl als christologisches Problem* (Gütersloh: G. Mohn, 1963); English trans., *The Lord's Supper as a Christological Problem* (Philadelphia: Fortress, 1970).

18. Rudolf Pesch, *Das Abendmahl und Jesu Todesverständnis,* Quaestiones Disputatae 80 (Freiburg: Herder, 1978); "Die Abendmahlsüberlieferung," in *Das*

Markusevangelium: Zweiter Teil; Kommentar zu Kap. 8,27—16,20, Herders theologische Kommentar zum Neuen Testament 2/2 (Freiburg: Herder, 1977).

19. Regarding the scare quotes ("Eucharists") in the heading to this section: Although I am following Chilton as a convenient guide, I am aware that his exegetical findings, especially his interpretation of the data, may be out of step with that of other exegetes. Is it accurate, for example, to label as "Eucharist" all identifiable instances of New Testament table fellowship? I claim, nevertheless, that Chilton's findings are sufficiently close to what historians of the liturgy and other exegetes find in order to justify the kind of reflections I offer in the third part of this article.

20. "See" or "read" would be more accurate words, for what Chilton "finds" has always been there in the texts for anyone to see—granted, of course, that Chilton sees there much more than many others see.

21. Chilton, "Eucharist and the Mimesis of Sacrifice," 143. For the exegetical details see *A Feast of Meanings,* esp. chap. 1, "The Purity of the Kingdom," 13–45.

22. Few will dispute that Jesus' "rules" for table fellowship seemed to be distinctive in their inclusiveness. But to specify these "rules" as, simply, "Israel as forgiven and willing to provide of its own produce" can be seen as interpreting beyond the evidence.

23. Chilton, "Eucharist and the Mimesis of Sacrifice," 146. For the exegetical details see *A Feast of Meanings,* esp. chap. 2, "The Surrogate of Sacrifice," 46–74.

24. Chilton, *Feast of Meanings,* esp. chap. 3, "The Covenantal Sacrifice of Sharings," 75–92.

25. Ibid., 88–89.

26. Chilton, "Eucharist and the Mimesis of Sacrifice," 147. See also Chilton, *Feast of Meanings,* esp. chap. 4, "The Passover," 92–108.

27. To call this a "Hellenistic refinement" is a bit puzzling, because there would seem to be at least as much evidence to suggest calling it a specifically Jewish refinement. See the section "Sin Offering and Atonement" in Robert J. Daly, S.J., *The Origins of the Christian Doctrine of Sacrifice* (Philadelphia: Fortress, 1978), 25–35; and the multiple references to sin offering in the index of Daly, *Chistian Sacrifice,* Studies in Christian Antiquity 18 (Washington: Catholic University of America Press, 1978).

28. Chilton, *A Feast of Meanings,* esp. chap. 5, "The Heroic Hata'at: Pauline and Synoptic Symposia," 109–30. But I also ask here the same question as in the previous footnote: do not the Jewish traditions regarding the messianic/eschatological banquet provide as much, if not more, background than Hellenistic ideas of a philosophical symposium?

29. Chilton, "Eucharist and the Mimesis of Sacrifice," 149. See also Chilton, *A Feast of Meanings,* esp. chap. 6, "The Miraculous Food of Paul and John," 131–45.

30. Chilton, "Eucharist and the Mimesis of Sacrifice," 149. In this same essay, Chilton goes on to say: "The meanings conveyed by words must be the point of de-

parture for a generative exegesis because those meanings are our only access to what produced the texts to hand. But having gained that access, it becomes evident that Eucharist is not a matter of the development of a single, basic meaning within several different environments [as I myself have previously assumed—RJD]. Those environments have themselves produced various meanings under the influence of definable practices. Eucharist was not simply handed on as a tradition. Eucharistic traditions were rather the catalyst that permitted communities to crystallize their own practice in oral or textual form. What they crystallized was a function of the practice that had been learned, palpable gestures with specified objects and previous meanings, along with the meanings and the emotional responses that the community discovered in Eucharist. There is no history of the tradition apart from a history of meaning, a history of emotional response, a history of practice: the practical result of a generative exegesis of eucharistic texts is that practice itself is an appropriate focus in understanding the New Testament" (149).

31. See above, my section on: The "Last" Supper.

32. *Post hoc*, however, does not necessarily mean *propter hoc*.

33. In "Eucharist and the Mimesis of Sacrifice," Chilton reads this action in the Temple not as a direct attack against the Temple cult, but as an attempt (not without precedent in the action of other rabbis) to change its purity regulations in order to make the sacrificial cult more easily accessible to ordinary Israelites. This made Jesus all the more a powerful nuisance whom the authorities would like to be rid of, but not yet the kind of direct threat that required immediate "neutralizing" action. This is, of course, a hypothetical reconstruction. Its main merit is not that it fills in the blanks and tells us with certainty what actually happened, but that it lays out a possible scenario. *Something* like this must have happened. Paradoxically, or ironically, this imaginative reconstruction, which sails closer to the line of "literary fiction" than "literal history," relies on the historicity of the chronology implied in these "fictions."

34. Chilton, "Eucharist and the Mimesis of Sacrifice," 147.

35. What is, for a traditional point of view, particularly startling about this is the official Roman Catholic affirmation of the validity of a eucharistic prayer that does not contain the words of institution. For an introductory account, see Robert F. Taft, "Mass without the Consecration?" *America* 188, May 12, 2003: 7–11. For a more detailed and scholarly account, see Robert F. Taft, "Mass without the Consecration? The Historic Agreement between the Catholic Church and the Assyrian Church of the East Promulgated 26 October 2001," *Worship* 77 (2003): 482–509.

36. See Edward J. Kilmartin, S.J., *The Eucharist in the West: History and Theology*, ed. Robert J. Daly, S.J. (Collegeville, MN: Liturgical Press, 1998), 346.

37. See Robert J. Daly, S.J., "Marriage, Eucharist, and Christian Sacrifice," *INTAMS Review* 9 (Spring 2003): 56–75, esp. 56–60; "Sacrifice Unveiled or Sacrifice Revisited: Trinitarian and Liturgical Perspectives," *Theological Studies* 64 (2003): 24–42; "Sacrifice: The Way to Enter the Paschal Mystery," *America* 188

(May 14, 2003): 14–17. Those familiar with recent developments in liturgical theology will recognize both in this article and in all my recent work on Eucharist and sacrifice the towering background influence of Edward J. Kilmartin, S.J. See especially his "The Catholic Tradition of Eucharistic Theology: Towards the Third Millennium," *Theological Studies* 55 (1994): 405–57, and, especially for this trinitarian understanding of sacrifice, *The Eucharist in the West*, 381–82.

38. See Robert J. Daly, S.J., "Robert Bellarmine and Post-Tridentine Eucharistic Theology," *Theological Studies* 61 (2000): 239–60.

39. Obvious instances of this are, to list a few: (1) what the Roman Catholic liturgical reform has learned from the Orthodox and Eastern Churches about the Epiclesis, and from the Protestants about the centrality of the Word in worship; (2) and from the other side, what the mainline Protestant churches have been learning from the Episcopalian, Catholic, and Eastern Churches about the broad richness of the liturgy; (3) the ecumenical membership, including their working groups and seminars, of the Societas Liturgica and the North American Academy of Liturgy; (4) the ecumenical structure and content of practically all recent hymnals; (5) the obvious (and acknowledged) ecumenical influence on the content and structure of the North American Presbyterian and Methodist worship books that also make them, in some respects, seem more "Catholic" than the Roman Catholic Sacramentary. For more on this topic, see Robert J. Daly, S.J., "Ecumenical Convergence in Christian Worship," in *Jesuits in Dialogue: "Ecumenism: Hopes and Challenges for the New Century," Secretariat for Interreligious Dialogue*, conference at Alexandria, Egypt, July 4–12, 2001; papers available from Curia S.J., C. P. 6139, 00195 Rome Prati, Italy.

40. See *Dialogue of Origen with Heraclides and His Fellow Bishops on the Father, the Son, and the Soul* 1–5, Ancient Christian Writers 54 (New York: Paulist, 1992), 57–61.

41. This is one of the major points of the impressive body of literature in "comparative theology" being produced by Francis X. Clooney, S.J.

42. See the articles listed above in n. 37.

SIX

Life after Death

Violence, Martyrdom, and Academic Life in Western Religions

ALAN F. SEGAL

There's nothing so American as a near death experience (NDE). According to a Gallup poll, eight to twelve million people in the United States have had one. That may not be a lot of people when compared with the whole population, but it is a sizeable minority. For instance, with that number we could populate a city about the size of New York. There are more NDE experiences in the United States than there are Jews. Abductions by aliens also contain many formal similarities to these stories and indeed the special effects in the movies are quite similar. So, for that huge majority of us who have never had an NDE, there is always education by television and the movies — the constant depiction of near death experiences in the media and the so-called "nonfiction" books, which explain them to us and instruct us on how to project our souls astrally so that we can have such experiences without risking a life-threatening trauma. Of course, I'm not counting the fact that everybody in New York has had a near death experience in a taxi cab. My classes and I have several times listed the number of films or TV programs that deal directly with the issue of the afterlife. It takes no more than five minutes to get a hundred or so recent films on the board.

I will just give one example, from the *Sopranos,* an ethnography of my adopted state, New Jersey. In it we see depicted a near death experience for an Italian gangster who sees the afterlife as an Irish Bar where every day is St. Patrick's Day. What makes Christopher Moltisanti's NDE so interesting is that it is a vision of hell, not heaven.

179

I don't think I would mind hell if it were an Irish bar, but then I'm not an Italian mobster. Had we been living in the Middle Ages, this vision of hell would have been the norm for a near death experience. Many people had dreams and visions of hell, often presented in literary fashion as a death-bed confession.[1] But Americans are different. Hell has practically fallen out of our religious imaginations. The worst that can happen is that we will need some therapy to adjust to the afterlife, as the film *What Dreams May Come* imagines. Apparently, life, liberty, and the pursuit of happiness means that the next life should be relatively as happy, making up for lost opportunities as well as injustices. Students of Eastern faiths take notice: life, liberty, and the pursuit of happiness depend upon three great ideas or illusions (depending on your perspective) of Western thought, the self (consciousness or the soul), free will, and the cosmos.

The Gallup poll's pervasive and helpful interest in American attitudes towards religion (and, believe it or not, the Gallup poll is our best source for quantified American religious attitudes) helps us clarify some crucial aspects of our religious life that Americans themselves often confuse. George Gallup (himself a religious man, which accounts for his constant interest) has authored two books on the afterlife, each with help from another scholar. Like the rest of us, Gallup is only able to produce hearsay reports. But they are interesting for what they tell us about ourselves. One is *The People's Religion: American Faith in the 90s.*[2] The other is *Adventures in Immortality.*[3] In them, the Gallup organization investigates various measures of what we Americans believe about our afterlife. If you trust me to evaluate their evidence, Americans almost always envision an afterlife in the form of immortality of the soul or some such similar carrier of identity after death. The numbers of Americans who believe in life after death is amazingly high: over seven in ten believe in it, a figure that is practically identical with the figures of half a century ago, and widely interpreted so as to dispute any notion that we Americans are losing our faith or that our society is secularizing. I actually think the detailed results show the opposite, but first let's look at the more amazing aspects of the polls: more Americans believe in a personal life after death than believe in a personal God. This belief is significantly higher than what statistics show for Canadians and most Europeans. To find similar results, you have to look to polls taken in Ireland and India. Spain and Italy, two traditionally Catholic European countries whose piety is often touted, come out far lower than we do. North European countries like England and Scandinavia are notable by their denial of such doctrines. Indeed, the whole issue of why we answer "Yes!" to such religious questions is an interesting area of speculation in itself.

Very likely, this affirmation of the afterlife is, in large part, due to the First Amendment to the Constitution, where our separation of church and state is proclaimed, thus throwing religion into the competitive marketplace where, if it is to exist at all, it has got to be vibrant and competitive. It also gives equal advantage to independent entrepreneurs and groups with media expertise, as anyone who watches late night television or Sunday morning programming can attest.

The place where secularization is likely to have taken place is in what has happened to our literal beliefs in the dogmas of our faiths that involve not immortality of the soul but resurrection of the body, quite a different notion of our ultimate felicity. The resurrection of the body is a fundamental belief of both Christianity and Judaism, as well as Zoroastrianism today. ("Now if Christ is preached as raised from the dead, how can some of you say that there is no resurrection of the dead?" asks Paul in 1 Cor 15:12). The rabbis warned that he who does not believe in *thyt hmtym* (let us call that "resurrection of the body" for the moment) from the Torah will not get it (Mishnah Sanhedrin 10). These are clear statements of the value of resurrection to these communities.

Immortality of the soul is, in fact, associated with rational religion in a way that resurrection is not. To give but one example: Moses Mendelssohn, the great eighteenth-century Jewish thinker who paved the way for Jewish entrance into European life, believed that resurrection was an irrational belief but that immortality of the soul was a rationally derivable doctrine. Reform Judaism, following Mendelssohn among others, removed all references to resurrection in its liturgy for much of the twentieth century but has recently put it back in the Hebrew. With Hebrew language mastery, I suppose, comes maturity in judgment. Many Americans of all denominations, in fact, assent to the statement that they believe in resurrection and actually mean upon scrutiny that they believe in immortality of the soul.

In fact, as George Gallup Jr. shows us, the notion of resurrection is only really characteristic of a sizeable minority of Americans—those on the right side of the line that separates the fundamentalist and evangelical churches from the liberal and mainline ones. A traditional, strong, and literal view in resurrection of the body is, in fact, a very strong indicator that the person is on the evangelical fundamentalist or orthodox side of the line. And that line is the big story of American religion at the beginning of the twenty-first century. Americans on the left of that line—let us call them the liberal, mainline religions for lack of a better term, be they liberal Jews, Protestants, Catholics, Muslims, or from the great Asian faiths—actually have more in common in terms of attitudes towards political, economic, and moral questions than they do with their coreligionists across that line. Of course, we have known for a long time, at least since the work of Gerhard Lenski's *The Religious Factor,* that religion is as important, indeed a much more important variable than many, in predicting American attitudes as economic, political, racial, or geographical differences.[4] The news of the twenty-first century is that the religious factor can sometimes be simplified into two basic, all-encompassing stances regarding religion in the United States.

Asking people whether they believe in immortality of the soul or resurrection of the body is one way to find that basic rift in American life and to ask how the social differences that we see as so much a part of that rift came about. I can't go into the reasons for the social differences I have outlined in American life; nor am I competent to analyze them completely. What I propose to do instead is to take these observations back to the past. Why should we not try to find the social patterning, functioning, and structuring in the past, and why then should that not help us understand what we are expressing when we speculate about our life after death?

I'm not going to be able to go into much detail here, having done that elsewhere.[5] My basic point in what follows is that people's beliefs about life after death, in the present as in the past, influence their attitude toward life and help to account for a variety of attitudes toward asceticism and martyrdom as forms of self-sacrifice. Good deeds and ascetical practices of mortification for the sake of moral virtue are generally supported by the idea of the soul's immortality, whereas a belief in bodily resurrection more particularly supports (albeit in various ways, depending on the specific notion of the resurrected body) an acceptance, passive or willfully active, of martyrdom. The two beliefs are clearly distinguishable, but certainly not mutually exclusive. Indeed, in the long history of Judaism and Christianity, they often conjoin. In this essay I trace some of the points at which they have either parted ways or come together.

René Girard has struggled against the association of martyrdom with sacrifice—no doubt because of his concern that a sacrificial reading of Jesus' death has historically authorized forms of violence against oneself and others.[6] Picking up on that Girardian theme, Bruce Chilton has demonstrated that from ancient times the story of Abraham's sacrifice of Isaac, related in Genesis 22 and in the Qur'an, has inseparably connected the themes of sacrifice, martyrdom (in Isaac's putative self-offering at his father's hands), and belief in bodily resurrection (cf. Heb 11:17–19)—often with violent results.[7] What I want to emphasize here is that the intellectual and religious history is richly complicated. Sacrificial practices—religious and secular, past and present—are not necessarily tied to belief in a personal afterlife; martyrdom is more often than not (but again, not necessarily) associated with a belief in bodily resurrection; and belief in life after death does not necessarily (although it often does) entail belief in resurrection.

Life after Death: The Biblical Witness before Daniel

The surprising continuing importance of the conception of an afterlife in contemporary American society is all the more amazing when we note that the earliest parts of the Bible do not concern any life after death worth having. The Bible has no organized notion of a beatific afterlife before Daniel and at times even seems deliberately to avoid talking about it. Rather than discuss the notion of afterlife, as was quite common in the literature of Israel's neighbors, the advice of the Bible is curt and practical: "Teach us to number our days that we may gain a wise heart" (Ps 90:12). This life with its inevitable death is what the Bible wants to emphasize.

Any reader who systematically surveys the oldest sections of the biblical text becomes impressed with how the Bible studiously avoids the concept of life after death. The reasons for this silence must be supposed and cannot be demonstrated, but one sensible guess would be an editorial enmity for foreign cults and for the cult of the dead, which surely existed in Israelite culture, but was strictly opposed by the prophets. We know well that the Bible normally turns the objects of veneration in other neighboring countries into the material objects of God's creation. Thus the heavens of Hebrew life are not gods but the handiwork of God.

In the same way, we may assume that reticence to talk of life after death or ghostly existence reflects ancient Hebrew reticence to grant a realm or power in competition with God. Most likely, we find no extended discussion of the notion of life after death or the realm of the dead in biblical thought, not because it did not exist in popular Israelite thought, but because the editors of the Bible are suspicious of it. There is real and serious (though fragmentary) evidence of biblical syncretism, though it is discussed most often only by the prophets, and by the priestly and royal writers. Any quick survey of the world's notions of life after death shows that the belief in ghosts and spirits at least is almost universal in human experience, where it serves a myriad of different social purposes, perhaps the most important being retribution or the protection and respectful burial of the dead. Indeed, the notion of spirits is probably older than the human race itself, since we find grave goods in Neanderthal burial sites.

Divination and ancestor worship must also be mentioned as often supported by the notion that something of the dead personality has survived death. In Hebrew thought, the issue that brings out the biblical editors' sense of wrath against idolatry is divination. In the famous story of Saul and the witch of Endor (1 Sm 28:6–17), we see revealed something of what the Bible studiously avoids. Samuel is just as reticent as the medium to provide Saul with an answer to his question. From this passage and many others, we learn some things about the ancient and partly suppressed traditions of the afterlife. As in other cultures, there was in Israel an abode of the dead, usually called *Sheol* but sometimes called by other names suggesting a pit or waste. It was not a place of reward or punishment, but very much like the Greek Hades, a place where all the dead go. Unlike in the Greek Hades, however, the dead (or at least Samuel) do not have to wait for a word from above to know about human events, and this makes all the difference. Samuel already knows the future; indeed, a plausible derivation for the word Sheol may be found in the word "ask" or "inquire." And perhaps it is this quality of Ancient Near Eastern mythology that disturbs the writers most. Because of his supernatural powers, the ghost Samuel is called an *Elohim,* a *god* emerging from the ground. On the other hand, the plural verb may imply several "gods" or "supernatural judges" appearing, of which Samuel is one. In any event, the term suggests the reasons for the biblical silence on life after death.

So far as this passage of biblical narrative is concerned then, the dead can be recalled, but it is sinful to do so, probably because to do so suggests that they are divine beings, breaching the canons of monotheism (a slightly anachronistic way to express it—more likely something like it gives allegiance to a cult that YHWH hates). But, as Brian Schmidt shows in his recent study of the material, the Bible's reticence and condemnation of the behavior is closely associated with the Deuteronomic reform and may perhaps originate there.[8] The word witch (*mekashepa*) used to describe the enchantress in 1 Samuel is the same word used to describe the last of the enchanters in Deuteronomy (*Mekashep*) except that the gender is common (masculine) in the latter. The reason given for the prohibition seems to be that these practices "violate monotheism" by allowing the children of Israel to practice religiously like those who preceded them and were dispossessed by the Lord for their sinfulness—passing their sons and daughters through fire. What we might call the Hebrew impulse to monotheism then was consistent with the Deuteronomic suspicion of foreign cults and what seems to be a deliberate failure to spell out notions of life after death, lest it define powers in opposition to God or areas whence his rule does not extend.

Though the Psalms were written over a vast period of time, some possibly even when the notion of life after death had been encouraged by Hellenistic culture, most of the Psalms do not color the abode of Sheol morally, although there is some moralizing tendencies in statements like "the good will praise you" while the evil will be lost. Most of the Psalms use Sheol as a way to convince God not to kill the Psalmist in his distress (Ps 16:10). This plea is roughly equivalent to the remarks of Isaiah 38:18–19, which states that only the living praise God, while Psalm 49 goes into great detail in saying that the wealth of the sinners is evanescent. Though throughout the Bible there are some notions that the good remain with God, since God would not suffer his righteous to perish,[9] the general skepticism of the biblical writers continues even once Greek influence is felt in the land.

The book of Ecclesiastes, whose date is controversial but which is now usually thought to evince Greek and especially Stoic influence, does not see any necessity to invoke the Platonic notion of immortality of the soul (Eccl 9:3–10). This lack is especially interesting because Ecclesiastes appears to reflect not just ancient consciousness but self-conscious reflections by the narrator. There is a brief notion of judgment earlier, but it appears ironic: "For the fate of humans and the fate of animals is the same; as one dies, so dies the other. They all have the same breath, and humans have no advantage over the animals; for all is vanity" (Eccl 3:19).

All reward is this-worldly and evanescent. Kohelet's reaction to this knowledge is Stoic in form—not despair but *apatheia*, courageous indifference. It is not much different from the famous Stoic epitaph, which is so common in the Hellenistic period: "I was not, I was, I am not, I care not" (*Non eram, eram, non sum, non curam*). And this is part of the heroic facing of death in the ancient world that Freud admired so much. Like Sidduri in the Old Babylonian version of the Gilgamesh epic, Kohelet suggests a *carpe diem* theme. Enjoy life. Eat and drink with enjoyment; let your family give you pleasure; dress well. This life is all that we can know. Don't count on anything more. (And this is Job's answer as well, except that he has the unique privilege of appealing his case directly to the divine throne room.)

Even in the later, much more pious apocryphon *The Wisdom of Jesus Ben Sira*, we find similar notions that ignore life after death. All rewards and punishments are considered to be part of this life. Adversity is a test of one's faith; "Opt not for the success of pride; remember it will not reach death unpunished" (9:12). Even more important is Ben Sira's famous discussion of death:

> Give, take, and treat yourself well,
> for in the nether world there are no joys to seek.
> All flesh grows old, like a garment;
> the age-old law is: all must die. (14:16–17)

There are two ways, principally, in which a person outlasts death in Ben Sira's estimation. The first is through children (30:4–5). They will represent their parents after death. The other way is by means of a lasting good reputation (41:11–13). This approach to life, which Freud characterized as heroically facing death without illusion, continues in Hebrew thought principally amongst the Sadducees. They are aristocracy by birth, not talent, and they continue the most ancient traditions.

But there is evidence of the gradual imposition of the idea of life after death in the later prophets and psalms. One of the most famous passages occurs in Ezekiel 37, although the context suggests that it is meant to be the vehicle of a vision, not an actual happening (Ez 37:1–14). The other passage that is often brought in demonstration of ancient views of life after death in Israelite thought is in Isaiah 26:17–19.

> Your dead shall live, their corpses[10] shall rise.
> O dwellers in the dust, awake and sing for joy!
> For your dew is a radiant dew,
> and the earth will give birth to those long dead.[11]

It is the people who are the subject of the passage. The prophet points out the previous failures of the people. They have tried already to return to the LORD. But, as in Ezekiel 37, their endeavors were in vain. And it seems to me that this passage, like the one from Ezekiel, is meant to be a prophetic vision, not an actual prediction.

Resurrection in the Bible: The Later Biblical Witness

The first clear reference to life after death can be defined exactly, both with regard to its date and with regard to the specific circumstances that produced it:

> At that time Michael, the great prince, the protector of your people, shall arise. There shall be a time of anguish, such as has never occurred since nations first came into existence. But at that time your people shall be delivered, everyone who is found written in the book. Many of those who sleep in the dust of the earth[12] shall awake, some to everlasting life, and some to shame and everlasting contempt. Those who are wise shall shine like the brightness of the sky,[13] and those who lead many to righteousness, like the stars forever and ever. (Dn 12:1–3)

Here is the first explicit reference to resurrection in the Hebrew Bible. And we can fix its arrival. The date is 165 BCE or thereabouts, just before Antiochus Epiphanes comes back from Egypt. The sign of the resurrection is the arrival of Michael. It is a time of unprecedented, terrible tribulation. But the people whose names are written in the book shall be rescued. The book has never been explicitly mentioned before in Hebrew thought, though it may be derived from Exodus 32:32–33 and quickly becomes part of standard Jewish lore (similarly to the ascension of Is 9:21–22), as well as providing the central image for the liturgy of Rosh Hashanah (See m. Rosh Hashanah 1:1).[14]

Now this writer is aware of the previous writing on the subject. The language of Daniel 12:1–3 is taken directly from Isaiah 26:19. The writer of Daniel has certainly taken the ambiguous prophecy of Isaiah in a literal sense, saying that the sleepers in the dust will literally rise. But he has not taken the writing literally in every respect because he has some definite notions about the identity of the resurrected. He goes on to say that the righteous will not be resurrected alone. Also, some of those whose behavior has been reprehensible will be resurrected for eternal contempt and shame. Later discussions of resurrection will confine themselves to providing a reward for the righteous. This particular passage, the earliest *undoubted* reference to resurrection in the Hebrew Bible, suggests that both the righteous and the very evil need to be resurrected for the purposes of giving them their well-deserved rewards.

Besides the general resurrection and punishment, a very interesting special reward is promised to those who make others wise (*hamaskiyliym*). They shall shine like the brightness of the heavens (*k'zohar harakiya*), those who lead the many to righteousness, like the stars forever (*layolam vaed kakochaviym*) (Dn 12:3). They shall be luminous beings, shining as stars, which is the same as the angels, for stars and angels had been identified since earliest times (for example, Jgs 5:20 and Job 38:7). This vision serves as the basis for the doctrine of resurrection even in rabbinic Judaism. The term brightness or splendor is *zohar* and is likely the basis for the title of the most famous book of Jewish mysticism, *The Zohar*, written in the High Middle Ages. So there is no question that this passage is important to later mystical tradition.

Now there is no scriptural basis for this heavenly reward. Though scripture can be adduced in retrospect in support of the imagery of sleep and waking, we do not get a rational explication of the preceding scripture. Instead the passage is framed as a prophetic dream. This innovation in Hebrew thought is not decided by exegesis but by a specific revelation received by consciously or unconsciously manipulatable means. For me, this passage clarifies the social position by which the previous scriptures were reunderstood into a specific prophecy for resurrection. It was authored by revelatory dreams from prophets who beforehand must have been contemplating the meaning of the precedents in Isaiah and Ezekiel, but who did not explicate the past text but rather reexperienced it as revelation in dream visions. We have often seen that early Jewish mysticism has been found in apocalyptic and pseudepigraphical documents, as well as in Christian documents, by tracing various themes that later show up in Jewish mysticism. But little has been said about the methods by which revelations are achieved. The reasons for this lack of discussion are clear enough. It is very difficult to discuss consciousness from a text alone. But I would suggest that exegesis of the earlier texts in Ezekiel and Isaiah is not enough to explain the innovation of resurrection and life after death in this Daniel passage. One has to understand that the vision was given on the basis of prophetic dreams, but also that it is based on texts that came earlier. A word or two is necessary about how both can be possible at once.

Dreams are a special case of human consciousness. We all have them, several times a night, but usually we only remember a very few. And we can stimulate that remembrance either directly by waking up during the dream and reciting or writing it down or by consciously or unconsciously making conditions that disturb sleep indirectly—such as by eating or drinking too much or too little or by ingesting psychotropic substances or by vigils or prayer or otherwise predisposing the dream to be seen in a particular light. Finally, dreams are very much related to daily experience, both in content and emotional tone. That would mean that anyone who spent his or her time in careful exegesis of the texts that describe the heavens, the divine throne room, and the journey there would likely dream about the same details. Besides reflecting the "unconscious" issues of life, with training, people are actually consciously able to manipulate the content and even progress of their dreams. Lastly, oral reporting and literary processes are always available to subject the dream experience to correction when it goes far from the expected details. Certainly dream visions are one major means by which the imagistic relationship between earlier texts like Daniel and Ezekiel and the Hellenistic apocalypses can be explained.

We should note that a person who seeks out a dream and treats it as a revelation is relying, from our point of view, on ordinary reflex of human experience, but is choosing to treat the experience as a nonnormal state of consciousness and a divine message, in short, a religiously interpreted state of consciousness (RISC). Usually in cultures that posit a nonnormal state of consciousness for prophecy, dreams are also specially marked as having a divine origin. We certainly know that this is true in Hebrew society because of the famous dreams of Joseph and Daniel. So, from the perspective of the agent (where there is one) and the hearers of the stories, these are religious experiences, clearly understood to have religious consequences. And there is no reason to believe that people did not have these experiences. They are relatively common throughout the world and not especially uncommon in Judaism and Christianity today. And, of course, dreams are omnipresent.

Dreams were expected and prepared for by prophets and seers. Night vigils of lamentation are characteristic in some way of many of the same apocalypses, and they are also present in the later apocalypse, 2 Enoch. This occurrence seems to me to be far more than just chance. Whether they are isolated as specific techniques by the text is beside the point; dreams are peculiarly both within control and out of rational control, so they can easily be seen as authored messages from the deity. This understanding of dreams is almost universally accepted in the Hellenistic world. And dreams are the medium for revelation in these texts with remarkable frequency, no doubt because of Daniel.

Furthermore, in 4 Ezra there are three famous other techniques: fasting, eating flowers of the field, and drinking a fiery liquid. The last technique, however, should probably be excluded as an actual technique because the drinking itself occurs in the vision, as a way of re-membering scripture more than anything else, and it does not appear to be suggested as a waking technique for achieving revelation. None of the seers themselves are directed to do this before the vision starts. So this technique should probably be seen as a specific characteristic of that single vision.

Revelation in Judaism is also specific to historical circumstances. We think we know the specific events that produced the revelation of resurrection in Daniel. It was not written during the Persian period, as it purports to be, but during the persecution surrounding the Mac-cabean War. During this period, Jews were martyred for their faith. We note in 2 Maccabees 6–7 that the first martyr, Eleazar, refuses to eat pork, or even to eat acceptable food when the crowd has been told it was pork. So the old man Eleazar dies a martyr's death, even though he is offered a merciful and respectful way out, because in his last re-maining years he does not want to make a mockery of his entire life (2 Mc 6:18–31). Soon the seven brothers and the mother are put to the same torture. This gruesome story differs in several important ways from the story of Eleazar. Although the children are as valiant as the old man, their reasons for allowing themselves to be martyred are quite different. Several of the children make brave statements about a re-ward for martyrs in the world to come, all of which mention bodily resurrection fairly explicitly (2 Mc 7:9b, 11, 14) and seem to be an ex-plicit way of working out the problem in theodicy that the first brother outlines: "The Lord God is watching over us and in truth has com-passion on us, as Moses declared in his song that bore witness against the people to their faces, when he said, 'And he will have compassion on his servants'" (2 Mc 7:6). The issue that occasions resurrection and ascension is again, as it was in Daniel, theodicy. But recourse to theodicy was not occasioned by philosophical speculation. It was caused by a crisis of violence. As the consequence of a regime that killed people for their religious faith, we have the first biblical religious martyrdom.

The compassion of God, which makes the whole notion of resurrection necessary in the case of martyrdom, is a way of spelling out the prophecy that we have already seen in Daniel 12. Resurrection shows God's continuing mercy in vindicating those who suffer martyrdom. The resurrection will be bodily, in fact very bodily, as the third son's remarks make clear. The effect of this extreme attention to the body in the restoration of this world shows that the tradition of resurrection is not at all obligated to Platonic thought or even Greek thought, although 2 Maccabees is certainly a book that was written originally in Greek and uses Greek cultural norms in a variety of ways. The palpability of the bodily resurrection, wherever it comes from, has become a quintessentially nationalist Hebrew idea, organizing national liberation from the Syrian Greeks. Bodily resurrection is the remedy given by God to the Jews because of the cruelty and oppression of foreign domination, a notion that will carry on directly into the Roman period. And it is easy to see why it is stressed at this particular moment. The persecutors have destroyed the bodies of the young martyrs. But God's mercy guarantees that they will have them back and have the pleasures of their bodily existence again when God raises them. In the epitomist's comments in 2 Maccabees 12:43–45, we also see a similar interest in resurrection: "In doing this he acted very well and honorably, taking account of the resurrection (*anastasis*). For if he were not expecting that those who had fallen would rise again (*anastēnai*), it would have been superfluous to pray for the dead" (2 Mc 12:43–44).[15] We have come a great distance from the issues that occupied Deuteronomy.

In such protestations of earthly compensation for the pleasures foregone by martyrdom, one other important aspect of the tradition is often overlooked. The mother encourages her martyr sons in several ways, but nowhere more importantly than when she exalts God's creative powers (7:22) and even more clearly in 2 Maccabees 7:28: "I beseech you, my child, to look at the heaven and the earth and see everything that is in them, and recognize that God did not make them out of things that existed. Thus also mankind comes into being." This is, in most estimations, the first clear statement of *creatio ex nihilo*, the first time God is clearly praised as creator from nothing.[16] In Genesis, of course, God does not actually create everything—darkness (*hosheh*) and the deep (*tehom*) precede creation. The writers of the great prologue in heaven of Genesis 1 were not sensitive to the theological principles that we have inherited from Aristotelianism. Even Isaiah 45:7 only praises God as the creator of light and darkness. One normally thinks that Aristotelian principles suggest the necessity that God create out of nothing, lest anything that is coterminous with God be also considered as coequal with Him. But this passage in 2 Maccabees shows that the motivation for stressing creation from nothing was actually the growing notion of bodily resurrection. God needs the powers to create the martyrs' bodies again from nothing. In the previous examples, where resurrection is discussed, a bodily residuum remains. The dry bones knit together in Ezekiel, the corpses of those who rest in the dust, become the basis of the awakened and resurrected saints in Daniel. Here, the text seems impelled to stress that God can create as He will because in this power rests His promise to the martyrs. The martyrs will be resurrected from nothing just as all humans come from nothing. It is not the creation of the world that is stressed here, but the mysterious creation of each individual. The result of this assertion is the reassurance that God can certainly resurrect the righteous from dust and even from nothing, if nothing remains. There is no gainsaying the absolute innovation that the sudden importation of ideas of life after death found in Hebrew thought. Evidently, the Roman occupation radicalized many different parts of the population. And it makes necessary a reclarification of what will later be two distinct mystical topics—the deeds of creation (*bereshit ma'aseh*) and the deeds of the merkabah (*ma'aseh merkabah*).

The texts at Qumran show that this sectarian group also believed in resurrection and life after death, even as angels, as Josephus' description implies. Furthermore, the Qumran community apparently nursed many ascension traditions, as we are seeing in the more recently published Qumran material. Certainly, this belief in ascension is in line with Daniel's prophecy that those who make others wise will become stars in heaven. And ascension is just what Josephus reports about them. Yet, although it is clear that these promises of resurrection, ascension, and heavenly immortality as angels come from a sectarian background, the ideas were so attractive to the culture as a whole that they spread out far more broadly than the sectarian conventicles of first-century Judaism. They appear in writings of the Pharisees—who are hardly a millennarian sect, though they apparently do have a distinct group identity.

The Influence of Greek Philosophy on Judaic Ideas of Immortality

Behind this seeming anomaly lies the ambiguity of the existence of a second doctrine of life after death in Judaism. The idea of the immortality of the soul was entering Jewish life from the other end of the social spectrum. Immortality of the soul enters with Greek philosophical contexts—in particular, Platonic notions of the immortal soul. Judaism does adopt these notions, but the first social classes to adopt them during this period are not the same as those who adopt notions of resurrection. Indeed, these classes are in some ways polar opposites. Resurrection is the product of the alienated, the martyrs deprived of life, just as the priestly aristocracy of Qumran was deprived of access to the Temple. The alienated are, in Anthony Wallace's words, cut off from the redemptive media of the culture, a much more sophisticated concept than merely "relative deprivation."[17] Some people may follow the relative deprivation model—namely, the disenfranchised classes of people who cannot abide foreign domination and who adopt the standard position of revolutionary groups. But others are socially lacking in the wherewithal to achieve salvation. These others range from one extreme of purity to another, from priests who were evicted from the Temple by the Maccabean kings to the tax-collectors and prostitutes who were so visibly evangelized by the New Testament.

By contrast, immortality of the soul is mainly adopted by classes of people who learn Greek culture and benefit from it. They are people like Philo, Josephus, and the Pharisees, people we would call clients of the Roman overlords, people deeply involved in Greek intellectual ideas who need to see the continuity between the two cultures, people who combine Judaism with the intellectual currents of their day. Indeed, the Greek traditions themselves come already equipped with an application to martyrdom. Socrates is himself a kind of martyr because he willingly drinks hemlock rather than flee, as he had ample time to do but would thereby demonstrate a lack of courage in his convictions, and so, tacitly admit the charges against him, namely, that his ideas pervert the young. The martyrs who use this model for their martyrdom, however, are young aristocrats like the hapless Cato the Younger, who eventually gained the courage to commit suicide at the emperor's order by reading Plato, or at least this is the story related by Plutarch.

But let us concentrate first on the clear-cut contrasts before we discuss the mixture of the two concepts. The contrast in social class is clearly congruent with the contrast in conceptions of the afterlife. The apocalyptic writers promise to the young martyred men a return of the physical body that was denied them by their martyrdom, a fitting reward that returns their youth and strength to them. Sacrificing youth may desire a complete restoration of their bodies and their lives; the aged, having attained wisdom, have eschewed the pleasures of the flesh for philosophical reflection. Immortality of the soul, in both its Greek and Jewish versions, stresses the ideals of a more aged intellectual class and preserves a continuity of consciousness.

The intellectuals who adopt it from Greek society are those who need Greek society for their support. They are part of a client class or even part of the Greco-Roman elite. This group included Philo Judaeus, Josephus, several other Jewish philosophical writers, and, finally, the Pharisees, or more exactly, the rabbis, as they give up their sectarian status and become the ruling body in Jewish life. In so doing, they synthesize the notion of an immortal soul with the notion of bodily resurrection. Christianity also provides another meeting point for the two ideas, but in this context they do not blend quite as well, and so we are left with centuries of interesting attempts to synthesize these ideas.

It is hard to say that Philo is typical of anyone. His enormous wealth and power would suggest that he represents the cynosure of Jewish Hellenism, not a typical example of it. We also have more of his work than any other Hellenistic Jewish writer and perhaps any other writer of the period, with the exception of Plato and Aristotle. His enormous corpus of writing is unique in the Hellenistic Jewish world, and also unique in his attempt to synthesize Greek with Hebrew thought. His apologetic technique is very sophisticated, showing that the Hebrew Bible both clearly illustrates Greek philosophical truths in allegory (as do the *Iliad* and *Odyssey,* according to the Greek commentators) and morally surpasses them. Philo is mostly an exegete, writing commentaries on the biblical works. He rarely indulges in systematic philosophical exposition. So it is difficult to find a short and full exposition of his ideas on any subject; they must be gleaned from many different sources. All these characteristics mean that we have to be satisfied with a characterization of his writing on the afterlife rather than an extensive treatment of it.

Philo was born to a very wealthy Alexandrian family a fraction of a century before Jesus. He was a contemporary of both Jesus and Paul, possibly outliving both of them. Unlike Jesus, however, he was born in a major center of Hellenistic culture and brought up in one of the wealthiest families in the city. He presumably received private tutoring, probably also a gymnasium education, and participated in Greek athletics. At the same time, he sees nothing in these activities to detract from his perfect observance of Jewish law, though he evidently does not practice the Jewish law in conformity with his contemporaries in the land of Israel, the Pharisees. His life and writing make clear that Jewish observance and Pharisaism are not to be equated. There were many legitimate yet opposing ways to carry out the commandments that God had given Israel in this period. He lived long enough to accompany the Jewish delegation that interceded with Gaius Caligula, asking him to rescind the law that would put up his statue in all public places in the middle of the first century.

In terms of his ways of dealing with life after death, Philo is typical of the new Jewish intellectual class, well attuned to Greek philosophical traditions and explaining the Bible and Judaism by means of philosophical notions. Being a good Platonist, Philo discusses the immortality of the soul without ever broaching the resurrection of the body. The Septuagint evinces a distinct interest in resurrection but makes no obvious clear statement regarding the immortality of the soul, forcing Philo to interpret against the grain, which, of course, he has no problem doing given his finely honed tool of allegory. No doubt, his Bible had no book of Daniel in it, or, if it did, he interpreted it allegorically.

For Plato, immortality must also be an inherent quality of the mind, which is the very nature of the human being. Conversely, mortality is directly related to our bodily nature. In direct opposition to Plato, Philo believes that the soul is immortalized by moral behavior so those who do not act morally are condemned to nonexistence at death. In other words, the immortality of the soul does not necessarily mean its indestructibility. Does this mean that Philo was not so impressed with Plato's proof of the soul's immortality? If so, he remains silent. Rather he is at pains to make the Platonic doctrine coincide with his biblical faith, and he uses his writings to demonstrate the full truth.

The knowledge (*epistēmē*) of God is the true consummation of happiness. It is also age-long life. The law tells us that all who "cleave to God live," and herein it lays down a vital doctrine: "For in very truth, the godless are dead in soul, but those who have taken service in the ranks of the God, who alone IS alive, [possess a] life [that] can never die" (*oi de tēn para tō onti theō tetagmenoi tachin athanatos bion zōsin*) (*De Specialibus Legibus* I, 345).

Philo supports his equation of immortality and knowledge of God with a reference to Deuteronomy 4:4: "but you who held fast to the LORD your God are all alive this day." The Greek for "you who held fast" (*oi proskeimenoi*) is fairly literal to the Hebrew (*v'atem hadveikiym*, Dt 4:4), so Philo allegorizes the term to mean those who have "conceived of" or "known" God.[18] Platonic influence obviously contributed to Philo's identifying immortality with moral behavior, though Philo's reading of the Bible is far more important in understanding his thinking here. Certainly, Plato notes that moral behavior is what perfects the soul for its intellectual adventure. However, for Plato all souls are immortal, no matter how heinous they may act.

The very sinful may be given special punishment in Hades, but they will eventually be reincarnated for further progress (see, for example, *The Republic* 10 [610a]). Philo's Jewish and religious commitment to a personal relationship between God and each human who seeks Him is what makes necessary his further development on the Platonic notion—a thoroughly individual and personal disposition of the soul, one that is strictly dependent on its earthly behavior. In any event, it is unclear just how personal is the immortality that Plato outlined: the soul is forced to forget everything personal when it is reincarnated, leaving only some basic innate categories as the continuity between lives. Furthermore, personal immortality certainly falls by the wayside in Aristotle's thinking. By contrast, personal immortality is central to Philo's understanding of biblical ethics, and so he corrects the philosophical error.

And reincarnation too must fall by the wayside in Philo's adaptation of Plato's thinking. Thus, we face for the first time in Jewish life an explicitly and fully personal, immortal soul whose center is the intellectual faculties. This is illustrated most clearly in Philo's notions of the reward and punishment of sinners. Although he sometimes interprets biblical passages to mean that the dead merely cease to exist, as the text itself seems to imply (*De Posteritate Caini* 39), when asked for his own opinion, he says that they will be punished: "Men think that death is the termination of punishment, but in the divine court it is hardly the beginning" (*De Praemiis et Poenis* 60). In other words, though Philo adopts the notion of the immortal soul from Plato, he equates moral living with the practice of philosophy and gives primacy to the kind of ethical behavior that is outlined by the Bible.

Why should a good Platonist even want a resurrection of flesh, when flesh corrupts just as all matter does? Philo believes that the perfection of the intellectual and moral faculties is what leads to the immortality of the soul, in a nonmaterial way. The continuity of consciousness most attracts Philo's observations. But Philo, alone among the Jewish writers of his day, also offers a critique of Plato. Plato thought of the soul as immortal by nature, but Philo resists this idea. Instead, he shows by biblical demonstration and logic that the soul is immortalized through the doing of righteous actions and brought to corruption by doing evil ones. Thus, he achieves a true synthesis of Greek and Hebrew thought.

The more usual way of dealing with the differences between the two thoughts is illustrated by Josephus and a number of other Hellenistic Jewish writers. They talk to their Greek-speaking audiences about the immortality of the soul, when logic would demand that they should talk about resurrection. This substitution is especially clear in the case of Josephus' description of the sects of Judea. He always expresses Jewish sects who believe in resurrection, like the Essenes and Pharisees, as preaching *anastasia*, immortality, or immortalizing the souls. This hermeneutic tactic is cruder than Philo's true synthesis, but it illustrates the tack that most Jews took. They just interpreted one in terms of the other.

Philo does not use the word *anastasis* nor its derived verb forms that signify *resurrection* in the Septuagint and the New Testament. He does not use any forms derived from *egeirō* to signify postmortem existence, as Paul likes to do. He either does not know or does not like the notion of a fleshly rising from the dead. Instead he almost exclusively uses the term *athanasia*, immortality. He scarcely mentions any messianic hopes about the Jews, defusing a political issue between pagans and Jews. But he does valorize Jewish martyrdom, saying that Jews accept death as if it were *immortality* (*De Virtutibus Prima Pars, Quod Est De Legatione Ad Gaius* 117.2) and says that when threatened by death Jews are given *immortality* (*De Virtutibus Prima Pars, Quod Est De Legatione Ad Gaium* 369.2). He says that Jewish youth seek liberty as eagerly as *immortality* (*Quod Omnis Probus Liber Sit* 117.4). It is clear, then, that Philo is partly accessing his Jewish knowledge, explicitly describing the Jewish notion of martyrdom, though he is describing it in Platonic garb.

He also makes central to his notion of the Bible's message an ascent to see God. In fact, for Philo, the name Israel is a designation for ascent and philosophical contemplation. For Philo, *Israel* means "the person who saw God": *ish shera'ah el* in Hebrew. This refers both to Jacob's wrestling with the angel (*el*) and to the people's quest for God in their religious writings. It is also applicable to any who pursue philosophy to its correct conclusion, a vision of God, and therefore functions in a universalistic way in Plato's writing.[19] And he outlines a clear mysticism based on the mystical ascent to heaven for prophecy and immortalization.

The souls of those who have given themselves to genuine philosophy "study to die to the life in the body, that a higher existence immortal and incorporeal in the presence of Him who is himself immortal and uncreated, may be their portion" (*meletōsai ton meta sōmatōn apothnēskein bion, ina tēs asōmatou kai aphthartō para tō agenētō kai aphthartō zōēs metalachōsin*) (*De Gigantibus* 14). Some of this sounds just like Plato, whose Socrates says that the truly philosophical live as already dead. But for Philo it is the process of moral education itself that brings us into the presence of God and transforms us into immortal creatures. There may be hints of our previously discussed resurrection and transformation motifs in these doctrines, but, if so, they are highly refined.

There are a few places where Philo even hints that he knows the more native Jewish interpretation of the afterlife, seemingly backing into a notion of resurrection—for instance, in the allegory of grief over a rebellious child, Israel. But he does not take the description to the point of contradiction:

> Then, like a fond mother, she will pity the sons and daughters whom she has lost, who in death and still more when in life were a grief to their parents. Young once more she will be fruitful and bear a blameless generation to redress the one that went before (*ep' anorthōma tēs proteras*). (*De Praemiis et Poenis* 158)

Philo's text is Isaiah 54:1,

> Sing, O barren one, who did not bear;
> > break forth into singing and cry aloud,
> you who have not been in travail!
> > For the children of the desolate one will be more
> > than the children of her that is married, says the LORD.

He characteristically understands these words as an allegory. It is probable that Philo is not actually thinking of bodily resurrection per se, but rather the apocalyptic end, which can suit his philosophical principles more exactly.

Philo thinks of the soul as a perfected body, sometimes implicitly described as made out of the same stuff as stars. He is therefore able to identify the righteous dead with the stars themselves, and hence as angels, as we have seen in the apocalyptic literature:

> When Abraham left this mortal life, "he is added to the people of God" (Gn 25:8), in that he inherited incorruption and became equal to the angels, for angels—those unbodied and blessed souls—are the host and people of God (*karoumenos aphtharsian, isos angelois gegonōs angeloi gar stratos eisi theou, asōmatoi kai eudaimones psuchai*). (*De Sacrificiis Abelis et Cain* 5)

It seems here as if Philo is giving us his own interpretation of the various apocalyptic traditions we have already seen. But he styles them not in terms of resurrection (they are unbodied souls), but in terms of incorporeal intelligences. Thus we learn that the stars and the angels are both incorporeal and intelligences:

> The men of God are priests and prophets who have refused to accept membership in the commonwealth of the world and to become citizens therein, but have risen (*huperkupsantes*) wholly above the sphere of sense-perception and have been translated (*metanestēsan*) into the world of the intelligible and dwell there registered as freemen of the commonwealth of ideas, which are imperishable and incorporeal. (*De Gigantibus* 61)

Notice that Philo does not use the standard vocabulary for resurrection in these passages, but rather makes up his own words to distinguish his thinking from standard resurrection vocabulary in other Hellenistic Jewish writers. In most passages, however, Philo explicitly regards death as the soul's liberation from the prison of the body. Here he seems rather to try to accommodate postbiblical interpretations to his brand of Platonism.

Philo also codes his philosophy according to gender. Matter is feminine (*hulē*) and passive to the masculine *logos* and *nous*. Unbridled sexuality is also a distraction and a detraction. The influence of women must be limited by human rules and regulation for the good of both sexes. Women, though theoretically the equal of men, and equally responsible for their actions, are simply not treated as the equal of men and certainly their will is viewed as weaker; their sexuality is degraded. This is a typical judgment of Platonism, but Philo seems more zealous than most. Philo points out the sexual abstinence and even celibacy of the Therapeutai, whom he admires and who are so similar to the Qumran group. As sexuality is such an important aspect of human life, gender coding is indeed quite frequent in other groups as well— including complete celibacy, which is characteristic of some Essenes, some Christians, and Manichaeans.[20]

Philosophically at least, Philo is committed to an equal and yet loftier view of the soul, which is resident in all humanity and hence transcends gender. Some particularly moral souls can go beyond the angels and stars to be with God himself. In *De Somniis* 1.4 and 23, Philo refuses to commit himself on the issue of whether the celestial bodies have souls and minds. This refusal appears to be a further example of Philo's sensitive Bible reading. For him, as for the Genesis text itself, the heavenly bodies are but creations of God, not entities in themselves, as in Plato. Furthermore, souls do not descend into nonhuman bodies, as they may in Hindu or Platonic thought. The highest expression of Philo's thought is, as usual, best expressed by the systematic treatment of H. A. Wolfson:

> While encased in the human body, the rational soul affects the life of the body and is affected by it. On the one hand, it helps the process of sensation induced into the body by the irrational soul within it, and, on the other hand, it utilizes the data of sensation for the formation of intellectual concepts. More especially does it exercise control over the body by its power of free will, with which it was endowed by God. But still, even while in the body, it never loses its character as a distinct entity, so that when the body with its inseparable irrational soul dies, the rational soul departs and enters upon its bodiless eternal and immortal life. The place where rational souls abide during their immortal life varies. Some of them go up to heaven, by which is meant the astro-

nomical heaven, to abide among the angels; some of them go up to the intelligible world, to abide among the ideas; some of them go up even higher, to abide in the presence of God. Immortality, however, is not due to rational souls by their own nature; it is a gift from God, and God who created them can also destroy them; consequently only the souls of the righteous who have earned the gift of immortality survive, while those of the wicked may be destroyed.[21]

Josephus uses the Greek notion of the afterlife to describe martyrs to Jewish religion. The most famous example is in Eleazar ben Yair's speech at Masada before the Zealots commit suicide rather than fall into the hands of the Romans (*War* 7.8.6–7). Ben Yair's speech recommending death over slavery is widely quoted. The speech is well ordered. The first appeal is to heroism. Clearly, God has determined that they should all die, since the Romans are close to vanquishing them, although they have had the best position possible and an enormous cache of supplies and weapons. On the other hand, God has graced them with information that many of their compatriots do not have — namely, the knowledge of their imminent capture. He therefore urges a noble death in liberty (*eleuthera d' ē tou gengaiou thanatou, War* 7.326) rather than slavery and dishonor.

What is not often mentioned is that this argument does not move the combatants to slaughter their own loved ones. According to Josephus, the argument that allows the defenders to justify violence against themselves is, in effect, a proof for the immortality of the soul: "Though many are convinced by the appeal of freedom in death over slavery in life, others are more compassionate for their wives and children. For this reason, Eleazar continues on to a discussion of the immortality of the soul" (*peri psuchēs athanasias, War* 7.341). Josephus reports that Eleazar argues: "Death truly gives liberty to the soul and permits it to depart to its own pure abode, there to be free of all calamity" (*outos men gar eleutherian didous psuchais eis ton oikeion kai katharon aphiēsi topon apallassesthai pasēs aumphoras apathies esomenas, War* 7.344).

Josephus continues by positing that the soul is the principle of life in the world — whatever it inhabits is alive and whatever it abandons immediately dies. He then tries to demonstrate that the soul is independent of the body in sleep and will be all the more so after death. This is pure Platonic thinking, which may have impressed Josephus's readers deeply. But it is unlikely to be anything at all like the ideas of immortality that the desperate defenders of Masada embraced. They, like all other Jewish sectarian groups of the day, were more attracted by the notion that they would be resurrected in their bodies completely to enjoy the rest of the life that had been denied them by faith.

In fact, all the nativist groups of the first century, Christianity included, embraced notions of a bodily resurrection, not the immortality of the soul. It is Josephus' use of Greek notions of immortality to describe the Hebrew notion of resurrection that has confused scholarship on the two different social backgrounds to the two ideas. Once we see where the two different notions come from, it is easy to disentangle the opposing notions and see Josephus' attempt to bring the two concepts together rather as the first of many. It was not easy.

Contemporary Connections

We can easily understand this connection from our own day. In Christianity and the Josephan examples, passive resistance elicits the notion of martyrdom. Josephus actually mentions some famous examples of the Jews resolving to die rather than allow their religious law to be violated. One is the famous example of Pontius Pilate's attempt to bring effigies of animals and humans into Jersualem on the Roman ensigns (*Antiquities* 18.3). In this case, the Roman relents, moved by the Jews' willingness to die. In another case, Jews take down the Roman eagle that was put up in the reign of Herod and willingly die for their crime (*Antiquities* 17.6.1–4). Since the Middle Ages, in both Christianity and Islam, soldiers who sacrifice themselves in a holy war have been granted special privileges in heaven. Christian holy warriors were forgiven their earthly sins in a plenary indulgence, while Muslim warriors actually attained the status of martyr (*shahid*) by dying in warfare. Jews, by contrast, have lacked armies until the mid-decades of the twentieth century and so were not given to such extremist sentiments. In fact, rabbinic Judaism is notable by its lack of encouragement to martyrdom.

When it comes to the abuse of martyrdom for political benefit, there are few heroes in the modern world. The martyr tradition has been so firmly fixed in the classical world, and in Judaism, Christianity, and Islam, that it feeds every spiral of religious violence in the world. All these traditions developed closely associated notions of martyrdom. All of them also were able to turn that religious notion into an instrument of the state and the furtherance of violence.

Now this should give us pause in our consideration of the very fertile and complex hypotheses that René Girard has given us. Obviously, the development of the notion of martyrdom follows Girard's line of thought. I leave it to those who are more familiar with the work to elaborate the details. On the other hand, the exclusive claim that only Christianity found a way out of the spiral of violence with the sacrifice of the perfect victim, it seems to me, is not supported by the historical evidence or even by philosophical reasoning. What seems to me to be closer to the historical evidence is that each tradition developed a notion of martyrdom, which was connected to the notion of resurrection or immortality of the soul. In the Christian and Jewish tradition, eventually, both resurrection and immortality of the soul were synthesized into the religious belief structure that made martyrdom meaningful. Each was able to use the notion of martyrdom to express the idea that sometimes a human life cut short by adherence to higher values of the sanctity of life achieves a transcendent meaning in history. Furthermore, each religious tradition shows that even this sacred tradition of the transcendence of values can be co-opted by the state to extend the spiral of violence and must be constantly critiqued.[22]

Notes

1. See Carol Zaleski, *Otherworld Journeys: Accounts of Near-Death Experience in Medieval and Modern Times* (New York: Oxford University Press, 1987); Ann W. Astell, "Near Death Experience and Julian of Norwich's Doctrine of Prayer," in *Women Christian Mystics Speak to Our Times*, ed. David B. Perrin, 109–28 (Franklin, WI: Sheed and Ward, 2001).

2. George Gallup Jr. and Jim Castelli, *The People's Religion: American Faith in the 90s* (New York: Macmillan, 1989), especially 58–59.

3. George Gallup Jr. with William Proctor, *Adventures in Immortality* (New York: McGraw Hill, 1982).

4. Gerhard Lenski, *The Religious Factor: A Sociologist's Inquiry* (Garden City, NY: Doubleday, 1961).

5. I refer you to my recent work on the social sources of the concept of life after death in the biblical societies of Egypt, Babylonia, Canaan, First Temple Israel, Persia, Greece, Second Temple Israel, apocalypticism, mysticism, early Christianity, the church fathers, the rabbis, and Islam. See Alan F. Segal, *Life After Death: A History of the Afterlife in Western Religion* (New York: Doubleday, 2004).

6. See, for example, René Girard, *Things Hidden since the Foundation of the World,* trans. Stephen Bann and Michael Metteer (Stanford, CA: Stanford University Press, 1987), 237–43.

7. See Bruce Chilton, *Abraham's Curse: Child Sacrifice in the Legacies of the West* (New York: Doubleday, 2008).

8. Brian Schmidt, *Israel's Beneficent Dead: Ancestor Cult and Necromancy in Ancient Israelite Religion and Tradition,* Forschungen zum alten Testament 11 (Tubingen: J. C. B. Mohr [Paul Siebeck], 1994), 294. It is possible to assent to Schmidt's observations about the linkage between Deuteronomy and this polemic without assuming that the polemic begins there. It seems to me that it is equally likely that the polemic is due to long-term social conflicts in the society that are recorded here in Deuteronomic form.

9. Note places where Psalms uses the term "forever" or "length of days" with exaggeration: Psalms 21:4, 22:26, 25:1, 31:5, 36:9, 37:18. For instance, "may your hearts live forever" in Psalm 22:26 probably does not imply anything more than a wish. Nor does the following imply anything more than Sheol, together with the hope that God will continue to guard him there: "Into your hand I commit my spirit; you have redeemed me, O Lord, faithful God" (Ps 31:5). The "forever" at the end of Psalm 23:6, "I shall dwell in the house of the Lord forever," is a tendentious translation of "length of days" in Hebrew: *l'ore yamim.* Nor does the motto of Columbia University in Psalm 36:9, "In your light we see light," help matters. Psalm 37:18, often quoted in support of life after death, seems to me to imply the opposite: "The Lord knows the days of the blameless, and their heritage will abide forever." Psalm 86:11 and Psalm 145:1 suggests that the faithful will glorify God's name forever, which may perhaps imply a moral reward after the grave. But it scarcely articulates anything resembling a "beatific" view of life after death. The best one can say is that in spite of the biblical reticence to spell out a detailed notion of life after death, several more popular notions creep into Jewish religious literature where the hand of the polemical editor was unlikely to be strongly felt, as in the independently redacted psalms.

10. Compare Syriac Targum: Heb. *my corpse.*

11. Heb. *to the shades.*

12. Or *the land of dust.*

13. Or *dome*.

14. My thanks to Steven Davis for having pointed out the connection with Exodus 32.

15. See also 2 Mc 7:9, 14 and also 12:38–46.

16. Sirach 24:8 also suggests the same, but it is normally dated a bit later.

17. See Anthony F. C. Wallace, "Revitalization Movements: Some Theoretical Considerations for their Comparative Study," *American Anthropolgist* 58 (1956): 264–81.

18. See Hans C. C. Cavallin, *Life After Death: Paul's Argument for the Resurrection of the Dead in 1 Corinthians 15, Part One, an Enquiry into the Jewish Background* (Gleerup: Lund, 1974), 135–36.

19. See Ellen Birnbaum, *The Place of Judaism in Philo's Thought* (Atlanta: Scholars Press, 1996).

20. See for example, Richard Baer, *Philo's Use of the Categories Male and Female*, Arbeiten zur Literatur und Geschichte des hellenistischen Judentums 3 (Leiden: E. J. Brill, 1970); also Dorothy Sly, *Philo's Perception of Women*, Brown Judaica Studies 209 (Atlanta: Scholars Press, 1990).

21. Harry Austryn Wolfson, *Philo: Foundations of Religious Philosophy in Judaism, Christianity, and Islam* (Cambridge, MA: Harvard University Press, 1968 [1947]), 415–16.

22. [Editor's note] Alan F. Segal (1945–February 13, 2011) passed from this life while the book was in immediate preparation for publication. We remain grateful for his remarkable life of distinguished scholarship, for his invaluable contributions to Jewish-Christian understanding, and for this essay, which we are honored to include here as his legacy to us.

SEVEN

Anti-Judaism, Josephus, and the Hellenistic-Roman Period

LOUIS H. FELDMAN

Everyone who deals with the subject of ancient anti-Semitism (an inappropriate term, of course, since it refers to families of languages rather than attitudes toward people) must approach it with a combination of humility and boldness: humility because we have such a small percentage of what was actually written (almost certainly not more than 1 percent, and who knows whether what was written was really representative of what people thought—especially since the rate of literacy apparently did not exceed 10 percent); and boldness because we dare to generalize from so small a sample.[1]

It is well to begin with some general considerations about the ancient world that distinguish it from our modern world. In the first place, the ancients could not have conceived of what we would call a separation of church and state. Even if we find individuals such as Caesar and Cicero, whose adherence to traditional religious beliefs is questionable (as we may see for example in Cicero's *De Divinatione*), officially, which is to say, when they are part of the government or commenting on political issues, they say the "right things" in so far as religious matters are concerned. The close of Cicero's first oration against Catiline (which he delivered in the Senate), illustrates this point. Once Catiline has left, Cicero says, "You, great Jupiter, who were established with the same rites as this city, whom we name rightly the establisher of this city and empire," will protect us.[2] In any codification of laws, stretching from the Twelve Tables to the Corpus of Justinian, there is no separation of civil law from religious law.

On the other hand, polytheism is, by definition, liberal and pluralistic, inasmuch as no pagan religion asserts that other religions and other gods are false. Less powerful yes, but not false. Although one could insist that the gods of one's own nation fostered the growth and success of one's nation, so that, as the revered Ennius put it, "Moribus antiquis res stat Romana viresque" ("the ancient state is founded on its ancient mores and its men"), there was always room in the pantheon for another god.[3] Judaism, however, insisted at least officially in the Torah, that all other religions and all other gods were false and, in fact, at least within the oral tradition, that the pagans, as children of Noah, were forbidden to worship idols. Hence, in the absence of a separation of church and state, Jews (constituting themselves something of a state), would seem to have as their goal, by definition as it were, the destruction of all other states. This idea might well be inferred for example (and however erroneously) from the fact that the Israelites are commanded in the Bible, upon entering the land of Canaan, to exterminate totally the seven nations of Canaan (see Dt 7:1–2).

Therefore, Apion, as cited by Josephus, would seem on the surface at least right in effect to ask why, if the Jews wish to become Alexandrian citizens, they don't worship the Alexandrian gods. One can go even further and ask how one can trust the Jews if their goal is to destroy the religious basis of the state. Intellectuals and philosophers can (and do) ask such questions. Both (such questions and such individuals) are logical. Fortunately, politicians then and now are not. And fortunately neither were many theologians. The biblical commandment to eliminate the seven nations of Canaan, like the commandment to eliminate the Amalekites, is subject to rabbinic interpretation and in practice not observed. Otherwise, how can we explain the Septuagint's translation of *Elokim lo tekallel* (Ex 22:27) as "You shall not curse gods," which both Philo (*De Specialibus Legibus* 1.9.3) and Josephus (*Antiquities* 4.207 and *Against Apion* 2.237) interpret to mean that one is not permitted to speak ill of other people's religions? Otherwise, how can we explain the Talmudic statement (*Sanhedrin* 96b) that the descendants of Haman, himself said to be a descendant of Amalek, studied Torah in Benei Beraq and thus became the ancestors of the present-day Haredim?

With rare exceptions, the Hellenistic and Roman rulers gave special permission to the Jews to observe their religious beliefs and practices (exceptions include Antiochus Epiphanes, Caligula, and Hadrian). With few exceptions, all the rulers of the Hellenistic and Roman world, from Alexander through his successors and the Romans, realized that the people from whom they themselves came were a minority in their realm and, realizing how numerous and economically important the Jews were, granted them special privileges. The intellectuals, the philosophers, and the theologians remained content with their logical arguments, wrote books (most of which have been lost), and gained promotions and tenure in the equivalent of their universities.

Let us examine some actual outbreaks against Jews in antiquity. What contributed to the suspicion of the Jews was their secrecy in refusing to allow non-Jews to enter the precincts of their great Temple in Jerusalem. Indeed, this seems to have been a factor in bringing about the very first pogrom of which we hear, namely, the one in which Ptolemy IV Philopator (3 Mc 5–6) in 217 BCE ordered the Jews to be massacred in Alexandria by a horde of elephants. He did this, it is said, because upon visiting Jerusalem, when he wanted to enter the Temple, he was mysteriously felled to the ground.[4] Inasmuch as the Ptolemies were themselves a minority in their own empire in Egypt and were regarded as interlopers by the native Egyptians, who were so proud of their long history, and inasmuch as Palestine was a constant battleground between the Ptolemies and the Syrian Seleucids during the third century BCE, Philopator may well have wondered what the Jews were hiding in the Temple when they excluded him.

Added to the secrecy of the Temple was the secret book (*arcano . . . volumine*), to which Juvenal refers (*Satires* 14.102), namely, the Torah. To be sure, Juvenal is a satirist, and satirists often use a sledgehammer to crack a nut. Moreover, the author of the *Letter of Aristeas* would have us believe that the Torah was known as a good and wise book. But the author of the *Letter* was probably a Jew; and, besides, there is only one passage (Pseudo-Longinus, *On the Sublime* 9.9, perhaps a Jew,[5] on Genesis 1:3, 1:9–10) or perhaps two (Hecataeus, *ap.* Diodorus 40.3.6)[6] from the entire Torah that are ever quoted or closely paraphrased in all extant classical literature. On the other hand, instances of gross ignorance of the Torah, even in such writers as Hecataeus and Pompeius Trogus and Artapanus, who are favorably disposed toward the Jews, are numerous. And when the elephants that Philopator had lined up to trample upon the Jews disobeyed his order and trampled upon those giving them, Philopator reversed himself, released the Jews, and returned to the previous policy of toleration.

A similar event (although some say that it is merely a duplicate of the event just described) occurred on the death of Ptolemy Philometor in 145 BCE, who had placed his entire army under the command of two Jews, Onias and Dositheos (Josephus, *Against Apion* 2.49).[7] When Philometor's brother, Ptolemy Physcon (Euergetes) seized the throne, Onias, true to the legitimate sovereign, Cleopatra II, took up arms against him (*Against Apion* 2.51). Thereupon, in a manner similar to that of Ptolemy Philopator, Physcon arrested all the Jews of Alexandria—men, women, and children—and exposed them, naked and in chains, to be trampled to death by elephants, which he is said to have made drunk. When, however, the elephants were given their orders in Greek, instead of rushing on the Jews they turned and trampled on some of Physcon's friends. It is this transference of blame from one individual—in this case, the general Onias—to all the Jews, that is a characteristic element of anti-Jewish bigotry. Such an incident of persecution by a ruler is, however, on the whole, exceptional, if, indeed, it is historical at all; and shortly thereafter Physcon apparently made his peace with the Jews (*Against Apion* 2.54–55).

The fact that Roman citizens of Jewish origin were exempted from military service (for religious reasons, notably observance of the Sabbath and dietary laws) from the time of Julius Caesar onwards (Josephus, *Antiquities* 14.226) may have seemed to the Romans an indication that the Jews were not fully loyal to Rome, especially since the Jews had a state of their own, Judaea, and, as we see from Agrippa I's triumphal march in Alexandria, were loyal to that state. Tacitus (*Histories* 5.13.2), Suetonius (*Vespasian* 4.5), and Josephus (*War* 6.312) mention a belief that someone from Judaea would become ruler of the world; and this was interpreted by the Jewish revolutionaries, says Josephus, to refer to someone, presumably a messianic figure, from their own people; and this would *ipso facto* require a revolution against the

Roman Empire. If someone, such as the Jew Tiberius Julius Alexander, did become part of the Roman military and political establishment, he was a renegade to his faith (*Antiquities* 20.100), since, with church and state never being separated, this accession to the establishment required worshipping the Roman gods.

The most striking case of what we would call a pogrom occurred in Alexandria, the most populous of the Jewish communities, with perhaps as many as 180,000 Jews,[8] in the year 38 CE.[9] Philo (*Legatio ad Gaium* 18.120) has an important comment, namely, that the hatred of the masses toward the Jews had been smoldering for some time. When a pretext was offered on the Jews' refusal to obey the decree of Emperor Gaius Caligula that he be worshipped as a god, the promiscuous mob, carried away with itself, let loose. The order of events was, first, long-standing resentment at the privileged position and influence of the Jews, whether political or economic; second, and more immediate, the accusation that the Jews were unpatriotic, inasmuch as they refused to participate in the state cults, which, like a flag, united all the diverse peoples of the empire; third, the rousing of the passions of the mob by professional agitators (though this appears to be exceptional); and fourth, the intervention of the government, ostensibly to preserve order while blaming the Jews for causing the riot. What determined the course of events in this instance was the behavior of Flaccus, the Roman governor of Egypt. During the first five of the six years of his administration, Flaccus (Philo, *In Flaccum* 1.2–3) had shown no signs of anti-Jewish animus and indeed was a model administrator. The change of attitude in Flaccus, and consequently the breakdown of the vertical alliance with the Roman administration, was due to the death of the Emperor Tiberius, who had appointed him and whose close friend he had been, and to the fear that, because Tiberius' successor Caligula had put to death Flaccus' friend Macro, his own position would deteriorate. In desperation, therefore, Flaccus, presumably assuming that the Jews would in their usual fashion remain loyal to the emperor, sought allies among his former enemies.

The immediate pretext for the riot was the visit of Agrippa I to Alexandria and his ostentatious display of his bodyguard of spearmen decked in armor overlaid with gold and silver. The mob responded to

Agrippa's majestic appearance by dressing up a lunatic named Carabas in mock-royal apparel with a crown and bodyguards and saluting him as *marin*, the Aramaic word for "lord." The implied charge clearly was that the Alexandrian Jews, in giving homage to Agrippa as a king, were guilty of dual loyalty and of constituting themselves, in effect, as a state within a state. The use of the Aramaic word would seem to be intended to emphasize the allegation that the Jews' first loyalty was to the Aramaic-speaking ruler of Palestine. Flaccus, according to Philo (*Legatio ad Gaium* 20.132), could have halted the riot in an hour if he had desired, but did nothing. That the Jew-baiters decried not merely the alleged lack of patriotism, but also, rather simply, the fact of Jewishness, can be seen in the treatment of the women, whom they seized and, when they refused to worship the image of the emperor, forced to eat pork (Philo, *In Flaccum* 11.96). In the end, however, what must have seemed to the opponents of the Jews like an instance of "international Jewish power" asserted itself: Flaccus was recalled in disgrace, banished, and eventually executed.

The next major eruption of anti-Jewish violence coincided, significantly, with the outbreak of the Jewish rebellion against the Romans in 66 CE, not unconnected, we may guess, with the charge of dual loyalty. Not unexpectedly, this most violent of all the outbreaks against the Jews occurred in Alexandria.[10] Our only source, Josephus, is hardly an impartial witness, especially because he had such an antipathy for Jewish revolutionaries. Yet, his account should be given serious weight, inasmuch as it is far from a whitewash of the murderous actions of the troops sent by the authorities. In recounting the event, Josephus (*War* 2.487) reminds us, as we had already seen in Philo, that there had always been strife between the native inhabitants and the Jewish settlers ever since the time when Alexander the Great, as a reward for the support that the Jews had given him against the Egyptians, had granted them *isomoiria*, that is, rights equal to those of the Greeks. Presumably, the Jew-baiters felt assured that the authorities would favor their cause against people who would now be perceived as unpatriotic rebels. The uprising was put down ruthlessly by the Roman governor, Tiberius Julius Alexander (Philo's nephew and a renegade Jew); and, according to Josephus (*War* 2.497), no fewer than 50,000 Jews were slain. Finally, Alexander gave the signal to his soldiers to cease; but so great, says Josephus (*War* 2.498), was the intensity of the hatred of the Alexandrians that it was only with difficulty that they were torn away from the very corpses.

As to the motives of the Jew-baiters in these pogroms, Josephus lists three (*War* 2.464, 478): hatred, fear, and greed for plunder—apparently a combination of economic jealousy and fear of Jewish power and expansionism. It is, moreover, revealing to note that in Caesarea, the chief point of conflict in Judaea, Josephus declares (*War* 2.268, *Antiquities* 20.175) that the Jews were superior in wealth—another indication of the importance of the economic factor in explaining the hatred of the Jew-baiters toward the Jews,[11] though we may remark that, generally speaking, ancient historians downplay economic factors in their view of the causality of events but rather highlight personality and military factors. Baron cites Josephus' extrabiblical comment (*Antiquities* 2.201–2), in his paraphrase of the Bible, that the oppression of the ancient Israelites by the Egyptians was due to the Egyptians' envy of the Israelites' abundant wealth and, most appropriately, suggests that this observation reflects contemporary realities with respect to the masses of the Egyptian peasants.[12] In this connection, we may cite a papyrus dated in 41 CE in which the author, a wholesale dealer in need of money, warns the recipient that if he fails to obtain a loan from the sources the author recommends, "like everyone else, do you, too, beware of the Jews" (*Corpus Papyrorum Judaicarum*, no. 152). The fact that the writer of the papyrus adds the gratuitous phrase "like everyone else" would seem to emphasize that, in his eyes, the warning to beware of the Jews is a general one, shared by the Gentile population at large, and that seeking loans from Jews was apparently customary.

That there was an economic factor in popular prejudice against Jews, based on Jewish prominence in trade, would seem to be indicated by the remark in the *Apotelesmatica* (2.3.65–66) by Claudius Ptolemy, the noted second-century CE Alexandrian astronomer, who was convinced that national characteristics are conditioned by the geographical and astrological situation.[13] His list of those people who are more gifted in trade than others starts with Idumaea, Coele-Syria, and Judaea; and he remarks that they are more unscrupulous, despicable cowards, treacherous, servile, and in general fickle. These people, he adds, are, in general, bold, godless, and treacherous. In referring to the inhabitants of these countries, he really has in mind only the Jews, because all three of these geographical areas are frequently identified with each other.[14] Another economic factor may be seen in Tacitus' bitter remark (*Histories* 5.5.1), alluding to the success of the Jews in winning others to convert to Judaism, that "the worst rascals among other peoples, renouncing their ancestral religions, always kept sending tribute and contributing to Jerusalem, thereby increasing the wealth of the Jews." Hence, it was not merely that Romans were abandoning their ancestral gods, who, in the view of writers such as Ennius and Livy, had enabled the Romans to build their great empire, but that they were even contributing monetarily to alien gods, who, in principle, found no place in their pantheon for the Roman gods. We thus see the combination of the economic factor and the alleged expansionism of the Jews as factors in Judeophobia.

Most of those who deal with this subject, including Peter Schäfer, in his extraordinary book *Judeophobia*,[15] concentrate on what the Greek and Roman writers say about the Jews. But aside from the fact that the citations in Menahem Stern's collection cover a period of a thousand years, to what degree do we get a representative picture? It is not until Herodotus in the fifth century BCE, in his *Histories,* that any extant Greek writer alludes to the Jews at all; and even he refers to them only obliquely, if indeed it is to the Jews that he is referring, when he discusses circumcision (2.104.2–3). Ezra is a contemporary of Herodotus, or perhaps of Plato, but neither of them as much as mentions him; and the first and only pagan writer who does mention him is Porphyry (*Adversus Christianos, ap.* Macarius Magnes 3.3) at the end of the third century CE. Indeed, one of the most important points to be made is the degree to which the Jews are simply ignored. A writer such as Cicero, who, to be sure, knew about Jews and refers to them in his oration *Pro Flacco* (28.66–69), ignores them completely in a work such as *De Natura Deorum,* where he deals at length with various theories concerning theology and where we might have expected some mention of them, inasmuch as the Jewish view of deity is, from a pagan point of view, so unusual. Stern's monumental three-volume collection of testimonia seems large;[16] but I have found a total of only 3,372 lines of actual text in Greek or Latin in volume 1 (covering the period from Herodotus through Plutarch in the first century CE) pertaining to the Jews; and this includes a good deal of information that is only peripheral to anything Jewish. In volume 2, covering through the sixth century CE, there are 5,006 lines. This comes to approximately 204⅓ pages for volumes 1 and 2, and a good deal of this consists of passages about the properties of the Dead Sea. When we consider that in the first century the Jews comprised perhaps as much as 10 percent of the population of the Roman Empire,[17] what surely must strike us, at least on the basis of what literature has come down to us, is that non-Jewish writers had little interest in the Jews. And it cannot be merely that the Jews were not in contact with non-Jews, since in Alexandria, at least, Philo was hardly unique in his knowledge of Greek literature and in his interest in attending sporting events and theaters. If anti-Semitism were more of an issue, one would expect a lot more attention.

If anti-Semitism was a burning issue, one would have thought that attempts would have been made by pagans to answer the one work that is devoted to refuting anti-Semites and that contains many debatable points and that had the sponsorship of the great bibliophile Epaphroditus and of the emperor Domitian, namely Josephus' essay *Against Apion*. But there is no such mention extant of the essay, let alone a refutation. If there was a widespread outcry of anti-Semitic comments among ancient intellectuals, we would have expected that some indication of this would be found among the thousands of scraps of literary papyri that have been found, but not a single such scrap has yet emerged. We would have expected to find at least some of the anti-Semitic statements of Manetho, Chaeremon, Lysimachus, Apion, or Apollonius Molon among the papyri; and while it is true that we have found fragments of Apion,[18] for example, none of the anti-Semitic comments have been found.

Moreover, though the *argumentum ex silentio* must be used with caution, if indeed anti-Semitism was rife among pagan intellectuals, we would have expected Philo, who was the head of what was in effect the Anti-Defamation League of Alexandria and who led a delegation to the Roman Emperor Gaius Caligula no less (*Legatio ad Gaium*), to have replied to their writings, and he does not. As to other Jewish writers (and there is doubt as to whether some of them are Jewish), namely, Demetrius, Eupolemus, Pseudo-Eupolemus, Artapanus, Cleodemus-Malchus, Aristeas, Philo the epic poet, and Ezekiel the dramatist,[19] none of them reply to anti-Semitic comments, and none of them are quoted by a pagan writer.

But, in all fairness, we must note that we know of at least seven writers—Alexander Polyhistor, Apollonius Molon, and Teucer of Cyzicus in the first century BCE; Apion of Alexandria, Damocritus, and Nicarchus in the first century CE; and Herennius Philo of Byblus in the second century CE—who are said to have written whole monographs on the Jews, most of which, to judge from the fragments, included anti-Semitic comments. Teucer's work, in particular, seems to have been very extensive, consisting, as it did, of six books. There may well be significance in the fact that none of these works has survived. Is this another indication of lack of interest in the Jews? If we had these works, how different would our picture be of the attitude of Greco-Roman intellectuals toward the Jews?

We must make one additional comment with regard to the attitude of pagan intellectuals toward the Jews, and that is that, unlike the influence of modern intellectuals, especially since the Age of the Enlightenment in the eighteenth century, pagan intellectuals seem to have had little influence upon public policy or upon mass movements in antiquity. How much influence did Alexander's tutor, Aristotle, who had such a negative view of barbarians, have upon Alexander the Great? Did Cicero, for example, who mentions the Jews as a pressure group in his speech *Pro Flacco* (28.66), despite his extremely important position in the Roman republic, have any influence on the republic's attitude toward the Jews? Did Seneca (*ap.* Augustine, *De Civitate Dei* 6.11), who refers to the Jews as a most accursed race (*sceleratissimae gentis*), have any impact on the policy toward the Jews of Nero, with whom, according to Tacitus (*Annals* 13.2), he had paramount influence, and who is defended by Josephus (*Antiquities* 20.154–55) against his detractors? How much influence did Tacitus, who was the son-in-law of the powerful Agricola (*Agricola* 3), and who authored the most extensive tirade against Jews that has come down to us (*Histories* 5.1–13), have upon public policy? What the Graeco-Egyptian and Greek authors made out of Jewish separateness, in point of fact, is mere rhetoric and quite unimportant. How much of a role did intellectuals play in inciting the rioters and justifying the pogrom in the year 38 CE? Did they produce anything like a "Protocols of the Elders of Zion" to set forth their theory of a monstrous conspiracy against all humanity, and did such a work play any role in outbreaks against Jews?

Let us examine the extant negative comments about Jews by Greek and Roman writers. In dealing with this evidence, however, we should heed several caveats. (1) Most of the passages come from fragments, and thus we are generally not in a position to know the occasion and original context of the remarks. (2) Many of the passages occur in Josephus, particularly in his essay *Against Apion*, or in church fathers, where there is often a question of their authenticity and, in any case, where the polemical nature of the work in which they are embedded is clear. (3) Many passages come from rhetorical historians or satirists, where the references are clearly colored and exaggerated. (4) We may note the patterns of ethnographical treatises that, especially under the influence of the Aristotelian Peripatetic school, had developed an interest in strange, foreign peoples and in their historical origins or in geographical oddities, as we see particularly in the large number of references to the properties of the Dead Sea.

In any case, the anti-Jewish remarks are to be seen in the context of their appearance. Thus, the anti-Jewish outburst in Cicero's *Pro Flacco* (28.66–69) is to be explained, at least in part, by the fact that he was a lawyer. And what else would you expect from a lawyer defending a client who had been accused of pocketing money that the Jews had collected for transmission to the Temple in Jerusalem? Cicero himself points out the difference between his true opinions and those that he uttered as a lawyer (*Pro Cluentio* 139). Moreover, the charge made against Jews that they are lazy—since, says Seneca (*ap.* Augustine, *De civitate Dei* 6.11), they spend one seventh of their lives in idleness—is also made against the Egyptians by Polybius and against the Germans by Tacitus. The charge that the Jews are superstitious because they refuse to fight on the Sabbath (Agatharchides, *ap.* Josephus, *Against Apion* 1.205–11; Plutarch, *De Superstitione* 8.169C: they allowed the enemy to capture Jerusalem on the Sabbath because they refused to fight on that day) is also made by Tacitus (*Germania* 39) against the Germans.

As to the alleged xenophobia of the Jews, we may note the statement, quoted in the name of the advisers to the Syrian king Antiochus VII Sidetes, in the first century BCE (Diodorus 34.1.1), that the Jews should be wiped out completely "since they alone of all nations avoided dealings with any other people and looked upon all men as their enemies." Even Hecataeus of Abdera (*ap.* Diodorus 40.3.4), in a passage that is otherwise very favorable toward the Jews, asserts that Moses introduced a certain misanthropic (*apanthrōpon tina*) and xenophobic (*misoxenon*) way of life. Polytheism is, by definition, pluralistic in its attitude toward other religious beliefs; and though earlier, as we see in such writers as Plato and Aristotle, the Greeks had looked down upon non-Greeks, whom they called barbarians, certainly after Alexander the liberalism and tolerance in religion extended to other peoples and other ways of life. Indeed, there were those, such as Hecataeus, who praised the Jews as led by men of the utmost refinement (*ap.* Diodorus 40.3.4), and Strabo (16.2.39), who extolled their lawgiver, Moses, as comparable to the great and much admired Spartan Lycurgus and as the composer of a laudable code of law.

However, is this negative attitude on the part of the Jews toward other peoples' culture really so very different from what Herodotus (2.35) says about the Egyptians: "As the Egyptians have a climate peculiar to themselves, and their river is different in its nature from all other rivers, so have they made all their customs and laws of a kind contrary for the most part to those of all other men. Among them, the women buy and sell, the men abide at home and weave; and whereas in weaving all others push the woof upwards, the Egyptians push it downwards, etc."? As to Peter Schäfer's claim that the charge of xenophobia is particularly made against the Jews,[20] Herodotus (2.41) says that "no Egyptian man or woman will kiss a Greek man, or use a knife, or a spit, or a caldron belonging to a Greek, or taste the flesh of an unblemished ox that has been cut up with a Greek knife."[21] Plato (*Laws*

12.953E) says that foreigners are prohibited by the Egyptians from participating at meals and sacrifices.

Gavin Langmuir, in his already extremely influential book,[22] distinguishes three kinds of hostile assertions: realistic hostility, where there is some basis in fact for the hostility toward the group; xenophobia, where the conduct of a minority of the members of a group is said to be true of all members of the group; and chimera, where characteristics attributed to the group have never been empirically observed. On this basis he concludes that chimerical (or irrational) anti-Semitism does not arise until about 1150 CE. In his long and incisive dialogue with Langmuir, Schäfer notes that the most salient example of chimerical anti-Semitism cited by Langmuir is the alleged Jewish custom of human sacrifice.[23] Schäfer objects that a similar charge is made by Apion and Damocritus against the Jews. According to Apion (*ap.* Josephus, *Against Apion* 2.92–96), the Jews would kidnap a Greek foreigner every year, fatten him up for a year, sacrifice his body with their customary ritual, partake of his flesh, and swear an oath of hostility to the Greeks. According to an historian named Damocritus (*ap.* Suidas, "Damocritos"), the victim was a stranger but not specifically a Greek, and the sacrifice occurred every seventh year.

One thinks of the parallel in the Gospels, which René Girard discusses in his essay "Is There Anti-Semitism in the Gospels?"[24] and where, similarly, the crowd is appeased at the expense of the innocent victim, a scapegoat, namely, Jesus. But, we may object, in any case, such a charge is not uniquely anti-Jewish, since we hear of other cannibalistic conspiracies, the most famous being that connected with Catiline.[25] Since such a charge is made against so many peoples, it hardly indicates that the Jews are to be regarded as a menace to society, especially since, as we see in Cicero, for example, it was understood, in those days, that rhetoricians were granted the license to exaggerate and, indeed, to do so even wildly. However, the main point to be made is that the charges made by Apion and Damocritus—and we may add that even Theophrastus (*ap.* Porphyry, *De Abstinentia* 2.26), in an otherwise very favorable notice about the Jews, says that the Jews were the first to institute sacrifices both of other living beings and of themselves—did not lead to outbreaks against the Jews, as did those in the Middle Ages. Apparently, the idea of a scapegoat who is then slaughtered, as Girard has pointed out to us, is so basic in religion that the fact that the Jews are accused of having this practice simply means that they are like everyone else. Hence, we do not have anti-Semitic outbreaks because of it.

Are we justified in using Langmuir's terminology in viewing Apion's and Damocritus' charges as chimerical? Yes, they are chimerical, but they are not part and parcel of ancient hostility, so far as we can tell. Significantly, several of the church fathers, notably John Chrysostom, are virulent in their antipathy toward the Jews and Judaizers, but none of them quote the blood libel as found in Apion, even though they are all acquainted with Josephus' works, where Apion's charge is made. Indeed, Minucius Felix (*Octavius* 28.2), in the late second century, mentions a charge against Christians that they devour infants. The pagan Celsus (*ap.* Origen, *Against Celsus* 6.27) actually asserts that it is Jews who spread abroad a malicious rumor that Christians sacrifice a child and partake of its flesh. In all the cases of overt hostility in antiquity, such as pogroms, we never hear the charge that Jews fatten up and kill non-Jews. When, in the High Middle Ages, some Christians bring the blood libel charge against the Jews, it is not the same as Theophrastus' remark, since the scapegoat, as Girard has so aptly noted, is said to be none other than Jesus himself.

We hear of expulsions of the Jews from Rome in 139 BCE and in 19 CE and perhaps again during the reign of Claudius, but these are provoked not by harangues or comments of intellectuals but rather by the success of the Jews in winning converts;[26] and, indeed, in each case, the Jews apparently return to Rome shortly after their expulsion despite the threat of Jewish proselytizing to the Roman way of life.

Cicero, as we have noted, is a lawyer who argued diametrically opposed points of view; in any case, his anti-Semitic comments, such as his reference to the Jews as a pressure group, are never cited by any other extant author—or, one might add, by the later church fathers—despite Cicero's unchallenged position as Rome's greatest orator, and, so far as we can tell, these comments had no influence on Roman governmental policy or the Roman masses. Seneca may have written bitter and nasty comments about the Jews; but though he was for a time the right-hand man of the Emperor Nero (Tacitus, *Annals* 13.2), he apparently had no influence on Nero's policy toward the Jews, if we may judge from Josephus. Juvenal was a professor of rhetoric, and fortunately in those days as in ours, professors were generally regarded as *luftmenschen,* a source of good jokes, and with little or sharply exaggerated understanding of reality. Though he has some incisive comments, his influence on public policy or the masses was fortunately nil. Tacitus may have held office under three emperors, may have been consul under Nerva, and may have been governor of the province of Asia under Trajan; but we know of no evidence that he carried his anti-Semitic views into practice in any of those positions. And, we may add, if Christians, at least in the West, were interested in appropriating from pagan literature charges against the Jews, the most obvious place to look was Tacitus' *Histories,* book 5, the most extensive and most intemperate extant pagan outburst against the Jews. It is significant that only one of the church fathers, Tertullian (*Apologeticus* 16.1–4), cites this passage, and he ridicules Tacitus. We come down to the fact that the Christians could not *ridicule* the Jews as such because in so doing they would be ridiculing themselves, since they claimed to be *verus Israel*; hence they had to insist, rather, that the so-called Jews have the wrong interpretation of the biblical texts.

If fear of the Jews because of their success in winning converts is seen solely in Roman literature, why are there no riots in Rome but rather, most notably, in Alexandria against the Jews? Indeed, according to Suetonius (*Claudius* 25.4) it is the Jews who are alleged to have made constant disturbances (*assidue tumultuantis*) in Rome, at the instigation of Chrestus; and these are said by Suetonius to have led the Emperor Claudius to expel the Jews from Rome. But we do not hear in Suetonius or in any other Roman source or in Josephus, who was a contemporary, or in any other Jewish source of popular riots by non-Jews against Jews at that time. It is furthermore significant that though we hear of cities in Asia Minor and Libya that did not honor the privileges that had been granted to the Jews by previous rulers and even confiscated money that the Jews had collected for transmittal to the Temple in Jerusalem, the Jews had their rights reaffirmed by Roman authorities; and, in any case, we do not hear of any riots or pogroms.[27] Rather, the anti-Semitism manifested itself in such acts as stealing money (*Antiquities* 16.45) that the Jews had collected in Asia Minor for transmittal to Jerusalem—acts that the civic magistrates apparently ignored.

Since the Romans were themselves a minority in their own empire and since the Jews constituted, as we have noted, as much as 10 percent of the population of the Roman Empire and as much as 20 percent in the eastern portion of it, the Roman policy of tolerance, even from a purely political point of view, made much sense. The attempt of the Emperor Gaius Caligula (*Antiquities* 18.257–309; *War* 2.184–203) to impose the imperial cult upon the Jews, since he hoped that this would be the one common denominator that would unite all the people of the Empire, was the exception; the norm was the decree of his successor, the Emperor Claudius (*Antiquities* 19.278–91), reaffirming the privileges of the Jews everywhere. Even the massacres of Jews in Damascus and other cities in Syria (*War* 2.559–61, 2.461–65) are isolated events, coinciding with the beginning of the Jewish war against the Romans. Another factor here appears to have been the success of the Jews, in a city such as Antioch, in constantly attracting multitudes of Greeks to their religious ceremonies. It is significant that this comment is made by Josephus (*War* 7.45), who generally is careful to soft pedal the conversion activities of Jews because he realized how sensitive the Romans were to such acts. In Damascus, we read (*War* 2.560) that the inhabitants "distrusted their wives, who were almost all addicted to the Jewish religion." Significantly, when the revolt of 66–74 CE ended and the people of Antioch (*War* 7.103–11) petitioned the commander-in-chief of the Roman army, Titus, when he visited the city, to expel the Jews, he refused; and when they asked that the privileges previously enjoyed by the Jews in Antioch should be rescinded, he likewise refused, this after four years of bloody war with the Jews. It is surely remarkable that, on the whole, after three great rebellions against the Romans, against Nero, Trajan, and Hadrian (the last, that of Bar Kochba, tied up a seventh of the entire Roman army in the tiny area of Judea),[28] the Roman government reaffirmed its policy of protecting the privileges of the Jews; and this eventually became the policy inherited even by Constantine and the Christian emperors who succeeded him.

According to Langmuir, the essential inferiority and powerlessness of the out group, that is the Jews, are a crucial factor in turning anti-Judaism into anti-Semitism. Schäfer correctly insists that this does not apply to the Jews of antiquity.[29] A people that produced a Herod, as well as four commanders-in-chief for the Ptolemaic armies; that produced a governor of Egypt (Tiberius Julius Alexander, who, to be sure, was no longer an observant Jew); that produced an Agrippa I, who was such a crucial factor in determining that Claudius should succeed Caligula as Roman emperor; that at one point was able to control the kingship of half a dozen states, petty though they might be, that was able to get Roman emperors time after time to side with them against their enemies, as we can see alike from the pages of Josephus, the Talmud, and the Acts of the Pagan Martyrs; that was able to get rights and privileges affirmed and reaffirmed in every part of the Graeco-Roman world; that, with its success in winning so many, came to embrace as much as 10 percent of the Roman Empire, was hardly powerless. Jews were feared and sometimes hated, but this is not the classic anti-Semitism such as we find in the Middle Ages and modern times. On the contrary, Jews were even admired by some of the greatest thinkers of antiquity—Pythagoras, Aristotle, Theophrastus, and Varro.[30]

In conclusion, it is time to revise the lachrymose view of Jewish history, at least for certain portions of the ancient period. Yes, Jews were envied because of their economic and political power and their special privileges but, by and large, they were protected by the government in power. They were accused of dual loyalty because Judea and Jerusalem and the Temple remained central in their thoughts and financial assistance. But despite occasional setbacks, Jews were doing well through gaining proselytes in large numbers, although this success, to be sure, did occasion resentment. Even among intellectuals, Jews were sometimes admired.

Notes

    1. See William V. Harris, *Ancient Literacy* (Cambridge, MA: Harvard University Press, 1989).

    2. *1 Catiline* 13.33.

    3. *Annales,* frag. 156 Skutsch = 500 Vahlen.

    4. See, however, my *Jew and Gentile in the Ancient World* (Princeton, NJ: Princeton University Press, 1993), 489n9; and Erich S. Gruen, *Heritage and Hellenism: The Reinvention of Jewish Tradition* (Berkeley: University of California Press, 1998), 222–36, who looks upon the whole incident as an appeal to amusement.

5. See my *Jew and Gentile in the Ancient World*, 533–34n21.

6. Perhaps, in the Septuagint, Dt 32:44, 28:69 (29:1 in the Septuagint), Lv 26:46, 27:34. See John G. Gager, *Moses in Greco-Roman Paganism* (Nashville, TN: Abingdon, 1972), 32.

7. See my *Jew and Gentile in the Ancient World*, 88–89.

8. See Diana Delia, "The Population of Roman Alexandria," *Transactions of the American Philological Association* 118 (1988): 286–88.

9. For an account of this incident, see my *Jew and Gentile in the Ancient World*, 111–16; Erich S. Gruen, *Diaspora: Jews amidst Greeks and Romans* (Cambridge, MA: Harvard University Press, 2002), 54–64.

10. For an account of this riot, see my *Jew and Gentile in the Ancient World*, 117–18.

11. See my *Jew and Gentile in the Ancient World*, 107–13.

12. Salo W. Baron, *A Social and Religious History of the Jews*, vol. 1, 2nd ed. (New York: Columbia University Press, 1952), 383n35.

13. Claudius Ptolemy, *Tetrabiblos*, 2.3.65–66, ed. F. E. Robbins, Loeb Classical Library (Cambridge, MA: Harvard University Press, 1940), 29–31.

14. See Menahem Stern, ed., *Greek and Latin Authors on Jews and Judaism*, 3 vols. (Jerusalem: Israel Academy of Sciences and Humanities, 1974–84), 2:163.

15. Peter Schäfer, *Judeophobia: Attitudes toward the Jews in the Ancient World* (Cambridge, MA: Harvard University Press, 1997).

16. Stern, *Greek and Latin Authors on Jews and Judaism*.

17. See Baron, *A Social and Religious History of the Jews*, 1:371–72n7.

18. Some of Apion's glosses on Homer have been found (P. Rylands 1.26), and a few first-century scholia on Homer's *Odyssey* (Literary Papyri, London 30; British Museum inv. 271) mention his name among other commentators. See my "Pro-Jewish Intimations in Anti-Jewish Remarks Cited in Josephus' *Against Apion*," *Jewish Quarterly Review* 78 (1987–88): 238–39.

19. On Eupolemus, see Carl R. Holladay, *Fragments from Hellenistic Jewish Authors*, vol. 1 (Chico, CA: Scholars Press, 1983), 98n2; on Pseudo-Eupolemus, see 162n13; on Artapanus, see 194n6; on Cleodemus-Malchus, see 248nn5–8.

20. Schäfer, *Judeophobia*, 170–79.

21. Herodotus, *Histories*, ed. and trans. A. D. Godley, Loeb Classical Library (Cambridge, MA: Harvard University Press, 1920).

22. Gavin Langmuir, *Toward a Definition of Antisemitism* (Berkeley: University of California Press, 1990).

23. Schäfer, *Judeophobia*, 198–211.

24. See René Girard, "Is There Anti-Semitism in the Gospels?" *Biblical Interpretation* 1, no. 3 (1993): 339–49, 351–52; also published in *The Girard Reader*, ed. James G. Williams (New York: Crossroads, 1996), 211–24, as "The Question of Anti-Semitism in the Gospels."

25. See Elias J. Bickerman, "Ritual Murder and the Worship of an Ass: A Contribution to the Study of Ancient Political Propaganda " in his *Studies in*

Jewish and Christian History: A New Edition in English Including "The God of the Maccabees," 2 vols., trans. Amram Tropper (Leiden: Brill, 2007), 1:497–527.

26. See my *Jew and Gentile in the Ancient World,* 300–304.

27. These reaffirmed rights have been very conveniently collected, with an excellent commentary by Miriam Pucci Ben Zeev, in *Jewish Rights in the Roman World: The Greek and Roman Documents Quoted by Josephus Flavius* (Tübingen: Mohr Siebeck, 1998).

28. See Emil Schürer, *The History of the Jewish People in the Age of Jesus Christ,* vol. 1, rev. by Geza Vermes and Fergus Millar (Edinburgh: Clark, 1973), 547–48n150.

29. Schäfer, *Judeophobia,* 201–11.

30. See my *Jew and Gentile in the Ancient World,* 201–32.

EIGHT

Beyond Anti-Judaism
Louis Feldman and the "Lachrymose Version" of Jewish History

ERICH S. GRUEN

In the preceding chapter, "Anti-Judaism, Josephus, and the Hellenistic-Roman Period," Feldman choses boldly and forthrightly to challenge the standard "lachrymose version" of Jewish history. Rightly so. I find his essay sound, cogent, and plausible. Such adjectives mean, of course, that he shares my own view (at least in large part). The whole notion of anti-Judaism, let alone anti-Semitism, among the pagans of antiquity is overblown and misconceived. Insofar as I disagree with Feldman, it is only that he does not go far enough. My own take on the subject might be labeled the "cheery version" of Jewish history.[1] Too sunny for most, even for Professor Feldman. But it is worth pushing his thesis a bit further.

A healthy portion of the most vitriolic comments about Jews comes, as Feldman notes, in Josephus' *Contra Apionem*, which is ostensibly a polemical counter-attack against Gentiles who had some nasty things to say. But how seriously should one take that treatise as an accurate reflection of pagan opinion? The principal accusation, according to Josephus, is that Jews are a relatively new phenomenon in the Mediterranean world: they don't go back to distant antiquity, so they can be dismissed as trivial. He devotes a good portion of the book to refuting that proposition.[2] But this is a set-up. The accusation appears nowhere else, it is absurd on the face of it, and Josephus rejects it without difficulty—though at great length. Space does not allow us to pursue the matter in detail here. Suffice it to say that the criticisms of Jews ascribed by Josephus to various pagan writers are extracts and selections, divorced from context, chosen or manipulated so as to leave them as easy targets for Josephus' rebuttals. He racks up an array of straw men.[3] That holds also for the notorious "blood-libel,"according to which Jews fattened up a Greek each year to sacrifice and devour him.[4] The charge appears in only one other text in all the Greco-Roman literature of antiquity. Josephus seems to have plucked out that slander precisely because it is preposterous. Few can have believed it. And it hardly represents pagan perceptions of Jews. Josephus' agenda predominates.

Feldman correctly observes that outbreaks of hostility against Jews are few and far between. They are fewer indeed than he himself allows. The miraculous escape of Jews from the thunderous herd of drunken elephants loosed by Ptolemy IV comes in a work of transparent fiction. And the happy ending, with the king coming around as champion of the Jews, gives the fable an upbeat quality that belies any notion of persecution.[5] The pogrom of 38 CE in Alexandria was certainly a horrendous one, but highly unusual and, in most ways, unique. Feldman correctly notes the complex and peculiar situation in that city. And one might observe that the perpetrators of the riots were largely Egyptians, who had special reasons for resenting the privileges of Alexandrian Jews.[6]

Feldman, however, believes that two factors did cause concern and distress among pagans when they thought about Jews (which they did not do very often): their economic and political power, and their dual loyalty (allegiance to Rome conflicted with adherence to the Temple). On these matters Feldman slips away from the cheery toward the lachrymose. But the worry may be unnecessary. Evidence for Jewish wealth or authority in the Greco-Roman world is so scanty as to be negligible. Tacitus' complaint about money being sent to the Temple is directed primarily against converts.[7] And Roman satirists more commonly compare Jews with beggars than plutocrats.[8] As for dual loyalty, did the Romans ever lose sleep over it? That Jews sought guarantees for the practice of traditional customs, like observance of the Sabbath, dietary laws, even exemption from military service, hardly amounts to dual loyalty—and the Romans were perfectly happy to give those guarantees.[9] It is particularly notable that Roman officials more than once assured Jews that they had every right to send moneys from all over the diaspora to the Temple in Jerusalem.[10] No sign here of any Roman worry about dual loyalty. Amidst the myriad complaints made about Jews for their antisocial behavior, their peculiar customs and rites, and their rigid exclusivity, the claim that they were unpatriotic appears almost nowhere. Of course, Jews declined to participate in the imperial cult. They could not square that with their religious obligations. But Rome had long been accustomed to the Jewish prohibition and had long made allowance for it. Jews would sacrifice to Yahweh on behalf of the emperor; they just would not sacrifice to the emperor himself. The Romans had no trouble with that.[11]

Instead of anti-Semitism then, do we have philo-Semitism? Professor Feldman expressed a wish to discuss the latter subject, though he confined himself largely to the former. But both concepts are strained and artificial. Pagans rarely gave serious thought to the Jews. They were not particularly worth hating or loving. As Feldman correctly observes, polytheism is by definition liberal and pluralistic. Hence, even the notion of "tolerance" may be off the mark. For a religious outlook that is inherently inclusive, the very idea of tolerance (or intolerance) has no substance. The "Roman policy of tolerance," as Feldman puts it, is therefore a misnomer. And the further postulate, that Romans pursued such a policy with the Jews because they were apprehensive about their own minority status in the empire while Jews enjoyed substantial numbers, seems not only implausible but quite unnecessary.

Feldman's essay merits commendation on numerous fronts, a refreshing response to conventional laments about Jewish experience in the classical world. He rightly reminds us that pagan authors took little notice of Jews who could go their own way, that expressions of hostility were rare, often a matter of rhetoric and not dissimilar to clichés directed toward other alien folk, that numerous admiring comments can also be found, and that actions against Jews stemmed from ad hoc circumstances and were regularly reversed. We need now only to take the next step: to dispose of misleading and anachronistic terms like "anti-Semitism," "anti-Judaism," and "Judeophobia." We don't even need "tolerance." Jews kept to their own ways, but they were part and parcel of the larger world of the Mediterranean.

Both Professor Feldman and I have emphasized the heterogeneity of the Hellenistic world and the ability of the Jewish people in diaspora to maintain their distinct identity in a multicultural universe characterized by contact with others. Feldman has focused attention on the ways in which Jewish narratives appropriate for their heroes the qualities admired by the dominant culture, while yet asserting the superiority of Judaism (in part, because of its greater antiquity). I have called special attention to legendary histories, written by Jews, declaring kinship between Jews and Spartans, Abraham and Herakles, and Moses and Mousaios (the mythical teacher of Orpheus).[12]

These and similar cultural appropriations in the Hellenistic-Roman world inevitably involved substitutions. Jews living in diaspora in the wake of the conquests of Alexander maintained their strong ties to the homeland not by living there, but through the ritualistic offering of an annual tithe in support of the Temple and through pilgrimages to it.[13] The dominant society, for its part, also accepted substitutions. Jewish prayers for the emperor substituted for their praying to him. According to Saint Augustine, the Roman grammarian Varro considered the god of the Jews the equivalent of Jupiter.[14] Others explained the Sabbath as a day honoring Saturn.[15] According to what is perhaps the most memorable of all the legends recorded by Josephus, Alexander the Great himself journeyed to Jerusalem, where he offered sacrifice to Jehovah and attributed his own military success to the Jewish god.[16] The Jewish legend puts the Macedonian general at the service of Yahweh. Where such substitutions, translations, and transpositions (real and imaginative) flourished, neither anti-Judaism nor anti-Semitism could easily arise.

Notes

1. See Erich S. Gruen, *Diaspora: Jews amidst Greeks and Romans* (Cambridge, MA: Harvard University Press, 2002).

2. Josephus, *Contra Apionem* 1.1–218.

3. See E. Gruen, "Greeks and Jews: Mutual Misperceptions in Josephus' *Contra Apionem*," in *Ancient Judaism in Its Hellenistic Context*, ed. C. Bakhos, 31–51 (Leiden: Brill, 2005).

4. Josephus, *Contra Apionem* 2.89–96.

5. The story is told in 3 Maccabees. See the analysis by Gruen, *Heritage and Hellenism: The Reinvention of Jewish Tradition* (Berkeley: University of California Press, 1998), 222–36; S. R. Johnson, *Historical Fictions and Hellenistic Jewish Identity* (Berkeley: University of California Press, 2004). Josephus' account, *Contra Apionem* 2.49–56, is surely a variant version of the same tale.

6. Cf. P. Schäfer, *Judeophobia: Attitudes toward the Jews in the Ancient World* (Cambridge, MA: Harvard University Press, 1997), 143–45; Gruen, *Diaspora*, 63–65.

7. Tacitus, *Historiae* 5.5.1.

8. Martial, 12.57.13; Juvenal, 3.10–16, 3.296, 6.542–47.

9. For example, Josephus, *Antiquities* 14.226–32, 237, 240–46, 259–61; 16.162–73.

10. Ibid., 16.163, 166–67, 169–71.

11. Philo, *Legatio ad Gaium* 133, 157, 232, 280, 356; *In Flaccum* 49; Josephus, *Bellum Judaicum* 2.197, 409; *Contra Apionem* 2.77.

12. See my "Cultural Fictions and Cultural Identity," 1993 presidential address to the American Philological Association, available at http://apaclassics.org/images/uploads/documents/gruen.pdf.

13. Gruen, *Diaspora*, 121, 243–46, 247, 249, 252. Bruce Chilton argues that Saint Paul sought to include gentile converts to Christianity within the worship of the Temple through their monetary contribution to the Church in Jerusalem. See his *Rabbi Paul: An Intellectual Biography* (New York: Random House, 2004), especially chap. 10, 222–46.

14. Gruen, *Diaspora*, 43; Augustine, *De Consensu Evangelistarum*, 1.30, 1.31, 1.42.

15. Gruen, *Diaspora*, 48; cf. Tacitus, *Historiae* 5.4.4.

16. Josephus, *Antiquities* 11.317–39.

NINE

Mimesis, Scapegoating, and Philo-Semitism
Reading Feldman and Girard

STUART D. ROBERTSON

Taking up Louis Feldman's passing observation that René Girard is right about the ubiquity of sacrifice in antiquity (and thus that Jewish scapegoat sacrifices would not have incited anti-Semitism at that time), I would like to compare and contrast the approach of Feldman to that of Girard. In his essay, Feldman graciously emphasizes his agreement with Girard. But how is it possible at a deeper level, I would like to ask, for Girard's notion of the societal scapegoat to be reconciled with Feldman's thoughts about ancient philo-Semitism? Feldman argues that Jews were not treated as scapegoats because they did not suffer from the sweeping anti-Jewish malice in the ancient world that we have seen in more recent European history. Feldman's inferences challenge modern assumptions that anti-Judaism today stems from the same bias at work in ancient times. Though on the surface this view might seem contrary to Girard's, even this apparent disagreement may be seen as a support of it. How so? Because for Girard, what is primary is not evidence but appropriation, the taking on of the perspective of another through whose eyes the world is observed and from which perspective evidence is subsequently derived. Girard offers a "grand unified theory" in the tradition of Freud, Durkheim, Einstein, and other scientific thinkers, a theory that, by definition and inherent design, embraces all the evidence within a psychological, sociological, or mathematical schema of the universe conceived as prior to it.

For Girard, the history of the Jews offers a prime example of scapegoating. Anti-Semitism demonstrates the effect of mimetic desire. It is the driving force behind supersessionism in the church, a dialectical energy Girard believes is more evidently inherent in the world than evolution is in nature. What developed historically into rivalry and persecution, however, began in the first century CE in an initially close, fraternal relationship between Jews and Christians. This historical process thus illustrates for Girard "triangular or mimetic desire" in which "our desires are copied from models or mediators whose objects of desire become our objects of desire. But the model or mediator we imitate can become our rival if we desire precisely the object he is imagined to have. . . . Jealousy and envy are inevitably aroused in this mimetic situation."[1]

Following Girard, Christian anti-Semitism could be understood as a failed form of Christianity, deriving from an unconscious appropriation of and subsequent rejection of Judaic modes. The same objects begin to be desired and rivalry ensues on the part of anti-Semites. Hence supersessionism and persecution.

Although he is careful in his essay to speak only of the inadequacy of thinking there was a widespread anti-Semitism in the ancient world, Feldman elsewhere emphasizes an early philo-Semitism. Eschewing the term "anti-Semitism" as referring to "families of languages rather than to attitudes toward people," Feldman has argued, to the contrary, that "Jews were even admired by some of the greatest thinkers of antiquity—Pythagoras, Aristotle, Theophrastus, and Varro" because of their "espousal of the four cardinal virtues."[2] Feldman cites Josephus' *Against Apion* to demonstrate that the Jews' wisdom and piety ranked above all other philosophers, "presumably including even Socrates and Plato" (*Against Apion* 1.162). Josephus deliberately compares his people with the finest of the Gentiles. Josephus' portrait of Abraham, the patriarch, shows "a man of extreme sagacity, gifted not only with high intelligence but with power to convince his hearers on any subject which he undertook to teach, he introduced [the Egyptians] to arithmetic and transmitted to them the laws of astronomy . . . whence they passed to the Greeks" (*Antiquities* 1.166–68). The *Antiquities* has been compared to the publications of the Anti-Defamation League, which, though written to dissuade those who defame them, are read more by Jews. But *Against Apion* is an apology for the Jews and Judaism brief enough to draw more widespread interest. There is no evidence, however, from ancient writers that they read his apology for Judaism.

Indeed, some would question the strength of Feldman's larger case for a predominant philo-Semitism in the ancient world of which his essay is a part.[3] Feldman supports his view in the face of the opening paragraph of *Against Apion*, where Josephus writes: "I observe that a considerable number of persons, influenced by the malicious calumnies of certain individuals, discredit the statements in my history concerning our antiquity, and adduce as proof of the comparative modernity of our race the fact that it has not been thought worthy of mention by the best known Greek historians." Whether Josephus was correct or not, he envisages "a considerable number of persons" who think ill of his people. The ill thought has to do with more than their alleged lack of antiquity. Josephus acknowledges their *amixia*, their not mingling easily in the societies of their exile. He defends his people against various canards and misunderstandings circulating in the Hellenistic-Roman world.

Feldman observes that only a small fraction of what was written in the ancient world survives. And he offers formidable evidence that included in this fragmentary corpus is very little that can be deemed anti-Jewish. Indeed, the evidence for sweeping cultural and official anti-Judaism is simply not there. But this absence does not count against Girard's theory, because, for Girard, an originary desire for the admired Other is the wellspring of later persecution: "The theory of the surrogate victim is paradoxical in that it is based on facts whose empirical characteristics are not directly accessible. . . . The inaccessible character of the generative event is . . . an essential part of the theory."[4] To be sure, Girard does not take up Feldman's examples of philo-Semitism and turn them in favor of his own theory, since the historical is less his theme than the anthropological, and the extent to which Jewish and Christian scriptures offer us an anthropological reading of primitive religion and culture. But putting the two side by side, we may observe that Feldman's arguments, which could otherwise appear contrary to Girard's mimetic theory, could also be received as evidence supporting triangular mimetic desire.

To compare Girard with Feldman, in other words, requires assessing evidence with contrary if not opposite assumptions. Feldman's thesis rests on evidence. He offers an empirically based argument rather than an appropriation based argument. Though it would impose upon him a humanly impossible impartiality to say that he is not guided by a theory, we can say that his theory is not so iron-clad as Girard's. Girard's theory is a theory of the primacy of appropriation, not the primacy of evidence. Girard postulates a theory that follows from his reading of the great European novelists and other great writers of the Western tradition (Shakespeare, Dostoyevsky) and a vast body of anthropological literature (found in Mauss, Durkheim, and others) that necessitates the unconsciousness of the processes at work. No scapegoaters declare that they are scapegoating, he is fond of saying. To the extent that such knowledge becomes available, it undermines the efficacy of the scapegoating process. The mystery of witch hunts is not, in his view, that they occurred but that we know about them. If we have survived for two thousand years with that knowledge, it can only be because some source of light has made that knowledge available to us—a transmission he assigns to Jewish and Christian scriptures. His mimetic theory in many ways displays the difference between an a priori and an a posteriori argument, one that comes at the beginning point, prior to the evidence and in the midst of human relations, and one that comes at the end point, as a consequence of human relations that inspects "evidence" presumed to be external. Girard himself arrived at his theory after having inspected historical, literary, and anthropological texts, and these texts are the evidence to which his theory bears witness.[5] His apodictic style, his certainty about the value of his theory is as unswerving as that of any great thinker and could seem unduly appropriative itself to readers unaware of the stakes of the argument—no less than a theory of order and disorder in the primitive and modern universe founded around sacrificial substitution. By contrast, Feldman begins from the bottom up, modestly offering an account of ancient attitudes toward Judaism.

To compare Feldman with Girard is therefore a precarious exercise. Not only do they hold different views, they begin from different epistemological assumptions. Girard offers, for example, a reading of the Incarnation that he sees, along with the Passion, as the announcement of the end of scapegoating. Although Girard's personal faith is Christian, his anthropological views and his views about the potential of scripture as anthropological reading have been accepted by non-Christians as well.

Similarly, Feldman's views of ancient Jewish-Christian relations are evident in many articles that describe Josephus' retelling to the non-Jewish world the stories of biblical characters clad in the cardinal virtues admired by the Greeks. He says boldly that Josephus' apologetic utilized the idealism of the ancient world. He draws evidence from Josephus' writing, placed along images of heroic virtue drawn by Greek writers. Does he overdraw the parallels between Josephus and the Greek writers? Even though his view is derived from close study of the evidence, does he perhaps overstate the case, because he is sure what was in Josephus' mind? Girard, having set forth his conviction of the ubiquitous operation of mimesis, would probably defend Feldman's view of the evidence for literary imitation by Jews of Gentiles, and vice versa, as an expression of mimetic desire, culling support from a mimetic reading of the evidence. Girard's approach can seem procrustean to one who does not share his view. One wonders, though, whether the violent pogrom that occurred in Alexandria did not take place precisely because an unusually high degree of mutual emulation between the Jews and Gentiles of that city had turned into a Girardian mimetic rivalry.

Notes

1. James G. Williams, ed., *The Girard Reader* (New York: Crossroad, 1996), 3.

2. See *Jew and Gentile in the Ancient World* (Princeton, NJ: Princeton University Press, 1993), 201.

3. See, for example, Erich Gruen, who argues in the preceding chapter, "Beyond Anti-Judaism: Louis Feldman and the 'Lachrymose Version' of Jewish History," that Jews were neither particularly admired nor condemned in the ancient world but regarded as members of a pluralistic, polytheistic community.

4. Williams, *Reader*, 20.

5. His dissertation was on medieval history in Provençal France. His first major book was on five European novelists. And his work since then has been on cultural anthropology and the genesis of modern understanding of sacrifice and scapegoating derived from our religious scriptures and great literature.

PART 2

Scripture

Hebrew Scripture: Genesis 22

TEN

Creation and *Akedah*

Blessing and Sacrifice in the Hebrew Scriptures

MATTHEW PATTILLO

According to Girard's mimetic theory, the Hebrew scriptures trace the history of a people who progressively transcended the human sacrifice prevalent among the Near Eastern peoples from whom Abraham and his descendants emerged. Initially, in the patriarchal stage of Hebrew history, an animal was substituted for the human victim. During the Passover stage of Israel's history, the postsacrificial communal meal becomes emphasized over the ritual killing aspect of sacrifice. In the later prophetic critiques, all sacrifice is denounced as displeasing to God. The full revelation of the true nature of sacrifice comes in the Gospel texts that record one man's victory over mimetic rivalry and the victimary mechanism. The Gospel revelation, though, is not alien to the Hebrew scriptures; it is already detailed there, according to Girard, in a number of narratives—for example, the stories of Abel, Joseph, Job, and the Judgment of Solomon—and inscribed in the Psalms and the prophets.[1]

Against Girard's position, it has been argued that these anti-sacrificial texts never formed the heart of the Judaic revelation. The main text for Judaism, the argument goes, was always the Torah, a unified and consistent whole, the center of which—and the intended center of religious life in Israel—is sacrifice. To the extent that mimetic theory traces the displacement of sacrifice and the "sacrificial way of thinking"[2] in its recounting of biblical history, the canonical narrative that mimetic theory develops is unavoidably supersessionist (Girard's critics say) in character. Girard and his disciples invite, in fact, the charges of anti-Judaism and triumphalism,[3] because mimetic theory, like much of Christian theology, relegates God's historical relationship to Israel to a propaedeutic function whose purpose has been superseded by Christian revelation.[4] This supersession or displacement of Israel, in turn, renders Israel and its history largely indecisive for matters of faith,[5] and even counterproductive to the Church's proclamation of redemption through Christ, to the extent the Jewish people insist on a distinct and continuing role for Israel in God's interaction with the world.

Two other criticisms of mimetic theory are closely related to the charge of supersessionism. The first is the contention by some that Girard is anticreationist, that mimetic theory is irreconcilable with *ex nihilo* creation by God.[6] The second is that the interpretation of Abraham's binding of Isaac (*Akedah*) in mimetic theory is the work of an "impoverished religious imagination"[7] that can discern no meaning in the *Akedah* apart from a polemic against child sacrifice. Indeed, relative to other texts in the Hebrew scriptures, mimetic theory and its proponents devote little attention either to the creation and Edenic accounts in the opening chapters of Genesis or to the *Akedah* in Genesis 22. The lack of attention indicates that for these critics these texts are indecisive for mimetic theory, but the foundational character of these texts for Torah and for Judaism calls for a closer reading. Girard writes, "the illusion that there is difference within the heart of violence is the key to the sacrificial way of thinking,"[8] but "illusions" as well as clarity concerning sacrifice in Israel are rooted in the Genesis texts detailing God's creation and the origins of sacrifice in Israel.

In this essay I focus on the relationship between Adam and Abraham, between creation and the *Akedah,* as defined by scripture itself and by the Jewish and Christian interpretive traditions surrounding these key passages. Drawing upon both mimetic theory and classical rabbinic exegesis, I argue, first, that Abraham's binding of Isaac in Genesis 22 signals God's liberation of Abraham and his descendants from the world of violence inaugurated by Adam's idolatrous disobedience, his rivalry with God, and, second, that the Temple sacrificial system, erected at the memorial site of the *Akedah,* symbolizes the continuing preservation and reenactment of divine redemption for Israel through its practice of obedience. In Christ's crucifixion and resurrection, finally,

God extends the *Akedah*'s revelation from Israel to the nations, offering to all people across time the Abrahamic reversal of Adam's sin and exile.

Economy of Sin and Redemption within the Economy of Blessing and Consummation

Christian theology has tended historically to construe its Bible within a framework that begins with the sin of Adam and Eve and finds its resolution in redemption through Jesus Christ. The biblical narrative, however, begins not with the disobedience of Adam and Eve but with God's original creative acts and purposes. Wesley Theological Seminary's R. Kendall Soulen has proposed that the economy of redemption is but a secondary matter where the larger biblical narrative is concerned. He places the antithesis of sin and redemption within a "more basic narrative context, namely, the unfolding of God's work as the Consummator of human creation."[9] As consummator, God's work "revolves around God's blessing and its power to communicate life, wholeness, well-being and joy to *that which is other than God*."[10] In the Torah, Soulen suggests, sacrifice functions in the service of God's overarching purposes as creator and consummator of creation, because sacrifice directs creation in its obedient return to God, at whose word it first came into existence.

The creation account of Genesis 1:1–2:3 records the inauguration of the "economy of mutual blessing between those who are different."[11] The primary relation of difference and mutual blessing between God and humanity is defined in Genesis 1:26–28, with God entrusting the management of his creation to the male and female he has created. It is a partnership between humankind and God, though, in light of God's place as creator and issuer of commandments,[12] the partnership must be qualified as a *submitted* partnership. The relationship between man and woman is likewise one of interdependence for the purpose of mutual blessing,[13] the divinely intended relationship between God and humankind, man and woman, parent and child, and humankind and nature. One may be reluctant to describe God as being interdependent with men and women, yet within the Genesis account God is portrayed as relying on humans to care for his creation. God even takes the form of a servant in the creation account, bringing the animals to Adam so that Adam can name them and find a suitable partner and then fashioning that partner by God's own hand.

The Genesis account of creation is clear that "the Lord's blessing is available only through the blessing of an other."[14] God blesses his creation[15] and is, in turn, blessed by that which is other than himself. In Soulen's words, "God's own activity as one who blesses what is other and who is blessed in return"[16] is the essence of the "image and like- ness" of God to which humanity conforms. Girard describes positive mimesis in similarly reciprocal terms, as "the opening out of oneself" toward another, an "extreme openness" that is "the basis of heroism and devotion to others."[17] Interdependence for mutual blessing is, for Girard, at once the "desire for God" and the "positive desire for the other"[18] defining positive mimesis.

In his command to "be fruitful and multiply," God establishes the relationship of interdependence for mutual blessing from parent to child and from generation to generation. The real theme of Genesis 2–11 is genealogical in nature,[19] tracing the fulfillment of God's com- mandment to extend the mutual blessing of the other throughout the world. In Genesis 12, God again initiates a relationship of mutual blessing among those who are different, when he separates Abraham and his descendants as a people and promises that through this family all families of the earth will be blessed.[20] The relationship of differ- ence among families of the earth is already anticipated in the creation account when God blesses the seventh day and sets it apart as the Sabbath. As this command is later given to Israel in the wilderness at Sinai, the creation of the Sabbath and its blessing form the true cli- max of the creation account, for the distinction between Israel and the nations is intrinsic to God's creative purposes.[21] The relationship be- tween Israel and the nations is not occasioned by the economy of sin and redemption, but is instead part of God's design for creation from the beginning.[22]

The Genesis prehistory records humanity's interference with God's creative purposes, but God's purposes are never thwarted. Humanity resists giving and receiving the blessing of the other, and the intended blessed relationship often becomes a cursed relationship instead. Nevertheless, the current of Genesis 1–12 makes clear that God's original purposes for creation do not change. Despite human rebellion, God's economy of redemption will be worked out in a way that accords with and furthers his work as creator and consummator of creation.

Mimetic Rivalry

Having established in its first two chapters the primacy of positive mimesis, the Bible records in Genesis 3 the entrance of negative mimesis—mimetic rivalry, or sin. The serpent, embodying mimetic rivalry with God, questions Eve concerning God's proscription against the tree of the knowledge of good and evil. In mimetic theory, desire is always mediated by an other, and until the serpent enters the scene, God mediates Eve's desire toward the tree. It is tempting to think God's prohibition must have provoked the very desire he wanted to restrict, but according to the Bible it is the serpent who suggests God's restriction is motivated by rivalry. Rather, God's prohibition should be interpreted as a model for Eve's aversion to the tree. Eve mimetically adopts the desire of her model, Adam, who has adopted his own aversion to the tree from his model, God.

When he first arrives on the scene, the serpent is already in mimetic conflict with God, a rivalry explicated by Christian tradition in the story of the revolt and judgment of the archangel Lucifer. Christianity often inserts this story between the first and second days of creation, whereas Jewish tradition sometimes places the entrance of mimetic rivalry into the world on day two, believing the separation of the waters indicates the introduction of strife.[23] Regardless of placement, the Genesis account assumes the potential for rift or rivalry as a fact of creation. The Jewish Sages hold the disobedience and exile of Adam and Eve happens the very day of their creation, the sixth.[24] Even this early rivalry, though, does not prevent God from bestowing on the seventh day a blessing upon all of creation: "So God blessed the seventh day and hallowed it, because on it God rested from all his work which he had done in creation" (Gn 2:3). The human capacity to refuse negative mimesis and to choose instead submitted partnership with God is always assumed.

The interaction of Eve, the serpent, Adam, and God is a detailed account of mimetic theory in action. The serpent appears to be in mimetic conflict with God, evidenced by his accusation that God is himself a jealous rival. Eve, though already under the influence of Adam's model, is persuaded by the appearance of a new model who is the rival of the first model. As "metaphysical desire is eminently contagious,"[25] Eve adopts the desire of her new model. Adam falls prey to the contagion, modeling his desire on Eve and so rivaling his creator. Of the players in the drama, God alone remains unaffected by mimetic rivalry.

Adam forfeits his relationship of submitted partnership with God by choosing rivalry with God. This rivalry spreads mimetically to all humanity inasmuch as all humans make the same choice to participate in rivalry with God and, consequently, with one another. The penalty for this choice is death, in that antagonistic mimesis leads to violent contagion, setting in motion the mechanism in which a single innocent victim is executed. The story of Cain and Abel completes the cycle of mimetic rivalry, violent contagion, and the victimary mechanism, as Girard explains these ideas. Acquisitive mimesis gives way to antagonistic rivalry for God's blessing, which is resolved by murder. Cain represents the mob that unanimously kills the innocent victim, Abel. That Cain becomes the founder of the first city confirms the hypothesis that the victimary mechanism is the cornerstone of culture and civilization.

The stories of Adam and Eve, and of Cain and Abel, as read by Soulen, portray individuals refusing the blessing of the other—that is to say, in Girardian terms, refusing the reciprocity of positive mimesis. Adam and Eve refuse the blessing of God that is contingent upon maintaining a distinct otherness between God and humanity. They are tempted to become "like God,"[26] tempted to erase any distinction. Similarly, by cutting off Abel from the realm of blessing, Cain cuts himself off as well, for it is through the other, Abel, that God intends to bless Cain.[27] Mimetic rivalry between humanity and God and within the human family increases exponentially in the Genesis account until "the earth was filled with violence."[28] God decides he will not "strive with man"[29] forever, destroying the world in an all-consuming flood. Preserving his economy of blessing in the ark with Noah and his family, God reaffirms his blessing on the human family at Noah's disembarkment and reasserts his intention that they "fill the earth."[30] Later, the families of the earth again rebel against God's command on the plains of Shinar, attempting to "exploit the unity of the human family in order to frustrate God's intention to bless through difference."[31] However, God prevents their unanimous revolt and restores difference — and therefore the potential for blessing — by confusing their languages. "Like the narrative of God's creation of woman from man's side," Soulen argues, "the story of Babel portrays the movement from sameness to difference as mandated by the logic of divine blessing."[32]

The negative mimetic tendencies of humanity thus never consume the potential for positive mimesis that God intends for humanity in the Genesis prehistory. God's order of difference and mutual blessing is complicated by mimetic rivalry — the renunciation of the blessing of the other — but is never defeated. The theme of Genesis 1–11 is God's established order of difference between the divine and the human, man and woman, humanity and nature, parent and child, and generation and generation. With the call of Abraham, God establishes a relationship with Israel as doubly different. On the one hand, it is different from other nations. On the other, God works through Israel for the blessing of all the world, and that is the unifying theme of the Hebrew Scriptures from Genesis 12 on. The Gospel revelation must also be understood in this context.

Taken out of the context of God's order (which is characterized by difference and mutual blessing), negative mimesis and its resultant violence, as described in Genesis 1–11, seem catastrophic. The biblical record, though, contextualizes the economy of redemption within the economy of consummation without minimizing the tragic effects of sin. Neither does mimetic theory lose any of its explanatory power when recontextualized in the same way. The mimetic rivalry described in the Garden of Eden and the founding murder recorded in the story of Cain and Abel remain intact, and the preceding creation story is allowed to contextualize both.

The Reversal of Mimetic Rivalry: Abraham as New Adam

The Genesis stories accurately describe mimetic rivalry and its consequences within the human family, but the source of rivalry among humans is always rivalry with God. "Every victim of metaphysical desire,"
Girard writes, "covets his mediator's divinity,"[33] and thus are Adam
and Eve victimized, with the tantalizing promise of being "like God,
knowing good and evil" (cf. Gn 3:5). Adam and Eve seek to erase the
difference between themselves and God, and by so doing, cut themselves off from the blessed relationship of otherness to God. Mimetic
rivalry, or sin, is "not simply an act of disobedience against God but an
attempt to overthrow God by making man into a God-like creature."[34]

In the Garden of Eden, Adam and Eve are tempted to appropriate for themselves that "blessed self-sufficiency, which is in the
last analysis the quality possessed by the deity."[35] The "blessed self-
sufficiency" in the garden is the "knowledge of good and evil," the
quality of God by which he judges the good to be good and the evil to
be evil. The prohibition against the tree indicates, in the words of Michael Wyschogrod, that "God does not wish man to have this knowledge. He is to obey God in order to obey God and for no other reason."[36] Having eaten from the tree, however, Adam and Eve begin to
make their own judgments about what is good and what is evil and
as such "are no longer dependent on God's command as the exclusive
source of guidance in moral matters."[37]

The first evidence of Adam and Eve's misappropriated authority
is their judgment that they should do something to remedy the predicament of their nakedness.[38] Finding them after their transgression,
God asks them, "Who told you that you were naked?" He realizes that
Adam and Eve have eaten from the tree and are now making moral
judgments for themselves. Thus, God's banishment of Adam and Eve
from the garden mirrors and magnifies the humans' prior dismissal of
God from their lives, for "when man develops a morality not based on
God's commandment . . . an act of expulsion has occurred."[39]

Adam and Israel, Jacob Neusner claims, are mirror images, and
the story of humans in the Garden of Eden parallels the tale of Israel
in its land.[40] Whereas Adam and Eve took upon themselves the right

to decide good and evil, right and wrong, Abraham demonstrates in his binding of Isaac a sole and radical obedience to the commandments of God. While Adam and Eve are evicted from the garden, Abraham and his promised descendants are invited by God to take up residence in "the land that I will show you" (Gn 12:3). The themes of exile and return dominate the Hebrew scriptures. The Christian notion of a "fall" infers an ontological loss, a fall from a higher to a lower condition. Exile, on the other hand, refers not to the diminishment of the person but to the loss of intimacy with God; return signifies the restoration of the damaged relationship between God and humanity.

Through Abraham's (and, the rabbis say, Isaac's) obedience, the *Akedah* represents the reversal of mimetic rivalry with God and therefore the reversal of God's expulsion of humankind from paradise. In the Hebrew scriptures, in Levenson's view, "there is no category at all of 'the ethical' in the sense of a universal set of moral claims independent of the Deity's command."[41] Consequently, although God intervenes at the last moment to prevent Abraham from immolating his beloved son, Wyschogrod argues, "Jewish consciousness did not infer from this episode that the ethical in some way rules independently and therefore serves to check God's arbitrary demands, but rather it deduced a model of human behavior definable as obedience."[42] Abraham reestablishes a relationship with God based on obedience and submission to God, and Abraham's descendants are the continuing incarnation of this relationship.

The prohibition against murder in the Noachide laws (Gn 9:6) and the condemnation of Cain's murder (Gn 4:10–15) argue against the view that the *Akedah* is a mere polemic against murder or human sacrifice. Furthermore, the tacit approval of animal sacrifice earlier in the Genesis text by Abraham, Noah, Abel, and even God himself (when he covers the man and woman with animal skins in the garden) renders the deflection of violence from human to animal victims inessential to the meaning of the *Akedah*. Similarly, the prohibition elsewhere in the Torah against child sacrifice makes the *Akedah* superfluous as a condemnation of child sacrifice.[43] (Sadly, as Bruce Chilton has pointed out in his book *Abraham's Curse*, not every age has recognized either that superfluity or the profoundly anti-sacrificial message of the offering on Mt. Moriah.)[44]

What, then, is the essential meaning, the revelation, of the *Akedah*? Prior to the *Akedah*, God attaches to Isaac by name (Gn 17:19), even before his birth, the promise of the fulfillment of God's purposes as consummator of creation. God has thus established an order of dependence and blessing between parent and child, one generation and the next, thereby creating a relationship between Abraham, Isaac, and their descendants that transcends blood relations. It is God, too, who has promised Abraham that Isaac will be the vehicle of blessing to Israel and the nations. Abraham's relationship with Isaac is, Wyschogrod writes, "radically different from the relationship of any other father to any other son," and thus Abraham's sacrifice "must be understood above all as self-sacrifice or, more accurately, sacrifice of what is even more precious than the self." [45]

Abraham renounces mimetic rivalry with God, choosing instead to be the "friend of God."[46] Abraham obeys God "in order to obey God and for no other reason,"[47] Wyschogrod asserts, an obedience establishing Israel, long before the event at Sinai, as the people of God. Abraham repudiates the serpent's mediation and renounces the pride of usurpation and auto-apotheosis.[48] Renouncing the rivalry with God (negative mimesis) of Adam and Eve and their slavery to sin, Abraham reestablishes submission to God (positive mimesis) as the model for the human relationship to God and becomes the father of Israel. God reaffirms the promise of Genesis 12:1–3,[49] but now incorporates Abraham's obedience into the divine promise.[50]

The Resurrection of Sacrifice in the Hebrew Scriptures

Abraham's obedience to God is mirrored and magnified in Isaac's obedience to Abraham. From Isaac's point of view, the *Akedah*, in Wyschogrod's perspective, "lays down the principle that to be loved by God requires the willingness to accept death at the hand of God."[51] This acceptance of death is not the acceptance of a just punishment meted out by God, but rather a submission to the fate of death that awaits all those born into God's creation. It is an acknowledgement of God's work as creator and an affirmation of the goodness of creation in all of its aspects, including death.

Raymund Schwager observes that "in the course of the Old Testament, the notion of sacrifice (not the hidden sacrifice-mechanism) was progressively linked to the idea of obedience."[52] In the *Akedah,* however, obedience becomes the permanent foundation for sacrifice in Israel, Wyschogrod notes, "the original sacrifice to which all subsequent sacrifice points."[53] All subsequent sacrifice in Israel, Levenson concurs, is "a continuing commemoration and reenactment of the radical obedience" of the *Akedah.*[54] Consequently, to be Jewish, to be a son or daughter of Abraham, is to obey God in imitation of Abraham.

To be a son or daughter of Abraham, though, is to be a sacrificial victim. Willingly submitting himself to sacrifice in obedience to his father, Isaac takes the form of the innocent victim in the *Akedah.* Isaac's identity is forever that of the victim, and Israel's identity is also that of the victim. Indeed, Israel is identified both with Abraham in his radical obedience to the commandment of God and with Isaac as the innocent victim and cooperative sacrificer. Even though Abraham's hand was stayed against Isaac, Jewish tradition credits Abraham as though he had sacrificed Isaac. Similarly, although Isaac is spared, it is as though he had been immolated, and he becomes a living sacrifice.[55] Just as Israel is described as a nation of priests in its identification with Abraham, the great high priest of the human race, Israel can be described as a nation of living sacrifices in its identification with Isaac. After the *Akedah,* God incorporates identification with the victim into the divine promise of Genesis 12:1–3.

"We will worship and then we will come back to you," Abraham prophesies.[56] Resurrection is closely related to the idea of return: Abraham returns Isaac to God who had given him; God then returns Isaac to his father, with the promise of even greater future returns. Abraham's offering of Isaac is not disinterested sacrifice, but obedience in the hope of receiving Isaac again.[57] God's later offering of the Messiah, God's own son, is likewise, from a Christian point of view, no masochistic self-denial, but the answer in kind to Abraham's offering.[58]

"All social structure, the entire scapegoating machinery, is revealed as delusional," Sandor Goodhart observes, "a delusional quality we are not permitted to see fully unless we observe the victim 'after death' so to speak."[59] It is the resurrection of Isaac that converts Abraham. Isaac's "apparent resurrection," Girard writes, "is the subjective correlative of something most objective and real, (Abraham's) renunciation of (Adam's) bad desire."[60] Neither Abraham nor Isaac was divinized in Israel, nor were they found guilty of any crime. The innocence of the victim upon which Cain founded the first city is forever revealed *for Israel* in the resurrection of Isaac, and the people of Israel are the incarnation of the *Akedah* revelation.[61]

Levitical Sacrifices and the Prophetic Critique of Sacrifice

The Levitical sacrifices prescribed by the Torah have meaning to the extent that they participate in the meaning of Isaac's self-sacrifice and are offered in the spirit of Abraham's self-sacrificial obedience. The nature of the Levitical sacrifices—innocent animals, kosher and unblemished—strengthens the identification with Isaac as innocent victim. The insistence that the sacrifices be offered only on Mount Moriah, the present-day Temple Mount, underscores the physical connection between the *Akedah* and the Levitical sacrifices.[62] The Temple sacrificial system contemporizes the *Akedah* in Israel's history, preserving revelation in Israel until the Messiah would proclaim revelation to all the world. In this sense Israel, as the carrier of God's blessing and revelation, is preserved through sacrifice, and the world, in turn, is preserved through Israel.[63] The Levitical sacrifices are of a qualitatively different nature than those practiced among the nations for the temporary expulsion of violence.

Careful analysis of the later prophetic critique of sacrifice reveals, in Wyschogrod's words, that "they were directed at sacrifices without repentance and not at sacrifices as such."[64] The prophetic critique decries any sacrifice that has renounced the spirit of the *Akedah* and has become instead a mere imitation of what mimetic theory terms the victimary mechanism. The fourfold spirit of the *Akedah* (understood from a Girardian perspective consistent with Israel's own) consists of obedience to God, repentance for participation in mimetic rivalry with God (a form of idolatry) and the scapegoating of others, submission to the will of God even to the point of death, and, finally, identification with the victim. Consequently, the prophets condemn sacrifice to the extent that it does not partake of the meaning of the *Akedah* revelation.

Alongside the many prophetic passages condemning sacrifices,[65] however, stand numerous prophetic passages extolling the virtue of obedient sacrifice and predicting the triumphant return of faithful sacrifice in Israel.[66] The relationship between the sacrifices commanded by and acceptable to God and the prophetic critique of sacrifice is clearly defined in Psalm 51. The context is David's adulterous transgression with Bathsheba and his subsequent murder of Uriah the Hittite. When confronted by God, David admits the source of sin—his rivalry with God: "Against thee, thee only, have I sinned, and done that which is evil in thy sight" (Ps 51:3–4). His rivalry with God has resulted in rivalry with Uriah, in turn leading to the Hittite's murder. He appeals to God to free him from his mimetic rivalry: "Take not thy holy Spirit from me . . . uphold me with a willing spirit" (Ps 51:11–12). The willing spirit for which David prays is the spirit of Abraham, who was willing to obey God at all cost. The "holy Spirit" of which he speaks is the spirit of Isaac, the spirit of the victim and the defender of victims.

David realizes sacrifice alone cannot save him—"For thou hast no delight in sacrifice; were I to give a burnt offering, thou wouldst not be pleased" (Ps 51:16)—and that his salvation requires repentance: "The sacrifice acceptable to God is a broken spirit; a broken and contrite heart, O God, thou wilt not despise" (Ps 51:17). The sacrifice acceptable to God is self-sacrifice, a sacrifice of the heart and the spirit, and as such, David's hope of salvation is in the identification of his own heart and spirit with the heart and spirit of Abraham/Isaac. David submits to the will of God—"Thou art justified in thy sentence and blameless in thy judgment" (Ps 51:4)—and in turn recognizes the blood guilt of mimetic rivalry with others (Ps 51:14). In the end, David renounces mimetic rivalry with God: "Cast me not away from thy presence . . . restore to me the joy of thy salvation" (Ps 51:11–12).

To omit the final lines of the psalm is to do violence to the full revelation of God: "Do good to Zion in thy good pleasure; rebuild the walls of Jerusalem, then wilt thou delight in right sacrifices, in burnt offerings and whole burnt offerings; then bulls will be offered on thy altar" (Ps 51:18–19). It will be contended, Girard notes, that later Temple scribes added these lines to David's "in order to give his work an appearance of religious orthodoxy,"[67] but the conclusion is crucial to the psalm's prophetic reassertion of the true spirit of sacrifice, the spirit of obedience and repentance that attends every true sacrifice in Israel, the same spirit inspiring and informing the *Akedah* revelation. The Levitical sacrifices preserve revelation in Israel until the *Akedah* would be proclaimed for all the world in the Messiah, son of David.

Akedah and Gospel

The Gospel revelation is that Jesus entered and brought to light that dark place in our culture where we accuse and execute innocent victims to relieve our own confusion, violence, and sin. The heart of the victimary mechanism is dark because its true nature is concealed, as it must be in order to be effective. The veiled reality of this mechanism finds a parallel in the holiest place of the Temple, set apart by a veil, and the Gospels record the rending of the veil at the very moment of Jesus' death, forever opening that dark place to the light of truth. Israel, however, always knew what was going on behind the veil in the Temple, even if the revelation remained mysterious in its effects: when the veil was finally removed, the mystery of the *Akedah* was exposed to all the world. The Gospel revelation is a mystery, but it, too, is a mystery revealed. The once-secret knowledge of the victimary mechanism is now forever brought to light: the *Akedah* was the Gospel preached to Israel; the Gospel is the *Akedah* for the nations.

All of the elements of the Christian notion of sacrifice are present in the *Akedah*: obedience, nonviolent love, identification, intercession, and conversion.[68] The *Akedah* is Abraham's priestly intercession for the coming of the Messiah; the Levitical sacrifices are fourteen centuries of priestly intercession for the coming of the Messiah. In his life, death, and resurrection (so Christians believe), Jesus Christ echoes and confirms all of the great realities of the *Akedah*. In his perfect submission to the will of God and self-sacrificial love toward all people, Jesus embodies positive mimesis, mirrors and magnifies Abraham's positive mimesis, and amplifies the blessings of the *Akedah* from Israel to the nations, as promised in Genesis 12:1–3.

Although every victim of the victimary mechanism is innocent of the charges leveled against him, everyone, including the victim himself, is indebted to the cycle of rivalry, violence, and murder upon which all culture is founded and sustained. Jesus, as second Adam, new Abraham, and new Isaac, is a man who in no way participates in this mimetic rivalry and its subsequent violence and murder. Jesus resists Satan's enticements to rivalry with God in a direct confrontation with the enemy in the wilderness,[69] and also in an indirect challenge through his own disciple Peter.[70] Jesus refuses to join in the condemnation of the woman caught in adultery and of others ostracized by reason of physical or spiritual contamination.[71] Ultimately, Jesus selflessly and willingly becomes the single victim of the violent contagion, but, as the Gospel proclaims, Jesus is innocent — not only of the false accusations brought against him but also of any guilt or debt at all in relation to mimetic rivalry and the victimary mechanism. The Gospel revelation of his innocence and obedience to God extends the revelation of the *Akedah*.

In his conversation with David Cayley, Girard has described the *Akedah* as *against sacrifice,* as evidence of God's work within the sacrificial system to transcend sacrifice.[72] The profoundly anti-sacrificial revelation of the *Akedah*, I argue, is that submission to God is the victory over mimetic rivalry with God, and that identification with the victim is the victory over the victimary mechanism. "That the blessing of Abraham might come upon the Gentiles" (Gal 3:14), God offers in Christ the *Akedah* for all the world, a sacrifice against sacrifice.

Extending the Anti-sacrificial to the World

The relationship of interdependence for mutual blessing between Israel and the nations is ultimately intrinsic to God's revelation to the world. "The Gospel text," Goodhart observes, "is fundamentally Jewish . . . reconceiving the Mosaic revelation . . . for a wider audience."[73]

God's invitation goes out from Israel to all the families of the earth to embrace the self-sacrificial character of the innocent victim and to join the family of God in submission and obedience to God, extreme openness and devotion to others. The differentiated unity of the *Akedah* and the Gospel mirrors the divinely intended and enduring relationship between Israel and the nations, and the reflection of God's revelation in the world is, finally, nothing less than life from the dead.

Notes

1. René Girard, *Things Hidden since the Foundation of the World* (Stanford, CA: Stanford University Press, 1978); René Girard, *I See Satan Fall Like Lightning* (Maryknoll, NY: Orbis Books, 1999); René Girard, *The Scapegoat* (Baltimore: Johns Hopkins University Press, 1986).

2. Girard, *Things Hidden,* 266.

3. Walter Wink, *Engaging the Powers: Discernment and Resistance in a World of Domination* (Minneapolis: Fortress Press, 1992), 153–55.

4. For the Girardian version of supersessionism, see Robert G. Hamerton-Kelly, "Sacred Violence and the Curse of the Law (Gal. 3:13): The Death of Christ as a Sacrificial Travesty," *New Testament Studies* 36 (1990): 98–118; also Robert J. Daly, S.J., "Is Christianity Sacrificial or Antisacrificial?" *Religion* 27 (1997): 231–43; For a response to the accusation of anti-Semitism, see René Girard, "Is There Anti-Semitism in the Gospels?" *Biblical Interpretation* 1, no. 3 (1993): 339–52.

5. R. Kendall Soulen, *The God of Israel and Christian Theology* (Minneapolis: Fortress Press, 1996), 31.

6. René Girard, "Violence, Difference, Sacrifice: A Conversation with René Girard," interview by Rebecca Adams, *Religion & Literature* 25, no. 2 (Summer 1993): 20–21.

7. J. D. Levenson, "Abusing Abraham: Traditions, Religious Histories, and Modern Misinterpretations; Post-Kantian Analysis of the Aqedah as Rational Theology," *Judaism* 47, no. 3 (1998): 259–77.

8. Girard, *Things Hidden,* 266.

9. Soulen, *The God of Israel and Christian Theology,* 115. For a treatment of the relation of violence to blessing from a Girardian point of view, see Vern Neufeld Redekop, *From Violence to Blessing: How an Understanding of a Deep-rooted Conflict Can Open Paths of Reconciliation* (Ottawa: Novalis, 2002).

10. Soulen, *The God of Israel and Christian Theology,* 116.

11. Ibid.

12. Gn 1:28: "And God blessed them, and God said to them, 'Be fruitful and multiply, and fill the earth and subdue it; and have dominion over the fish of the sea and over the birds of the air and over every living thing that moves upon the earth'"; Gn 2:17: "But of the tree of the knowledge of good and evil you shall not eat, for in the day that you eat of it you shall die." For biblical citations, I use RSV, unless otherwise stated.

13. Gn 2:18: "Then the Lord God said, 'It is not good that the man should be alone; I will make him a helper fit for him.'"

14. Soulen, *The God of Israel and Christian Theology*, 117.

15. Gn 1:22: "And God blessed them, saying, 'Be fruitful and multiply and fill the waters in the seas, and let birds multiply on the earth'"; cf. Gn 1:28; Gn 2:3: "So God blessed the seventh day and hallowed it, because on it God rested from all his work which he had done in creation."

16. Soulen, *The God of Israel and Christian Theology*, 135.

17. Girard, "Violence, Difference, Sacrifice," 24.

18. Ibid., 25.

19. Soulen, *The God of Israel and Christian Theology*, 118.

20. Gn 12:1–3: "Now the Lord said to Abram, 'Go from your country and your kindred and your father's house to the land that I will show you. And I will make of you a great nation, and I will bless you, and make your name great, so that you will be a blessing. I will bless those who bless you, and him who curses you I will curse; and by you all the families of the earth will bless themselves.'"

21. Soulen, *The God of Israel and Christian Theology*, 118.

22. Ibid., 117–18.

23. *The Chumash: The Torah, Haftaros and Five Megillos with a Commentary Anthologized from the Rabbinic Writings*, ed. Rabbi Nosson Scherman, 9th ed. (Brooklyn, NY: Mesorah Publications, orig. pub. 1994), 5.

24. *Chumash*, 15.

25. René Girard, *Deceit, Desire, and the Novel: Self and Other in Literary Structure* (Baltimore: Johns Hopkins University Press, 1965), 96.

26. Gn 3:5: "For God knows that when you eat of it your eyes will be opened, and you will be like God, knowing good and evil."

27. Soulen, *The God of Israel and Christian Theology*, 142.

28. Gn 6:11: "Now the earth was corrupt in God's sight, and the earth was filled with violence."

29. Gn 6:3 (KJV): "And the LORD said, 'My spirit shall not always strive with man, for that he also is flesh: yet his days shall be an hundred and twenty years.'"

30. Gn 9:1: "And God blessed Noah and his sons, and said to them, 'Be fruitful and multiply, and fill the earth.'"

31. Soulen, *The God of Israel and Christian Theology*, 143.

32. Ibid., 119.

33. Girard, *Deceit, Desire, and the Novel,* 182.

34. Michael Wyschogrod, "Sin and Atonement in Judaism," in *The Human Condition in the Jewish and Christian Traditions,* ed. Frederick E. Greenspahn (New York: Ktav, 1986), 106.

35. Girard, *Things Hidden,* 415.

36. Wyschogrod, "Sin and Atonement in Judaism," 105.

37. Ibid., 107.

38. Gn 3:11: "He said, 'Who told you that you were naked? Have you eaten of the tree of which I commanded you not to eat?'"

39. Wyschogrod, "Sin and Atonement in Judaism," 110.

40. Jacob Neusner, *Confronting Creation: How Judaism Reads Genesis* (Columbia: University of South Carolina Press, 1991), 103–6.

41. Levenson, "Abusing Abraham," 270.

42. Michael Wyschogrod, *The Body of Faith: Judaism as Corporeal Election* (New York: Seabury Press, 1983), 21.

43. Lv 20:1–5: "The Lord said to Moses, 'Say to the people of Israel, Any man of the people of Israel, or of the strangers that sojourn in Israel, who gives any of his children to Molech shall be put to death; the people of the land shall stone him with stones. I myself will set my face against that man, and will cut him off from among his people, because he has given one of his children to Molech, defiling my sanctuary and profaning my holy name. And if the people of the land do at all hide their eyes from that man, when he gives one of his children to Molech, and do not put him to death, then I will set my face against that man and against his family, and will cut them off from among their people, him and all who follow him in playing the harlot after Molech.'"

44. See Bruce Chilton, *Abraham's Curse: Child Sacrifice in the Legacies of the West* (New York: Doubleday, 2008).

45. Wyschogrod, *Body of Faith,* 22.

46. Jas 2:23: "And the scripture was fulfilled which says, 'Abraham believed God, and it was reckoned to him as righteousness'; and he was called the friend of God."

47. Wyschogrod, "Sin and Atonement in Judaism," 105; see also Samson Raphael Hirsch, *The Collected Writings,* vol. 2 (New York: Philipp Feldheim, 1985), 61.

48. Girard, *Deceit, Desire, and the Novel,* 294: "Repudiation of the mediator implies renunciation of divinity, and this means renouncing pride. . . . In renouncing divinity the hero renounces slavery."

49. Gn 22:15–18: "And the angel of the Lord called to Abraham a second time from heaven, and said, 'By myself I have sworn, says the Lord, because you have done this, and have not withheld your son, your only son, I will indeed bless you, and I will multiply your descendants as the stars of heaven and as the sand which is on the seashore. And your descendants shall possess the gate of their

enemies, and by your descendants shall all the nations of the earth bless themselves, because your have obeyed my voice.'"

50. Scott Hahn, "Kinship by Covenant: A Biblical Theological Study of Covenant Types and Texts in the Old and New Testaments" (Ph.D. diss., Marquette University, 1995), 200.

51. Wyschogrod, *Body of Faith*, 20.

52. Raymund Schwager, "Christ's Death and the Prophetic Critiques of Sacrifice," *Semeia* 33 (1985): 121. See also Raymund Schwager, S.J., *Jesus in the Drama of Salvation: Toward a Biblical Doctrine of Redemption,* trans. James G. Williams and Paul Haddon (New York: Crossroad, 1999), 180–82.

53. Wyschogrod, *Body of Faith*, 19.

54. Levenson, "Abusing Abraham," 273.

55. Paul may also allude to Isaac in Rom. 12:1: "I appeal to you therefore, brethren, by the mercies of God, to present your bodies as a living sacrifice, holy and acceptable to God, which is your spiritual worship."

56. Gn 22:5; see Rabbi Abraham ben Isaiah and Rabbi Benjamin Sharfman, eds., *The Pentateuch and Rashi's Commentary: Genesis* (Brooklyn, NY: S. S. & R. Publishing Company, 1995), 233.

57. Isaac's resurrection is referred to in Heb 11:19: "(Abraham) considered that God was able to raise men even from the dead; hence, figuratively speaking, he did receive him back."

58. Edward Kessler has studied the mutual influence between Jews and Christians in their respective interpretations of the *Akedah,* which Christians took to be a prefigurement of Christ's death on Calvary. See Edward Kessler, *Bound by the Bible: Jews, Christians, and the Sacrifice of Isaac* (Cambridge: Cambridge University Press, 2004).

59. Sandor Goodhart, "'We Will Cling Fast to Your Torah': A Response to René Girard's Contribution to [Willard Swartley's] *Violence [Renounced],*" *Bulletin of the Colloquium on Violence and Religion,* no. 19 (November 2000): 16. This essay is accessible at http://www.uibk.ac.at/theol/cover/bulletin/archive/bulletin19.pdf.

60. René Girard, "The Crime and Conversion of Leontes in *The Winter's Tale,*" *Religion & Literature* 22, nos. 2–3 (1990): 218.

61. Many of the passages in the Hebrew scriptures concerning resurrection seem clearly to refer to the return/resurrection of Israel, e.g. Ez 37:1–4; Hos 6:1–3, 13:14. The suffering servant passages of Isaiah also contain a corporate element, although Christian exegetes have interpreted these as references to the suffering and resurrection of the Messiah. While both Elijah and Elisha perform resurrections in the Scriptures (1 Kgs 17:17–24; 2 Kgs 4:31–37; 2 Kgs 13:21), the first unmistakable reference to the resurrection of individuals from the dead seems to be Dn 12:1–3. Jesus cites the Torah for proof of resurrection from the dead, contending that because God refers to himself as "the God of Abraham,

the God of Isaac, and the God of Jacob" (Ex 3:6) these three must have been resurrected, for God "is not a God of the dead, but of the living" (Lk 20:38). Maimonides, on the other hand, contended immortality of the soul is taught in the Torah, but resurrection of the body is a miracle that can only be proclaimed by a prophet, and the Israelites were not ready to hear it until the later prophets. See Moses Maimonides, *Treatise on Resurrection* (Northvale, NJ: Jason Aronson, 1997), 45–48; also Robert Martin-Achard, *From Death to Life: A Study of the Development of the Doctrine of the Resurrection in the Old Testament* (Edinburgh: Oliver and Boyd, 1960).

62. *Rashi*, 238; *Chumash*, 101; see also Moses Maimonides, *The Code of Maimonides, Book Eight: The Book of Temple Service* (New Haven, CT: Yale University Press, 1957), 10.

63. This connection is clear in the sacrifices of the feast of Sukkoth, when seventy bulls were sacrificed, representing the seventy nations of the world.

64. Wyschogrod, "Sin and Atonement in Judaism," 123.

65. See, for example, Mi 6:6–8; Is 1:10–17; Jer 6:20; Hos 5:6, 6:6, 9:11–13; Am 5:21–25.

66. Mi 4:1–2: "It shall come to pass in the latter days that the mountain of the house of the Lord shall be established as the highest of the mountains, and shall be raised up above the hills; and peoples shall flow to it, and many nations shall come and say: 'Come, let us go up to the mountain of the Lord, to the house of the God of Jacob; that he may teach us his ways and we may walk in his paths'"; Is 56:6–7: "And the foreigners who join themselves to the Lord, to minister to him, to love the name of the Lord, and to be his servants, every one who keeps the sabbath, and does not profane it, and holds fast my covenant—these I will bring to my holy mountain, and make them joyful in my house of prayer; their burnt offerings and their sacrifices will be accepted on my altar; for my house shall be called a house of prayer for all peoples"; Jer 17:24–26: "But if you listen to me, says the Lord, and bring in no burden by the gates of this city on the sabbath day, but keep the sabbath day holy and do no work on it, then there shall enter by the gates of this city kings who sit on the throne of David, riding in chariots and on horses, they and their princes, the men of Judah and the inhabitants of Jerusalem; and this city shall be inhabited for ever. And people shall come from the cities of Judah and the places round about Jerusalem, from the land of Benjamin, from the Shephelah, from the hill country, and from the Negeb, bringing burnt offerings and sacrifices, cereal offerings and frankincense, and bringing thank offerings to the house of the Lord"; Jer 33:17–18: "For thus says the Lord: David shall never lack a man to sit on the throne of the house of Israel, and the Levitical priests shall never lack a man in my presence to offer burnt offerings, to burn cereal offerings, and to make sacrifices for ever."

67. Girard, *Deceit, Desire, and the Novel*, 291. Girard's discussion of novelistic conclusions is instructive here.

68. Schwager, "Christ's Death and the Prophetic Critiques of Sacrifice," 121.

69. See Mt 4:1–11.

70. See Mt 16:21–23; also Girard, *The Scapegoat,* 156–58.

71. See Jn 8:53–9:11; Mt 9:9–12.

72. David Cayley, *The Scapegoat: René Girard's Anthropology of Violence and Religion,* audiocassette (Canadian Broadcasting Company, 2001). A transcript of this interview is available with the tape.

73. Sandor Goodhart, review of *Things Hidden since the Foundation of the World,* by René Girard, *Philosophy and Literature* 14, no.1 (1990): 173.

ELEVEN

The Unbinding of Isaac

STEPHEN STERN

Face as mortality, mortality of the other beyond his appearing;
nakedness more naked, so to speak, than that which the unveiling
of truth exposes; . . . a victim's abandonment.

—Emmanuel Levinas

Imagine a father taking his son's life for his own ends. The blade is raised. The son silently calls for help. The mother cannot be found. There is no human witness to his misery or his life. How does one show the father how to *bear witness* to his son when he cannot even see or hear his son? This is the problem for God with Abraham. God is trying to teach Abraham to take responsibility for his son, Isaac. Abraham is not the only student, however. God is also teaching Isaac that he is not only responsible for Abraham, but additionally for building something new out of Abraham's traditions. This is the purpose of God's test.

> God put Abraham to the test. [God] said to him, Abraham, and he answered, "Here I am." [God] said, "Take your son, your favored one, Isaac, whom you love, and go to the land of Moriah, and offer him there as a burnt offering on one of the heights which I will point out to you."[1]

Without protest, Abraham leaves with Isaac the next morning. On their way up to Mount Moriah, Isaac asks his father, "Where's the sheep for the burnt offering?" Abraham says, "God will see to the sheep for [God's] burnt offering, my son."[2]

Christian tradition calls this episode "the Sacrifice." Jewish tradition calls it "the Binding of Isaac." In a way, it is both. There is a sacrifice of a ram and of Abraham's fatherly control of Isaac, both of which are preceded by Abraham binding Isaac. However, this is all precipitated by God's test for Abraham. This test is obviously significant for Abraham and for biblical teaching in general, yet the purpose of this test has been debated for centuries.

The debate emerges not only from the facts in the biblical text, but from in between the facts, where one finds gaps or a lack of explanation in the Bible. For example, the text does not tell us why God tests Abraham. This lack of explanation leaves an interpretive space for the reader or biblical commentator. In the rabbinic tradition, such spaces are often filled with a midrash that brings out meanings of the narrative. In the following essay, at times, I exercise a midrashic orientation to develop new meanings of Genesis 22. I do not limit my use of midrashic accounts, however, to the rabbinic tradition or to the Jewish people, but extend that orientation to other writing—for example, philosophic commentary.[3]

Perhaps the most famous non-Jewish account of this test is found in Søren Kierkegaard's *Fear and Trembling*, where Kierkegaard witnesses the test as an issue of faith. If we examine the nature of the test partly from the philosophy of Emmanual Levinas, however, Kierkegaard's conclusion does not necessarily follow. Before I disclose why I think the test is not an issue of faith, I will present Kierkegaard's notion of faith as offered in *Fear and Trembling*. Then I will show how the test is not about Kierkegaard's notion of faith. From there, I will examine the nature of the test through an analysis of the three people directly affected by the test, Abraham, Isaac, and Sarah. Through this analysis, we will find that the test is about Abraham's learning to take responsibility for the Other.

Kierkegaard's Notion of Faith

In a critique of Hegel in *Fear and Trembling*, Kierkegaard explains that faith does not emerge from an inability to prove the existence of God. It is not about skepticism or knowledge, by which Kierkegaard generally means Hegel's dialectic or system, wherein everyone is involved in the realization of the universal. According to Hegel, this universally true dialectic accounts for all subjects. Kierkegaard writes that for Hegel the subject

> has its telos in the universal, and the individual's ethical task is always to express himself in this, to abrogate his particularity so as to become the universal. As soon as the single individual wants to assert himself in his particularity, in direct opposition to the universal, he sins, and only by recognizing this can he again reconcile himself with the universal.[4]

In Kierkegaard's terms, Hegel's dialectic is unable to account for the faithful subject. This inability is not because the subject is sinning by asserting itself. It is because the universal cannot account for the subject's individual, particular, nonuniversal relationship with God. For Kierkegaard, one's relationship with God exposes the limits of Hegel's universal, not the other way around. Thus, he explains that one's faith is not less than this universal dialectic. It is more than the dialectic can hold. Kierkegaard writes: "Faith begins precisely where thinking [or the universal dialectic] leaves off."[5] Where thinking leaves off is where one finds oneself relating to God.

Since ethics is realized in Hegel's general or universal dialectic, Kierkegaard's notion of faith suspends the Hegelian ethical. Levinas writes: "The ethical means the general, for Kierkegaard. The singularity of the *I* would be lost, in his view, under a rule valid for all."[6] Thus, where thinking leaves off, where the I is not lost under a rule valid for all, the ethical is suspended by one's relationship with God. Kierkegaard justifies his reading of the sacrifice by noting that upon following God's command, where Abraham has a particular, nonuniversal relationship with God, Abraham is no longer bound by ethics. Ethics are suspended. In other words, the ethic of not murdering is suspended in Abraham's sacrificial gesture towards Isaac on behalf of God.

Finally, Kierkegaard's faith reveals the limits of this universal or of that which is knowable. The universal (as articulated by Hegel) is unable to account for the privacy of Kierkegaard's faith-based relationship. The faithful subject's private relation with God is beyond the scope of knowledge.

Critique of Kierkegaard's Notion of Faith

If the test is strictly about the faith presented by Kierkegaard, two general problems arise. First, Kierkegaard treats Sarah and Isaac as secondary to Abraham. Second, Kierkegaard colors Abraham with the self-indulgent dye God wants Abraham to wash off.

If the test is just between Abraham and God (Kierkegaard implies), then why does the test involve more than Abraham and God? What about Isaac? What about Sarah? In *Fear and Trembling,* Kierkegaard treats Isaac as a means to an end. Is his relationship with God secondary to that of his father? Kierkegaard does not address this matter. In addition, he does not consider that Isaac is a thirty-seven-year-old adult at the time of the binding. He pictures him as a boy. Yet, if the text is read chronologically, Isaac is thirty-seven, because in Genesis Sarah gives birth to Isaac at the age of ninety, and she dies right after the test, when she is 127 years old. Thus, at the time of the binding, Isaac is thirty-seven. Given Isaac's adulthood, the test is not merely showing Abraham something; it is also showing Isaac something. And what about Sarah? The test affects her. Nevertheless, Kierkegaard treats Sarah as a subordinate to Abraham, saying little about her relationship to the test or with God. In fact, Kierkegaard's commentary reads as if only Abraham is having a relationship with God. In writing solely about Abraham, Kierkegaard writes at the expense of the others.

Beyond Kierkegaard's secondary treatment of Isaac and Sarah, his account presents faith exclusively through Abraham; Kierkegaard's account of subjectivity is about Abraham and for Abraham. It is self-indulgent. If everything is about Abraham's faith, then Abraham is the subject for himself. In Levinasian terms, Abraham (the subject) is "tensing" upon himself.[7] One might say, God is the subject for Abraham, or he sees himself as the subject for God. Either way, he is idolizing God for *himself.* What I mean by idolatry here is a type of selfishness; it is what happens when one egotistically eclipses one's responsibility for the Other. Here, idolatry is understood as meaning to locate oneself within one's own indulgences. Ethical responsibility for the other individual is eclipsed by one's self-centeredness. This is what the Hebrew understands by sin, for the biblical God commands that one is responsible for the Other

I say idolizing God for himself, because in Kierkegaard's terms, Abraham's faith or relationship with God is at the expense of his responsibility for the other individual. His relationship with God serves himself. For example, if he murders Isaac because God says, "Do it," that murder reveals that he is idolizing his relations with God—and thus idolizing God—at the expense of Isaac. It is as if Isaac is to receive any action Abraham gives him on behalf of Abraham's faith, an objectification that creates the illusion that Isaac does not count. Therefore, if Abraham's relationship with God excludes Isaac, it follows that his relationship with God is about himself, not Isaac. There are traces in the narrative, however, that show Abraham is not completely this type of person and that God does not want Abraham to be this type of person.

Abraham's relationship with God is often about the Other, not at the expense of the Other. We know this from his protest on behalf of the people in Sodom and Gommorah. Levinas writes: "Kierkegaard never speaks of the situation in which Abraham enters into dialogue with God to intercede in favor of Sodom and Gommorah, in the name of the just who may be present there."[8] The dialogue between Abraham and God shows that in this particular narrative, God is not a God who commands doing something at the expense of an innocent human being, such as Isaac. If that were the case, God would be indistinguishable from the idols from which Abraham and Sarah made their exodus; Abraham would be murdering his most beloved son on behalf of a god. However, the test is not about idolizing God. It is about Abraham listening to God, who commands responsibility for the Other, the God who has promised Isaac as the heir of Sarah and Abraham, the first of many descendants.

Where Kierkegaard has Abraham transcending the ethical or suspending it, Levinas has God returning Abraham to the ethical, which is to say that Abraham is returned to the Other for whom he is responsible. As Levinas observes, Kierkegaard "describes the encounter with God as subjectivity rising to the religious level: God above the ethical order! His interpretation of this story can doubtless be given a different orientation. Perhaps Abraham's ear for hearing the [heavenly] voice that brought him back to the ethical order was the highest moment in this drama."[9] In other words, the test is not about Abraham's "existence as a care that a being takes for its own existence."[10] The test is about learning to witness the Other for whom one is responsible.

If the test is about Abraham's faith as defined by Kiekegaard, then Abraham is not returned by it to the Other for whom he is responsible. In *Fear and Trembling*, Kierkegaard's account of faith turns Abraham back towards himself, not towards the Other, exposing the irresponsibility of understanding this test as an issue of faith. Kierkegaard's explanation of faith has the subject (Abraham) tensing upon himself.[11] By suspending the ethical, Kierkegaard is able to justify Abraham's sacrifice of Isaac. Simply, Abraham's relationship with God is all about Abraham. It is all about Abraham relating to God, as if Abraham is opting for a mystical union with God at the expense of the other individual, that is, in this case, Isaac and Sarah. However, this explanation might not make sense. The test is not about Abraham's faith, for the test does not return Abraham to Abraham, or to a relationship with God at the expense of Isaac. As Levinas explains, the test returns Abraham to the other person, where one finds God's command for ethics.[12]

God, Abraham, and the Purpose of the Test

Jewish tradition often teaches that one purpose of the test is for God to show Abraham that human sacrifice on behalf of a god is no longer to be practiced. It is not enough for God to tell this to Abraham. Something this important cannot merely be spoken and heard; it must be learned through experience by Abraham acting out what he is not supposed to do and what he is supposed to do.[13] The test is an opportunity for Abraham's instructor, God, to show Abraham what he (Abraham) has learned and has not learned.[14]

For Abraham, the test is an opportunity to show understanding of what he has learned. Throughout the biblical narrative, Abraham is being taught to witness to the other person.

The question is whether Abraham understands this. If he does not, then Abraham is not beyond the self-indulgent violence of idolatry,[15] where one is out for oneself and treats the world as a receptacle for one's own activities. Concerning this idea, Levinas writes: "Violence is to be found in any action in which one acts as if one were alone to act: as if the rest of the universe were there only to receive the action."[16] Thus, the test is to see whether Abraham is beyond violence and whether he can offer peace. More specifically, the test shows him how to witness to the Other and, thus (as René Girard might say), to make an exodus out of human sacrifice.[17] If Abraham murders Isaac, Abraham is not a witness to Isaac's humanity. Murdering Isaac is to treat him as a thing. "A thing," Levinas states, "can never be presented personally and ultimately has no identity. Violence is applied to the thing, it seizes and disposes of the thing. Things *give*, they do not offer a face."[18] God is not instructing Abraham to treat Isaac as a thing or to present him as a thing. God is returning Abraham to ethics. It would be nonsense — not to mention barbaric — if murdering Isaac were the road to the ethical.

Taking the Test: When Peace Is Announced

> Abraham and Isaac arrived at the place of which God had told him. Abraham built an altar there; he laid out the wood; he bound his son, Isaac; he laid him on the altar, on top of the wood. And Abraham picked up the knife to slay his son. Then an angel of the Lord called to him from heaven: "Abraham! Abraham!" And he answered, "Here I am." And he said, "Do not raise your hand against the boy, or do anything to him. For now I know that you fear God, since you have not withheld your son, your favored one, from me."[19]

This passage raises three significant points that aid in further understanding the test. First, the angel of the Lord tells Abraham to do no harm to the boy. In other words, let the boy go. The key to why Abraham lets the boy go is not that the angel commands it. Midrashically speaking, the key is that as Abraham raises the blade to sacrifice Isaac, he takes notice of what he sees, the vulnerability of Isaac. This is inferred from the belief that when one is about to be stabbed or killed, one is vulnerable. When raising the blade, it's plausible to assume that Abraham, who is looking down, is looking into Isaac's face. When doing so, Abraham, we may infer, sees that Isaac, in the words of Derrida (talking about Levinas's notion of the "host" or "hostage"),

> is not reducible to its [READ: the face's] actual predicates, to what one [READ: Abraham] might define or thematize about it [READ: Isaac], anymore than the I [READ: of Abraham] is. It [READ: Isaac] is naked, bared of every property, and this nudity is also its [READ: Isaac's] infinitely exposed vulnerability: its [READ: his] "skin."[20]

Faced by his son's vulnerability, Abraham resists his violent memory, which manufactures Isaac into predicates, themes, or mischaracterizations. Isaac's face commands Abraham's resistance, that is by showing—teaching—Abraham to come out of his violent impulse. Isaac's face is this significant! Levinas emphasizes:

> The signifying of his [READ: Isaac's] face, defenseless nakedness, the very uprightness of exposure to death. Mortality, and at the same time the signifying of an order, a commandment [READ: to Abraham]: "Thou shalt not kill!"[21]

In other words, in Isaac's face, Abraham finds the divine command, "Thou shalt not kill." That command comes to mean for him "Thou shalt cause thy neighbour [READ: Isaac] to live."[22] This ethical imperative commanded by God discloses that Abraham approaches God through Abraham's relationship with Isaac. Levinas continues:

> This original ethical signifying of the [READ: Isaac's] face would thus signify—without any metaphor or figure of speech, in its rigorously proper meaning—the transcendence of a God not objectified in the face in which he speaks; a God who does not "take on body," but who approaches precisely through this relay to the neighbor [READ: between Abraham and Isaac].[23]

At this moment, Abraham finds that his love and devotion to and for God is in his love for Isaac.[24] He realizes that killing Isaac on behalf of God is to violate God. This means that Abraham's relation to God is "inseparable from the recognition of the other person [in this case, Isaac]." The relation to God is already ethics, or as Isaiah 58 would have it, the proximity to God, devotion itself, is devotion to the other."[25] Thus, as said, when Isaac's face carries Abraham out of a violent, idolatrous past, Abraham finds that he approaches God and that God approaches him. Isaac's face both assigns Abraham responsibility for his son and signifies that Abraham is in proximity to God.

Abraham is then chosen and elected through this proximity;[26] he is returned to the ethical, where he finds himself devoted to Isaac's life and to God. Abraham's devotion to God is devotion to Isaac. In other words, here we find that Isaac's face signifies Abraham's infinite responsibility for his son. The Infinite is signified in Isaac's face.[27] Levinas highlights this idea, declaring, "the Infinite then has glory only through subjectivity."[28] He continues:

> The Infinite then has glory only through subjectivity, in the human adventure of the approach of the other, through the substitution for the other, by the expiation for the other. The subject is inspired by the Infinite, which, as illeity, does not appear, is not present, has always already past, is neither theme, telos, nor interlocutor. It is glorified in the glory that manifests a subject, is glorified already in the glorification of its glory by the subject, thus undoing all the structures of correlation. Glorification is saying, that is, a sign given to the other, peace announced to the other, responsibility for the other, to the extent of substitution.[29]

To picture what Levinas means by this, we briefly turn back to the test. As the blade is raised, recall, it seems that Abraham would be looking into Isaac's face. Here, perhaps for the first time, Abraham witnesses Isaac and is *inspired* to substitute the other individual for himself, possibly finding himself substituting his concern for himself with his concern for Isaac. At this climatic moment, we can infer that the Infinite is signified in Abraham's approach toward Isaac. In his approach, Abraham witnesses the vastness of his infinite responsibility for Isaac; in so doing, he approaches the Infinite.

Through his unbinding, Isaac's vulnerability brings strength into the weaknesses of Abraham's memory, strength that partly unbinds Abraham from his past. The power of Isaac's face unsays Abraham's memory, saying what has not been said. The Infinite is signified in Isaac's facial saying or in the relay between Isaac and Abraham where one finds "a sign given to the other, peace announced to the other, responsibility for the other, to the extent of substitution."[30] Now Abraham no longer objectifies Isaac as an object to be possessed or owned. He sees Isaac as independent or autonomous. This moment for Abraham—in which he recognizes that Isaac is a single person, an other individual and, thus, autonomous—is the moment in which peace is announced in the infinite approach. As Levinas writes, "Peace [i]s the incessant awakening to that alterity and to that uniqueness."[31] This moment of peace is addressed in the Talmud's *Mishnah Sanhedrin* 4,5:

> Man was created alone, to teach you that whoever destroys a single Israelite soul is deemed by Scripture as if he had destroyed a whole world. And whoever saves a single Israelite soul is deemed by Scripture as if he had saved a whole world. And it was also for the sake of peace among people, so that someone should not say to his fellow, "My father is greater than your father."[32]

The second helpful point of the original passage comes when the angel of the Lord says to Abraham, "I know that you fear God." Here, I would argue fearing God means fear of hurting, or perhaps one should say fear of violating or injuring God, not just fearing God's retribution. In her introduction to Abraham Joshua Heschel's *The Prophets,* Susannah Heschel explains, "Divine Pathos indicates a constant involvement of God in human history but insists that the involvement is an emotional engagement: God suffers when human beings are hurt, so that when I hurt another person, I injure God."[33] Thus, by Abraham showing that he fears harming Isaac, he shows (my argument requires that we accept) that he fears violating or injuring God.

To be with God, Abraham must witness Isaac as independent of himself. Abraham must protect his son's independence; to do otherwise is to violate God. It is as if the unbinding of Isaac is the unbinding of the violent bonds between father and son. This unbinding separates Isaac from Abraham, allowing for a social bond between father and son. They are able to welcome one another as other individuals, signifying they are for one another. It is radical alterity. About this, Jacques Derrida writes: "There would be neither welcome nor hospitality without this radical alterity, which itself presupposes separation. The social bond is a certain experience of the unbinding without which no respiration, no spiritual inspiration, would be possible."[34] Here, we find Levinas' understanding of peace: "Peace [i]s the incessant awakening to that alterity and to that uniqueness" of the Other.[35]

Finally, the third clarifying point is made with God's comment, "you have not withheld your son, your favored one, from me." In witnessing Isaac, Abraham has given Isaac to God, the God who creates life. Thus, Isaac is given his life. The sacrifice is constituted first by Abraham giving up ownership of Isaac (as well as ownership of his memories of Isaac) and then freeing him. This gesture is realized in not withholding Isaac from God; which is to say, this is realized in giving Isaac over to God. The biblical commentator, Rashi, explains that God may appear to have changed his mind at the binding. First God wants Isaac sacrificed; then God does not want him sacrificed. God's "apparent 'change of mind' about the sacrifice," however, is not necessarily supported by the narrative.[36] Rashi explains: "[God] did not say to him, 'Slaughter him'; because the Holy One Blessed be He did not desire to slaughter him, but only to bring him up to the mountain in order to prepare him as a burnt offering. But after Abraham had brought him up, He said to him, 'Take him down.'"[37] In other words, as Avivah Zornberg writes, Rashi interprets God to say: "'Take your son,' I will not change what I have uttered. For I did not tell you, 'Slaughter him,' but 'Take him up.' Now you have taken him up—take him down."[38]

Pushing beyond Rashi, let us look at the Hebrew word God uses when he commands Abraham to offer his son as a burnt offering and to take him up. The Hebrew word used for "burnt offering" (in the biblical passage) is *olah*, the root of which is the verb *alah*, which means "to go up, ascend, climb." Biblically, *olah* is often used for a burnt offering, which is why it is regularly translated that way. There are, however, biblical passages where forms of the verb are used for "going up" in other ways. For example, in Jacob's dream in Genesis 28:12, when the angels are going up and down the stairway, the word used for "going up" is derived from the root *alah*. We also see a form of *alah* used in Exodus 19:20, when God calls Moses to the top of Mount Sinai. Perhaps God's intended command in Genesis 22, then, is not for a burnt offering but for an ascension. Regardless, Abraham lets go of Isaac, and God blesses that release. In Abraham's approach towards the Infinite, in Isaac, peace is announced. The world now unfolds for Isaac. Biblical scholar W. Gunther Plaut remarks,

> The story may thus be read as a paradigm of a father-and-son relationship. In a way every parent seeks to dominate his child and is in danger of seeking to sacrifice him to his parental plans or hopes. In the Biblical story, God is present and can therefore stay the father's hand. In all too many repetitions of the scene God is absent and the knife falls. Thus is the "Akedah" (the binding of Isaac) repeated forever, with its test and terror.[39]

Isaac's Lesson

We conventionally spend so much time trying to understand what the test means for Abraham that the oddity of Isaac's compliance to be bound often goes without notice. Although thirty-seven years old, by rabbinic count, Isaac is a child when faced with the traditions or memories of his father. By commanding the performance of the test, God is showing Isaac that he is to build tomorrow out of today. As Franz Rosenzweig writes: "we are, as Scripture puts it, 'children'; we are as tradition reads it, 'builders.'"[40] For Isaac to become a builder, he must witness Abraham, and unlike a child, he must move out of the shadow of Abraham to become independent. Isaac is the builder who approaches Abraham (the tradition), to begin the act of building beyond tradition.

What this language of approach shows is that Isaac is not completely located in tradition—he is too novel for it, yet he cannot live without it either. He is both constructed by tradition and approaches it. In other words, he simultaneously emerges from tradition and transcends it.

By unbinding Abraham's traditional bonds upon Isaac, God is teaching Isaac that he stands apart from his father, witnessing Abraham from beyond Abraham's grasp. Isaac has something to say or live that Abraham has not said or lived. Levinas explains that memory and history are often lived as a "totality determined like matter, a present without fissures or surprises, from which becoming is expelled, a present largely made up of representations, due to memory and history."[41] Isaac is otherwise to Abraham's memory and history. His life is a surprise to memory and history, a saying to what has been said, a becoming that is not fixed by tradition; neither is it expelled by tradition, but instead approaches tradition. In becoming Isaac, Isaac finds himself approaching Abraham.

In their approach towards each other, Isaac finds that he is not to be used as a piece of evidence disclosing Abraham's faith. *Ein Sof,* a kabbalistic reference to God, the Infinite, is disclosing for Isaac that "the witness belongs to the glory of the Infinite. It is by the voice of the witness that the glory of the Infinite is glorified."[42] By bringing Abraham to ethics, and introducing Isaac to ethics, the Infinite, God, is glorified. As said, Isaac is now independent, and in turn, he is able to approach Abraham as Other, and vice versa. In other words, when the knots are untied, Abraham and Isaac are able to have an ethical relationship. With this, more sense emerges from Levinas' explanation when pitted against Kierkegaard's.

Thus, the test is not about faith in God. The test signifies God returning Abraham and bringing Isaac to ethics, where one understands that one is responsible for the other individual. It is this responsibility for the Other that glorifies God, not a relationship in which ethics is suspended by one's faithful relationship with God. Here Isaac finds

the order in my [READ: his] response itself, which, as a sign given to the neighbor, as a "here I am," brings me [READ: Isaac] out of invisibility, out of the [READ: Abraham's] shadow in which my [READ:

Isaac's] responsibility could have been evaded. This saying belongs to the very *glory* of which it bears witness.[43]

Now that the inferred lesson God is teaching Isaac is clear, we turn to Isaac's response to the test.

Isaac's Liberation

In Genesis 22:19, it is written that Abraham returns from Moriah. The text does not say that Isaac returned with him. However, in this space where Isaac is not mentioned, one may see that Isaac let his father go, no longer hanging on to Abraham's robes. In Plaut's words, "Isaac now became a man who for the first time could let his father go and who would return later, at his own choosing."[44] Isaac now begins to understand that, for his sake, the world was created. This does not mean treating the world as a receptacle for any action. It means that Isaac is responsible for the world, for the peace of the world. He is to realize, like his father, the Mishnaic teaching (as noted earlier) that pervades Levinas, that a single person is created for the sake of peace.

Finally, through having once been bound both by and to his father's memory, Isaac witnesses his father and the violence of his father's idolatrous memory. The binding shows Isaac that he is ethically separate from his father. Isaac and Abraham are most loved when asserting separateness, by saying to one another what their history does not or perhaps could not hold. Here we find humans making their ethical world. Where Abraham as a predecessor threatened the world with strangulation of the new, Isaac's liberation signifies a time from which a new world can be created.[45]

In other words, the son is no longer condemned to live the same life as his father. Isaac now has the opportunity to build a new community, to create a house beyond the violence of memory, a house that is not merely for oneself but for the Other also. As more than memory, the house, as Levinas might say, will not be constituted from only "traces of memory."[46] This is not to suggest, however, that the house will be memory free. Isaac will build from tradition that which tradition does not anticipate. As he begins his journey as a builder, Sarah also begins a new, yet different journey.

Sarah's Light

> Sarah's lifetime—the span of Sarah's life—came to one hundred and twenty-seven years. Sarah dies in Kiriath-Arba—now Hebron—in the land of Canaan; and Abraham proceeded to mourn for Sarah and to bewail her.[47]

Sarah's departure from life exposes the problem of her life.[48] Rashi explains, in Zornberg's account, that the "death of Sarah is narrated directly after the Akedah, the Binding of Isaac, because, as a result of the tidings of the Akedah—that her son had been fated for slaughter, and had been *all-but-slaughtered*—she gave up the ghost [lit., her soul flew away] and died."[49] Zornberg writes, "Here, Rashi is succinctly summarizing a complex Midrashic tradition, which holds at its core a poignant thesis: Sarah is the true victim of the Akedah, her death is its unexplicated, inexplicable cost."[50] This being said, the joy one feels for Isaac, Abraham, and perhaps God in this situation must be mitigated. Joy is "undercut by Sarah's death."[51]

Sarah understands that God would not command the literal, murderous sacrifice of Isaac—an understanding that finds support in the concluding moments of Abraham's test. From Sarah's response, we learn that Abraham could have challenged God's order. It is somewhat bewildering that he does not protest, regardless of what God commanded. Even if Abraham misunderstands the command as prescribing the killing of Isaac (since *l'olah,* meaning "to go up" also means "burnt offering"), he should question God's command. A protest on behalf of God's promise for an open future in time would not be difficult for a man who listens and at first questions God's decision to wipe out Sodom and Gommorah.

Moreover, Abraham understands that God has promised Isaac's life as an heir, not as a dead man. If God commands the killing of Isaac, then Abraham might at least ask God, "Why are you going back on your promise?" Whatever he is being shown by God, the fact that he has to be shown—in the manner in which he is shown—is reason enough (in review of the rabbis) for Sarah's anguish to suffocate her, enveloping her in death.[52] It is her anguish that exposes the depth of Abraham's egoism in agreeing to take the test.

By this agreement, Abraham kills the community of Sarah, Abraham, and Isaac with one another. This is the community that Abraham and Sarah are commanded to build for Isaac, not only because of God but because Isaac's face commands them to provide him with this. Moreover, their journey seems to be moving towards this community; making an exodus from their homeland is the simultaneous construction of a community built not for oneself but for one another and their creation, Isaac. Isaac is born out of their love for God and, therefore, for one another, not out of the self-indulgent idolatry from which they have made an exodus. Abraham and Sarah's love creates that which is not remembered or confined to idolatry, a beginning.

Thus, when Abraham goes up to Moriah, he violates Sarah by killing their community. The very peace for which Abraham and Isaac were created seems to violate Sarah. One might say that if Sarah does not resist Abraham's agreement, there is no way for him to know he is violating Sarah. And although we have no direct evidence that Sarah resists Abraham's agreement to take the test, we do have evidence that she does not stand by. Midrashically speaking, Sarah leaves Abraham over the event.[53] Note that Abraham appears to be in Beer Sheba while she dies in Kiriath-Arba. Can we not conclude that she may have died as a result of the binding of her son?

Whether or not Sarah dies over the binding—as Jewish tradition often suggests—such a grief stricken death does not exclude the possibility that she leaves Abraham before her death. The assumption that Sarah departs disables any account that Abraham might give of the episode, just as a woman who escapes domestic violence stands beyond her husband's characterization of their problems. In considering the narrative potential that Sarah's departure is independent of Isaac's death, we are led to expand the customary view of Sarah's death to be a sovereign response or testimony to Abraham's breaking up the community. Not only is Abraham shown through her departure that his memories do not own Isaac (and do not account for Isaac), but upon his return, he is shown by Sarah that he owns neither her nor their community. When he returns, his life is not how he remembers it. Sarah is not there.

With the taking of the test, Abraham finds that the conditions for their community slip away. Sarah's assumed exodus exposes that before she dies, she lives as a historical refugee, in exile or asylum. Evidence for this is found in Genesis. She dies in the land of the Hittites, a foreign land that is not home for her, Abraham, and Isaac. Sarah's possible exile exposes that the test is a negation of her life with her husband and son. Here, Zornberg writes, there "has to be a suspension of belief and affirmation, a kind of philosophical schizophrenia, in which the theoretical optimistic conclusions of faith are ignored, and only the cries and wails of nothingness are heard."[54]

Finally, by rising above the local setting, Sarah regains her fullness through exile. Moreover, it is only when Abraham is hospitable to her (in the way he provides for her burial and mourns her death) that we find the conditions of the community for Isaac. And what about Isaac? In her parting, Sarah does not leave Isaac; she has left her space for him. Isaac will find refuge in his mother's exile, inheriting Sarah's space. Indeed, later in the biblical narrative, Isaac moves into Sarah's house.[55] Her exile is thus a separation that welcomes Isaac to a world beyond Abraham. Sarah's parting gesture also shows us that, like Isaac, we do not have to live in the cave of the remembrance of Abraham's traditions, memories, and characterizations. When remembering Sarah, we might look to Levinas when he writes about God commanding Abraham to obey whatever Sarah says in Genesis 21:12; "in prophecy itself," Levinas writes, "a possible subordination of the male inspiration to the female" occurs.[56]

From the present account of Sarah, we find Abraham's inspiration to take the test subordinated to Sarah's response. One can hear, witness, and testify that Sarah's inferred departure is forever a sovereign response or testimony to Abraham's violent betrayal, showing that neither Abraham nor the biblical commentators own her. As an exile or refugee, Sarah stops one from slipping into the idolatry of patriarchy,[57] disrupting Kierkegaard's reading of the narrative in which the female is subordinated to the male, or, perhaps I should say, forgotten.

Through highlighting Sarah, one might conclude that Abraham fails the test. Peace may be announced, but it is not manifest. Sarah stops us from "neutralizing the terror" she sees when Abraham leaves with Isaac for Mount Moriah.[58] Yet, through Sarah's departing gesture from Abraham's violence, justice is shown to us, witnessed, so to speak. Thus, Sarah's disruptive light still shines from beyond Abraham's shadowy, smothering ego.

> When all work is brought to a standstill, the candles are lit. Just as creation began with words "Let there be light!" so does the celebration of creation begin with the kindling of lights. It is the woman who ushers in the joy and sets up the most exquisite symbol, light, to dominate the atmosphere.[59]

Abraham and the Ethical Test

In this narrative, there is a problem in Abraham's relationships with Isaac and Sarah that becomes clear when God commands him to take the test. If Abraham is readying Isaac to be sacrificed for God, to serve God, then we are seeing Abraham idolizing his relations with God—and thus idolizing God—at the expense of Isaac. For example, let us say Abraham's answer for the test is to give Isaac as a burnt offering. The answer is given because Abraham wants to give the right answer; he wants to please God. However, if that is his answer, he is mistaken in giving this answer to God. Offering Isaac as a burnt offering is done for Abraham, not for God. It is as if Isaac is to welcome any action Abraham gives him, as if Isaac does not count, as if he is not there. All that counts is Abraham's relationship with God. If this is the case, Abraham is an idolater. Everything is about him and his relationship with God, showing that Abraham is self- or subject-centered. (As implied above, one of the many problems with biblical idolatry is that it is self- or subject-centered.) Thus, if Abraham presents a murdered Isaac, it is clear Abraham is not a witness.

Offering Isaac as a burnt offering is to treat him as a means to an end; it is to treat him as a thing, so to speak. As quoted earlier, "A thing can never be presented personally and ultimately has no identity. Violence is applied to the thing, it seizes and disposes of the thing. Things give, they do not offer a face."[60] Is Abraham defacing Isaac? Yes, if he offers him as a burnt offering (which seems like a form of murder); he is misunderstanding what God wants from him. God does not want Isaac treated as a thing to be killed. Nowhere in the narrative are we given reason to think that God finds Isaac (the child God chose for Abraham) a faceless thing. Therefore, if Abraham murders Isaac, he fails the test. This *failure* would expose and reemphasize that if Abraham's ego silences Isaac (treating Isaac as an object for himself or a receptacle for his actions), he is being idolatrous and barbarically violent towards Isaac. "Violence is to be found," Levinas notes, "in any action in which one acts as if one were alone to act: as if the rest of the universe were there only to receive the action."[61]

From here, we can see that the test is a test of whether Abraham is beyond violence. In other words, the test is about Abraham's ethics. In fact, this is first indicated right before God commands the test, when God asks, "Abraham?" and Abraham answers, "Here I am." God's question is not merely about Abraham's physical proximity, finding out where Abraham is physically standing. God is asking where Abraham is ethically standing, as Abraham's ethical motivations are not clear. Perhaps they are clear for God, but they are not necessarily so for Abraham or for those of us who read this narrative. What is clear is that Abraham does not lower the blade into Isaac.

While holding the blade above Isaac, looking into Isaac's defenseless, naked face, Abraham suddenly ascends beyond his past, recognizing and witnessing that Isaac is independent: a single person for whom the world is created, for whom Abraham is infinitely responsible. Levinas captures this moment when he writes:

Face as mortality, mortality of the other beyond his appearing; nakedness more naked, so to speak, than that which the unveiling of truth exposes; beyond the visibility of the phenomenon, a victim's abandonment. But in that very precariousness, the "Thou shalt not kill" that is also the meaning of the face; in that *directness* of exposure, the proclamation—before any verbal sign—of a right that peremptorily

calls upon my responsibility for the other man. It assigns me and demands me, as if the invisible death which the face of the other faces—
uniqueness separated from any whole—were *my business.*[62]

Upon Abraham's hearing the heavenly voice, we find that Abraham
is not indifferent; he puts down the blade and unbinds his son. Instead
of violence, Abraham gives Isaac peace. Abraham receives his son. Here
we find the Mishnaic teaching that pervades Levinas: a single person is
created for the sake of peace. Because of Isaac, Abraham learns peace;
because of Abraham, Isaac is given peace. In this infinite approach, we
find that God has returned Abraham to ethics, to the Other, to Isaac.[63]

Conversely, by agreeing to take the test, Abraham betrays Sarah,
giving her violence, not peace. For Sarah to remain her own person,
she leaves Abraham, vanishing from his world. When he returns from
the unbinding, he does not find what he remembers. The love of his
life is gone. In the wake of Sarah's exodus, Abraham learns that the
future will not be constituted by what he remembers. There will be
no future with Sarah. He now finds ambiguity or perhaps darkness
stretching out before him. Abraham feels sorrow, sorrow that we witness when he mourns Sarah's death.

In conclusion, the very process through which Abraham learns
peace violates the peace he has with Sarah. As Abraham learns peace,
learns not to constitute the future from traces of a violent memory, so
Sarah's light challenges this peace. In her light, there is no peace (or
essence) as result of the unbinding of Isaac, no fixed truth, and thus
no fixed characterization. No one gets to own the characterization of
this narrative by hedging it into a single theme. The highlight from this
biblical passage is best put by Levinas when he paradoxically writes:
"Do not constitute the future from traces of memory, mistrusting new
things and even the miracle required for universal peace."[64]

Notes

    1. W. Gunther Plaut, ed. *The Torah: A Modern Commentary* (New York:
Union of American Hebrew Congregations, 1981), 146.
    2. Ibid.

3. See below, for example, my treatment of Derrida's reading of Levinas's notion of the hostage in application to Genesis 22, upon which text in fact Derrida is not explicitly commenting, or my use of Levinas's own discussion of the face in the citation immediately following.

4. Soren Kierkegaard, *Fear and Trembling* (New York: Penguin Books, 1985), 83.

5. Ibid., 82.

6. Emmanuel Levinas, *Proper Names*, trans. Michael B. Smith (Stanford, CA: Stanford University Press, 1997), 76.

7. Ibid.

8. Ibid.

9. Ibid., 74.

10. Ibid.

11. Ibid., 76.

12. Ibid., 74.

13. For example, this way of learning is present when one learns to drive. One does not merely learn to drive from reading the driver's manual or from merely being told how to drive. One learns to drive by getting behind the wheel of a car. Like driving, God is teaching Abraham through experience or performance.

14. Another possible reason for God needing to show this to Abraham is that God does not want Abraham imitating or performing God's destructive gestures towards others, e.g., wiping away Sodom and Gommorah. Such a wrong, destructive imitation of God and of Abraham as sacrificer has occurred historically, as Bruce Chilton shows in *Abraham's Curse: Child Sacrifice in the Legacies of the West* (New York: Doubleday, 2008).

15. Genesis does not directly speak about the issue of idolatry. It is not until the book of Exodus that the problem is directly addressed. But analyses of Genesis often assume idolatry as an implicit issue.

16. Emmanuel Levinas, *Difficult Freedom*, trans. Seán Hand (Baltimore: Johns Hopkins University Press, 1997), 6.

17. René Girard views the Bible as being "permeated by a single, dynamic movement away from sacrifice"; see *Things Hidden since the Foundation of the World*, trans. Stephen Bann and Michael Metteer (Stanford, CA: Stanford University Press, 1987), 239. He points to "the sacrifice of Abraham" as marking a "world in which the only legitimate blood rites are circumcision and the burning of animal victims."

18. Levinas, *Difficult Freedom*, 8.

19. Plaut, *The Torah*, 147.

20. Jacques Derrida, *Adieu to Levinas*, trans. Pascale-Anne Brault and Michael B. Naas (Stanford, CA: Stanford University Press, 1998), 111.

21. Emmanuel Levinas, *In the Time of the Nations*, trans. Michael B. Smith (Bloomington: Indiana University Press, 1994), 171.

22. Emmanuel Levinas, *Alterity and Transcendence,* trans. Michael B. Smith (New York: Columbia University Press, 1999), 127.

23. Levinas, *In the Time of the Nations,* 171.

24. Ibid.

25. Ibid.

26. Emmanuel Levinas, *Otherwise Than Being, or Beyond Essence,* trans. Alphonso Lingis (Pittsburgh: Duquesne University Press, 1981), 145.

27. The meaning of Infinite is *Ein Sof,* God. *Ein Sof*—the Infinite—is the name for God in Jewish mysticism. On the Kabbalalistic tradition, see Gershom Scholem, *Major Trends in Jewish Mysticism* (New York: Schocken, 1961) and *On the Kabbalah and Its Symbolism* (New York: Schocken, 1965), and more recently Daniel Matt, *Essential Kabbalah: The Heart of Jewish Mysticism* (San Francisco: HarperSanFrancisco, 1995), and Elliot Wolfson, *Along the Path: Studies in Kabbalistic Myth, Symbolism, and Hermeneutics* (Albany: State University of New York Press, 1995).

28. Levinas, *Otherwise Than Being,* 148.

29. Ibid.

30. Ibid.

31. Levinas, *Alterity and Transcendence,* 138.

32. *The Mishnah,* trans. Jacob Neusner (New Haven, CT: Yale University Press, 1988), 591.

33. Susannah Heschel, "Introduction," to Abraham Joshua Heschel, *The Prophets* (New York: Perennial Classics, 2001), xviii.

34. Derrida, *Adieu,* 92.

35. Levinas, *Alterity and Transcendence,* 138.

36. Avivah Gottlieb Zornberg, *The Beginning of Desire* (New York: Doubleday, 1996), 131.

37. Rabbi Benjamin Sharfman et al., eds., *The Pentateuch and Rashi's Commentary,* (Brooklyn, NY: S. S. & R. Publishing, 1976), 200.

38. Zornberg, *The Beginning of Desire,* 131.

39. Plaut, *The Torah,* 151.

40. Franz Rosenzweig, *On Jewish Learning,* ed. Nahum N. Glatzer (New York: Schocken Books, 1955), 91.

41. Levinas, *Otherwise Than Being,* 5

42. Ibid., 146.

43. Ibid., 150; my italics.

44. Plaut, *The Torah,* 152.

45. See Zornberg's discussion in Zornberg, *The Beginning of Desire,* 123–43.

46. Levinas, *In the Time of the Nations,* 86.

47. Plaut, *The Torah,* 156.

48. See Zornberg's discussion in Zornbereg, *The Beginning of Desire,* 123.

49. Ibid.

50. Ibid.

51. Ibid., 126.

52. Ibid.

53. See the discussion in Rabbi Joseph Telushkin, *Jewish Literacy* (New York: William Morrow, 1991), 38.

54. Zornberg, *The Beginning of Desire,* 129.

55. Plaut, *The Torah,* 166.

56. Levinas, *In the Time of the Nations,* 86.

57. What I mean by "the idolatry of patriarchy" is twofold and stretches what one may normally mean by it: (1) women are generally subordinated to the men in the biblical narrative and in traditional interpretations of the narrative, which I find to be the case in Kierkegaard's lack of reflection on Sarah; (2) I am suggesting that one traditional Christian reading, which sees Genesis 22 as fore-shadowing God's (the Father's) sacrifice of his son on behalf of humanity, also suffers from the patriarchal standpoint often read into the Bible. In this paper's account, in which Sarah is not forgotten, Abraham's faith in God is not the sole focus. Further, Sarah's standpoint ruptures reading Genesis 22 as foreshadowing God's sacrifice of his son.

58. Zornberg, *The Beginning of Desire,* 132.

59. Abraham Joshua Heschel, *The Wisdom of Heschel,* trans. Ruth M. Good-hill (Toronto: Collins, 1986), 313.

60. Levinas, *Difficult Freedom,* 6.

61. Ibid.

62. Levinas, *Alterity and Transcendence,* 126–27.

63. Levinas, *Proper Names,* 74.

64. Levinas, *In the Time of the Nations,* 86.

TWELVE

Blessing and Binding

A Response to Pattillo and Stern

SANDOR GOODHART

The essays of Matthew Pattillo and Stephen Stern offer a fruitful basis for comparison and contrast. Pattillo examines the whole of Hebrew scripture in relation to Girard's reading of the Christian gospel as an exposure of the scapegoat mechanism, while Stern focuses in upon one key moment of the Hebrew Bible from which all else in his view (and my own) may be deduced. Moreover, although these two writers are diametrically opposed in their view of that one text, their views reflect divergent angles of approach to it that remain consonant, I would like to suggest, with both Hebrew scripture as the rabbis read it, and with the thinking of René Girard.

Pattillo begins with Girard's seminal insight that all of Hebrew scripture is a move away from the sacrificial, and his essay is an attempt to delineate precisely how that takes place. His discussion moves from a consideration of creation, to one of Adam and Eve, to Abraham and the *Akedah*, to Leviticus, and finally to the later prophets. He cites (to advantage, in my view) the argument of Kendell Soulen that all of the Hebrew Bible may be read as an extension of creation, a creation conceived primarily as about blessing. Soulen's view offers, Pattillo affirms, a positive understanding of mimesis, one that complements Girard's critique of runaway mimetic desire and appropriation as a process necessarily entailing the decay of the sacrificial mechanisms founding all culture. The Hebrew Bible is not only about the end of the primitive sacrificial, the argument asserts, but about what we may do in its stead. Understanding creation as culminating in Genesis 1:28, "And God blessed them" (an intent refined in God's commandment to Abraham in Genesis 12:2 to "be a blessing"), the episode of Adam and Eve would then tell the story of disobedience and its fruit, of the negative imitation of God expressed as the substitution of man for God as model, a gesture leading (in the wake of the Cain and Abel episode) to the Deluge and universal idolatry, violence, and death.

In this connection, the *Akedah* would then reverse this earlier chronicle of runaway mimetic behavior and signal a return to the primacy of blessing. Leviticus would similarly articulate the positive value of obedient submissive behavior modeled on the spirit of Isaac: on obedience to God, repentance for past mimetic rivalry, extreme openness or submission to God's will, and identification with the position of the victim.

And finally, if the prophetic texts denounce sacrifice, they denounce in Pattillo's view only the "bad sacrificial," the sacrificial gone wrong. What good are all your sacrifices if while you do them you are thoroughly mimetic in the primitive sacrificial way? the texts would ask. On the other hand, if you give up these emulations of the victimary mechanism and become obedient to the law, the Torah, the teaching or instruction of God, then all bodes well.

Jesus in this reading would come along to complete the process begun in the Hebrew Bible: to restore the primacy of creation, to reinstall blessing and the value of positive mimetic behavior as the new (or return of the old) order of the day. Here is what you are to do, he would be understood as saying. Imitate me. Refuse violence. Obey the father, submit to the will of God, as Abraham learned to do, as Isaac did, as Leviticus affirmed, and as prophets reiterated amidst unthinkable historical catastrophe.

Pattillo's reading is brilliant. He has taken a Girardian insight and amplified it to the point where it constitutes a full and illuminating itinerary of the entirety of Christian scripture—from the "Old Testament" to the Gospel, one, moreover, that is significantly harmonious with Jewish rabbinic understandings. Creation is the center, as Franz Rosenzweig makes clear. Genesis 2–11 registers the misunderstanding of creation in the primitive sacrificial sense (in the form of a generalizing usurpation of the divine with the human) and leads to unmitigated disaster—worldwide idolatry, violence, and death. The life of Abraham in Genesis 12–24 turns the corner with its signature commandments, "get thee gone" and "be a blessing," and its climactic moment in Genesis 22. On its basis, Leviticus works out a program for the anti-sacrificial structure of ritual observance. And the later prophetic texts are less outright rejections of sacrifice than criticism of ritual performed in the spirit of the primitive sacred, a body of critical literature that again links suffering, victimage, and sacrifice gone wrong with idolatry on the one hand, and creation, responsibility, and the ethical with anti-idolatry on the other, and thereby looks forward to a day when Torah will be lived as flesh, blood, and heart. Christianity in this interpretation would be one version of that future, one imagined from within the prophetic understanding, a reaffirmation of the creational gesture of which all of Torah is an extension, a working out of the details of a positive mimetic ethical position only sketched in Girard's work.

Stephen Stern similarly focuses upon Genesis 22 as a critical moment of the Hebrew Bible, but instead of examining it within the panoramic view Pattillo adopts, he reads it at close range to examine both its successes and its failures in unexpected ways. "How does one show [a] father how to bear witness to his son," Stern asks initially. "This is the problem for God with Abraham." There is also another, Stern asserts: how does God teach the son that he is responsible both for the father and for building something new out of a tradition? Upon these issues (and a third raised later) Stern builds his reading. Pursuing these questions through the interpretive quandary of the significance of the test, the essay considers first a non-Jewish view, then a traditional Jewish view, before offering an examination of each of the four major players.

Kierkegaard serves for Stern to witness the test as an issue of faith. Kierkegaardian faith in his view is not about skepticism or knowledge. The individual for Hegel (in Kierkegaard's view as Stern reads both) must abrogate particularity and express himself through the universal and the ethical founded upon it. Opposition to this universal is sin. But for Kierkegaard, faith suspends this Hegelian ethical, which remains unable to account for the privacy of an individual's faith-based relationship with God.

On the other hand, Stern tells us, reading the *Akedah* via Kierke-gaard, two problems arise. Sarah and Isaac are treated as secondary. And Abraham comes off as self-indulgent, and therefore idolatrous, from a biblical point of view. If the test is about Abraham's faith in Kier-kegaard's terms, Abraham is not to be found with the other individual for whom he is responsible but returned back upon himself.

Read within the Jewish tradition, on the other hand, the test is an opportunity for Abraham's instructor to show Abraham what he has learned and what he has not. Abraham is taught how to witness to the Other and thus make an exodus from human sacrifice, an insight that aligns Stern's reading with Girard's. Murdering Isaac means treating Isaac as a thing. "Things give, they do not offer a face," Levinas writes. In this way, "God is returning Abraham to ethics."

The mountaintop episode raises three points that in Stern's view enable us to understand the test. The angel says let the boy go, and Abraham does so. But he does so, Stern notes, not in response to the angel's command, but because as Abraham raises the blade to sacrifice Isaac, he notices Isaac's vulnerability, his naked face. Abraham realizes that killing Isaac on behalf of God is in fact violating God. One ap-proaches God, Levinas tells us, through the relay of the neighbor and not as a third party. Proximity to God is proximity to the other indi-vidual. Isaac's face signifies for Abraham infinite responsibility for that other, even to the extent of substitution. Isaac is unbound, as a re-sult, not just from the sacrificial cords that tie him to Moriah, but from living as only a projection of Abraham's subjectivity; Isaac's alterity is recognized and accepted.

The angel says something else: "I know you fear God." Susannah Heschel writes, "God suffers when human beings are hurt," and Stern links the two ideas. Fearing God becomes fearing for God. Thus, Stern asserts, when Abraham refrains from harming Isaac, he is refraining from harming God. Finally, the angel says in effect: "You have not with-held your son, your favorite one, from me." Witnessing to Isaac, Abra-ham has given Isaac to God. He gives up ownership and thereby gives new life to Isaac.

In this way, Stern notes, Abraham learns to witness to the Other. What about Isaac? Isaac is thirty-seven years old by rabbinic count, and a "builder" according to Franz Rosenzweig. At thirty-seven, to become a builder, Isaac must witness Abraham and move out of the shadow of Abraham to genuine independence. Witness belongs to the glory of the infinite, not to the father's subjectivity. The test, Stern says, is not about faith in God but about returning Abraham and Isaac to ethics. It is responsibility for the other that glorifies God, not a relationship in which ethics is suspended by one's divine faithfulness to God.

What is Isaac's response to this lesson? The text does not say Isaac returned with Abraham. In this space where Isaac is not mentioned, Stern argues, one may recognize that Isaac lets his father go. Gunther Plaut writes: "Isaac now became a man who for the first time could let his father go and return later at his own choosing." The son is no longer condemned to live as his father did. He has the opportunity to build a new community.

But someone is condemned nonetheless—and here is the third issue mentioned above. Sarah's death, narrated shortly after the *Akedah,* "exposes the problem of her life" for Abraham. The traditional Jewish reading is that she died of grief, that when she learned Isaac had been *all-but-slaughtered,* she "gave up the ghost." In this regard, Sarah, in Aviva Zornberg's words, "is the true victim of the Akeidah; her death is its unexplicated, inexplicable, cost." Through her death, we learn that Abraham could have challenged God's order as he did at Sodom and Gomorrah. Abraham might at least have asked God, "Why are you going back on your promise?" Her anguish exposes the depth of Abraham's egoism in agreeing to take the test in the first place. In doing so, Abraham kills the community of Sarah, the community they are commanded to build by virtue of Isaac's face. When Abraham ascends to Moriah, he violates Sarah. And she does not stand idly by. She leaves Abraham over the event.

Does she leave even before the event? Stern notes that when Abraham returns she is not there. She dies in the land of the Hittites—a land that is not her home. Abraham returns to Beer Sheba and appears to be there while she dies in Kiriath-Arba. And she leaves space for Isaac. He moves into her tent later in the narrative. Sarah's death disrupts Kierkegaard's Abraham-centered reading. And we get to witness the beginning of a sketch of justice.

There is a problem, Stern concludes, in Abraham's relationship with Isaac and Sarah that becomes clear when God commands Abraham to take the test. In so far as Abraham readies Isaac for sacrifice, he idolizes his relations with God at Isaac's expense. If Abraham presents a murdered Isaac, Abraham witnesses only his own egoism. He defaces Isaac. If Abraham murders Isaac, he fails the test. The test is about Abraham's ethics, about where he is ethically, about whether he is beyond violence, not about the teleological suspension of the ethical understood in Kierkegaardian or Hegelian terms. Looking into Isaac's defenseless face, Stern tells us, Abraham suddenly transcends his past, recognizing and witnessing that Isaac is independent, a single person for whom Talmud teaches the world is created, and for whom Abraham is infinitely responsible. The "face as mortality," Levinas writes, is equivalent to "a victim's abandonment." "Hearing the heavenly voice, Abraham puts down the knife, and finds peace for himself and for Isaac."

But in agreeing to take the test at all, he also betrays Sarah, giving her not peace but violence. To remain her own person, we may infer, Stern tells us, Sarah leaves Abraham, vanishing from his world. When he returns, he does not find what he remembers. If Abraham and Isaac appear to be successful in their relationship with God and with each other, the relationship of Sarah with both would appear tenuous. And her death will be less easy to overcome than the near loss on Moriah.

Drawing upon Levinas's notion of our infinite responsibility for the other human being, in other words, and our access to that responsibility through the face of the other individual, Stern argues that if the *Akedah* does not reject sacrifice entirely, it rejects killing Isaac as a demonstration of faithfulness, either as Kierkegaard defines that term or as the Jewish tradition of anti-idolatry (understood in the popular sense) defines it. In that way, the text remains profoundly anti-sacrificial. And in that way Stern's reading joins the reading of Pattillo as a move away from the sacrificial postulates by which primitive culture would organize itself. It looks forward to a world founded upon ethics, and leading to justice.

Stern's view is audacious, if not so much in its result as in its method of arriving at that result. Levinas is a powerful reader of the Jewish tradition along just the lines Stern cites, and Stern is one of a number of critics who have begun to employ Levinas's ideas — and the Jewish renewalist context from which they come in Martin Buber and Franz Rosenzweig — to biblical reading. Moreover, in so far as a critique of victimage is at the heart of both, his reading would appear compatible with René Girard's. Finally, there is a way in which as readers of the biblical text we must find the fulfillment of the sacrificial expression of the commandment unacceptable, and in which, to the extent that he does attempt it, Abraham fails the test, a failure signaled forcefully in Stern's essay in his account of Sarah's death.

Pattillo and Stern thus arrive at their anti-sacrificial views in very different ways. In Pattillo's view, Abraham's obedience to God is positive and in Stern's view Abraham's rejection of God's sacrificial commandment is positive. Are these views not at odds? In fact, if we recognize the drama in which each of these writers are engaged, we may see that they articulate the same position, although, in the first case that perspective yields a positive reading of the sacrificial and in the second case a negative one. Pattillo is concerned with the way the *Akedah* refuses the disobedience of earlier Genesis episodes and reorients us toward an anti-sacrificial conclusion. Stern telescopes the details of that obedience, identifying through a series of narrative inferences a midrashic way of explaining Abraham's anti-sacrificial behavior. Like the rabbis, Stern argues it is both a test of Abraham's capacity to behave in an anti-idolatrous fashion and a repudiation of Abraham's gesture of raising his knife to "slaughter" Isaac. Although couched within a seemingly linguistic debate, Rashi finds a way of saying that Abraham fails the test no less than Stern does, asserting that Abraham is wrong in so far as God never said slaughter. It would be as much a misreading of Stern's view to see it as rejecting the traditional perspective as it would be a misreading of Pattillo's to see it as endorsing Abraham's sacrificial behavior rather than his rejection of imitative rivalry.

And of course that is how both Girard's view and Levinas's view come together. The face of the other individual upon which Levinas depends is the face of the victim upon which Girard depends. All of Levinas's work is geared toward rejecting the victim, toward finding oneself in the position of the accused, an accusative that precedes the nominative, in Levinas's language, an assignation we are assigned before becoming a subject of consciousness. The suffering of the other individual (by which Levinas understands the victimage of the other individual) is never meaningful for Levinas, never redemptive; only my own suffering may be assigned a meaning. And only this insight is capable of founding the ethics of interhuman groups. "Face as mortality, mortality of the other beyond his appearing, . . . the 'Thou shalt not kill' that is also the meaning of the face," is the equivalent of "a victim's abandonment." Endorsing the voice of the victim, the position of the victim, whether expressed in voice or face, and understanding God through that victimage (and not as a third party to it), is Judaism itself. "*La position des victimes,*" the position of victims, the condition of being a victim, Levinas writes, "is Judaism." "Israel has become once again a religious category."[1]

Looked at close up, in other words, whether read via the critique of the idolatrous sacrificial in René Girard, or read via our mimetic appropriation of God's infinite responsibility for the other individual and the position of the victim (through his or her face) vis-à-vis Levinas, the Hebrew Bible continues to inaugurate the systematic rejection of the sacrificial gone wrong as idolatry, violence, and suffering, a rejection that operates in an especially elusive way when the rejection itself shows up as the newest idolatry. It delineates a movement toward the rabbinic position that articulates, in the midst of a new crisis in the ancient world, a view of the former one. And it continues to endorse the anti-sacrificial movement in which the thinking of René Girard, of Emmanuel Levinas, and of the rabbis coincide: in the place where we used to sacrifice, we now pray and read.

Note

1. "La position des victimes dans un monde en désordre, c'est-à-dire dans un monde où le bien n'arrive pas à triompher, est souffrance. . . . La souffrance du juste pour une justice sans triomphe est vécue concrètement comme judaïsme. Israel—historique et charnel—redevient catégorie religieuse"; "The position of victims, the condition of being a victim, in a world that is in disorder, which is to say, a world where the good does not triumph, is suffering. . . . The suffering of the just individual for a justice that is without triumph is lived concretely as Judaism. Israel, historical and carnal, becomes again a religious category," my translation. See Emmanuel Levinas, "Aimer la Thora plus que Dieu," *Difficile liberté* (Paris: Albin Michel, 1983), 191.

Holy Writings: The Book of Job

THIRTEEN

Mimesis, Sacrifice, and the Wisdom of Job

CHRIS ALLEN CARTER

The poetry of Job . . . allows multiple possibilities of interpretation . . .
corresponding to the open, unresolved tensions in the author's vision of reality.
—Moshe Greenberg

No sooner had the West developed in the eighteenth century the techniques of modern historicism than they were applied to its own earliest religious traditions, with the result that today, after two and a half centuries of research, more is known about the birth and growth of the Hebrew Bible, and that knowledge is more widely dispersed, than in those years when the Second Temple of Jerusalem first shone in all its splendor.[1] Likewise, modern historical study of the Christian Gospels gives us a fuller picture of these documents than ever before, and, despite having been thrown into crisis by Albert Schweitzer's *The Quest for the Historical Jesus,* has now regrouped and proceeds enriched by new archaeological finds at Nag Hammadi, Qumran, and other sites.

Meanwhile, this broad historicist trend has spun off an epiphenomenon of more ahistorical, more literary approaches to our religious texts. Kenneth Burke's 1961 *The Rhetoric of Religion,* Frank Kermode's 1967 *The Sense of an Ending,* Robert Alter's 1981 *The Art of Biblical Narrative,* and Northrop Frye's 1982 *The Great Code* are all inspired applications of the increasingly sophisticated techniques of secular criticism, especially the practice of "close reading" and the revelation of "blind insight," to Judeo-Christian scriptures. Other New Critical and deconstructionist works could be listed here, but this is a sample of the books that continue to introduce the movement to many. As James

Williams once put it, literary criticism and critical theory "[open] up biblical texts in new ways."[2]

It is among such crosscurrents that René Girard's 1985 *La route antique des hommes pervers* appears, translated two years later as *Job, the Victim of His People*.[3] This very independent text disregards some current trends while turning others to the demonstration of its own technique. Mimeticist criticism chooses to emphasize the human tendency to copy the other. But because by copying the other, human beings often copy the other's aggression (a reciprocal aggression that so frequently escalates), the mimeticist usually discovers contagions of violence and commemorative rites that mimic that violence in the texts under study. Mimesis, sacrifice, and victimage are key words in the mimeticist lexicon. Girard has made a career out of his theory of imitative behavior, creatively using it to elucidate difficult passages ancient, medieval, and modern, putting to work aspects of texts left lounging in the dim corners of other readings.[4]

In *Job, the Victim of His People*, Girard tackles one of the more recalcitrant interpretive problems of the Bible. In his analysis of the book of Job, history deepens into crosscultural anthropology, while the criticism of myth and psychology are employed in the service of a moral vision urging the reduction of our levels of victimization. Thus literary criticism, including some deconstruction, takes an ethical turn. Without neglecting the history of the text, Girard compares the treatment of Job in the Hebrew Bible to the treatment of Oedipus in Greek tragedy in order to stress the ubiquity of victimage and the implications of such chaos and violence for our own times. I propose to highlight Girard's ethical approach by contrasting it with the approaches of Moshe Greenberg, Robert Alter, and Stephen Mitchell, approaches in which historicist dissection of the text is declined in favor of a more New Critical and more organic interpretation. Afterwards, I will return to Girard's analysis of Job in more detail.

Job Before Girard: Greenberg, Alter, and Mitchell

Moshe Greenberg, in his chapter "Job" in Robert Alter and Frank Kermode's 1987 *A Literary Guide to the Bible*, does not try to hide certain

characteristics of the book of Job that might be taken as indications of
a serial composition, including its "sudden shifts of mood and role,"
its "reversal and subversion," its "rhetoric of sarcasm and irony," and its
portrayal of more than one Job.[5] He opens his essay with a paragraph
acknowledging "the complexity of the character set forth in the book
that bears his name." He admits that "the book's representation of Job
seems to some modern scholars so disharmonious as to warrant the
hypothesis that two characters have been fused in it." Once upon a time
there was a primitive folktale whose pious hero, "Job the Patient,"
offered a model of simple virtue. Sometime between the seventh and
fifth centuries BCE, "the hypothesis continues, a far more profound
thinker (perhaps a survivor of the Babylonian exile and its crisis of
faith)" split the parable and inserted poetic dialogues whose central
figure, "Job the Impatient," loudly protests his fate and thus "radically
challenges . . . the conventional wisdom of the tale [now the prose
frame]." Later redactors of the work, be they poets, dramatists, or pres-
ervationist scribes, were persons in whom emotional alienation, if not
physical dislocation, created a need to alter the traditional stories. The
history of the book of Job seems to be the history of a series of documents, born in a land of turmoil, riven by contradiction, and allowing
"multiple possibilities of interpretation."[6]

However, the rest of Greenberg's essay is a studied attempt to refute this documentary hypothesis. "The contrast between the folktale
and the artful poem," he cautions, "must not be overdrawn."[7] The origins of the text are so obscure no critic should be confident of his or
her "ability to reconstitute the original."[8] The assumption of multiple
authors is based on an assumption of multiple texts, and this premise
of a multitext is based on the most fundamental expectations of "sim-
plicity, consistency, and linearity" that, once violated, prod a leap to
conclusions of serial composition. On the contrary, the text, as Greenberg views it, is a weave of diverse elements, and its difficulties can better be explained as the tactics of a single poet whose purpose is to disrupt the functioning of linear logic and to present a panorama of divine
creativity that spreads beyond human reason. In other words, the dis-
unity of the text is an illusion deliberately fostered only to be dispelled.
Just as antievolutionists sometimes claim that the so-called facts of the

fossil record, rather than evidencing a long, staged growth of life, are instead false clues planted by God to test our faith, Greenberg claims that the so-called discrepancies of the Job text are false clues planted to tempt us to an overdependence on logic. Instead, they can be safely incorporated into a unified reading, and any long, complicated history of textual development safely ignored.

Greenberg chooses to emphasize both that the "vastness and complexity of God's work" dwarfs the mere mortal and that "God's amazing creativity" outruns mere earthly calculation.[9] One can almost picture the human accountant, complete with green eyeshade, hunched over his desk, oblivious to his position on a small planet orbiting an insignificant sun spinning through an obscure arm on one of a billion billion nondescript galaxies. Against this spectacle of nature, symbolized in God's climactic speeches to Job not only by the lion and the war-horse and the Behemoth and the Leviathan and other creatures real or imagined, but also by the famous astronomical reference to the founding of the universe "when the morning stars sang and the angels shouted for joy," "man is incidental."[10] In these speeches, the human is no longer the crown of creation or its telos: "Job, representing mankind, stands outside the picture, displaced from its center to a remote periphery." These divine pronouncements at the culmination of the book of Job, Greenberg argues, reject "the anthropocentrism of all the rest of Scripture."[11] By the time Greenberg concludes, the primary message of the work has become our duty to copy Job, yielding all dominion to God. The receptive reader, surprised by his or her sins of misreading, should humbly repent.[12]

Some of this is irrefutable. True, nature is "an astonishing panoply of creatures created and sustained in ways unfathomable to the human mind."[13] True, no human "can comprehend God, whose works defy teleological and rational categories."[14] And after the documentarians have chopped the text into separate pieces, they should take the time to put it back together again; it was, after all, read for millennia as some kind of finished product. Purely secular historians of the text are their own most telling counterexample, textual bookkeepers trying to account for this piece or that piece of the document without ever looking up at the larger picture, much less feeling awe at the spectacle.

But there are problems with Greenberg's argument as well. To begin with, it is not *some* modern scholars but *most* modern scholars who accept the split-parable theory, and it is not an emotional attachment to minor consistencies that generates postulates about split texts, but a major gap between the Job of the prosaic prologue, who says meekly we must accept from God the bad along with the good, and the Job of the poetic dialogues, who refuses ever to yield. There is something faintly pagan about the original "unsplit" parable with its gods who inflict suffering, its humans who serve as their playthings, and a divine test that gets carried away. It was perhaps inevitable that such a tale would provoke a rebuttal at that moment when the scholarship was available and the scribes were ready to force new meanings. Greenberg may still not be ready. He gives away the game when he somewhat disingenuously offers that his intention is "not to assert the infallibility of the text in hand, but rather to confess our inability to justify on grounds other than individual predilection the alternatives proposed to it."[15] Yet a decision to focus on the text as a fallible product of human history and on the issues of justice raised by the possibility of God's working through that history would be no more arbitrary than Greenberg's decision to escape from history into authority.

Greenberg is directly influenced by Robert Alter, whose 1985 *The Art of Biblical Poetry* also seems to sympathize initially with the assumption of a serial composition and a split protagonist.[16] Alter opens his essay with a couple of paragraphs acknowledging a stark contrast between the "impeccably God-fearing" Job of the naïve folktale and "the poetic Job" who wishes "he had never been born."[17] He admits that the voice from the whirlwind has "troubled many readers over the centuries" as "an attempt to overwhelm poor Job by an act of cosmic bullying."[18] By "not deigning to explain why innocent children should perish" and "decent men and women writhe in affliction," and by instead sarcastically "asking Job how good he is at hurling lightning bolts, making the sun rise and set, causing rain to fall, fixing limits to the breakers of the sea," and so forth, this God seems to "ignore the issue of justice."

He—this autocratic, patriarchal ruler of the heavens—is not the only one. The rest of Alter's essay has nothing to say in defense of divine justice (theodicy) or human justice (anthropodicy?) in the course of making a case for the book of Job as a crafted unity. The text, as Alter views it, is not a series of documents; it is a carefully designed interlace of anticipations and retrospectives. The speech of Yahweh responds image-by-image to the earlier complaint of Job; the "jejune and superficial" phrases of Eliphaz and the "stereotyped language" of Zophar serve as rungs up to the more exalted rhetoric of the Lord Himself; even the Hymn to Wisdom and speeches of Elihu set the stage for the utterances of the divine voice. All evidence the tight control of a single artistic hand, Alter claims.[19]

Alter chooses to emphasize that "the uniquely vivid descriptive poetry" of the two discourses of God "enables Job to glimpse beyond his human plight an immense world of power and beauty and awesome warring forces."[20] This world presents to our human eyes only "a welter of contradictions, dizzying variety, energies and entities that [we] cannot take in."[21] Were we omniscient, however, we could see an order that harmonizes both creative and destructive forces. Again, it would be difficult to refute that the divine plan is "truly uncanny," "truly inscrutable," or that certain aspects of this overarching scheme possess "a rare beauty in the midst of power and terror and strangeness."[22] Such has long been the very definition of the holy or the sublime. Nor would it be wise to deny that God's vision is all encompassing, "contrasted with man's purblind view."[23] The awesome mystery of this vast world eludes us just when we are about to grasp it as the Leviathan of the poem, just when the poet is about to capture it for us in words, "churns out of our field of vision, leaving behind a foaming wake that, like his mouth and eyes, shines."[24] By the time Alter concludes, the overarching message of the work has become our duty to copy Job, realizing the limits of our mortal imagination. The receptive reader, surprised by his or her sins of impiety, should humbly repent.

Again there are problems. Alter makes a valiant effort to lace together a divided text, but his essay is left riven by contradiction: Job fighting for justice versus Job crushed by a God beyond justice. Alter is too quick to assume the theocentric perspective, and he speaks somewhat too casually of "God's vision," "God's poetry," and "God's speech."[25] He refers to the "revelation" that roars out of the whirlwind as the

portrayal of a providence that "defies moral categorizing."[26] He tips
his hand when he adds, "The most crucial respect in which such defiance makes itself felt is in the immense, imponderable play of power"
that informs creation, especially, that creates and sustains the "constant clash of warring forces."[27] But few theorists still worry about the
morality of the impersonal forces of nature. They realize these infrahuman systems lay the basis for higher-level human systems and their
sense of black humor. What we must worry about is the constant clash
of the human factions around us. We do not judge the volcano or the
hurricane good or evil; we judge what humans do to each other. Alter
presents the divine lecture series as a sequence of cosmogony, meteor-
ology, and zoology.[28] Apparently, some kind of deficit, fiscal or moral,
forced ethics to be dropped from the curriculum.

A few years before Alter and Greenberg, in the introduction to
his 1979 translation of the book of Job, Stephen Mitchell also celebrated a realm beyond good and evil. He concludes that the message
of the work is the desirability of a mystical union with the divine.[29] His
receptive reader is surprised by nirvana. We are to copy Job yielding to
a cosmos swirling with creative and destructive energies.[30] Mitchell
chooses to emphasize Job's final lapse into silence.[31] By the end of the
poem, the hero moves beyond the ego, beyond "personal will," beyond
words.[32] This is not a case of a penitent "beaten into submission," but
of one who has "surrendered into the light."[33] Interestingly, Mitchell
accepts the serialization of the text. In fact, so convinced is he of the
"belatedness" of the Hymn to Wisdom and the speeches of Elihu that
he drops these from his translation![34] But whatever its discrepancies,
the Job story basically organizes a "spiritual transformation."[35] Even the
much-maligned folktale-ish epilogue is seen to have been redacted to
help effect this transvaluation of values, celebrating as it does "peace,
abundance, and a specifically female kind of grace" beyond judgmen-
tal reason and "the male compulsion to control."[36]

Different as they are—Alter and Greenberg neoorthodox right,
Mitchell more or less Nietzschean left—all three end up, explicitly
or implicitly, to one degree or another, dismissing human history, the
emergence of equal rights, and the documentary record of that ethical
struggle.[37] This is not a matter of theological correctness but of em-

phasis. Might not we stress *both* Mitchell's private vision *and* our public responsibilities? We could learn to shuttle back and forth between mystical union with the divine and our roles as individual egos or personalities clashing (cooperating?) in the battle for social justice. The former may refresh us for the efforts of the latter. Might not we be as awestruck at the moral power explored in the book of Job and at the unresolved tensions expressed on the interface of its documentary fragments as Greenberg and Alter are awestruck at the raw power of the animal kingdom? If the multiple possibilities of interpretation opening in the vision of a single text are a marvel, so much more the new meanings arising across cultural lines, as with the synthesis of Hebrew, Greek, and Christian multitexts. The human language-user emerges out of a caldron of infrahuman forces into a drama of choice and responsibility, a spectacle awesome in its own right. From an admittedly anthropocentric perspective—and it is not easy to adopt honestly any other—cultural developments are *more* inspiring than natural developments.

Girard's Reading of Job

Such are the kinds of texts available when René Girard makes his book-length contribution to the discussion on Job. Unlike the religio-aesthetic critics, he does not oppose the documentary hypothesis. The discrepancies between the earliest and latest layers of the document are basic to his argument. Acknowledging that the text remains riven with conflicts and divisions papered over (papyrused over?) since the foundation of culture, he spares us any pleas to treat the text as an interlaced whole. Yet while he assumes a serial composition, he is not particularly interested in the details of this process as usually presented, at least not in his *Job, the Victim*. He chooses instead to emphasize what came before and what comes after. His approach might be said to be "anthropological" and, insofar as he is digging down through layers of texts, "archaeological." If he is correct about the primeval story that predates the rest of the Job text, the most insightful of its redactors were not working with a *tabula rasa* when they composed their masterpiece.

What was used to split the traditional parable was not entirely new material. In the shifting literary landscape of the time, all the editing and reediting, all the sociopolitical turmoil and artistic experimentation, created openings that produced something dramatically new, something that would only emerge more fully in the Gospels centuries later. In brief, Girard recontextualizes the Job story, but to do this he has to give us still another Job or two.

Girard zeroes in on the dialogues, and there he finds not existential skepticism and anxiety but a scapegoat pursued by armed attackers. He notes that Job seems less interested in settling the philosophical question of evil or decoding the inscrutable divine than in avoiding a lynch mob. At times Job complains more pointedly about the meanness of people than about the providence of God. In a last survey of his condition, he regrets that he is the "laughing-stock of . . . the young people" (30:1), that he has become the "talk of the town" (30:9), that even the lowly rabble of his society encroach as a mob "to [the] right of [him]" (30:12).[38] He reels from wave after wave of terror, his attackers bursting upon him.

> They move in, as though through a wide breach,
> and I am crushed beneath the rubble.
> Terrors turn to meet me,
> my confidence is blown away as if by the wind;
> my hope of safety passes like a cloud. (30:14–15)

Strangely, his diatribe omits mention of the preemptive strikes that supposedly wiped out his house and barns and children. The Job of the dialogues who here summarizes his calamities seems oblivious to the events of the prologue. As Girard puts this, "the more obstinately Job remains silent on the subject of his lost cattle and his other good reasons for complaint, the more he insists on portraying himself as the innocent victim of those around him."[39]

While Job's main worry seems to be the attack from human assailants on the ground, Job and his enemies frequently resort to an epic imagery of celestial marauders to describe their fears (15:20–23). A hail of arrows from above — that is the fate reserved for the wicked

(20:23 and 20:29).[40] But in the prologue was there not a division among the gods between those who were assigned to test Job and those who were awaiting the results? Job was supposedly chosen to be pursued by one divine faction because he was so good, not because all the gods were angry with him, much less determined to swoop down with their combined minions to punish him. Girard records that Job's interlocutors provide neither the friendship nor the sympathy nor the comfort forecast by the prologue. They do not really engage Job in a debate; if they hear him, they do not really listen to him; instead, they harangue him and, worse, incite violence against him.[41] The rhetoric of their accusations comes close to being formulaic and even liturgical; their words "are couched in the style of religious epic."[42] These orators are a throwback to the hierophants of a ritual sacrifice. This seems another odd note in terms of the prologue. Nor is Job just another prosperous rancher of unimpeachable character, as the prologue indicates, but closer to an actual ruler, once respected, deferred to in council, feared if not loved, who has been subsequently accused of abuses of power and pulled down from his perch on high.

> If I smiled at them, it was too good to be true,
> they watched my face for the least sign of favour.
> In a lordly style, I told them which course to take,
> and like a king amid his armies,
> I led them where I chose. (29:24–25)

In short, the Job of the dialogues, as these are excavated by Girard, is not the subject of a divine experiment or the exemplum of an ethical debate. This Job is essentially the victim of his people.[43]

These gaps between the prologue-epilogue and the dialogues are taken by Girard as evidence of a serial composition, and he uses them to imply a new theory of the development of the story. In the beginning were accounts of an actual stoning or stabbing or lynching, in other words, scapegoat narratives about an actual mimetic crisis. These stories told how the world was founded upon the sacrifice of a victim-hero-god. In terms of Girard's theory of the mimetic cycle, these were commemorative myths that, along with rituals and taboos, perpetuated tribal traditions. Formed when the culture was at the level of the spoken word, these myths were held in the cultural memory as rhythmic verse and often included such special effects as verbal duels between orators who face off against each other in bombastic challenge, most powerfully, duels between an accused and his accusers. Lifted to the level of the written word, this style of confrontational dialogue was preserved, as with the war councils in the *Iliad.* The dialogues of the book of Job would appear to be based in an oral poetry belatedly recorded, specifically, in a late variation of the primeval scapegoat myth in which a victim was surrounded and condemned by a barrage of verbal attacks. At long last, but now in a newly inscribed version, the accusers are once again on the brink of an assault on the accused. Knives will soon flash or stones fly, this time between the lines of a written document.

At this stage of the story's development, we cannot assume its main character is named Job. We could call this "Ur-text" "Edomus the Persecuted" or "Edomus Rex," suggesting both its local origins in some non-Hebrew version of the scapegoat myth (the protagonist is said to hail from Uz, a city in Edom, the desert territory southeast of the Dead Sea) and its similarity to another famous myth of the same genre. *Oedipus Rex* (or *Oedipus the Persecuted,* as it could just as easily be called) tells the story of another highly respected decision maker, deferred to in council, feared if not loved. Its main character, too, is accused of "abominable crimes" and pulled down from his perch on high.[44] His "career collapses" in the kind of terrors described by Job's friends. He, also, is an idol transformed into someone "accursed, defiled, and stricken with plague."[45] Behind the Sophoclean tragedy is a similar local epic of divine vengeance, a myth commemorating the founding sacrifice. Oedipus, as excavated by Girard, is essentially the victim of his people.[46]

But what strikes Girard is the difference between the Greek and the Near Eastern stories. The latter breaks open the primeval form and lets the victim speak. Unknown redactors have amplified the story by expanding the role of certain characters and have granted the main character the right to protest. Just as in the rise of Athenian tragedy over a hundred-year period, in which first one actor, then another, steps forward out of the chorus and begins to speak on his own or to answer others, the Edomite drama allows at least four characters, an accused and three accusers, to emerge from the ceremonial background. But here the protagonist goes a step further. He does not just separate himself as a developing personality or soliloquist; he adopts an interpretation of the basic situation that differs from the rest of the citizenry. In dialogue with other characters, he vehemently protests his fate, proclaiming his innocence to the end. The verbal duels of the earlier myth become a logomachy over the issue of justice.

What the student of mimesis or imitative behavior notices is that this victim does not copy others. As the crowd closes in expecting him to cower, he instead turns and fights, fights with words. Unlike previous victim-hero-gods, silenced for millennia under a pile of rocks or hail of knife-points, this victim speaks in his own defense. Perhaps we should say he *writes* in his own defense because he specifically requests that his plea be etched on a tablet or inscribed in a book and answered in kind. As Mitchell translates this passage, "If only my cry were recorded, and my plea inscribed on a tablet—carved with an iron stylus, chiseled in rock forever (Job, 19:23)."[47] In effect, this victim issues a challenge, hoping that his more permanent marks will survive long enough to reach someone outside the circle of persecution, someone less in the grip of passion, someone more objective, someone who will not copy those delivering blows but will instead copy him in the act of protesting the system of injustice. As James Williams puts this in his analysis of the development of the myth, the victim gambles that writing "will become the means of his deliverance."[48]

At this point, I would choose to emphasize that what Job is hoping written words will do for him, the written word was just beginning to do for the larger community. The introduction of the alphabet into this region and the evolution of communication from oral to written during this period are producing greater distance between subject and object, greater detachment between knower and known, and greater knowledge of the self and the other. These new relationships form the basis for a new rationalism and individualism and a sense of the worth of each soul.[49] Such new perspectives eventually throw into question the scapegoat process. Read in a metalinguistic mode, the enhanced scapegoat myth symbolizes the possibility of this group deliverance. With the strokes of a stylus, "Edomus the Persecuted" becomes "Edomus the

Unrepentant" or even "Edomus the Innocent." In contrast, the Sopho-clean protagonist protests at first but then yields. "Oedipus the Perse-cuted" does *not* become "Oedipus the Unrepentant," much less "Oedi-pus the Innocent." The mythic fallen king ends up admitting "that he is," in Girard's words, "accursed, evil, and an enemy of God and that he deserves all the acts of vengeance that will be committed against him."[50] This admission, Girard claims, allows the scapegoat myth to function conventionally, namely, to confirm the guilt of the victim, to justify his persecution and sacrifice, and to commemorate the order founded upon his death. But in the later Near Eastern version, the de-nials of the protagonist disrupt the functioning of the scapegoat sys-tem. It is as if, in the passing of traditions held holy in the cultural memory, the sacred cup has been deliberately dropped.

The comparison of the two myths enables us to see that in the Near Eastern dialogues the usual pattern has been "mishandled" by a "more demanding and radical inspiration."[51] When this is sublated into the project of splitting the simple parable "Job the Patient," the insight is retained:

> The [traditional scapegoat] myth is [the victim's] story told entirely by his persecutors. The Dialogues of Job are an Oedipus story in which the victim forever refuses to add his voice to those of his per-secutors. . . . Job [as successor to the outspoken victim I have been calling Edomus the Innocent] derails the mythology that is meant to envelop him by maintaining his own point of view in the face of the formidable unanimity surrounding him. By remaining faithful to the truth revealed by the victim, [this new kind of protagonist becomes] the true hero of knowledge rather than Oedipus, who is perceived as such in the philosophical tradition.[52]

Thus the great Greek tragedy, long considered a monument of self-revelation, is surpassed by the developing Near Eastern tradition, which breaks the pattern of, and then goes beyond, the traditional scapegoat myth or tragedy. For perhaps the first time in human history, a story achieves the level of an explicit knowledge of the innocence of the vic-tim and then proceeds to proclaim this innocence most vehemently.[53]

We will probably never be able to reconstitute the series of events by which regional folktales and myths were transformed into the great poem of Job. We can guess that it was a collective effort and that each development in communication and knowledge added new levels of meaning. What is important is that the veritable palimpsest handed down to us (handed up to us?) sketches "the truth of the victim."[54] Always before, the persecutors had told the story proclaiming themselves blameless and the victim guilty. But this was a lie, a lie designed to establish order. Now we have the words of Job, and they must not be put "on the same level" as that of the persecutors.[55] Argues Girard, "Job's discourse must be preferred over the others; the revelation of the scapegoat must be taken seriously."[56] The friends are perfectly sincere, but their speeches mystify what is actually an attempted assassination. The truth of Job, on the contrary, is "unconditional, absolute truth."[57] Girard does not equivocate: "the truth of the victim that we at last possess is the greatest, most fortunate event in the history of religion and the whole of humanity."[58]

Thus Girard challenges the ahistorical trend of the mid-eighties by stressing the social justice agenda advanced by the book of Job. He preserves the history of the work from the mythic patterns of victimage that informed the earliest pre-Judaic and Judaic traditions to the extension of the story into Christian times, especially, into the fuller presentation of the innocence of the scapegoat in the Gospels. Had he approached the text as if all its fissures had been sealed, issues of divine and human justice would not have been raised. Had he collapsed the different voices of the poem's serial composition into one voice (*the* voice?), important new statements about the divine treatment of the infradivine, the treatment of men and women by each other, and the developing relationship among them all would have been muted. Had he silenced, as so many other critics have done, the dissent of the protagonist of the dialogues with the authoritative utterances of the voice from the whirlwind, with those oratorical pronouncements of the greatness of God and the insignificance of the human, the real mimeticist significance of the work would have been lost. Girard chose not to do so.

Finally, Girard issues a warning for our own times. He notes that Job puts his audience, whether listeners or readers, on the spot. Those who do not come to his aid, in effect, take a stand for persecution: "Remaining neutral is a deception."[59] The caution is a caution against impassivity, and Girard applies it to today's poets, dramatists, redactors, scribes, and members of all other intellectual priesthoods: "Any pretense at impassiveness, whether stoic, philosophic, or scientific, perpetuates the status quo, prolongs the occulting of the scapegoat, and makes us effective accomplices of the persecutors."[60] We must take a stand against persecution; we cannot avoid participating either for or against the practices of our times. But by copying each other in the act of protesting any system of injustice, our efforts may become a self-fulfilling prophecy in the cause of mercy, and by the time we conclude, if not before, we may be surprised by our own empathy.

Notes

1. An earlier version of this essay was delivered at the Colloquium on Violence and Religion held at Purdue University, June 5–8, 2002. My thanks to the other members of the panel, Sandor Goodhart and Fritz Cohen.

2. James G. Williams, "On Job and Writing: Derrida, Girard, and the Remedy-Poison," *Scandinavian Journal of the Old Testament* 7, no. 1 (1993): 32.

3. René Girard, *Job, the Victim of His People*, trans. Yvonne Freccero (Stanford, CA: Stanford University Press, 1987). For Girard's fullest presentation of his own theory, see his *Things Hidden since the Foundation of the World*, trans. Stephen Bann and Michael Metteer (Stanford, CA: Stanford University Press, 1987), especially the first chapter, entitled "The Victimage Mechanism as the Basis of Religion," 3–47.

4. For one brief summary of Girard's mimetic theory, see C. Allen Carter, *Kenneth Burke and the Scapegoat Process* (Norman: University of Oklahoma Press, 1996), 21–22 and 84–88, where Burke's theory of the scapegoat is contrasted with Girard's, the main difference being Burke's emphasis on symbolic language as opposed to Girard's emphasis on mimesis.

5. Moshe Greenberg, "Job," in *The Literary Guide to the Bible*, ed. Robert Alter and Frank Kermode (Cambridge, MA: Harvard University Press, 1987), 283.

6. Ibid., 303.

7. Ibid., 285.

8. Ibid., 283.

9. Ibid., 298, 297.

10. Ibid., 298. See Jb 38:7.

11. Greenberg, "Job," 299.

12. I have in mind here (and elsewhere) a theory about how the experience of reading is incorporated into the meaning of the text. See Stanley Fish, *Surprised by Sin: The Reader in "Paradise Lost"* (Cambridge, MA: Harvard University Press, 1967).

13. Greenberg, "Job," 298.

14. Ibid., 299.

15. Ibid., 284.

16. See Robert Alter, *The Art of Biblical Poetry* (New York: Basic Books, 1985), 85–86.

17. Ibid., 85.

18. Ibid., 86.

19. Ibid., 96–102, 88–89, 91–94.

20. Ibid., 104, 110.

21. Ibid., 110.

22. Ibid., 109.

23. Ibid., 108.

24. Ibid., 109.

25. Ibid., 108, 110, 97.

26. Ibid., 106.

27. Ibid.

28. Ibid., 94.

29. Stephen Mitchell, *The Book of Job* (Garden City, NY: Doubleday, 1979; rev. 1987; New York: Harper Collins, 1992), xiv–xv. In his analysis of Job, Mitchell has in mind the *Bhagavad Gita*, Jakob Böhme, and the engravings of William Blake.

30. Ibid., xxiv.

31. Ibid., xxvi–xxviii.

32. Ibid., xxviii.

33. Ibid., xvi and xxviii.

34. Ibid., 97.

35. Ibid., xxx.

36. Ibid.

37. For another of Alter's neoorthodox allies, see J. Gerald Janzen, *Job: Interpretation, A Bible Commentary for Teaching and Preaching* (Atlanta: John Knox Press, 1985), 22–24. Alter, Greenberg, and Janzen should all be read in contrast with Marvin H. Pope, who summarized the documentarian position in his introduction to a new translation, *The Anchor Bible Job* (Garden City, NY: Doubleday, 1965), xxi–xxviii.

38. These passages are taken from Job as translated in *The Jerusalem Bible* (New York: Doubleday, 1966), edited by Jones et al.

39. Girard, *Job*, 6.

40. See the fourth chapter, "The Celestial Armies," in Girard *Job*, 21–28. See also Job 20:23–29.

41. Girard, *Job*, 23.

42. Ibid.

43. See Girard's first chapter, "Job the Victim of His People," and his second chapter, "Job the Idol of His People."

44. Girard, *Job*, 33.

45. Ibid.

46. See Girard's sixth chapter, "Oedipus and Job."

47. Mitchell, *Book of Job*, 49.

48. See Williams, "On Job and Writing," 42. Just as Girard argues that the book of Job has an appreciation for the victim lacking in Greek tragedy, Williams argues that the book has an appreciation for the development of writing and legal objectivity lacking in Plato, or at least in parts of Plato.

49. For a discussion of these matters, see Walter J. Ong, *Interfaces of the Word: Studies in the Evolution of Consciousness and Culture* (Ithaca, NY: Cornell University Press, 1977).

50. Girard, *Job*, 36.

51. Ibid., 35.

52. Ibid.

53. See Girard's sixteenth chapter, "A Totalitarian Trial."

54. Girard, *Job*, 107.

55. Ibid.

56. Ibid.

57. Ibid.

58. Ibid., 108.

59. Ibid., 107.

60. Ibid.

FOURTEEN

The Expulsion of Complaint from Early Jewish Worship

WILLIAM MORROW

René Girard is unique among modern commentators in describing the religious dilemma addressed by the book of Job as a "sacrificial crisis." According to Girard, the voice of Job in the dialogues (Jb 3–27) is that of an archetypal victim of social persecution and ostracism. There is actually no indication as to what led to the downfall of this paradigmatic social leader, as it is a mistake to read the dialogues in conjunction with the prologue. The Job of the dialogues is a solitary individual pitted against the unanimity of the crowd whose mimetic desires for the high status the downfallen Job once enjoyed unleash the dynamics of the scapegoat mechanism. But Job, unlike Oedipus, is a failed scapegoat because he refuses to agree with his persecutors that he is guilty or deserves punishment at the hands of those convinced of the sacred character of their own collective violence towards him. To this end, Job's speeches and prayers develop an unprecedented appeal to a God of the victims who is opposed to the God of the persecutors. In Girard's view, this creative rhetorical strategy is compromised by theologizing additions to the dialogues consisting of the speeches of Elihu and YHWH, and the prose prologue and epilogue.[1]

The purpose of this essay is to connect Girard's thesis about sacrificial crisis in Job with the demise of the genre of individual lament in early Jewish worship. Girard's contribution to the interpretation of Job deserves appreciation but also requires modification. First, Girard offers an unusual account of the literary history of Job to support his position. I will assess Girard's contribution within the context of a more accepted account of the composition of the book in biblical scholarship. Second, the nature of the sacrificial crisis portrayed in Job needs to be reframed. I support Girard's perception that all the responses to Job's speeches refuse to legitimate his complaints against God. The rejection of Job's protests is bound up with the history of the complaint against God in early Judaism. The complaint against God was not only tolerated but permitted in informal and formal acts of prayer from preexilic (First Temple) times.[2] But by late Second Temple times, this motif had vanished from liturgical usage.[3] Such momentous change requires explanation. What could lead to the elimination of this unique expression of biblical faith? It is my opinion that the sacrificial crisis marked by Job has to do with doubts about the legitimacy of complaint against God in an era experiencing such significant social and religious transformations that it has been dubbed "the Axial Age."

The Literary History of Job

A thorough discussion of the literary history of Job extends beyond the scope of this study and is, in any case, open to controversy. The odd mixture of narrative and poetry, the organization of the speeches in Job 22–27, the appearance of a previously unmentioned speaker (Elihu) in Job 32–37, and difficulties in the cohesion of the YHWH speeches in Job 38–41 are some of the book's significant puzzles.[4] There are grounds for assuming that the poem on wisdom in Job 28 and the Elihu speeches are later additions.[5] But the task still remains to explain the book of Job as a meaningful communication in its final form.[6] The insertion of sizeable additions into a shorter original gives the impression that the book as it now stands ought to be read as an anthology of reflections and possible solutions to the problem of divine justice and human suffering.[7]

Job 1–27, 29–31, and 38–42 substantially comprehend the original version of the book.[8] The author of Job probably took over a traditional folktale about an exemplary person who patiently endured the trials and tribulations of life.[9] But he adapted it to suit his own needs. There are other Ancient Near Eastern books with a prose prologue and epilogue framing an extensive section of poetic dialogue. Therefore, one can assume some meaningful relationship between the discourse in the dialogues and the prose frame. For example, the prose prologue sets up verbal criterion for apostasy: Job must curse God to his face (1:11; 2:5). Job can actually be quite critical of the divine character without crossing this line.[10] The prose epilogue also identifies the use of right speech as the criterion by which Job is approved and Eliphaz and the others censured (42:7). This provides another link between the narrative frame of Job and the poetic dialogues in Job 3–27. After an opening soliloquy in Job 3, the confrontation between Job and his three friends, Eliphaz, Bildad, and Zophar, takes place in three cycles of speeches: Job 4–14, 15–21, and 22–27.[11] The YHWH speeches logically follow on Job's dramatic declaration of innocence and self-curse in Job 29–31.[12]

Job was composed during the exilic or postexilic era (that is, between the sixth and fourth centuries BCE).[13] The destruction of the First Temple by the Babylonians plunged the religion of Israel into great theological turmoil. Restoration of the Second Temple (dedicated in 515 BCE) brought with it numerous problems about the (re-) organization of religious life.[14] Many scholars perceive that Job registers a spiritual crisis related to that historical context.[15]

Job and the Rhetoric of Individual Complaint

It is sometimes thought that the character of Job personifies suffering Israel. Job's protests, therefore, would symbolize the quandaries of the nation struggling to make theological sense of the loss of the Temple during the exilic period (597–539 BCE) and the difficulties of national reconstruction after the return to Judah in the late sixth century BCE Support for this opinion points to two developments in exilic and postexilic literature: the use of individual complaint imagery to represent the voice of the community (for example, Lam 3) and the emergence of a literature that reacts to the destruction of Judah and Jerusalem by the Babylonians.[16]

Despite those arguments, I find no grounds for interpreting Job as a symbol of national distress. Job's language resonates clearly with the language of individual complaint psalms.[17] As with these psalms, one should assume that Job's complaints represent the voice of an individual unless there is strong evidence to the contrary.[18] In this respect, there is simply no unambiguous reference to national catastrophe in Job. This absence sets the book apart from other exilic and postexilic literature that explicitly wrestles with the destruction and exile of Jerusalem and Judah (such as, Ezekiel, Lamentations, and Isaiah 40–55).

I agree with Girard, therefore, in the perception that at the heart of Job is a distressed individual who appeals to his God using the language of the complaint psalms.[19] This genre of prayer has various designations in biblical scholarship: psalms of lament or complaint,[20] the law-court pattern of prayer,[21] and prayers of protest.[22] For the sake of variety, I will use these terms interchangeably. This tradition of biblical prayer typically gave a voice to victims of violence that allowed them both to affirm their innocence and to protest the violence they experienced. The psalms of individual complaint were originally used in private or semipublic services for suffering individuals conducted by liturgical experts, but not necessarily in sacred space.[23]

Job's words and arguments show the influence of the lament genre throughout,[24] especially with psalms emphasizing the innocence of the petitioner (cf. Jb 6:28–30, 16:16–17, 23:10–12, and 27:2–6 with Ps 17:3–5 and 26:2–7).[25] Particularly significant is the use of an oath formula in Job 29–31, in effect calling on God to curse the poet if his righteousness is not established (cf. Jb 31:5–40 and Ps 7:4–6/3–5). Such a procedure would have been considered highly risky unless the guiltlessness of the afflicted party was beyond doubt.[26] Also indicative is the description of Job's God as personal creator in 10:8–12 (cf. Psalm 22:10–11/9–10). Appeals to God as personal creator and protector mark the genre of individual complaint as distinct from community prayers.[27]

A key to Job's refusal of the status of scapegoat is the articulation of a distinction between the God of the victim and the God of the persecutors (cf. Jb 16:18–22, 19:25–27, and 23:5–7).[28] According to Girard, this perception is part of the originality of Job, as if the author "is articulating things never heard before."[29] But this thesis of Girard requires modification. Job was able to arrive at a distinction between the God of the victim and the God of the persecutors because this ambiguity was already implicit in the social and theological context of the law-court pattern of prayer.

The ambiguity of Job's protest resides in the perception that God is the divine enemy who persecutes him but also the witness who will defend him.[30] A similar ambivalence appears in a number of psalms of complaint. For example, Psalms 6, 13, 22, 35, 42–43, 88, and 102 directly protest suffering as unjustified divine action. They contain no confession that suffering is due to sinfulness on the part of the petitioner. Psalms 13, 22, 35, and 42–43 complain about divine inaction while Psalms 6, 88, and 102 remonstrate against divinely directed affliction. In all of these cases, God is held against God.

In order to understand how the lament psalms could operate with this ambiguity, we need to underscore how recent psalm scholarship agrees with Girard in emphasizing the motifs of social ostracism, abandonment, and violence as key forms of suffering to which the complaint tradition responds. Lea Jakobson has carefully compared the dominant motifs of suffering of representatives of the Mesopotamian lament tradition with biblical examples. Akkadian compositions such as "I will praise the Lord of Wisdom," the Babylonian Theodicy, and the Sumerian "Man before his God" describe the sufferings of high-ranking persons who are thrust down into the lowest levels of social status as a result of misfortune and disease. Sickness, however, is not what they primarily complain of. Motifs of social ostracism and persecution by former friends, colleagues, and companions dominate these works. Connections with imagery in the individual complaint psalms are strong.[31] Erhard Gerstenberger has also suggested that much of the enemy language in the psalms of individual complaint reflects the bitter social rivalries of village life.[32] Loss of status, for whatever reason, was explained as divine judgment and afforded a pretext for violence and ostracism by members of the larger group.

One might say that the dilemma encountered by the protest prayer tradition was of conflicting perceptions regarding divine justice. The persecuting community regarded the victim as already judged by God. How to counter the impression that God has caused the psalmist's suffering? The individual appealed to God to bring the unjust suffering caused by the crowd to an end. One view of divine justice, therefore, was held against another. A primary goal of the complaint psalms was to rehabilitate the individual to the larger group (who also worship YHWH) by affirming the undeserved suffering of the petitioner, an affirmation that is intended both to arrest his social exclusion and the justification of group violence against him.[33]

By the end of the dialogue, the confrontation between Job and his dialogue partners has reached an impasse. Both parties are entrenched in their theological positions. This situation stands in contrast to the social effects of complaint rhetoric in the Psalms. There, the language of complaint and affirmation of innocence were tactics used by ostracized people to win support from a hostile or indifferent community. Protest against undeserved suffering functioned to rehabilitate individuals into their local support group. What has happened to make Job's theologically motivated protest so ineffective? And why does the accompanying assertion of innocence not move Job's former support group to accept him?

The Sacrificial Crisis in the Book of Job

A sacrificial crisis arises in a society when traditional institutions for managing collective violence begin to lose their legitimacy.[34] Job indicates that the law-court pattern of prayer was no longer able to manage collective violence. The turmoil surrounding the reconstruction of Israel's religious life in the exilic and postexilic eras provides a plausible context for the collapse of traditional institutions. We have already seen, however, that Job does not explicitly refer to national disaster. Another perspective is required.

The sacrificial crisis of Job reflects social, political, and theological shifts in Israelite religion that came about as biblical faith entered the "Axial Age." According to the philosopher Karl Jaspers, the Axial Age encompassed 800–200 BCE, with a center at approximately 500 BCE.[35] Jaspers used the epithet "Axial" because this epoch heralded fundamental and revolutionary changes in human social, religious, and intellectual history. Many civilizations were affected, including those of ancient Israel, Greece, Iran, China, and India.

Axial Age civilizations perceived a large degree of tension between the transcendental and mundane orders of reality. This tension emerged and was expressed in ways that distinguish these societies from their predecessors. Human societies typically perceive the divine or spiritual realm as somewhat different, usually higher and more powerful, than everyday reality. In pre–Axial Age civilizations, this higher world was symbolically structured according to principles very similar to the mundane or lower one. In other words, the two worlds were thought to operate by similar principles and accessed by similar means. By contrast, in the Axial Age there developed the perception of a sharp disjunction between the everyday and transcendent worlds. The divine reality was no longer simply human reality writ large. Such a distinction created numerous problems in the construction of social institutions with respect to the cosmic order.[36]

Axial Age social, political, religious, and intellectual processes were closely connected with the emergence of new social elites. Examples include the Jewish prophets, Greek philosophers, the Chinese scholar-class, and Buddhist monks. They created new institutions and practices to manage the perceived tension between the transcendental and mundane orders. These new types of thinkers differed from the elites that had been ritual, magical, and sacred specialists prior to their society's Axial Age revolution.[37] Radical changes in the nature of knowledge partly account for the rise and influence of these new religious specialists. The Axial Age did not simply involve transformations in social structures; it portended significant changes in the conceptual worlds of human beings. In fact, these new elites produced the first true ideologies in that they offered comprehensive views of the world and how people should live in it.[38]

What does the Axial Age have to do with the composition of the book of Job and the questions it poses? Chronologically, the exilic and postexilic eras can be located within the emergence of the Axial Age. During this time, Israelite religion was subject to ideological innovation. The emergence of early Judaism into the Axial Age is associated with the development of its monotheistic faith into a universal religious claim.[39] Though there are antecedents, the late exilic prophet called the Second Isaiah (Is 40–55) can be considered the endpoint of the evolution of an unambiguous and universal monotheism in Israel.[40] Second Isaiah proclaimed YHWH not only sovereign over Israel, but the sole existing deity whose sway was universal (Is 45:14–25). Moreover, YHWH was immeasurable, unteachable, and incomparable (for example, Is 40:12–26).[41] These characteristics suggest a sharp distinction between transcendent reality and the human world.

This theology was the product of a history of intellectual speculation that had been taking place among Israel's prophetic elite. One has only to compare the more anthropomorphic picture of YHWH in Isaiah 6:1–3 (mid-eighth century) with that of Ezekiel 1:22–28 (early sixth century) to realize that a belief in a more transcendent deity, less amenable to the human imagination, had been developing for some time. The result was a deity more transcendent and more powerful than the one envisaged in the complaint psalm tradition, an imperial deity: king not only of Israel but unmatched emperor of the universe. The faith tradition reflected in complaint psalms accepted the possibility of inexplicable and even arbitrary absences of the divine presence.[42] But Israel's religious imagination required the construction of a less compromised God in the Axial Age. To a certain extent, in the Axial Age, YHWH's absence was structured into the universe because of his greater transcendence. But as an imperial deity, ruler of the universe, YHWH had to be portrayed as completely righteous and completely powerful. Consequently, all of YHWH's absences must be defensible; such a deity's actions were not to be subject to criticism by mere mortals.

Throughout the dialogue both Job and his friends assume that God is primarily responsible for Job's predicament. At stake is whether Job's suffering is justified or an exercise of divine power that can be challenged. In his speeches, Job continually protests the assumption that his suffering is warranted. The position of Job's erstwhile friends is that God acts justly, treating persons as they deserve.[43] The theological perspective of Job's friends was common in educated circles of the Ancient Near East. It is associated with the ideology of wisdom. Wisdom thinking often endorses a doctrine of divine retribution in which there is a predictable cause and effect relationship between order and chaos, justice and suffering.

The intransigent refusal of Job's comforters to entertain the force of his complaint against God and his declarations of innocence points to their engagement with Axial Age influences. In the preexilic period, wisdom discourse existed alongside complaint rhetoric. It is the assertion of wisdom theology to the exclusion of complaint rhetoric by Job's comforters that marks a theological turning point in the history of biblical thought.

Girard sees a rejection of Job's creative appeal to a God of the victim as stemming from a reassertion of the point of view of the persecutors.[44] But the issue, in terms of the development of the biblical tradition, is more complex. Instead of inventing a tradition of invoking God against God, the voice of Job in the dialogues is not that of an innovator but of a traditionalist. Job forcefully advances his argument using preexisting categories of complaint and petition in early Jewish liturgy. Ironically, it is those who voice the traditional (wisdom) categories of retribution (the comforters) who are on the theological *avant-garde*. They are possessed of a theology in which God is so much in control of creation that the tradition of complaint, which holds a place for questioning divine action and divine absence, has no credibility.

Girard and the Loss of Lament in Job

Girard is correct to view the various responses to Job's speeches as unsupportive of his complaints against God. Besides the replies of the friends, Job 28 and the speeches by Elihu and YHWH all reveal Axial Age influences that undermine the legitimacy of lament. Most ambiguous is YHWH's response in Job 38–41, which can be associated with the original version of the book.[45] In fact, the YHWH speeches support the position of neither Job nor his comforters. Despite, or perhaps because of, their imperious tone, they force Job to take stock of reality in a new way, to look seriously at the world that God as creator has brought into being.[46]

The YHWH speeches undermine an anthropocentric worldview assumed by both traditional complaint and wisdom theologies. They challenge the idea that the cosmos operates with human interests at its center. In the natural world, human-centered moral categories are shown to be nonoperative. Neither the weather (38:25–27) nor the wild animals (39:5–18) reflect human values.[47] Though a nonanthropocentric vision of creation might be upsetting to a religious person in Job's culture, it possesses therapeutic potential. A view of the cosmos that does not have humanity at its center relieves suffering persons from having to interpret every situation as a potentially blameworthy response to their own actions.[48]

Job's dialogue partners assume that the created world perfectly reflects the character of God, thereby repressing any moral ambiguity in the cosmos. This supposition is refuted in the YHWH speeches.[49] Texts such as 38:13, 38:15 and 40:8–14 confront Job with a world where the unjust thrive as well as the just.[50] Their misdeeds do not make them simply (unwitting) agents of divine retribution.

Like wisdom thinking, complaint theology also relies on an opposition between chaos and order. One of the central metaphors for chaos was the wild, untamed natural world. This imagery is used to describe the enemies in the individual complaint psalms (for example, Ps 7:3/2, 17:12, 22:14/13, 35:17, 57:5/4, and 59:7/6). Another symbol of chaos and suffering in the psalms is deep and raging water (for example, Ps 42:8/7, 69:2–3/1–2, 88:18/17, and 130:1). The contrast between chaos and order can be maintained only by repressing the knowledge that "chaos creatures" are also the creations of God. The YHWH speeches force Job to reevaluate conventional images of chaos. These include various manifestations of water in 38:8–38 and wild animals in 38:39–39:30. Both categories of wildness are claimed as products of the creative activity of God. Finally, Job is challenged to contemplate the huge water monsters thought to occupy creation (Jb 40–41), praised as pinnacles of YHWH's creative power.[51]

YHWH's transcendence, a typical Axial Age doctrine, is affirmed in Job 38–41 by increasing his distance from the created world. The deity depicted in the YHWH speeches is not simply a human being writ large. His creatures and his actions are often unfathomable according to human categories. The moral order and the natural order are distinguished in a way that neither pre-Axial wisdom nor complaint theologies envisaged.

In my opinion, the writer of Job 1–27, 29–31, 38–42 did not intend to resolve questions regarding the propriety of protest as a response to suffering in Israel's Axial Age. This version of the book works primarily as a vehicle to confront its readers with the paradox that faces all those who refer their existence to a single and righteous deity: the experience of unjust suffering in a world made by a God supposed to love justice. Traditional complaint rhetoric and wisdom discourse are juxtaposed in a way that defies resolution. Readers are left to infer their own solutions to the dilemma. Carol Newsom has observed that the book of Job not only ruptures the ideological closure of retribution thinking but that its structure actually resists all closure and all resolution of contradiction.[52] I follow that observation here. The YHWH speeches support neither the tradition of complaint prayer nor retribution theology. But they refrain from articulating a vision to take the place of either theological construct.

The ambiguity and lack of clarity of Job 38–42 may well have been the reason why later hands added the Elihu speeches and the poem to divine wisdom in Job 28. Job 28 places an emphasis on the distance between the divine and human realities that is characteristic of Axial Age theology. Nothing in creation knows the way to wisdom, not even the preternatural realms of death and the grave (28:20–22). As for human beings, not only have they not found wisdom, it is so much beyond their attainment that they are not even able to assess it properly (28:16–19). Such distancing dissolves any analogy between human and divine wisdom. From the point of view of Job 28, it is category confusion to talk of human and divine wisdom as if they were the same thing.

A subtle detail in vocabulary helps to convey this impression. It is wisdom with a definite article ("the wisdom," that is, Wisdom) that God possesses in 28:12, 20. It is a less definite wisdom with no article ("wisdom") that is accessible to humanity (28:28). The content of these two sorts of wisdom is different. In the case of human beings, wisdom is the fear of YHWH; it is not ultimate knowledge about the nature of creation.[53]

Elihu's reasoning essentially represents the positions of Job's friends in the dialogue. But he offers a more sophisticated theological defense for the rejection of the arguing-with-God tradition. He reaffirms the thesis that God is always righteous and human suffering is connected to wrongdoing.[54] Elihu ends his speeches with lengthy praise to this exalted and ever righteous deity. He concludes that God is not within human reach, thereby emphasizing divine transcendence. By reason of his power and righteousness, God is to be feared and reverenced. But the divine being has no accounts to render to human beings (37:19–24).[55] Obviously, protests or doubts in connection with divine faithfulness or justice cannot be entertained in such a worldview.

The Expulsion of Complaint Prayer and Its Aftermath

One objection to my account of the sacrificial crisis of Job is that a sacrificial crisis is usually occasioned by expressions of empathy for the victim that undermine the moral legitimacy of institutions of collective violence and the mythology that supports them.[56] Here we seem to have the reverse situation: a preexisting tradition of empathy for the victim is shut down by new theological developments. My thesis also seems to run counter to the Girardian view that biblical literature reflects a gradual development in critique of the scapegoating mechanism at the heart of culture. As Girard notes, despite some indicators to the contrary, the final form of Job voices an orthodoxy that "does not perceive the abyss between the God of executioners and the God of victims."[57] But unlike Girard, I have not located empathy for the voice of the victim with the creativity of Job, but claimed its genesis belongs in a preexisting genre of psalmody.

One response to a sacrificial crisis, however, can be a new assertion of control by the powers-that-be in an attempt to shore up a morally ambiguous situation.[58] Divine integrity in the Axial Age was purchased at the cost of expelling the tradition that called it into question. The sacrificial crisis was resolved by dispensing with an increasingly problematic institution: protest prayer.

The elimination of complaint prayer can be analyzed in Girardian terms. An important precursor was a process of mimetic rivalry. As we have seen, it was the prophets who were responsible for taking the God of a small independent state and making him into a universal deity.

They did so under the pressure of, and partly in reaction to, imperial imagery and claims made by Israel and Judah's overlords and conquerors: the empires of Assyria, Babylon, and Persia.[59] In this triangular process, the common object of desire of both Israelite and Ancient Near Eastern intellectuals was a deity competent to control history. The politics of empire was an impetus for the emergence of the Axial Age and the need for vision of a sufficiently transcendent order to comprehend this new international reality.[60] Second Temple Judaism asserted its theological, if not social, cohesion by identifying religious elements thought to compromise the newly discovered sense of divine transcendence and expelling them. For example, the postexilic era witnessed the elimination of healing rituals from the idealized priestly temple described in Leviticus.[61] Similarly, the complaint against God was suppressed by late Second Temple times.[62]

But does the book of Job simply record a retrograde step in progress towards unveiling the scapegoat mechanism? What happened to the voice of the innocent sufferer in Israel's Axial Age? Did it simply disappear? Despite the demise of the lament genre, there is no reason to believe that the impulse that gave rise to it vanished. There was still a need for protests against unjust attacks upon suffering persons by enemies. There was still an occasion for private or semi-public services for suffering individuals conducted by liturgical experts. In the late Second Temple period and beyond, this picture is valid for exorcism.

In making this observation, there can be no question of deriving early Jewish prayers for exorcism from the complaint genre. Where the genre has relationships with psalmody, the point of reference is with magical statements of blessings such as Psalm 91.[63] My argument rests upon a psychological basis alone. The demise of lament created a pastoral or therapeutic vacuum that other forms of liturgy at least partially filled.[64]

The expulsion of the complaint against God may have actually paved the way for a more thorough exposure of the scapegoat mechanism than was possible while the tradition was liturgically valid. Recall that the God of the complaint psalm was simultaneously a God of the innocent and of the persecutor (understood as village rivals). This ambiguity was resolved in favor of a totally righteous God in Axial

Age religion and the transposition of the prayer of the righteous innocent into the words of one under demonic attack. In other words, on the mythical level a resolution was achieved between the righteous (and innocent) one and the monstrous crowd. The demonic metaphor allowed for a greater precision in identifying the true cause of innocent suffering, as Girard's analysis of the Gerasene demoniac shows.[65]

Lament and the Revelation of the Scapegoat Mechanism

I have examined Girard's thesis that the book of Job registers a sacrificial crisis in Israelite religion using an account of its literary history more accepted in biblical scholarship. As a result, I agree that Job marks an important moment towards the unveiling of the scapegoating mechanism, but I differ in my account of how this happens. The opposition between the God of the victim and the God of the persecutor, which Girard discovers in Job's speeches, is not original to this book but depends on a preexisting tradition of lament. The book of Job attests to the emergence of social and theological dynamics that worked to suppress the complaint against God in Second Temple times. The expulsion of protest prayer from early Jewish worship took place under the aegis of the Axial Age. But Girard is correct to claim that the spirit of complaint would not be denied. The dissimulation of its therapeutic potential into liturgies for the demon-possessed played an important role in unveiling the scapegoat mechanism in the Gospels.

Notes

1. René Girard, *Job, the Victim of His People* (London: Athlone, 1987), 83.

2. Claus Westermann, "The Complaint Against God," in *God in the Fray: A Tribute to Walter Brueggemann*, ed. T. Linafelt and T. K. Beal (Minneapolis: Fortress, 1998), 233–35.

3. Claus Westermann, *Praise and Lament in the Psalms* (Atlanta: John Knox, 1981), 213.

4. See the list in Andrew E. Steinmann, "The Structure and Message of the Book of Job," *Vetus Testamentum* 46 (1996): 87–89.

5. Yair Hoffman, *A Blemished Perfection: The Book of Job in Context,* Journal for the Study of the Old Testament: Supplement Series 213 (Sheffield: Academic Press, 1996), 281–84, 289–93; Leo. G. Perdue, *Wisdom in Revolt: Metaphorical Theology in the Book of Job,* Bible and Literature Series 29 (Sheffield: Academic Press, 1991), 80–83.

6. C. R. Seitz, "Job. Full Structure, Movement and Interpretation," *Interpretation (Int)* 43 (1989): 10; D. J. A. Clines, *Job 1–20,* Word Biblical Commentary 17 (Dallas: Word Books, 1989), lix.

7. Yair Hoffman, "The Creativity of Theodicy," in *Justice and Righteousness: Biblical Themes and Their Influence,* ed. H. G. Reventlow and Y. Hoffman, Journal for the Study of the Old Testament Supplement Series 137 (Sheffield: Academic Press, 1992), 127–28.

8. Leo G. Perdue, *Wisdom and Creation: The Theology of Wisdom Literature* (Nashville: Abingdon, 1994), 124.

9 James L. Crenshaw, "Job, Book of," in *Anchor Bible Dictionary* (New York: Doubleday, 1992), 3:863.

10. Y. Hoffman, "Ancient Near Eastern Literary Conventions and the Restoration of the Book of Job," *Zeitschrift für die alttestamentliche Wissenschaft* 103 (1991): 410.

11. The third speech cycle is not complete. Many commentators believe that its contents are distorted and disorganized, likely due to an error in transmission. See Hoffman, *Blemished Perfection,* 276–86. Though Hoffman acknowledges the majority position, he demurs and suggests the third speech cycle was simply never finished.

12. Claus Westermann, *The Structure of the Book of Job: A Form-Critical Analysis* (Philadelphia: Fortress, 1981), 105.

13. This is a common scholarly opinion. See, Crenshaw, "Job," 863–64; Anson Laytner, *Arguing with God: A Jewish Tradition* (Northvale, NJ: Jason Aronson, 1990), 34.

14. Rainer Albertz, *A History of Israelite Religion in the Old Testament Period,* vol. 2, *From the Exile to the Maccabees,* Old Testament Library (Louisville, KY: Westminster John Knox, 1994), 458–64.

15. See, e.g., James L. Crenshaw, *Old Testament Wisdom: An Introduction,* rev. ed. (Louisville, KY: Westminster John Knox, 1998), 103–4; Perdue, *Wisdom and Creation,* 124.

16. See Laytner, *Arguing with God,* 34–37.

17. John E. Hartley, "The Genres and Message of the Book of Job," in *Sitting with Job: Selected Studies on the Book of Job,* ed. Roy B. Zuck (Grand Rapids, MI: Baker, 1992), 68–69.

18. See John Day, *Psalms,* Old Testament Guides (Sheffield: Academic Press, 1996), 25.

19. Girard, *Job,* 8.

20. Day, *Psalms*, 20.

21. Laytner, *Arguing with God*, xvii–xviii.

22. David R. Blumenthal, *Facing the Abusing God: A Theology of Protest* (Louisville, KY: Westminster John Knox, 1993), 249–52.

23. Erhard S. Gerstenberger, *Psalms: Part 1 with an Introduction to Cultic Poetry*, Forms of the Old Testament Literature 14 (Grand Rapids, MI: Eerdmans, 1988), 13–14.

24. Westermann, *Structure of the Book of Job*, 31.

25. John E. Hartley, "From Lament to Oath: A Study of Progression in the Speeches of Job," in *The Book of Job*, ed. W. A. M Beuken, Bibliotheca Ephemeridum Theologicarum Lovaniensium 114, 79–100 (Leuven: Leuven University Press, 1994), 90–91.

26. Gerstenberger, *Psalms*, 65.

27. Rainer Albertz, *Persönliche Frömmigkeit und offizielle Religion: Religionsinterner Pluralismus in Israel und Babylon*, Calwer Theologische Monographien Reihe A: Bibelwissenschaft 9 (Stuttgart: Calwer, 1978), 37–38.

28. James G. Williams, *The Bible, Violence, and the Sacred: Liberation from the Myth of Sanctioned Violence* (New York: HarperSanFrancisco, 1991), 167–69.

29. Girard, *Job*, 138–39.

30. Williams, *The Bible, Violence, and the Sacred*, 164.

31. Lea Jakobson, "The Individual's Suffering in Psalms and in Mesopotamian Narratives," *Beit Miqra* 168 (2001): 33, 39–55.

32. Erhard Gerstenberger, *Der bittende Mensch: Bittritual und Klagelied des Einzelnen im Alten Testament*, Wissenschaftliche Monographien zum Alten und Neuen Testament 51 (Neukirchen-Vluyn: Neukirchener Verlag, 1981), 144–46; Gerstenberger, *Psalms*, 53.

33. Gerstenberger, *Der bittende Mensch*, 156–60.

34. Gil Bailie, *Violence Unveiled: Humanity at the Crossroads* (New York: Crossroad, 1995), 24–28.

35. Karl Jaspers, *Vom Ursprung und Ziel der Geschichte* (Zürich: Artemis-Verlag, 1949), 19.

36. S. N. Eisenstadt, "The Axial Age Breakthroughs—Their Characteristics and Origins," in *The Origins and Diversity of Axial Age Civilizations*, ed. S. N. Eisenstadt, SUNY Series in Near Eastern Studies (Albany: State University of New York, 1986), 1–3. This description is most valid for Judaism. New relationships between society and the cosmos were worked out in various ways in Axial Age civilizations. See Björn Wittrock, "The Meaning of the Axial Age," in *Axial Age Civilations and World History*, ed. J. P. Arnason, S. N. Eisenstadt, and B. Wittrock, Jerusalem Studies in Religion and Culture 4 (Leiden: Brill, 2005), 73–76.

37. Eisenstadt, "The Axial Age Breakthroughs," 4–6.

38. Peter Machinist, "On Self-Consciousness in Mesopotamia," in *The Origins and Diversity of Axial Age Civilizations*, 183.

39. S. N. Eisenstadt, "Introduction: The Axial Age Breakthrough in Ancient Israel," in *The Origins and Diversity of Axial Age Civilizations*, 128–29.

40. Benjamin Uffenheimer, "Myth and Reality in Ancient Israel," in *The Origins and Diversity of Axial Age Civilizations*, 168; John J. Scullion, "God in the Old Testament," in *Anchor Bible Dictionary*, 2:1042–43.

41. Scullion, "God in the Old Testament," 1043.

42. Samuel E. Balentine, *The Hidden God: The Hiding of the Face of God in the Old Testament* (Oxford: Oxford University Press, 1983), 166.

43. Carol A. Newsom, "Job," in *The Women's Bible Commentary*, ed. Carol A. Newsom and Sharon H. Ringe (Louisville, KY: Westminster John Knox, 1992), 132.

44. Girard, *Job*, 141–45.

45. Though there has been much discussion about their literary integrity, the YHWH speeches can be read as transmitted; see Perdue, *Wisdom in Revolt*, 83; Westermann, *Structure of the Book of Job*, 108.

46. Matitiahu Tsevat, "The Meaning of the Book of Job," *Hebrew Union College Annual* 37 (1966): 100. See also N. C. Habel, *The Book of Job*, Old Testament Library (London: SCM, 1985), 535; Fredrik Lindström, *God and the Origin of Evil: A Contextual Analysis of Alleged Monistic Evidence in the Old Testament*, Coniectanea biblica: Old Testament Series 21 (Lund: CWK Gleerup, 1983), 156–57.

47. Newsom, "Job," 135; Tsevat, "The Meaning of the Book of Job," 100, 102.

48. For a larger discussion of the therapeutic value of the YHWH speeches, see William S. Morrow, "Toxic Religion and the Daughters of Job," *Studies in Religion* 27 (1998): 272–74.

49. P. W. Nimmo, "Sin, Evil, and Job: Monotheism as a Psychological and Pastoral Problem," *Pastoral Psychology* 42, no. 6 (1994): 436–37.

50. Tsevat, "The Meaning of the Book of Job," 99.

51. Ibid., 100. See also Athalya Brenner, "God's Answer to Job," *Vetum Testamentum* 31 (1981): 133–34.

52. Carol A. Newsom, "Cultural Politics and the Reading of Job," *Biblical Interpretation* 1 (1993): 136.

53. Hoffman, *Blemished Perfection*, 278–81.

54. Westermann, *Structure of the Book of Job*, 147.

55. Édouard Dhorme, *A Commentary of the Book of Job* (London: Thomas Nelson & Sons, 1967), lvii.

56. Cf. Bailie, *Violence Unveiled*, 26.

57. Girard, *Job*, 145.

58. Bailie, *Violence Unveiled*, 266.

59. Moshe Weinfeld, "The Protest against Imperialism in Ancient Israelite Prophecy," in *The Origins and Diversity of Axial Age Civilizations*, 178–81.

60. Marcel Gauchet, *The Disenchantment of the World: A Political History of Religion* (Princeton, NJ: Princeton University Press, 1997), 41.

61. See Hector Avalos, *Illness and Health Care in the Ancient Near East: The Role of the Temple in Greece, Mesopotamia, and Israel,* Harvard Semitic Monographs 54 (Atlanta: Scholars Press, 1995), 370–71.

62. See the discussion of the late history of lament in Westermann, *Praise and Lament,* 201–13.

63. Émile Puech, "Les deux derniers psaumes davidiques du rituel d'exorcisme, 11QpsApa IV 4–V 14," in *The Dead Sea Scrolls: Forty Years of Research,* ed. D. Dimant and U. Rappaport, Studies on the Texts of the Desert of Judah 10 (Leiden: Brill, 1992), 78. Psalm 91 does not belong to the complaint genre; see Hermann Gunkel and Joachim Begrich, *Introduction to the Psalms: The Genres of the Religious Lyric of Israel* (Macon, GA: Mercer University Press, 1998), 147. By the time of Qumran, Psalm 91 had become a psalm of exorcism; see Hermann Lichtenberger, "Ps 91 und die Exorzismus in 11QpsApa," in *Die Dämonen: Die Dämonologie der israelitisch-jüdischen und frühchristlichen Literatur im Kontext ihrer Umwelt,* ed. A. Lange et. al. (Tübingen: Mohr Siebeck, 2003), 420.

64. For further discussion, see Willliam Morrow, *Protest Against God: The Eclipse of a Biblical Tradition* (Sheffield: Sheffield Phoenix Press, 2006), 190–95.

65. René Girard, *The Scapegoat* (Baltimore: Johns Hopkins University Press, 1986), 165–83.

FIFTEEN

The Book of Job and the Problem of Evil

Reading from Theodicy to the Ethical

SANDOR GOODHART

There was once, among the gentile people, a chassid *whose name was Iyov. He was placed into this world with only the purpose that he might earn his just reward. God exposed him to suffering and [rather than submitting quietly] he began to curse and to blaspheme. Because of this, God doubled his reward in This World so that he might be driven out of the World to Come.*

—Bava Batra 15b

R. Yochanan said: Iyov was among those who returned from the Babylonian exile, and his Beit HaMidrash is situated in Tiberius.

—Bava Batra 15b

René Girard's view of the book of Job is successful, I would argue, in unexpected ways, successful not only in Christian and secular terms where this book has often been read, but equally so in classical Jewish terms where it has been read in fact less often. Girard's thesis is that apart from the dramas in which we usually frame it—a God who seems oblivious to the question Job raises, a heavenly machinery that seems closer to Greek mythology than religious scripture, an attitude on the part of the friends that seems more bound to institution than people—there is another drama afoot, one that has more in common with the scapegoat dynamics of Greek tragedy than it does with the scriptural dynamics of the Hebrew Bible to that point.

Girard's Job is more like Oedipus than Abraham, and what is given voice in the long middle section of the book is more akin to the tradition expressed in the book of Psalms and some of the prophetic texts than the formulaic institutional conceptions of religion that would identify evil with the commission of sin.[1] Job is a scapegoat, a victim of his people, and the book gives voice to that victim more than to the institutional formulas in which it appears. Job appeals to God as his advocate and fleshes out that appeal in Girard's view in ways that make those other traditions pale by comparison. What is new in this book, from Girard's perspective, what locates it somewhere between Greek tragedy and Christian scripture (where the full articulation of scapegoat dynamics or defense for the victim will be offered, and which, in retrospect, confers upon this book, for Girard, the status of an early expression) is the articulation it gives to the voice of the victim.

The sense that among the other books of the Hebrew Bible the book of Job is closest to Greek tragedy has of course a long history, and one of Girard's innovations has been to show us precisely why, namely, as a result of the expression both give to scapegoat dynamics. And within the secular Jewish tradition, the insufficiencies of God's answer to Job's questions about human justice (by comparison, for example, with other scriptural passages in which such questions are fully addressed) have long been felt, and in this sense as well Girard's thesis strengthens that sense of incommensurability. If the idea that the book of Job looks forward to New Testament accounts of scapegoat dynamics would be a hard sell among the rabbis (if only for the reason that for the rabbis, of course, there is no "New Testament"), the idea that articulations about sacrifice and about scapegoat dynamics that show up in some of the prophetic texts (Isaiah, for example) may find expression in the book of Job is not at all unwelcome and adds to our sense of the proximity of theoretical conception of these texts.

In the essay that follows, I would like to show that Girard's thesis on the book of Job may play a much more decisive and fundamental role with regard to classical rabbinic conceptions of the book, that in some ways it may articulate a position that is critical to the rabbis' view of it, although to show how this is true necessitates understanding more fully their position. Put succinctly, Girard's view fleshes out the consequences of a book that has in effect from the rabbi's point of view expelled Judaism. By comparison with Second Isaiah, where the law of anti-idolatry is identified at once with suffering and creation, the book of Job leaves these two ideas in effect without a connection. Girard's reading bears witness to a text that, if taken on its own, must of necessity fail as an account of human advocacy.

Put in other terms, what if the insufficiencies of the answers the text provides (from a humanistic point of view) to the questions it raises is not a deficiency but its very point, one it shares with a great many other texts among the Holy Writings (or K'tuvim), texts whose goal is to show what happens if one or another element of Judaism is subtracted from the equation? You can subtract Judaism from the equation if you like (the book would then be saying to us), but are you sure you want to do that? Girard's demonstration (namely, that if we do subtract Judaism, the book looks very much like the tragedy of Oedipus) only confirms this rabbinic reading and strengthens our perception of the choice the book offers us, a choice regarding the ethical integrity we require if we are to negotiate a world in which suffering and creation, accidents of fortune and sacrificial institutional politics, inevitably play a role.

Girard has in short unexpectedly extended the rabbinic view of the book that identified it—and Job—as not Jewish, a non-Jewishness reflected in the contrast it offers between four perspectives in the ancient Greek world—mythological, institutional, humanistic, and creational—from which in each case Judaism has been extracted. The book of Job in this way is like the book of Esther—another late canonical entry—where Judaism is present but God is absent. Judaism for the rabbis is the law of anti-idolatry. The absence of Torah from the book of Job is like the absence of God from the book of Esther. Both partake in the questions the rabbis feel remain after the giving of the law: namely, what if the law of anti-idolatry itself becomes the newest source of idolatry? The law, the Torah, the teaching, is the law of anti-idolatry, and that insight is a great advance. But what prevents that law or instruction itself from becoming the newest danger, an even greater danger than before, since now (once the law is given) we have no external agency to which we may appeal its transgressions?

From the rabbinic view, that is the problem of the modern world, and all of the so-called Holy Writings—which is to say, the writings apart from Torah proper, and the Prophetic Books (or Neviim)—may be understood as accounts of some of the ways in which that idolatry of anti-idolatry may be enacted.

In what follows, I will show first how this alternative conception of the book of Job I have outlined addresses all of the difficulties we have customarily raised about it, referring to Martin Buber's four-fold reading of this text as a way of considering interpretations of the text. Then I will turn to Emmanuel Levinas's post-Holocaust reflections as a way of asking about the position from which we read today. In the conclusion, I will return to René Girard's thesis to refine our understanding of that position, to speak more precisely about the theodicy, the mythological, and their relation to the sacrificial and what Girard calls "the scapegoat mechanism," as a way of amplifying the rabbinic conception of the Book.

Job in Christian and Jewish Interpretation: Arthur Hanson and Martin Buber

In an important essay on the book of Job, Arthur Hanson lays out for us quite succinctly the interpretive problem, namely, that none of the explanations customarily presented allows us to account for the unprovoked and unmitigated suffering and evil that occurs.

> What has made Job a book of such an enduring value? Couched in its prose and poetic expression is an examination of a question that has deep religious significance. In simplest terms, how does one account for undeserved or innocent suffering? In one way or another, religions across the world and across centuries have tried to deal with this problem. It is often expressed simply as "The Problem of Evil." From this perspective, the Book of Job is a theodicy, a word which has roots from *theos*, God, and *dike*, justice. In a broad sense, theodicy is an attempt to vindicate the ways of God in view of evident suffering in the world and innocent suffering in particular.[2]

Hanson is responding in part to William Rowe, whose work has played an important part in the ongoing discussion of the problem of evil (and around whose work the conference at which Hanson read his paper on Job was constructed).[3] He signals the three themes foremost in our minds: the problem of evil, the way the book of Job poses that problem (by asking how one accounts for undeserved or innocent suffering), and the problem of "theodicy" (as shorthand for thinking about the problem of evil). He concludes that "if we look to Job for rational solutions to the problem of innocent suffering we will not find them."

Martin Buber was one of the first to articulate what in particular those explanations or reputed solutions were.[4] Buber pointed out that there were in effect four versions of God in the book of Job, four relationships between God and human beings, that are presented to us. We are offered initially a mythological God, a bet-making God, whose playful engagements with the arch accuser—*ha-satan* (the word *ha-satan* in Hebrew means, of course, "the accuser")—determine the fate of human beings (in this case Job).[5] Then we are offered the God of the three friends, a God who is little more than a divine cause and effect machine. You do this; that happens. You do that; this happens. If you have this state of affairs, it is because of that cause. Job suffers; therefore, Job must have sinned. The only problem with which we need to concern ourselves is uncovering what his particular transgression is.

We are presented in the third place, Buber tells us, with Job's God, the hidden God, the God who does not respond, the God to whom Job appeals for some sense of justice or of just design behind the social, psychological, and physical misfortune we experience. "The wicked prosper; and the good die young and unfortunate," Job in effect complains. "I am innocent of any misdeed, and I steadfastly hold," Job says in retort, "that there is a just design behind all this difficulty; but I fail to understand what it is. Show me what it is, because it is not that easy for us here to figure it out." This hidden God never responds to Job in Buber's account of these relationships.

And, then, Buber says, we are presented, finally, in chapters 38–42, with a fourth version of God. In the form of an unexpected intervention of a stranger (in a passage some critics claim to be a late invention), Elihu shows up (32–37) and basically denounces everyone, saying exactly what God will say a moment later: "You guys are all idiots," he says in effect, "and in fact, I didn't say anything before this moment because I was respectful of you. But now I'm going to say it; you are all self-justifiers, and you are all in the same ballpark. None of you understand the God of creation; and He is going to speak now. In fact, here He is." After this intervention, after Elihu, we are presented with a God of elemental creation, a God who appears and says: "Where were you when I created the universe?" (38:4).

How do you answer a question like that? Do you say: "I'm out"? "Call me next time; I'll try to be there"? Or a question like the following: "Can *you* catch Leviathan with a fishhook?" (to which you reply: "No, not me, sorry. That's not my job"). Or a question like: "Can *you* yoke Behemoth?" "Can *you* cause the seas to open its doors or command the seas to close its doors?" (38:8). And then, finally, in the second portion of God's response, how do we respond to God's implied challenge (40:8): "How dare *you* justify yourself before Me! Come back when you can do what I can do, and then we'll talk!" (40:8–14), a set of remarks that seem entirely inadequate to the questions Job has been asking, but equally to the God of the friends. It seems more a return to the bet-making God of the prologue — and somewhat of a divine bully — than the repository of heavenly wisdom responding to sincere human inquiry.

How do you deal with a God like that? Each one of these explanations — the mythological God, the cause and effect God, the hidden God of social justice, the elemental bullying God of natural creation — would seem on the surface inadequate to account for the situation that we have in front of us: injustice, evil, suffering. Job experiences all these qualities of injustice and evil not only around him but in his own body. At one point he says, "One moment I was the center of attention, and now I am forced to live with jackals. I am worse off than the ostriches" (30:29). Apparently, Job does not like ostriches very much. Earlier in the narrative, he found himself to be one of the beautiful people, one of the in-crowd, and now he finds himself on the outside, and he is fairly upset about that.

We would seem to be given, then, four Gods, or four schematized relationships with God. And they are presented to us in ways that are cumulative and increasingly comprehensive — so that the text itself is something of a scene of instruction. The mythological, which is the first, is undoubtedly the least powerful explanation, and Judaism certainly the most distant from it. The cause and effect God we find in the book of Ezra, among other places. This God reflects what Buber elsewhere calls the "apocalyptic," a kind of institutionalization of mythic thinking, and he will reject this explanation as distinguishable from what he will identify as "prophetic" conceptions.[6] But this cause and effect God is closer at least to Judaism (in this case, quite literally, since we know there is a cause that Job does not know about). Job's hidden God of social justice is more powerful than either of these first two, because it takes account of them and yet goes beyond them in its probing the human situation. And the most powerful and comprehensive God of all is the God of elemental creation, which has the potential at least to open us to vistas barely imaginable at the human level.

But none of these four interrelationships between God and human beings answers the problem of evil. If evil is a problem before we read this text, it is even more of a problem after. If this text is to be regarded as an example of theodicy (as Hanson invokes that word above), as the potential direct intervention of God in matters of human affairs and matters of justice, it is a failed theodicy. It is a record of four failed theodicies, if you like, for each of these explanations are really versions of theodicy in themselves, similar accounts of such intervention and interaction: mythic theodicy, a theodicy of sin or transgression, a negative theodicy or atheist theodicy of social justice, and an elemental creationist theodicy. And all are failures. All of them fail by virtue of their plurality alone — if for no other reason — and all raise at least as many questions as they answer.[7]

Arthur Hanson's observation, therefore, seems to me entirely justified. There is finally no rational explanation that is adequate: "If we look to Job for rational solutions to the problem of innocent suffering we will not find them." What the book of Job reveals to us is simply that there is no rational way of explaining evil. The text is a dismantling of all possible ways of explaining evil and suffering by rationality. There is nowhere in the text to put our feet down, to ground ourselves. Hanson's view seems to me an articulation of the only legitimate starting point for reflection upon the text.

So what then do we do with a text like this? Certainly, the fact that the text has not satisfied readers has not stopped readers from insisting that we look further, and from finding one or another of these four perspectives to be the dominant one. Job's perspective tends to be the playground of the greatest number of individuals, perhaps the most popular way of trying to understand the book, and Carl Jung's *Answer to Job* is a good example of a reading that adopts Job's perspective.[8]

But there are other perspectives to which we can turn among these four. The classical Jewish response to the book of Job affirms God's position—that what we have here is only a glimpse of the divine scheme of things, that if we knew more, we might agree with (or at least understand) God's plan. And so from this view the answer to evil is that it is too early to tell.

The perspective of the friends, the second of the four perspectives, seems to have attracted considerably less interest as the center of the book's gravity. But in the recent Artscroll edition of the book, which offers a good deal of the classic rabbinic commentary translated into English, we are informed, surprisingly enough, that the sages frequently argued against Job and for the friends—not for God, which is the more familiar modern Jewish response. In this particular book, the older tradition of scriptural commentary is at odds, the editor tells us, with the view derived from a more cursory reading of the text, and so the friends in some way do Job a service: Job sinned, therefore he is the cause of his own experience.[9]

And fourthly, and lest we think that the mythological perspective does not offer us any starting place for modern reflection about this text, has not the documentary tradition in the so-called "higher biblical criticism"—which regards the story as simply a product of a wisdom tale—done precisely that? Has not the wisdom tradition of the book of Job identified it as little more than a parable within the Jewish tradition? It's just a wisdom tale; we are not to think of it as anything more than that. The tale is bound by mythology. It's one more way of placing the center of gravity not on Job, not on God, not on the friends, but on the mythological. The fact that some of the language of the text seems to suggest a second millennium origin for portions of it is often recalled in this connection.[10]

But what if we find none of these perspectives acceptable? Then we are left with a problem, one to which I would now like to suggest a solution. I think I have identified an answer, if not to the problem of evil and suffering in the world, then at least to the problem of the book of Job.

My solution involves basically four steps. The first is to assume — as we have been assuming — that the book of Job is entirely meaningless if what we are looking for is some core lesson about suffering or evil that can assist us in dealing with it. Rather, in its primary form, the book of Job is a dismantling or a deconstruction of all possible (or all known or all available, which is to say, all the most powerful) reigning explanations for evil or suffering in the time in which it was written (probably the period of the Babylonian exile, even though scholars identify some parts of the text with the early second millennium). That is step one, to make this assumption — that the text itself is not satisfying.

Step two. What if instead of looking for meaning in the book of Job as we have been doing traditionally, we ask a different question: namely, why would the rabbis choose to include the book of Job in the canon of the twenty-four books of the Hebrew Bible? Why would the rabbis decide to include such a strictly performative text, or more precisely, such a negatively performative text, in the canon, performing all these theodicean explanations only to undo them? What meaning could we assign, not to the book of Job, but to their gesture of including it? In this connection, I will talk about their "prophetic" reading (and I will define that term in a moment), in the wake of the fall of the First Temple, a prophetic reading in which they see the book of Job in its negatively deconstructive way as the exclusion of Judaism; which is to say, the exclusion, as I understand Judaism, of the law of anti-idolatry.

For what is Judaism for the rabbis? It is the law of anti-idolatry. Judaism is *mitzvot*, commandments. Judaism is Torah; Torah is *mitzvot*; *mitzvot* is the law of anti-idolatry. This interpretation of Judaism is a prophetic reading the rabbis developed six hundred years after the Babylonian exile, when they started their movement amidst the tumult of their own time, one in which the Second Temple is collapsing. In other words, the rabbis who are reading this text look back six hundred years earlier to a former moment of the collapse of the Temple to explain, in some way, their own catastrophe. One situation of catastrophe explains another situation of catastrophe.

And once we have asked that question—why include such a deconstructive text?—we are led to a third question, namely, why are we interested in the problem today? Outside of purely academic interest, why in the beginning of the twenty-first century have we become concerned with the book of Job? Or, more precisely, with the rabbinic reading of the book of Job? And here, as you might imagine, the Holocaust and our post-Holocaust wars and reflections provide the starting point.

And then finally step four. If the rabbis read prophetically in the context of their own time (and I claim that they do), and if we read prophetically today after the Holocaust (and I suggest that we do, namely, that we read prophetically both the rabbis and the book of Job in the context of our own moment), it is legitimate to ask whether the experience of the modern reader may include these prophetic signposts, these readings, as she or he moves through the text. In other words, we can ask whether the book of Job will allow us to do what I'll call a "double reading," a reading where we go back and look at the four successive failed theodicies and reconstrue them, offering them a positive role in the scene of instruction constituted by the reading of the book. In that case, we would recognize the mythological relationship to be already about accusation, and the book of Job as already telling us to reject accusation. All of the explanations would appear to us as forms of accusation: accusation of Job by *ha–Satan,* accusation of Job by the friends, accusation of God by Job, and accusation of Job and the friends by God.

We might then want to ask ourselves whether we can reconstrue the second framework, which is the framework based on cause and effect. Is not the book of Job speaking to us about cause? And here I am going to introduce the notion of infinite responsibility and the ways in which responsibility becomes a means of talking about causality. And then thirdly we can ask whether Job's concern with social structure, humanism, and justice may be identified as an egoistic, self-centered (and self-justifying) understanding, to be replaced (fourthly) by a cocreational participation in the creation of the universe.

That is to say, I am going to suggest that Job's perspective, which accuses God, and then God's perspective, which attacks Job, can speak to us at another level, which I will call "subjectivity," namely, the ways in which an ego goes out and returns to itself, returns to the same. Hegel, and many other philosophers, have talked about the ways in which we construct identity through this "ego-agent" that proceeds from the "self-same," goes out to the other, and returns to the self-same, intent upon constructing in this way a route back to the same. Emmanuel Levinas calls this round-trip movement by which we construct ourselves as subjects of consciousness an "Odyssean" move similar to the one Odysseus makes in Homer, and he contrasts it with the "Abrahamic" movement by which a subjectivity based upon responsibility and the ethical may be conceived.

We might want to ask, in other words, whether this egoistic self-centered structure by which modern subjectivity and identity is constructed might be displaced by a more radical subjectivity, one that requires of us an access to a "before" the ego. Levinas puts it in the following way. He talks about it as "a thou must that takes no account of a thou can."[11] The "where were you when I created the universe?" might be a legitimate question. Maybe, having laughed at it earlier as if it were posed in a kind of Woody Allen comedy, we need to return to that question, and we need to say, "Yes, I have to own my responsibility for what I never did, what I could not have done, what I never consented to, what was even beyond my power to do. I have to be responsible, in other words, infinitely. That is what Levinas is going to call "infinite responsibility," responsibility that has no finite terminus.

Job and Midrashic Reading

We will return to this double reading at the end of our essay. But we need first to ask a different question. Why would the rabbis choose to include such a deconstructive book as the book of Job in the canon of the books of the Hebrew Bible? The rabbis say repeatedly two things about the book of Job of which we are reminded in the first epigraph to this essay.

There was once, among the gentile people, a *chassid* whose name was Iyov. He was placed into this world with only the purpose that he might earn his just reward. God exposed him to suffering and [rather than submitting quietly] he began to curse and to blaspheme. Because of this, God doubled his reward in This World so that he might be driven out of the World to Come (*Bava Batra 15b*).[12]

This commentary is very strange to anyone not familiar with rabbinic readings of the book of Job, largely because of its negativity. We do not expect the rabbis to say that. We are used to thinking Job raises legitimate questions. Why would he be rewarded only to be driven out of the world to come? This seems to be a very curious idea.

The passage is widely interpreted to mean that "Job is not Jewish." I was fascinated to learn that there were other takes on this idea. I mentioned to a colleague that in the Jewish tradition, Job is not Jewish, and he replied, "But in the Christian tradition, Job *is* Jewish." Christians in other words regard Job as the other, as Jewish, while Jews regard Job similarly as the other, as not Jewish. For each tradition Job is something of an other.

So, which is it? Is Job Jewish, or is Job not Jewish? In fact, the midrashic text is ambiguous. We read: "There was once, among the gentile people, a *chassid* whose name was Iyov." What does that mean? Does that mean Job is a just man, a *tzaddik*, albeit a gentile, perhaps even a "righteous gentile," as we say sometimes, and therefore he is not Jewish in that sense? Or is he a Jewish individual, a *chassid*, a *tzaddik*, a just Jewish man, who happens to be living among gentiles although he is in fact Jewish? How are we to decide this issue?

In fact, of course, in midrash, we don't. In the midrashic literature, we always speak of two requirements. The first is that it fills the gap from which it sprang. A midrash is always a story that responds to a gap or tear or break in the text. For example, when God says to Abraham, "Take your son, your only son, whom you love, Yitzhak, and *v'aleihu sham l'olah*, bring him up as an offering up, offer him up as an offering up," there's a midrash that says: "Why does he say: 'Take your son, your only son, whom you love, Isaac'? Why does he say it four times? Why doesn't he just say 'Take Isaac'?" So, the midrash says:

"Well, you see, there was a conversation between God and Abraham. And God says: 'Take your son.' And Abraham says: 'I have two sons' [you recall that his first son is Ishmael]. 'Your only son,' God says. And so Abraham says: 'Each is an only son to his mother'; [you recall that Ishmael is an only son to Haggar, and that Isaac is an only son to Sarah]. 'The one you love,' God says. 'I love them both,' Abraham replies. 'Isaac!' God says finally. To which, Abraham says: 'Okay, all right. I can't get around that.' And so he has no choice."[13]

Midrash raises for us, in other words, interpretive potentials that would not be seen otherwise. It dislocates our energy. In the above example, it reminds us that Abraham has two sons, that each has a mother (who would have an opinion about what is going on), that he loves both his sons, and so forth. It is in fact the primary means by which the rabbis thought about these texts.

Where then is the ambiguity about which we have been speaking? In midrashic literature, we do not decide things because what we mean by midrashic literature is that it fills in a gap. But there is a second requirement, namely, that the means by which the gap is filled constitute a material extension of the text. It is clear how the midrashic story in our epigraph fills in the gap. If Job or his friends (or Elihu) are not Jewish, that fact could explain why they did not understand God's thinking on these matters. But of course the name Elihu is Jewish, a perfectly good Jewish name in fact. And there are other indications in the text that there are traces of Judaism there. If Job is not Jewish, why do the friends wait a certain requisite period of time before they intervene? Some rabbis say they are sitting *shiva* with Job before they interact with him, before they raise the question. So the midrashic text extends materially that ambiguity. Job may be Jewish, or he may not be Jewish.

What I propose, then, in order to answer the question, is to consider another midrash. That is sometimes what you do when you work with midrash. You accumulate accounts without deciding the issue. You accumulate more midrashim and hopefully that additional midrashic commentary will allow you to shed some light on the previous midrash.

Here is another piece of Rabbinic commentary. Rabbi Yochanan, as we read in the second epigraph (also from *Baba Metzia*), was reputed to have said: "Iyov was among those who returned from the Babylonian exile, and his Beit HaMidrash is situated in Tiberius." How does this text help us?

Rabbi Yochanan speaks, as one of our editors in the Artscroll edition says, as if the issue is for him a decided matter, as if it is a matter of fact, not a matter of conjecture. "Iyov was among those who returned from the Babylonian exile, and his Beit HaMidrash is situated in Tiberius," which of course is a Roman name.[14] Job in this midrashic statement is a product of the Babylonian exile. But the text contains its own ambiguity. How so? We read: "and his Beit HaMidrash is situated in Tiberius." The phrase we might expect to hear in the text is not "Beit HaMidrash" but "Beit HaMikdash." Why? Because "beit haMikdash" means "house of study." We are looking for where he lives. We are looking for the place. One rabbi says he lives in the time of Moses. Another says he lives in the time of Isaac. Another in the time of Joshua. And what we get in the text is "he lives in midrash," "he lives in story." His *beit*, his house, is the house of story, the house of interpretation.

We understand, then, what midrash is doing. Rabbi Yochanan states as fact that Job lives in midrash. The doubleness of midrashic thinking returns. What is the difference between a *beit haMikdash* and a *beit haMidrash*? A solid house, a Temple, a determinable locus, has been replaced by a story, by an interpretation. The midrash fills the gap and materially extends the text that it fills.

How then are we to interpret these statements with regard to the book of Job at large? The same way we read all such rabbinic commentary, the ways the rabbis themselves read, namely, midrashically. To say "Job is not Jewish" is to say that the book of Job is written in the wake of the fall of the First Temple in the ancient sixth century (in 586 or 585 BCE depending upon how we calculate), and that the rabbis are already asking what happens when Jews become non-Jews. What happens when no explanation is any longer available to account for disaster, and Jews begin to imagine the possibility of the impact of other cultures upon them, other cultures that surround them? What would their arguments look like? That is what the book of Job is staging for us, performing for us if you like, these failed arguments, arguments that from a Jewish perspective lack one thing, namely, Judaism.

It is hard today for us to imagine the impact of the fall of the First Temple upon Judaism, and the appearance during this period of time, as Buber and many others have pointed out, of prophetic thinking in texts like Second Isaiah. But if we do so, it allows us to understand the book of Job in an entirely new way. A prophetic reading of the fall of the First Temple demands of us that we observe the dramas, the set patterns, these individuals are enacting and the end of those dramas to which they are moving. Here is what will happen if you continue along the path you have been traveling. What do we mean by the prophetic? The prophetic is a recognition of the dramas in which human beings are engaged and a naming in advance of the end of those dramas in order that we may decide whether to go there or not. That definition involves in the first place recognizing dramas, set patterns, or routines by which human beings interact, so that in formulating the mode of the prophetic we are not invoking the idea of fortune-telling. The prophetic is not a means of predicting the future: here is the path you have been traveling; Jews have become non-Jews, and here is how they argue.

In other words, mythological thinking, cause and effect thinking, social justice arguments, elemental creationist arguments—in short, all the arguments of the ancient world outside of Judaism—are put forth in this book. And yet none allows the book to cohere. The problem of evil or suffering is not answered by mythology, nor by the cause and effect argument, nor by Job's concern with social justice argument, nor even by the argument adopting the point of view of God in 38–42, that it is all a matter of elemental creation.

Why? Because what is missing in all these instances is Judaism. The problem is that Job is not Jewish, or perhaps more precisely, that Job is *no longer* Jewish. Jews have become non-Jews. Judaism understood as the law of anti-idolatry is now absent.

How do we know that? How do we know that is the problem? Because we have other texts scholars consider contemporary with the book of Job in which the same arguments are made regarding mythological thinking, cause and effect thinking, humanism and social justice thinking, and creationist thinking, texts that involve suffering and creation, and at the center of all of it is Judaism, Judaism understood as the law of anti-idolatry.

The text of Second Isaiah is one example. Here is a famous passage in which suffering is overtly a theme.[15]

> He was despised, and forsaken of men,
> A man of pains, and acquainted with disease,
> And as one from whom men hide their face:
> He was despised and we esteemed him not.
> Surely our diseases he did bear, and our pains he carried;
> Whereas we did esteem him stricken,
> Smitten of God, and afflicted. (53:3–4)

We thought of him in other words as lodged within a theodicy. But in fact it was because of our human gestures that all of this happened.

> But he was wounded because of our transgressions,
> He was crushed because of our iniquities:
> The chastisement of our welfare was upon him,
> And with his stripes we were healed. (53:5)

Here, on the other hand, are some texts about creation, texts that sound very much like the book of Job (and there are a great many more I am not citing).[16]

> Who measured the waters in the hollow of his hand,
> And gauged the skies with a span,
> And meted earth's dust of the earth with a measure,
> And weighed the mountains with a scales
> And the hills with a balance? (40:12)

These words sound as if they were lifted straight from the book of Job, from 38–42. But then other words link this God of creation with the issue of idolatry.

> To whom, then, can you liken God,
> What form compare to Him?
> The idol? A woodworker shaped it,

And a smith overlaid it with gold,
Forging links of silver. (40:18–19)

Do you not know?
Have you not heard?
Have you not been told
From the very first?
Have you not discerned how the earth was founded? (40:20–21)

This language is very close to Job but with one difference: Judaism is present here. How do you liken an idol to God? This is the law of anti-idolatry, the Jewish law, that stands between suffering and creation. He "who measured the waters in the hollow of His hand" is the same God to which no one or nothing may be "likened."

These verses are extremely powerful and they are only a very small portion of a great many. The insistence, the urgency with which they speak of our lack of knowledge, as well as the thematic content that rhetorical urgency envelopes, must strike us as familiar. "Do you not know? / Have you not heard? / The LORD is God from of old, / Creator of the earth from end to end, / He never grows faint or weary" (40:28).

Keep this in mind, and stand firm,
Take this to heart, you sinner!
Bear in mind what happened of old;
For I am God, and there is none else,
I am divine, and there is none like Me,
I foretell the end from the beginning,
And from the start things that had not occurred. (46:8–10)

But this same God, "who laid the foundations of the earth," is included within a "book of consolation of Israel."

Comfort, oh comfort My people,
Says your God.
Speak tenderly to Jerusalem,
And declare to her

That her term of service is over,
That her iniquity is expiated;
For she has received at the hand of the LORD
Double for all her sins. (40:1–2)

Thus said the LORD your Redeemer,
The Holy One of Israel:
I the LORD am your God,
Instructing you for your own benefit,
Guiding you in the way you should go.
If only you would heed My commands!
Then your prosperity would have been like a river,
And your triumph like the waves of the sea.
Your offspring would be as many as the sand,
Their issue as many as its grains.
Their name would never be cut off
Or obliterated from before Me.
Go forth from Babylon,
Flee from Chaldea! (48:17–20)

Say: "The LORD has redeemed
His servant Jacob!" (48:21)

"There is no safety"—said the LORD—"for the wicked." (48:22)

Like Job, in other words, Israel (or Jacob) will receive "double" for her suffering (having already paid in full, paid "double" for any and all inquities) if only she will follow the commandments and live a life of Torah, which is to say, a life of anti-idolatry. The prophet is instructed to comfort his people, not chastise them. The Abrahamic promise is available at any and every moment to all who accept the commandments, to any who participates with God in creation by living such a life.

On the other hand, the end of the wicked is also available to us. "For lo," says the psalmist, "they that go far from Thee shall perish; Thou dost destroy all them that go astray from Thee" (Ps 73:27). A life of anti-idolatry is by the same token the way in which Judaism has devised to live in the face of suffering. To question suffering as a problem is to question Judaism, to question the law of anti-idolatry, to question creation itself, which is constituted in Judaism as a response to that problem.

In other words, when God says to Job in 38–42, "where were you when I created the universe?" we can hear it in one of at least two different rhetorical ways: (1) "you should have been there; where were you?"; or alternatively, (2) "there's an attention deficit here; don't you know that that is how the universe is created? Where were you when I created the universe?" How many times has your mother or your father said, "Where were you when they gave out brains?" "Don't you understand?" It's a rhetorical way of talking. It's a very Jewish rhetorical way of talking. "Haven't you been paying attention to the fact that Judaism is about creation?" How many jokes involving the book of Job turn on this point?[17]

In other words, to Job's question—what is the justice scheme behind all of this?—God could be heard to be saying to him: "Have you forgotten something? Have you forgotten Judaism? Have you forgotten the Judaism that is devoted to precisely that question? Your question is itself already a displacement or foreclosure of the answer that you seek. Your inquiry into the nature of human justice can serve perhaps to get you out of this moment, can allow you to imagine a position from which you can criticize Judaism, and that position may seem profound to you. But are you sure that the exclusion of the sacrificial relations in which you are engaged is where you want to go? Are you sure that you will be able to yoke Behemoth as you imagine, or catch Leviathan with a fishhook? For do we not see Behemoth and Leviathan all around us—the monsters of the land and the monsters of the sea?[18] Are you sure that your questioning of all religious structures will allow you to deal with the kinds of movements that are going to arise in the future?"

Historians inform us that all cultures in the Ancient Near East in the sixth century BCE were experiencing invasions of monstrosities of all kinds, both internal and external. Think about Greece and the Dionysiac invasion identified in Greek cultural studies as coming "from the East," and the mindless embracing of the sacrificial that is so thoroughly denounced by the Greek tragic playwrights. Or about the Greek rationalism, especially Platonism, that took over (and in fact thoroughly rejected) the sacrificial and ritual behavior and from which our own theology, and to some extent our own culture of philosophy, has in part at least derived. We are still within the impact of that ancient embracing and rejection of sacrificial, ritualistic structures to which the book of Job bears testimony.

The rabbis are saying that the book of Job is talking to us prophetically. You can certainly try to do without these sacrificial structures if you like and found a culture entirely on social justice, but are you sure you want to do that?

Why would the rabbis be interested themselves in this moment six hundred years earlier? Precisely because they were experiencing the same crisis in the wake of the collapse of the Second Temple and the establishment of the rabbinic academy—at Yavneh, for example. There is no place here to talk about the formation of the biblical canon, or the rise of text-centered Judaism associated with it, starting in the sixth century BCE and continuing at the beginning of the modern era. Suffice it to say that the rabbinic tradition as we know it was forged in a context in which the world they knew was once again collapsing, and so they turned to events six hundred years earlier—to the so-called "Persian period"—where the beginnings of the movements that would later culminate in the Pharisees and eventually the rabbinic tradition were happening.

Why do we reflect upon these matters today? Precisely again because of the Holocaust, because of the categorical exclusion, both within and without, in Auschwitz and at Hiroshima and Nagasaki that the Holocaust articulates for us. If we are interested in these matters today, in the rabbinic period around the turning of the common era, or in the era six hundred years earlier in which text-centered Judaism was formed, it is because of the Holocaust that we face.

And here my guidepost to these matters is Emmanuel Levinas. The Holocaust, Levinas argues, in a wonderful essay called "Useless Suffering," which bears much rereading, is the end of theodicy, the end of the idea that there is any chance of a God who rewards the good with prizes and who punishes the bad with chastisements.[19] If we ever needed any reminder, the Holocaust is that reminder, that there is no such God ever going to show up.

Here is Levinas asking a question about a modern text, written by Zvi Kolitz and pertaining to the Holocaust, which applies equally I suggest to the book of Job.

> What is the meaning of this suffering of the innocent? Does it not bear witness to a world that is without God, to a land where man alone measures Good and Evil? The simplest and most common response to this question would lead us to conclude in atheism. This is no doubt also the sanest reaction for all those individuals for whom up until that point a God, conceived a bit primitively, distributed prizes, inflicted sanctions or pardoned faults, and in His kindness treated men as eternal children. But with what narrow-minded demon, with what strange magician, have you thus populated your sky, you who currently declare it to be deserted? And why under such an empty sky do you continue to seek a world that is meaningful and good?[20]

And Levinas continues.

> The certitude of God . . . is revealed to us with a new force under an empty sky. For if man exists so alone, it is in order to feel upon his shoulders [the shoulders of human beings] all the responsibilities of God.[21]

Everything is given to God except the "fear of God," the rabbis say. Which means in rabbinic terms not the terror of God but, to the contrary, the love of God, the reverential awe or appreciation of God.

> On the path that leads to the unique God there is a relay point that is without God. True monotheism must respond to the legitimate exigencies of atheism. A God of an adult manifests himself precisely through the emptiness of the sky of a child. This is a moment when God withdraws from the world and conceals his face.[22]

The Holocaust, in other words, according to Levinas, like the experience of Job, could lead us to conclude in atheism, if we were to imagine a God who distributed awards and issued punishments, such as the
God of Job's three friends. But who said God was like that? It is only by
positing such a God to begin with—and thus distorting Judaism—
that we can arrive at such a conclusion. Calvin Schrag has commented
that perhaps some of the problems we discover in philosophy relative to
God derive as much from the way we go about constructing the God of
whom we then ask such questions as they do from anything external
to those questions.[23]

Who said God was like that? It is only by positing such a God that
we create these problems. The absence of God in the world or in the
sky, the concealment of God behind a veil, far from signifying His
nonexistence, is itself the surest proof, in fact the certitude, of that existence. For it is this very absence of God from the point of view of the
world that confers upon man all responsibility for his own existence, his
own destiny. It is not that there is no God but that there is no God to
the world, from the world's point of view. That is the meaning of the
law of anti-idolatry, of the externality or radical alterity of transcendence that defines Judaism. We must function as if there is no God, as
if all responsibility for human behavior and human relations falls upon
man himself. That is what it means to be an adult as opposed to being
a child and to have a religion of adults rather than a religion of eternal childhood. The possibility of atheism is the necessary step in the
process of assuming responsibility for one's own behavior. This is the
meaning of the hidden God who conceals himself behind a veil.

Thus Levinas answers Job's complaint in the very terms in which
it has been posed. The hidden God, "le Dieu qui se voile," the God
who hides himself or veils himself, far from a stumbling block to Job's
lament, is in fact its very answer, an answer we may want to argue that
God explicitly reveals by appearing to offer to Job the discourse of his
otherness, his exteriority to man, his elemental creational status.

But Levinas continues and in a brilliant series of remarks extends
this analysis of the hidden God to the precise terms of Job's human
experience of justice, an experience of suffering and an experience of
victimage.

A God who conceals his face is not, I think, a theological abstraction or a poetic image. It is a way of talking about the hour when the just individual no longer finds any external recourse, when no institution protects him, when the consolation of divine presence in childlike religious sentiment is similarly of no avail, when the individual can no longer triumph except in his own consciousness, which is to say, necessarily in suffering.[24]

We understand here the appearance of a Jewish monism that is in no way a dualism. For this suffering that defines this moment of the hiding of God's face, when both institution and the religious sentiment of the child fails, Levinas continues, is "a specifically Jewish sense of suffering, which never at any moment assumes the value of a mystical expiation for the sins of the world."

> The position of victims (*la position des victimes*) in a world in disorder, which is to say, a world in which the good does not triumph, is suffering. That position reveals a God who, renouncing all helpful manifestation, appeals to the full maturity of the integrally responsible human being. . . . The suffering of the just for a justice that is without triumph is lived concretely *as* Judaism. Israel—historic and carnal—has become once again a religious category.[25]

You see now why I have insisted that it is Judaism that has been expelled when we create a "problem" of the book of Job, or, more specifically, a "problem of evil." The God of Judaism is neither the simple-minded cause and effect God of the three friends nor the hidden God of Job and his poetic and social justice imagery, but a God who confers complete responsibility for our own actions upon the integrally responsible human being, the individual who gives up the perspective of a child and assumes upon his shoulders the responsibility for full consciousness. And that consciousness is always necessarily and sooner or later a moral consciousness, a consciousness of suffering.

Suffering, in other words, within the Jewish perspective is not a mystical purgation or substitution for the sins of the world, but a reading from the position of the victim, which is to say, from the position of one who is in the midst of struggle, a struggle in which justice does not triumph, in which what triumphs, perhaps, are precisely the childish perspectives of the friends or the atheistic and nihilistic perspectives of the Jobs who carry their own position to an extreme (and who are thus the negatives of the perspective of the friends). Suffering is the consciousness gained from the victim that finds the certitude of God in His seeming absence and that thus enables the responsibility that escapes childishness and atheism to be assumed.[26]

Suffering, in short, is a perspective. Suffering is not an aberration that somehow invades a consciousness that is otherwise good from the outside. Suffering is coextant with the world in which we function. And the answer to Job's question, for Levinas, is Judaism itself. The God of the sufferers, the defender or advocate of those who suffer, is the Jewish God, and has never in fact been any other. If we have imagined the Jewish God to be other—and thus able to be scandalized by the existence of evil or of human suffering in the world—it is because it is we who have distorted him in conceptualizing him as such to begin with. Far from it being the case that Judaism is scandalized by evil or human suffering, radical evil and human suffering is that to which Judaism and the Jewish God has always already been a response— by definition, as it were. The Jewish God is the God of suffering par excellence and only by substituting for that God another candidate have we been able to pose our problem at all, a problem with which we then ironically charge God! "The suffering of the just for a justice which is without triumph," Levinas writes, "is . . . Judaism."[27]

But to conceive of a Judaism that has never been anything other than a response to suffering (a creative response, if you like), and suffering as *la position des victimes* (the position of victims, the condition of being a victim), brings us right back to the work of René Girard. Do we understand now the importance of a thesis that says that at the heart of the book of Job is an insight about victims, and a rejection of the structures by which human communities have organized such victimage? Set free of the law of anti-idolatry, suffering understood as a matter of victims can only seem to us unanswerable. Creation understood as the only way out of a world of victims can only seem to us fatuous. The sacrificial advice of the friends can only seem to us oppressive, and the bet-making God of the prologue demonic.

How does Levinas's reading of the Holocaust enable us—we need finally to ask in order to bring this essay to a close—to read the rabbinic gesture of including the book of Job in the Hebrew canon? You understand by now of course that my view is that we may see the book of Job, following Levinas, as the end of theodicy, as in fact a deconstruction of all possible explanations for evil and for suffering.

If the gesture of the rabbis, therefore, is to include the book of Job in the canon as a commentary on the problem of evil or suffering, it is because evil is precisely not a "problem" per se for them. Or if you like, it is the only problem Judaism is concerned with. Evil as the lack of the good, as distance from God rather than proximity (or nearness) to God, is the problem of Judaism par excellence, the one to which all of Judaism responds. Evil is not a unique problem in Judaism, not one among many, not even a special problem among others. Evil in Judaism is not a part of a dualism (in which it may be opposed by something like the good) but rather (and precisely) a monism. Evil or suffering in this context is precisely the good gone wrong, a breakdown that is a natural part of the order of things rather than an invasion of them from the outside (or the inside), "a deficiency of the good" so to speak (to use words familiar to Augustinian theologians), and not a part of any Manichean opposition of the good to the bad, which is how evil and suffering has often been regarded in the history of philosophy.

As a consequence of there being neither a theodicy nor a dualism, evil and suffering from a rabbinic perspective are nonredemptive, and the suffering of another individual is absolutely useless and meaningless. The suffering of the other is always without meaning, Levinas tells us. The only suffering to which I can assign a value—and which as a consequence can serve as a foundation for interhuman groups—is my own suffering.

And finally as a consequence of these three ideas (that it is not a theodicy, is not a dualism, and is useless or meaningless as a foundation for a redemptive act), we are led to a "double reading" of the book of Job as a whole, one that will at once recognize the four narrative relationships we have identified (as the book unfolds) as a prophetic extension of the gesture of excluding Judaism, and at the same time credit midrashically each of those four perspectives, each of the four performative deconstructive and increasingly comprehensive perspectives, to which the reader is diachronically submitted.

What are those four newly creditable perspectives? In the first place, as the result of reading the book in the way I have suggested, the book of Job *may* indeed finally be about accusation and mythic sacrificial thinking after all. Secondly, the book of Job may indeed be about our relations with friends or neighbors, and our responsibility for the other human being, a responsibility that exceeds even my capacity. Thirdly, the book of Job may indeed be about justice and the giving up of the sacrificial perspectives that arise among friends or when engaged in abstract and mythic thought, perspectives that lead good to become evil and nearness to God to become distance from God. And fourthly, the book of Job may finally be about creation, although a creation conceived, as Franz Rosenzweig among others conceives of it, as ongoing and cognate at the human level with responsibility itself.[28]

Only such a radical reconception of responsibility (cognate with a creation conceived as ongoing) answers to the enormity of the Holocaust. Only such a radical reconception allows us to understand the prophetic reading the rabbis undertake in including the book of Job within the canon of the Hebrew Bible. And only such a radical reconception of responsibility allows us to understand a text that says to Job, who complains of the deficiency of social justice, that the answer is creation itself, a "thou must that takes no account of a thou can," a responsibility for the other individual to which I have neither consented nor was ever even conscious, and yet that is imagined, midrashically, as the creation of the universe itself. Here is Levinas speaking to philosophers about subjectivity, defined at least since Hegel and the nineteenth century as a subjectivity to consciousness, articulating its relation to an accusation prior to freedom and an "outside of being."

> We still reason as though the ego had been present at the creation of the world, and as though the world, henceforth in its charge, had issued from an act of free will. Such are the presumptions of philosophers, the presumptions of idealists. Indeed, it is for this that scripture reproaches Job. No doubt he could have understood his misfortunes had they been the result of his faults. But he never wanted to do evil! His so-called friends thought as he did; in an orderly world one is responsible only

for one's *own* actions. Ergo, Job must have been guilty of an oversight. But the meaning of the world is not inscribed in being as a theme that exhibits itself in this world. Job does not have at his disposal all that is required for deliberating in matters of justice. Entering too late into a world created without him, he is responsible over and above what he experiences. And yet, in the same way, he is *better* for not being a mere effect of this world. The distinction between the free and the non-free is not therefore ultimate. Prior to the Ego taking a decision, the *outside of being*, where the Ego arises or is accused, is necessary.[29]

It is to that potential—to the rejection of accusation conceived as an attack upon the divine, to the replacement of an autonomous, ego-driven, free subjectivity with a heteronymous, other-driven, obligated subjectivity that understands prior accusation as a responsibility for creation itself—that I would like to suggest to you the book of Job gives articulation. If René Girard can identify in that articulation a further development of the prophetic insights of the Greek tragedians regarding sacrifice and scapegoating (insights that he notes will find further articulation in midrashic and parabolic narratives coined later within a Jewish tradition as a "New Testament"), is it not because the four failed theodicies that, as Buber teaches us, make up the book of Job may be read as four failed versions of the sacrificial to which the book of Job also offers us an increasingly comprehensive positive scene of instruction: from satanic mythic accusation, to the primacy of relations with well-intentioned if flawed friends, to legitimate if unanswerable (because messianic) concerns with social justice, to ultimate concerns with creation itself understood as our infinite responsibility for other human beings. It is from that potential for an anti-sacrificial understanding of the book of Job, one that moves from theodicy to the ethical, that I would suggest we may continue to learn today.

Notes

1. On the close connection of the book of Job to the complaint or lament tradition, see William Morrow's astute essay, "The Expulsion of Complaint from Early Jewish Worship," in this volume.

2. Arthur G. Hanson, "The Book of Job and Its Legacy," unpublished manuscript, 1–2. This paper was discussed at the conference "The Problem of Evil," held at Purdue University, April 2, 2005.

3. See, for example, William L. Rowe, ed., *God and the Problem of Evil* (Oxford: Blackwell, 2001).

4. See Martin Buber, "Job," in *On the Bible: Eighteen Studies,* ed. Nahum Glatzer, 188–98 (Syracuse, NY: Syracuse University Press, 2000).

5. In this essay, all quotations from the book of Job are from *Job: The Soncino Books of the Bible,* ed. Rabbi Victor E. Reichert (New York: Soncino Press, 1978).

6. Cf. Martin Buber, "Prophecy, Apocalyptic, and the Historical Hour," in *On the Bible,* ed. Glatzer, 172–87. See also Buber, "The Dialogue Between Heaven and Earth," in *On Judaism,* 214–25 (New York: Schoken, 1967).

7. When I started writing this essay, I received a communication from an individual who had written his own essay on Job and wanted to draw my attention to it. His argument was that the book of Job is a defense of theodicy. My view in what follows will be exactly the opposite, that the book of Job is an account of the end of theodicy, that, despite appearances to the contrary, it is in fact a deconstruction of all possible theodicy-based explanations for evil and for suffering.

8. Carl G. Jung, *Answer to Job,* in *Collected Works,* vol. 11, trans. R. F. C. Hull (Princeton, NJ: Princeton University Press, 1991).

9. See Rabbi Moshe Eisemann, *Job: A New Translation with a Commentary Anthologized from Talmudic, Midrashic, and Rabbinic Sources* (Brooklyn, NY: Mesorah Publications, 2002), xxviii: "the Rabbinic tradition seems to be in absolute conflict with the impression created by the simple meaning of the text. . . . The friends . . . are elevated [by the Sages] from inept bunglers to Divinely inspired saints."

10. For a careful and illuminating reading of the connection of the book of Job to the wisdom tale tradition, see Chris Allen Carter's essay, "Mimesis, Sacrifice, and the Wisdom of Job," in the current volume.

11. Emmanuel Levinas, "Revelation in the Jewish Tradition," in *The Levinas Reader,* ed. Seán Hand (Oxford: Basil Blackwell, 1989), 205: "a 'you must', which takes no account of what 'you can.'"

12. Quoted in Eisemann, *Job,* xxiv–xxv.

13. For a collection of midrashic stories surrounding biblical episodes, see *The Book of Legends: Sefer Ha-Aggadah, Legends from the Talmud and Midrash,* ed. Hayim Nahman Bialik and Yehoshua Hana Ravnitzky, trans. William G. Braude (New York: Schocken Books, 1992). A version of this midrash is given on p. 40.

14. Cited in Eisemann, *Job,* xv.

15. See the 1917 JPS edition.

16. Unless otherwise indicated, all further citations from Isaiah are from the JPS 1985 translation.

17. I thank my colleague and friend Tom Ryba for this discussion.

18. In twentieth century terms, the "monsters of the land" and the "monsters of the sea" could be understood as the way we conceptualize invasions of Europe by demonic forces originating elsewhere. Compare Levinas's comments below on the Holocaust in relation to the book of Job.

19. Emmanuel Levinas, "Useless Suffering," in *Entre Nous: Thinking-of-the-Other*, trans. Michael B. Smith, 91–101 (New York: Columbia University Press, 1998). On theodicy, see especially 94–100. Levinas writes, for example, in a section titled "The End of Theodicy," "The disproportion between suffering and every theodicy was shown at Auschwitz with a glaring, obvious clarity" (97).

20. See Emmanuel Levinas, "Loving the Torah More Than God," in *Difficult Freedom: Essays on Judaism*, trans. Séan Hand, 142–45 (Baltimore: Johns Hopkins University Press, 1990). The passage above is my translation from "Aimer la Thora plus que Dieu," in *Difficile Liberté: Essais sur le judaisme*, 3rd ed., 189–93 (Paris: Albin Michel, 1983). The quoted passage is at "Aimer la Thora," 190.

21. Ibid., my translation.

22. Ibid.

23. See, for example, Calvin O. Schrag, *God as Otherwise Than Being: Toward a Semantics of the Gift* (Evanston, IL: Northwestern Univeristy Press, 2002).

24. Levinas, "Aimer la Thora plus que Dieu," 191.

25. Ibid., my translation, emphasis added.

26. Cf. Emmanuel Levinas, *On Escape [De l'évasion]*, trans. Bettina Bergo (Stanford, CA: Stanford University Press, 2003).

27. Levinas, "Aimer la Thora plus que Dieu," 191.

28. See Franz Rosenzweig, *The Star of Redemption*, trans. Barbara E. Galli (Madison: University of Wisconsin Press, 2005).

29. Emmanuel Levinas, "Substitution," in *Emmanuel Levinas: Basic Philosophical Writings*, ed. Adriaan Peperzak, Simon Critchley, and Robert Bernasconi, 79–95 (Bloomington: Indiana University Press, 1996), 93.

Christian Gospel: Matthew, Luke, and John

SIXTEEN

Luke and the Opportune Time

Reading the Temptation Story as Preface to Kingdom and Prologue to Passion

WILLIAM MARTIN AIKEN

> *When the devil had finished every test, he departed from him until*
> *an opportune time.*
>
> —Luke 4:13

Luke has a unique and remarkable account of the temptation story, in which the devil is portrayed (in Neil Forsyth's words) "as an actor, or what Aristotle calls an 'agent,' with a role to play in a plot."[1] Not content to portray the devil's actions as the personification of the devil's character nor to let that character suffice for the devil's story, Luke insists upon, or recounts to us Jesus' insistence upon, the extremity of the devil's situation. Because, as Eric Bentley observes, "drama is an art of extreme situations," the Lukan account of the temptations becomes a drama.[2]

Our own temptation to relate to the devil as the personification of his character is understandable, particularly since his character has often been taken to be the "embodiment of evil."[3] The devil's familiar Greek name in the Gospels in the early narratives (and especially the temptation story) is *diabolos* ("the opponent").[4] For instance, Luke's contemporary Matthew appears to focus on the devil's role as Jesus' opponent,[5] and so, in Matthew's world, the first and apparently dramatically sufficient order of business is for Jesus to resist the devil persistently and almost preemptively.[6] We are receptive to this preemptive behavior of course because we "know" the devil's character, and knowing that character, we expect the appropriate conduct from each of the others.

But is being informed about character sufficient for comprehending a drama, and especially the one that occurs in the desert between Jesus and his "opponent"? In the case of at least one great dramatist, in Bentley's words, we find that "Shakespeare often shows less interest in attributing qualities to people than in providing a demonstration that they are alive, that they are in the world. . . . What [his] drama lacks in character-drawing, it makes up for in a concrete rendition of the dynamics of living."[7]

No doubt Luke would be interested in showing that Jesus was "alive," that he was "in the world." He reminds us of this life when he tells us "that the events that have been fulfilled among us . . . were handed on to us by those who were from the beginning eyewitnesses" (1:3). Luke, it could be argued, has a dramatist's interest in portraying the devil as "alive . . . in the world," and as being involved in the "dynamics of living." Luke does this by "putting him back into history," where we can "see him as an actor . . . with a role to play in a plot."[8] Plot is "the means by which the playwright gets us into [extreme] situations and . . . out of them again."[9] I define an extreme situation as one in which no act is superfluous and no choice inconsequential. The temptations are the first, if not the last, extreme situation in which the more alive the devil and Jesus become to each other, the more dramatic the outcome of their relationship will be.

Drawing upon the work of René Girard and Hans Urs von Balthasar, Raymund Schwager, S.J., has argued that "The theological line of reasoning can be developed out of drama, since drama does not advance without end in epic manner, but expresses itself in conflict and its corresponding resolution."[10] The personation that brings characters dramatically to life in a play, moreover, involves actors and audience alike in the drama, challenging the division between the "stage" (real or imaginary) and the "world." In this chapter, I read the Lukan temptations closely and dramatically, from within their action—a method that consciously resists the tendency to keep these temptations at a distance as belonging, historically and literally, to another (either the devil as tempter or Jesus as tempted). I argue that Luke intends this dramatic process of personation and involvement in order to characterize the temptations precisely as concerning Jesus' personhood as Son of God,[11] an identity for which the devil offers a series of substitutes in his endeavor to tempt Jesus away from his very self.

Setting the Stage: Crisis in the Desert

> Every kingdom divided against itself becomes a desert,
> And house falls on house.[12]

Our understanding of the temptation story is blurred because of our familiarity with the text. If a reader whose senses have been sharpened and perspective changed by René Girard's insight into other "familiar" texts were to see a story that shared the outline of this text—a man being led into the wilderness, and, even though accompanied by an advocate for his innocence, led directly to an accuser, indeed *the* accuser[13]—then that reader would almost have to conclude that in this story of exclusion and accusation, the protagonist is an outcast destined to share the lot of either exclusion or sacrifice common among scapegoat dramas.[14] The presence of the Holy Spirit guarantees that this will not be a normal scapegoating story: indeed, the Holy Spirit is there precisely because of the story's scapegoating potential.[15]

Ironically, the person of Jesus keeps us from sensing immediately the presence of an outcast. We see "Lord" where the story seems to say "outcast." Our habitual reading sees a uniquely pious man, newly ordained as it were, on his way to achieve an almost inevitable victory over a mismatched antagonist, never considering what it was, and is, that brought them into relationship. Yet, the realities of Jewish society in first-century Palestine suggest that someone like Jesus could indeed become a functioning outcast.[16] As N. T. Wright has noted:

> What matters is not simply . . . "getting in" (how one becomes a member of the covenant) and "staying in" (how one remains a member of the covenant). What matters, when Israel's symbols are under threat—when the question of what it means to be a Jew is everywhere raised and nowhere settled—is staying in *at this time of crisis;* or, to put it

another way, staying in when there was a risk of finding oneself suddenly excluded outside, or perhaps, getting back in after finding oneself suddenly excluded. That is the situation that sects exploit. That is exactly the situation that we find in first-century Palestine.[17]

The "time of crisis" to which Wright refers is conditioned by Israel's belief that she is still in exile, an exile made even more problematic and painful because Israel remains in slavery to foreign overlords in her own land.[18] A natural consequence was a proliferation of "sects," in which each was intent upon claiming that theirs was the true identity of Israel, and just as intent upon excluding others as violators of Israel.

All sects agreed that the eschatological vindication coming for the true Israel would be the final act of salvation, "a matter of a new world, the renewal of creation."[19] Israel, beginning with Abraham, had been the creator's means of dealing with the sin of Adam. Now "Israel herself becomes the true Adamic humanity."[20] In the words of Qumran, where this view was pronounced but to whom it was by no means unique, "God has chosen them for an everlasting covenant, and all the glory of Adam shall be theirs."[21] Adam's true heirs will be the completion of God's work in Adam and the realization of the true Adam.

Luke tells us three things about Jesus' situation immediately prior to his entry into the wilderness. First, this is the beginning of Jesus' work (3:23). Second, Luke chooses to place the genealogy of Jesus here, whereas Matthew used the genealogy as a part of an extended introduction to the nativity. Luke inverts the Matthean order, choosing to begin with Joseph and ending with "Adam, son of God" (3:38). The emphasis clearly falls on Jesus as the descendant of Adam, son of God, and implies that the beginning of Jesus' work completes Adam's story. The blessing God bestows upon Jesus following Jesus' baptism and immediately prior to the temptation serves to emphasize this association. If we invert the Lukan blessing to make it read: "with you I am well pleased; you are my Son, the Beloved" (3:22, reversed), the initial clause "with you I am well pleased" hearkens back to God's observation in Genesis 1 that creation was good; the naming of Jesus as the Beloved recalls the blessings of Genesis accorded to Adam.

Most readers of the temptation episode see the wilderness setting as a reference to Israel's crossing of the wilderness in Exodus under the leadership of Moses. That it unquestionably is, but with nuances and additional references that may go unappreciated. Of immediate and absolute relevance to a Jew of first-century Palestine was Israel's existential exile under Roman rule. The Jewish people struggled to maintain in a compromised present an identity that was first given in the Mosaic past, then experienced throughout the Deuteronomic history. The promise was that the exile would end and the people of the covenant would once again reenter the promised land. The temptations themselves begin only after the forty days of fasting (4:2). They thus occur on a divide similar to the one between the years of exodus and the entry into the promised land, at the exact point in salvation history, in other words, where Israel maintained a precarious balance between exile and redemption. Jesus' return from the Jordan and into the wilderness actually follows in geographical outline the entry into the promised land.[22]

The promised land is always a new Eden. If God has promised a new Eden, why does the devil encounter Jesus, the new Adam, in a wilderness? Is not the wilderness a place in which one may feel abandoned by God? The wilderness setting makes sense vis-à-vis the devil because it represents the devil's choice to be separated from God. Adam had not been abandoned by God. God had redeemed Adam's heirs through the covenant and his adoption of Israel. But Israel in Jesus' time is now in torment, convinced that she is exiled once again.

The temptation story is an encounter between the old professional at separation, the devil, and the new Adam, Jesus. The temptations the devil offers to Jesus are strategies for dealing with separation. Jesus will give the devil two opportunities to replace his perspective on separation with the experience of a freely shared affiliation with "Deuteronomic" abundance. But the temptations are not just strategies for dealing with separation. They are a strategy to separate, designed to change the relationship between God and his creation. The third temptation will make it clear that this is a demonic strategy threatening Israel at that very moment. Exile has become not just a variety of ways of dealing with a perceived separation; exile threatens to become an instrument of separation. Jesus brings the temptations to a close by turning away from this seduction and walking towards the kingdom.

The First Temptation

Jesus has fasted for forty days, a period that has already served to acquaint Jesus with trials (4:2). When the forty days were over, "The devil said to him, 'If you are the Son of God, command this stone to become a loaf of bread.' Jesus answered him, 'It is written, "One does not live by bread alone."' Then the devil led him up and showed him . . . the world" (4:3–5).

Jesus in Luke does not say what Matthew's Jesus says and almost every ear insists on hearing: "but by every word that proceeds out of the mouth of God" (Mt 4:4). The absence of that phrase in Luke makes this the first exchange in a genuine dramatic encounter between Jesus and the devil. Unlike Matthew's Jesus, Jesus in Luke has left open the question of just what it is that man will "live by": "One does not live by bread alone" and then, *silence.* In a good drama, and in real life, such a silence allows the revelation of character to take place. What is important is not just what may have been said by Jesus' silent conclusion, but what it is the devil may hear about Jesus and show about himself in that same silence. The devil can hear in that silence one of two questions, either "Do you hear what I am telling you," or, "What do you have to offer me?" Whichever question the devil thinks he hears Jesus saying reveals the devil's character.

I think the best way to understand Jesus' response to the devil is to call it an invitation. Jesus turns both the devil's desire and the devil's diagnosis of their situation on their ears. First we rearrange Jesus' words "Man does not live by bread alone" to read, "By bread alone man does [READ: will] not live." In other words, Jesus is saying, we risk putting ourselves in an even more precarious situation were I to give that commandment ("command this stone to become a loaf of bread"). It is actually safer here by me (READ: Jesus) where we have no bread. Jesus is not being pious; he is being practical. Jesus is inviting the devil to enjoy a greater security.

The whole point of Israel's manna episode in the desert was that the manna that God supplied was not-bread, just as hunger is not-bread. God "afflicted you and made-you-hungry, / and had you eat the *mahn . . . in order to make you know* / that not by bread alone do humans stay-alive, / but rather by all that issues at YHWH's order do humans stay-alive" (Dt 8:3).[23] To understand *mahn* ("manna") you must understand that both *mahn* and the affliction that accompanies it are the same things. The hunger and the non-bread are the same. *Mahn* did not satisfy hunger: *mahn* and hunger both pointed to the same ultimate source of satisfaction. Manna's exotic nature was not there to draw attention to its divine origin as a substitute for bread in a precarious situation but to transform the understanding of the situation's precariousness. Affliction is described in positive terms. Its "non-breadness" was to show the extent to which one could commit one's life to an absolute dependency upon God. This seems to be a consistent currency of exchange in a divine economy where accepting irony is the key to the transaction. Jesus is actually telling the devil that it is safer here by his side where there is no reliance on commanding that stones become bread; instead of that command, there is an absolute dependence on God. Jesus is encouraging the devil to join him in a satisfying abundance by embracing absolute dependence.

The devil doesn't get it. His fundamental mentality is a "scarcity mentality," which he projects upon Jesus.[24] The question he hears Jesus asking him in that pregnant silence is "What do you have to offer me?" To the devil's ear, "Man does not live by bread alone" means Jesus is pointing to an appetite left unsatisfied, exactly the opposite of the satisfaction we can hear in Jesus' voice. The devil concludes Jesus needs something more and is willing to consider whatever the devil might have to offer: for instance, "the world." The second temptation is composed of just such an offer from the devil. This only serves to whet the devil's appetite. Nothing so stimulates the devil's appetite as the discovery of another appetite.

The Second Temptation

Then the devil led him up and showed him in an instant all the kingdoms of the world. And the devil said to him, "To you I will give their glory and all this authority; *for it has been given over to me, and I give it to anyone I please.* If you then will worship me, it will all be yours."

Jesus answered him, "It is written, 'Worship the Lord your God, and serve only him.'" (Lk 4:5–8, italics mine)

I would first like to note some of the differences between Luke's passage and Matthew's. First, Matthew has the offer of a kingdom as the third and not the second temptation, interrupting any dramatic continuity between this episode and the first. Keeping Jesus and Satan separate, at arm's length, would not be out of character for Matthew. He has as Jesus' first words after hearing the devil's offer, "Away with you, Satan, for it is written" (Mt 4:10), words that unmistakably convey opposition to the devil's offer. It is only in Luke that the italicized phrase above appears. This phrase, "for it has been given over to me and I give it to anyone I please," could be said to serve as the devil's property deed. Matthew omits the phrase and has Jesus respond to the devil's offer of the kingdoms with an antagonistic dismissal of the devil's claim, as we have seen.

I want to suggest that the best way to read Luke's version is to accept that (1) the devil has made an offer to give something to Jesus that has already been given to him; (2) Jesus has listened to that offer and considered it legitimate, specifically, the claim to have "all the kingdoms of the world" to give, as well as the right to dispose of them as he chooses; and (3) Jesus has suggested, actually reminded, the devil that the best place to carry through on his offer "to give" is to give it to God.

The best support for my interpretation can be found in the antecedent self-contained passage in Deuteronomy that concludes Jesus' response to the devil:

10 Now it shall be
    when YHWH your God brings you to the land that he swore
            to your fathers, to Avraham, to Yitzhak, and to
            Yaakov, *to give you,*
    towns great and good that you did not build,
11 houses full of every good-thing that you did not fill,
    cisterns hewn out that you did not hew,
    vineyards and olive-groves that you did not plant,
    and you eat and are satisfied,

12   *take-you-care,*
      lest you forget YHWH
      who brought you out of the land of Egypt, out of a house of serfs.
13   *YHWH your God you are to hold-in-awe,*
      him you are to serve,
      by his name you are to swear!

(Dt 6:10–13, italics mine)[25]

Jesus' response to the devil's offer is a quotation of verse 13. The preceding verses of Deuteronomy describe an extraordinary act of giving. They also recognize, at the end of verse 11, that the act of giving will inevitably result in a moment of crisis for the relationship from which the giving originates. When you eat and are satisfied— the sense seems to be "having eaten your fill"—then, at that very moment, you are at risk, and you must "take-you-care."[26] Not eating and apparent dissatisfaction had provided the occasion for the dramatic conflict of the first temptation and led to the temptations of the second. Deuteronomy locates this time of peril, it is worth noting, at the very period we have identified as the historical parallel of both Israel's then-contemporary situation and the temptation setting: balanced between exodus/exile and the entry into the promised land. In the second temptation, Jesus is positioned within this Lukan drama to play the role that "take-you-care," which is prescribed by our transition verse, fulfills structurally in Deuteronomy.

How is it that you are to "take care" at this time of crisis? In the simplest sense, you must not allow what one has been given to cause one to lose sight of the "giver," YHWH himself. Verses 12 and 13 can be rephrased "Hold not to what you have, but hold God in awe." In effect, the verses are saying, do not let what you have been given through the relationship compromise the relationship.

I commented earlier that in the second temptation we see the increase of the devil's desire. How is it that the devil's appetite can increase? What is it he can lack, since he obviously has so very much: "all the kingdoms of the world" are his, he assures us. In Matthew, Jesus and the devil concentrate on a view of the kingdoms from a mountain vista with all the clarity such a perspective offers (Mt 4:8). In Luke it is only for "an instant" that the actual kingdoms are in view. We have the devil referring to his possessions so often the actual kingdoms are blurred behind the cloud of his possessiveness. The desirability of the devil's possessions blurs into the desirability of his desire. The devil's every effort is focused on getting Jesus to desire the devil's desire. The devil's desire to be worshiped is the surfacing of an appetite that can only be satisfied by another appetite. Luke has given us a textbook demonstration of the cloud of mimetic possession and the reality of mimetic desire.

Luke may or may not have been a student of mimetic desire. He was a witness to the abundant faithfulness of God, and a student of what disposition of man would place him in the most intimate relationship to that God. He has twice in the temptation narrative given the same answer: if you have nothing, take away even more so that you can have abundantly; if you have been given much, give it all away so that you can receive. Luke has identified as the very heart of the right relationship to God the Deuteronomic affirmation of the desire of God and the discovery of the wayward desire of man. That was the gift that was received during Israel's affliction in the wilderness. To become a "you-are," you are "to serve him" (Dt 6:13, rearranged). Jesus has yoked himself to the Deuteronomic relationship. Fidelity to Deuteronomy is at the heart of Jesus' effort to offer the devil guidance, even relationship. Matthew will observe that this same fidelity is one of the cornerstones of Jesus' later ministry: "Take my yoke upon you, and learn from me" (Mt 11:29). Accepting—as if receiving a gift—and becoming a "serve-him *you-are*" is to yoke yourself to God, to know yourself as the work of another.

The devil, by contrast, holds his possessions in awe—"their glory and all this authority"—and is insistent upon maintaining his own disposition towards these possessions, the most precious of which to him are the appetites that surround him. The next temptation will give a hint of the ultimate outcome of that disposition. The third temptation makes an explicit reference to the Passion. It "refers" to the Passion as "an opportune time." Jesus has been treating the temptation episodes as an opportune time for the devil. By insisting upon framing his own opportune time the devil will set in motion a string of events where, irony of ironies, his assertion of ownership and *opportunity* to give will be fulfilled. The devil will indeed ultimately "hand over." But obviously "none of the rulers of this age understood this; for if they had, they would not have crucified the Lord of Glory" (1 Cor 2:8).

A Hypothesis

It is no surprise that the "rulers of this age" misunderstood Jesus' identity. The great problem of this age was to understand and fulfill Jewish identity. If the age's answers to that problem left Jesus unsatisfied, then Jesus was likely to remain incomprehensible to the age. The devil may have even been gratified by their misunderstanding and included it in his calculations: the greater Jesus' isolation, the more likely Jesus can be convinced to take matters into his own hands. The third temptation is not the devil's last all-or-nothing chance to entrap Jesus. It will be the devil's most opportune time, during this encounter at least, to convince Jesus that he alone is in control of his identity and his destiny.

N. T. Wright offers a useful summary of the identities that were available to a Jew of first-century Palestine:

> With a certain oversimplification we can trace easily enough the three options open to Jews in Jesus' day. . . . First, the quietist and ultimately dualist option, taken by the writers of the Dead Sea Scrolls at Qumran: separate yourself from the wicked world and wait for whatever God is going to do. Second, the compromise option taken by Herod: build yourself fortresses and palaces; get along with your political bosses as well as you can . . . , and hope that God will validate it somehow. Third, the zealot option [among whom Wright includes the Pharisees]: . . . say your prayers, sharpen your swords, make yourselves holy to fight a holy war, and God will give you a military victory that will also be the theological victory of good over evil, of God over the hordes of darkness, of the Son of Man over the Monsters.[27]

I would like to suggest that the temptation story provides a Lukan synopsis of Jesus' encounters with these three identities that characterized first-century Palestinian Jews, with an emphasis on the Essene-like community at Qumran. For instance, the Qumran community believed they should be separate from the world and removed themselves to the desert. Jesus, of course, immediately after his baptism by John in the Jordan, enters the wilderness. If Jesus was baptized by John at Bethabara (considered one of the two most likely baptismal locations), then Jesus entered the wilderness in very close proximity to Qumran.[28] I began by showing that Jesus may be in the wilderness as an outcast. The Essenes viewed themselves as the elect; this idea has as its corollary that there are the nonelect. This paradigm of election became the most intense in the expulsion of former members. The expelled ones became like outcasts, a life-threatening position to be in for one who had sworn to eat no food except that of the Essene community.[29] The devil comes upon Jesus in just such a life-threatening situation. We also saw how Luke linked Jesus to Adam (for example, the genealogical kinship that Luke elaborates immediately prior to Jesus entering the desert). Consider Luke's juxtapositions alongside this self-reflection from Qumran: "to the penitents of the desert . . . to whom all the glory of Adam shall belong."[30]

Almost no imaginative effort is required to see the affinity between accepting the devil's second temptation offer to Jesus of kingdoms and the choice represented by Wright's "compromise option" of entering into power-sharing relationships with the Romans, as Herod and the Jerusalem priests chose to do. For the average first-century Jew, it would have taken no imagination whatsoever to conclude that the devil had been given the kingdoms of the world: the too visible presence of so many Romans was proof enough. All that remained was to exchange the right Jewish leader for the wrong Roman ones, a trade the devil for his part appears willing to make.

The Essenes had two beliefs that would complicate leading an Essene sympathizer to the Temple. They considered the current Temple illegitimate and refused to participate in the Temple cult.[31] And while the Essenes "looked forward to a dramatic change in the future, . . . [namely,] the *eschaton*,"[32] which would lead to God's return with a new Temple to follow, they also followed a praxis that did not allow active revolt.[33] If the devil did first encounter Jesus in an Essene setting, the devil had to be especially pleased with the opportunity Jesus gave them to leave the desert by being willing to be shown "the world." The devil's practical problem, now that the Temple is in sight, is to find a way to have Jesus jump at the opportunity for "dramatic change" that is waiting for him near the Temple, where a party of insurrection is waiting for the opportunity for its own eschaton.

The Third Temptation

> But there arose no further prophet in Israel like Moses,
> Whom YHWH knew face to face.[34]

The third temptation can seem bizarre. As if its near-continuous awkwardness were not frustration enough, there is also the failure of most interpretations to explain the prominence in the story of the phrase "you will not dash your foot against a stone" (4:11). This is perhaps *the* signature Girardian phrase,[35] and to let it pass without explanation is as incomplete an account of this temptation as a portrait of Mae West would be that doesn't explain "Why don't you come up and see me sometime?"

Luke continues his account:

> The devil took him to Jerusalem, and placed him on the pinnacle of the temple, saying to him, "If you are the Son of God, throw yourself down from here, for it is written, 'He will command his angels, concerning you, to protect you,' and 'On their hands they will bear you up, so that you will not dash your foot against a stone.'" Jesus answered him, "It is said, 'Do not put the lord your God to the test.'" When the devil had finished every test, he departed from him until an opportune time. (Lk 4:9–13)

While it is not entirely clear what Jesus would receive by accepting the devil's offer, it becomes clear later what acceptance here would have made it possible to avoid. By rejecting this opportunity Jesus will later find himself in the demonic grip of a different "opportune time":

Then Satan entered into Judas . . . and began to look for an opportunity to betray him. . . . Suddenly a crowd came and the one called Judas . . . was leading them. . . . When those who were around him saw what was coming, they asked, "Lord, should we strike with the sword?" Then one of them struck the slave of the high priest and cut off his right ear. But Jesus said, "No more of this!" . . . Jesus said to the chief priests . . . "When I was with you day after day in the temple, you did not lay hands on me. But this is your hour, and the hour of darkness." Then they seized him and led him away, bringing him into the high priest's house. (Lk 22:47–54)

The following outline should help to make the structural parallels clear:

Temptation	Arrest
I. A. He will command his angels, concerning you, to protect you.	II. A. Those who were with him . . . asked, "Lord, should we strike with the sword?" . . . But Jesus said, "No more of this!"
I. B. On their hands they will bear you up, so that you will not dash your foot against a stone, that is, so that no offense is taken at you.	II. B. "Day after day . . . you did not lay hands on me. But this is your hour." They seized him and led him away (in order to find an offense with which to charge him).

I have added the clarifying clause "so that no offense is taken at you." The word Luke uses, *proskope*, translated in the NRSV as "dashing your foot against a stone," is better translated "an occasion for taking offense."[36] "Taking offense" to Jesus almost literally describes what occurs at the betrayal, arrest, and crucifixion.

Jesus responds to the devil's offer by quoting once again from Deuteronomy: "It is said, 'Do not put the Lord your God to the test.'" But while we as readers of the entire gospel know what the structural successor to the third temptation will be—an arrest that leads to the cross—we do not yet know here what the third temptation is or why it represents a temptation at all. The presence of the devil, as we saw in the first two temptations, is not enough to identify an option as a temptation and disqualify it as a choice.

Our best guide to the temptation is to rely upon Jesus' insight into the situation. Jesus quotes from the Deuteronomic injunction that was derived from the wilderness incident at Meribath-Kadesh, where Moses intervened to relieve a life-threatening thirst for Israel and a life-threatening crisis for him by striking a rock and bringing forth water (Ex 17:1–7). This incident had left a stain because Israel had asked, in the words of Moses, "Is the Lord among us or not?" In other words, Israel had doubted the presence of God, and Moses himself was not without blame in addressing Israel's doubt.

The situation posed by the devil would now seem to be fairly easy to understand. If we begin with Jesus' answer (and keeping in mind that in the Deuteronomic context "testing God" means doubting his presence), the devil appears to have placed Jesus in a risky situation and then challenged Jesus to ignore the risk and jump. Jesus' willingness to jump would be the sign that Jesus trusts God to be present to protect him.

Why does Jesus not "throw himself down . . . here?" The devil is offering Jesus an opportunity, an occasion to accomplish something visibly, if only Jesus will "throw himself down." But this is a very hard "throw" to catch. We have considered the possibility that the word simply means "jump," jump being a one-word summation of "throwing yourself off a cliff." Jumping, though, would represent, if anything, the consequence following upon a decision, not the act of choice itself. Luke is clearly focused on Jesus' intentionality.

The verb "throwing" as it is used here does have the quality of intentionality we would expect. If we examine the Greek text we find that *ballo*, here *bale*, is predominantly a verb of intentional, directed throwing, as in throwing one thing at another with a goal in mind. *Seauton* ("yourself") is in the accusative, indicating the object thrown. The object thrown has to be first chosen and then taken in hand. The phrase *bale seauton*, given the accusative case of *seauton* and the transitive nature of *bale*, could easily be translated "Decide upon yourself, and throw." Luke is referring in principle to the pitcher whose decision about what pitch to throw is crucial. The act of throwing in which the pitcher's choice becomes embodied is the origin of every play.

Who is the "yourself" that is to be decided upon? It is not as simple a question as it seems. A better question would be "*What* is *your-self*?"

Seauton, once again, is in the accusative. *Seauton's* accusative case tells us that it occupies a grammatical spot, the accusative case where what is thrown is named, that could be occupied by another, that is, something else could be thrown. The only constant is throwing, which is really choosing. We still do not know what the devil's strategy is, but it seems to depend upon keeping hidden that there is a choice involved. The better other possibilities are kept hidden, the more likely that Jesus will agree with the devil that "your-self" is the thing to "throw." Since telling someone what their "your-self" is can provide such good camouflage for keeping the possibility of other opportunities or choices out of sight, "your-self" can offer ample opportunities for the devil to practice the deceptions that are his stock-in-trade. Even though choosing "yourself" seemed straightforward, it was not. Choosing "yourself" in fact represents a crucial choice.

Near the end of the chapter in which the temptation story occurs, Luke, in another departure from Matthew, has a story remarkable for the transparency it brings to the very type of problem we have in the temptation. Whereas the devil had suggested that Jesus "throw" himself down, in this story a demon must throw down the man he is possessing because Jesus has ordered him to "be silent and come out of him." The story gives us insight not only into what "throwing down" may mean, but also how it may have a role in the putting together, or the taking apart, of a man's self:

> In the synagogue there was a man who had the spirit of an unclean demon, and he cried out with a loud voice, "Let us alone! What have you to do with us, Jesus of Nazareth? Have you come to destroy us? I know who you are, the Holy One of God." But Jesus rebuked him, saying, "Be silent, and come out of him!" *When the demon had thrown him down before them, he came out of him without having done him any harm.* (Lk 4:33–35, emphasis mine)

Luke has a delightful literary touch that supports an exegetical link between these two stories. *Bale,* the manner of throwing in the temptation, is intentional, directed, as if one were throwing a spear at a target. The *throwing* in the casting out/healing is *hripsan,* which is much more a "throwing about" or "casting away," with nuances suggesting, for instance, a soldier throwing away his weapons to hasten his retreat, or, in this story, a demon losing control of that over which just a few seconds earlier seemed to be enough his own that he could use it as a part of himself.

What the demon has experienced as enough his own that he can use as a part of himself is the very thing the possessed man seems to experience as "his-self" since "he" appears to have been submerged by being possessed. The demon knows that he and the man may be joined in one identity now, but he also knows that they are distinct, that they can be separated from one another, and that at least one of them is capable of returning to "him-self." The critical factor in the demon's self-identification appears to be whether he can speak as a crowd or is forced to speak to an individual. This explains the demon's change from "destroy us" to "I know" when talking about *himself* to Jesus (4:34). What the demon has known all along becomes objectively clear to the people of Capernaum only with Jesus in their midst: the self can harbor an intruder astute enough to the ways of the self to present itself as the self. Where at the point we first entered the story there appeared to be only one man, there were in fact three selves: the man-with-the-demon, the demon, and the man. Their unity and their distinctness crystallized side-by-side and instantaneously in that infinitesimal moment into which they were thrown.

Let us return to the third temptation and see whether this schematic Luke has laid out for us is of any use in understanding the devil's scheme. After bringing Jesus to where he wants him, the pinnacle of the Temple, the devil then immediately introduces the exact kind of triad Jesus uncovered in the healing/exorcism we have just examined: "you"; "Son of God"; and the identity we have been treating as elusive, "yourself." By itself, "yourself" appears innocuous, just as the devil's proposal centered on "you" and "Son of God" seems straightforward. Jesus either is or is not the Son, and if he is, he either will or will not jump. Whatever he decides, it would seem obvious enough that Jesus' decision comes down to following an ethical guideline, not making a personal decision about how he will get along in the world. But, for comparison, does the possessed man face an ethical decision or a personal problem?

We know from seeing the means by which a person's identity can be corrupted that Jesus' decision is entirely about personhood. We see it again in the devil's attempt to insinuate that to be "yourself" you only need to let the "Son of God" come into "you," just as for the man the "demon" had gone into "him," leaving "himself" divided. But the devil, skilled in seduction as he is, waits to introduce the real opportunity with which he is trying to seduce Jesus. The first mention of "Son of God" was a generality, meant to whet the appetite. Now the devil pulls out a picture of what Jesus can have: "He will command his angels concerning you, to protect you" (4:10).

Let's concentrate on what this sentence is truly about. It reflects a more developed effort by the devil to get Jesus to accede to and participate in the devil's primary aim, to get this flesh-and-blood Jesus ("you") to accept into himself the "Son of God" and become the self-possessed ("yourself") self that will throw itself down. Like a good salesman, the devil keeps the pressure on Jesus non-stop; notice how he entices by doubling the "you." This "you" is clearly his "customer." The promised benefactor "he" is also doubled: "He" will do this for "you," as will "his" agents do this for "you." Clearly, the devil wants to focus Jesus on what this "he" can do. This is nothing new; the temptations to this point could be renamed "the devil trying to convince Jesus what he can do."

There is one candidate who fulfills the requirement of being both a benefactor for Jesus and an appeal to Jesus' ego: the Son of God. The devil is not focused on convincing Jesus of the benefits of being the Son of God. He is determined to convince Jesus that being the Son of God makes it possible for Jesus to be his own benefactor.

To help us understand how crucial having the right attitude towards sonship is in this story, we can turn to another story focused on sonship and relationship to the father, namely, Luke's story of the prodigal son and his father. The younger son already enjoys, as heir, the use of his property, which Luke names *ousia,* his *being.* The only concession he must make toward his property, his being, as Jean-Luc Marion has elegantly pointed out, is that he must acknowledge that he receives the property as a gift, through another, the father.[37] This acknowledgement, though, is the very concession the son is not prepared to make. He is not content with just the use of property to be his own; he wants his *ousia,* his being, to be his own. The son is not satisfied by being able to enjoy the property, the *ousia* the father shares with him. Only having his being to dispose of by himself will satisfy the prodigal.

The devil is urging Jesus to follow the same road to satisfaction that the prodigal had traveled. The temptation we normally face in reading this passage, this third temptation, is to assume that the "he" with whom the devil entices Jesus by quoting scripture is God. Ironically, by reading the temptation this way, we make Jesus' faithfulness to the Father the same as the faithfulness of the elder son to their father. The elder son is proud because he limited his exposure to temptation. What he failed to realize was that he was also limiting his enjoyment of his father's generosity. The devil wanted to position Jesus to be one of these two sons. But Jesus would not take his Sonship in hand as if it were purely his own to dispose of as he might choose. Jesus hears the Father speak to him as the prodigal's father had spoken to his sons: "Son, you are with me always, and all that is mine is yours" (Lk 15:31). For this Son there will be no question of the presence of God.

We have seen how crucial this decision about sonship is. But why does the devil use this setting, the pinnacle of the Temple, and this offer, the immunity provided by being the Son of God, to "stumbling," to do his testing? There must be something in the larger setting that would potentially make Jesus more willing to give in to the devil's desire to corrupt the Sonship of the son.

From the pinnacle where the devil had placed him, Jesus would see Israel still in exile. There was at least one other figure in Israel's history that had been brought to a pinnacle to look upon an Israel not yet in the promised land. God had ordered Moses to the top of Mount Nebo, from which the promised land could be seen, but would allow Moses to go no further: "Although you may view the land from a distance, you may not enter it" (Dt 32:52).

Why was Moses not allowed to cross over into the promised land? In fact, his situation was much more drastic than simply not being allowed to accompany the people. God tells Moses that "you shall die there on that mountain that you ascend." God had ordered Moses to ascend the mountain. The unmistakable implication is that God in some way passed judgment on Moses' death, even if the details of that judgment are left somewhat vague. God is explicit, though, in telling Moses what his sin was:

> because you . . . broke-faith with me
> in the midst of the Children of Israel
> at the waters of Merivat Kadesh, . . .
> because you did not treat-me-as-holy
> in the midst of the Children of Israel.
> Indeed, at-a-distance you shall see the land,
> but there you shall not enter.
>
> (Dt 32:51–52)[38]

Why would Moses' punishment be so much greater than that of the people he led? Their sin would, if anything, appear to be greater than that of Moses. Every incident in the wilderness seems to include Moses as a beleaguered leader responding to the "testing" into which the people continually fall. But God appears tender towards the people; twice he calls them "children," even as he sends Moses up the mountain to his death. What could Moses have done that God will not forget; how did Moses "break faith" and fail to "treat-God-as-holy"?

The third Exodus temptation begins as expected. The people find themselves in a perilous situation and almost immediately begin to doubt that they are in God's care: "The people quarreled with Moshe, they said: / Give us water that we may drink!" (Ex 17:2). What happens next does not follow the form of the previous temptations. Moses responds to the people with "For-what do you quarrel with me? For-what do you test YHWH?" (17:2). Moses has equated quarreling with him with testing God.[39] Our own temptation as readers is to give Moses the benefit of the doubt and assume he is cautioning against testing and mentions himself only to add emphasis. But the Deuteronomic judgment forces us to accept that Moses has come dangerously close to considering himself the face of God. At Mara, at the moment of the first wilderness temptation, when the people complained of the bitter water, Moses had cried out to God, but he did not put himself before God among the people (15:24–25). God had already decided upon his response to the peoples' grumblings at Sinai before he ever spoke with Moses (16:2–8). Now here at Massah, Moses has the confidence of "his" past successes; he is no longer empty-handed in the presence of God.

God does not intervene, and the people redouble their complaints against Moses. Moses suddenly loses his confidence. His focus becomes the people's quarrel with him, and Moses starts to fear for his life: "What shall I do with this people? / A little more and they will stone me!" (17:4).

We immediately see that Moses has let fear for his life compromise his witness to the presence of God, but Moses and Israel's crisis is much more desperate than this. Israel is on the verge of stoning Moses. This potential stoning is a much more lethal threat to the journey to the promised land than a simple crisis in leadership relationships. If the people were to stone Moses, there is enormous risk that the stoning of Moses would be the new source of the peoples' cohesion. They would no longer be the people of the promised land. The people of Israel would have become the people gathered around Moses' grave. Peace would descend on this turbulent group. And Moses would be dangerously close to being regarded as a divinity. This averted result may be one of the great triumphs of God's forming of his people. Deuteronomy refers to this triumph in a way that we easily overlook: Moses was buried in a valley in the land of Moab "but no one knows his burial place to this day" (34:6, NRSV).[40] Moses' solitary death and lost grave may represent one of the great triumphs, as well as the great tragedy, of Deuteronomy. In any case, Deuteronomy regards the crisis at Massah as a time of such momentous importance that it ties Moses' fate to it.

Returning to Jesus' temptation, we recall that the devil regarded it as so momentous for Jesus that speaking of it properly required the devil to make promises for Jesus' fate. If we think about Moses as we listen to the devil's promises to Jesus, it suddenly sounds as if the devil has designed his promises to allay concerns very much like those the fateful crisis of Moses would bring to mind. Where Moses had found himself in danger of being stoned, the devil assures Jesus "that angels [will] protect you," that Jesus will not even have to risk "dash[ing his] foot against a stone." In fact, Jesus can circumvent even the possibility of this risk. Moses had had to trust in the presence of God in order to make his way in the wilderness. When the people made a sudden claim on Moses, demanding what only the presence of God could provide, Moses found himself in a precarious situation. The devil tells Jesus that as the Son of God he runs no such risk, because as the son, he has the right to demand his *ousia* from his Father and cut the tie of dependence on the Father.

The third temptation, and with it all three temptations, now comes into focus. From Mount Nebo, as he approached his own death, Moses looked out on a people about to enter the promised land, but at great cost to himself. From the pinnacle of the Temple, Jesus looks out on an Israel once again in exile, waiting for a new leader to lead the return to the new Israel, but at an unknown cost. The devil has his answer ready: "For the Son of God, at no cost." The devil concentrates Jesus' attention on both the plight and promise of Israel, and the wonderful future that awaits Jesus, at no cost to himself, if only Jesus will take himself in hand as Son of God and "throw himself down." But this son is not tempted by the seduction of ending the exile, because he already knows "the Father is with him always and all that the Father has is his." Talk of exile can only be a fiction, another seduction from the seducer.

Notes

1. Neil Forsyth, *The Old Enemy: Satan and the Combat Myth* (Princeton, NJ: Princeton University Press, 1987), 4. Forsyth discusses the need to see Satan always as an actor in a story; it is my own contribution to see Luke's temptation story as uniquely satisfying Forsyth's observation. I follow tradition throughout and refer to the authorship of the Gospels by their attributed authors.

2. Eric Bentley, *The Life of the Drama* (New York: Applause, 1991), 32.

3. Forsyth, *The Old Enemy*, 4.

4. Ibid.

5. There is general agreement, though not unanimity, that Luke dates from 80–85 CE, and Matthew from 85–90 CE. See Bruce M. Metzger and Michael D. Coogan, ed., *The Oxford Companion to the Bible* (New York: Oxford University Press, 1993), 472, 502–3.

6. I say "appears" because it may be more our focus than Matthew's. Matthew's language may take the form it does because he acquired an immunity to the risk involved that we have since lost.

7. Bentley, *The Life of the Drama*, 61.

8. Forsyth, *The Old Enemy*, 4.

9. Bentley, *The Life of the Drama*, 32.

10. Raymund Schwager, S.J., *Jesus in the Drama of Scripture: Toward a Biblical Doctrine of Redemption*, trans. James G. Williams and Paul Haddon (New York: Crossroad, 1999), 12.

11. The very term *persona*, so important to Trinitarian theology, is related to the *dramatis personae* of theater. See Mary Hatch Marshall, "Boethius' Definition of *Persona* and Mediaeval Understanding of the Roman Theater," *Speculum* 25 (1950): 471–79.

12. Luke 11:17. All quotations are from the New Revised Standard Version of the Bible unless otherwise specified.

13. See, for example, Forsyth, *The Old Enemy*, 4.

14. See, for example, René Girard, in *The Girard Reader*, edited by James Williams (New York: Crossroads, 1996), especially part 4, "The Scapegoat and Myths of Persecution," 97–144.

15. René Girard, "Are the Gospels Mythical?" *First Things* 62 (April 1996): 27–31.

16. In both senses: (1) managing to function as oneself, while (2) filling a functional role for another.

17. N. T. Wright, *The New Testament and the People of God* (Minneapolis: Fortress Press, 1992), 335–36. The emphasis is Wright's, who credits the use of E. P. Sanders' categories.

18. Wright, *New Testament and the People of God*, 268–69.

19. Ibid., 337.

20. Ibid., 262.

21. Ibid., 265.

22. Yohanan Aharoni and Michael Avi-Yonah, *The Macmillan Bible Atlas* (New York: Macmillan, 1968), plates 54, 227.

23. Everett Fox, ed., *The Five Books of Moses: Genesis, Exodus, Leviticus, Numbers, Deuteronomy*, vol. 1 of *The Schocken Bible*, trans. Everett Fox (New York: Random House, 1995), 888–89; italics mine.

24. I would like to give a general credit to Stephen Covey for his insights into "scarcity mentalities"; see *The Seven Habits of Highly Effective People* (New York: Free Press, 1989, repr. 2004) and *Living the Seven Habits: The Courage to Change* (New York: Free Press, 2000).

25. Fox, *The Five Books of Moses*, 881.

26. Ibid.

27. N. T. Wright, *The Challenge of Jesus: Rediscovering Who Jesus Was and Is* (Downers Grove, IL: InterVarsity Press, 1999), 37.

28. Aharoni and Aui-Yonah, *The Macmillan Bible Atlas*, plates 224, 227; N. T. Wright, *Jesus and the Victory of God: Christian Origins and the Question of God*, vol. 2 (Minneapolis: Fortress Press, 1996), 161.

29. Wright, *New Testament and the People of God*, 207.

30. Quoted in ibid., 265.

31. Wright, *Jesus and the Victory of God*, 411.

32. E. P. Sanders, quoted in Wright, *The New Testament and the People of God*, 208. Sanders makes clear that he considers the *eschaton* to be primarily a category applied by modern scholars to aid classification of first-century belief.

33. Wright, *The New Testament and the People of God*, 206.

34. Deuteronomy 34:10, in Fox, *Five Books of Moses*, 1014.

35. See, for example, René Girard, *Things Hidden since the Foundation of the World*, trans. Stephen Bann and Michael Metteer (Stanford, CA: Stanford University Press, 1987), 416–31.

36. David McCracken, *The Scandal of the Gospels: Jesus, Story, and Offense* (New York: Oxford University Press, 1994), 193–97.

37. Jean-Luc Marion, *God Without Being: Hors-Texte*, trans. Thomas A. Carlson (Chicago: University of Chicago Press, 1991), 95–100.

38. Fox, *Five Books of Moses*, 1008.

39. See Fox, *Five Books of Moses*, 351: "Notice how the text equates quarreling with Moshe and testing YHWH."

40. Cf. Fox, *Five Books of Moses*, 1014: "He buried him / in a valley in the land of Moav, / opposite Bet Pe'or, / and no man has knowledge of the site of his burial-place until this day" (34:6).

SEVENTEEN

A Gospel That Preaches Nonviolence and Yet Provokes Violence

GÉRARD ROSSÉ

As a biblical scholar, I would like to offer a few reflections on the gospel, which I understand to be a message of peace that could, nonetheless, provoke a violent reaction.[1] In this way, I hope to engage in an implicit dialogue with the thesis of René Girard.

It is well known that the central proclamation of Jesus concerns the proximity of the kingdom of God, definitively awaited at the end of time. Jesus did not, however, limit himself to this simple announcement. Those who entered into contact with him and opened themselves to his message experienced this proximity of the kingdom in both his words and his deeds. For these people, the proximity of the kingdom proclaimed by Jesus already began to produce its effects in history: God revealing his love, realizing his salvific will, and inaugurating his kingdom, a kingdom of grace and mercy. In his person, Jesus brought about the direct intervention of God into the society of human beings in a way that was for his contemporaries rather upsetting. Before the God who acts in Jesus, they understood, one must make a choice, and undertake an existential decision.

From whatever vantage point we might consider Jesus' proclamation, its social character is virtually incontestable. Jesus was not merely satisfied with the conversion of a few individuals; his aim instead was the renewal of Israel as a people. Moreover, the beatitudes in their original forcefulness demonstrate that Jesus does not have in mind simply an interior and spiritual reality, but also a concrete situation of social injustice. The coming of the kingdom of God must lead to a new society, to new interpersonal relations that are based upon a love that requires the acceptance of the other, thus going beyond the relationship of dominance and submission.

But in order for this new society to come about, Jesus does not envision the necessity of overturning the Roman administration and driving them out in order to make way for his own political agenda. Instead, Jesus explicitly distanced himself from movements advocating the use of violence, such as that of the Zealots. The social revolution that he proposed, by way of contrast, was to begin in the heart of human beings, in the seat of individual self-consciousness and the locus where profound decisions are made. Jesus strongly urged human beings to open themselves to the nearness of God he was announcing, to welcome divine pardon, to experience the personal and freeing love of God. In this way, the human being was called to a radical conversion.

Moreover, this transformation of the human heart did not mean that Jesus intended the human being to be simply a more virtuous or more pious individual. Rather, Jesus desired to recreate the human being altogether, to give him the capacity to love, to pardon others, and thus to create new relationships and alliances, whether those relationships be pleasant or unpleasant, and whether they take place among individuals who are white or black, rich or poor, and so forth. The encounter with the God of Jesus, these followers understood, compels the individual to move beyond the logic of a competitive mimesis.

In this regard, the parable of the unforgiving servant in Matthew 18:23–35 is important. The king, who has forgiven the servant's enormous debt, does not send him to the Temple to pray but invites him to act similarly with those who are in debt to him. In other words, Jesus suggests through the parable a new sort of mimesis, a mimesis of God. This divine imitation becomes possible because the servant has already experienced God's unconditional pardon. In all interpersonal relationships among human beings, God is an interested party, whose presence makes it possible to transcend any interpersonal obstacles that may arise.

It is well known that Jesus had a predilection for marginalized individuals. Yet he did not incite them to rebellion; more exactly, he stood in solidarity with them in assuming their state of legal impurity. Jesus' solidarity with the marginalized, however, does not mean that he wished

to constitute a proletariat that do battle with the leisured class. Historically speaking, the intention of Jesus was to integrate the poor into
the Israel of God, because they, too, are the sons of Abraham. On a
deeper level, the encounter with the God of Jesus, who loves each individual personally—regardless of one's merits, or even one's social or
religious situation—has transformed those who were socially marginalized by the "right thinking" society, by giving them back their proper
human dignity. In coming into contact with the God of Jesus, they re-
discovered dignity, liberty, and hope. Jesus fostered within them the
consciousness of the priority of the human being as a person, over and
above any power of domination, whether that domination be political
or religious.

This solidarity of Jesus with the marginalized was certainly provocative in the eyes of both the political elite and other religious movements. Not only did his solidarity question the established order, it concretely demonstrated his conscious strategy of *integration* rather than
the exclusion often practiced by other movements of the day. Jesus
sought to construct a society that affirms its own identity, not in dis-
criminating against but in welcoming each and everyone in their diversity in so far as all are children of the same Father. In acting in this
manner, however, Jesus created for himself numerous enemies among
the leaders of the country and other religious currents. Jesus' proclamation of the kingdom thus provoked violence against himself. It
was, therefore, precisely his message of nonviolence that gave rise to
violence.

The Sermon on the Mount, Love of Enemies, and Nonviolence

Jesus proclaimed the law of the kingdom of God to be a love without
boundaries and an unlimited forgiveness that, in turn, becomes the
foundation for a revolution of universal brotherhood, inviting each person to overcome the violence that is present within the human heart.
The crux of this teaching is found in the demand to love one's enemies and in the appeal to nonviolence, which is summarized in what

is usually referred to as the Sermon on the Mount (Mt 5:38–48; Lk 6:27–36). This catechesis comes from the Q source, but the primitive core no doubt goes back to the historical Jesus. It bears his characteristic imprint: his radicalism, concreteness, and universality.

In this chapter, I wish to deal neither with the numerous practical questions connected with the demands Jesus makes nor to focus on the concrete problems that would naturally arise in applying them to different social and political situations.[2] Instead, what particularly interests me is the fact that, in Jesus' proclamation of the kingdom, the demand to love one's enemies is tightly bound up with the novelty of the *proximity* of the kingdom of God. The demands of the sermon, therefore, must characterize the behavior of the human being in the times inaugurated by the irruption of the *eschaton*, which is to say, the end of time. The sermon is not the formulation of a political strategy. Rather, Jesus places the human being who welcomes the kingdom of God prior even to the demand to love, a demand that actualizes itself each time that the disciple lets himself be seized by the reality of the kingdom and consequently behaves as a son of God.

Matthew's last two antitheses in his Sermon on the Mount are particularly meaningful. With respect to the *lex talionis*, Jesus counters with nonretaliation; that is, to the hatred of one's enemies, he responds with the demand to love one's enemies. In order to counteract violence, Jesus exhorts his disciples to respond in a contrary fashion. In this way, the chain of violence is interrupted by an equally great force of nonviolence, and the disciple shows himself to be a son of the Father. In the sermon, Jesus exhorts his listeners to "love your enemies . . . in order to be a son of your Father who is in Heaven, since he causes the sun to rise upon the evil-doers and the good, and the rain to fall upon the just and the unjust" (Mt 5:44–45). Indeed, the motif of mimesis is clearly affirmed, but it must be noted that it is a question of conscious imitation of a God who is essentially antimimetic (which is to say, not to be perceived as a rival) and who gives the gifts of life, like the sun and rain, to each and every person, even to those who do not return his love.

Love for one's enemy and the renunciation of violence when put into practice by the disciple mediate and reveal the face of a God who does not correspond to human conceptions of God. To follow the God of Jesus demands a deep transformation, a conversion, that changes the individual from within, disarming the violence he bears within himself. This conversion carries with it the experience of divine pardon, an experience that reveals man to himself, although at the same time freeing him and opening him to love. Love becomes the new mode of *being;* one essentially receives one's self in the gift to the other, in being a son of God.

Divine Sonship in the Pauline and Johannine Letters

To be a "son of God" is not just a simple metaphor. In the relationship between the God revealed by Jesus, who is close at hand, and the individual who welcomes him is born a *perichoresis,* an interior reciprocity, which makes of the believer a new creation (2 Cor 5:17). The human response to this love is neither mechanical nor coldly rational, but rather, the human being experiences this *perichoretical* encounter as an interior demand emerging from the depths of one's being, as a call from God.

The theological reflection of Paul speaks of "the love of God deposited in our hearts by the Holy Spirit, which has been given to us" (Rom 5:5), and John, too, affirms that Jesus communicates, to those who are his own, the love of the Father for the Son, in order that it might circulate among his disciples (Jn 15:9). In addition, John does not hesitate to say that "he who loves is born of God" (1 Jn 4:7). Love appears, therefore, as a vital demand that arises from the very being of the believer who is born from God.

To sum up briefly what we have said thus far, it is the nearness of God that changes relations among people. Human relationships are no longer simply formed between one person and another. More precisely, they are characterized by the presence of God himself in the relationship. This understanding is important when considering the system of mimesis and the expiatory victimization that René Girard has brought to light. The nearness of God impels one to love as a personal demand. One can very well understand from this perspective the sentence in 1 John 3:14–15: "He who does not love abides in death. Any one who hates his brother is a murderer, and you know that no murderer has eternal life abiding in him." The same author also cites the example of Cain and Abel: "We should love one another, and not be like Cain who was of the evil one and murdered his brother. And why did he murder him? Because his own deeds were evil and his brother's righteous" (1 Jn 3:11–12). Cain is guilty, and his violence is brought to the fore; the "mechanism of victimization" does not work. John remains coherent with the gospel of Jesus, and he has unveiled the extreme consequences: love is a question of life or death.

The Death of Jesus

Does not the salvation that he proclaimed already provide a solution capable of neutralizing the homicidal violence that sometimes dwells in the human heart? Moreover, must we not take into consideration the possibility that God can communicate love as the gift of his own divine life, and that this love is capable of generating for the believer new life? In order to understand how this communication happens, let us examine the death of Jesus, which the tradition of the Church unanimously affirms to be the salvific event par excellence.

Jesus announced a God who loves everyone without discrimination, who renounces demonstrating his own power but who nonetheless imposes radical demands upon human beings (for example, the love for one's enemies), and in this way breaks into the affairs of human beings. Such a God could not but upset the established order. Jesus was not subject to any illusions about the reactions of others, as certain of his parables show us. Jesus responds for example to the "grumbling" of the scribes and Pharisees in his audience by providing them with a mirror in the reaction of the workers of the first hour in the parable of the workers in the vineyard (Mt 20:10–12) or the reaction of the faithful son in the parable of the Prodigal Son (Lk 15:25–32). These reactions reflect the upset that the God of Jesus can occasion, by putting the last first and showing mercy to the sinful. Was Jesus deemed to be dangerous by other religious movements in Palestine, not to mention the Roman occupier, as a consequence of these teachings?

Historically, it is likely that Jesus' prophetic stance within Judaism and in particular his discourse about the Temple provoked his arrest.

In this regard, I would like to recall simply that Flavius Josephus' *Jewish Wars* credibly recounts that a certain Jesus, a son of Ananius, prophesied against the Temple and against Jerusalem shortly before the Jewish War. His sentence for that crime was flagellation. For Jesus, however, the son of Mary, condemnation to death seems from a political point of view to have been inevitable. The civil and religious authorities saw in him more than just an isolated madman!

The second part of the Gospel according to Mark is oriented toward the Passion, punctuated by the announcement of Jesus' suffering, death, and resurrection in a characteristic formula: "The Son of Man must suffer many things" (Mk 8:31). Undoubtedly this texts and others do not wish to present Jesus as submitting to an inexorable fate or to suggest that the Father willed that he die. Instead, Mark's reflection intends to explain the faithfulness of Jesus to the salvific design of God, namely, his free adherence to a divine will that wishes to reunite with human beings in their hearts, their hearts being both the foundation of their interpersonal relations and the place where evil and violence dwell. The Passion and death of Jesus are seen essentially as an experience of unity between Jesus and his Father. Where you find Jesus, you find the Father, and the two of them, by nonviolent means, penetrate to the roots of division and violence, namely, wherever God is absent.

Already in the pre-Marcan Passion narrative (imagined by biblical scholars), a central place is assigned to the cry of abandonment in the comprehension of Jesus' death: "My God, my God, why have you abandoned me?" (Mk 15:34). According to Mark and the passion narrative that preceded him, these are the only words spoken by Jesus on the cross. The opening of Psalm 22 is placed on the lips of the one crucified in order to explain in the form of a personal experience the scandal of a death by crucifixion understood as a divine malediction (cf. Dt 21:23).

Jesus' unconditional adhesion to the plan of the heavenly Father on behalf of humanity has brought him to the point of experiencing in his own person the absence of God that characterizes the sinful human condition. One could say that Jesus totally identifies himself with man at the moment when his love was wholly oriented towards God. Jesus lived his death under the sign of the absence of God at the moment of his greatest unity with the salvific will of the Father. In other words, in his death Jesus introduced his extreme solidarity with the human experience of the absence of God into his full filial communion with the Father. Through his obedience, even to the point of death lived as abandonment, Jesus has, so to speak, brought the Father into the human experience where the lack of relationship—and as a consequence rivalry, violence, and evil—reign.

In the person of the crucified one who cries out: "My God, my God, why have you abandoned me?" God has established his definitive presence among men. The God of Jesus has loosened all the bonds and undone all the barriers erected by the Mosaic law, superficially understood, in order to penetrate into the depths of human relations and to manifest his universal proximity. Henceforth, God is there where no one expects him to be. Moreover, he is present not as the God-Judge who wishes to punish evil-doers and condemn them to the pains of hell, but as the God who loves his enemies and pardons seventy times seven. He is the God capable of bringing different groups together and reuniting men among themselves.

One cannot see in the crucified Jesus only a victim of human violence. The crucified Jesus speaks candidly to humanity and reveals its situation to be a lie and its relationships false. Understood positively, the crucified Jesus reveals the presence of God in all those situations characterized by the absence of God so typical of the human condition. This means that everything that is dead, empty, separated, and marked by the absence of genuine relationships has been filled by the same love that originally caused it to be. The force of the resurrection is life, and it acts as a life force. In whatever situation one may be, one has the possibility of encountering God and of discovering one's own authenticity.

The novelty of the gospel is found in the proclamation of a God who loves without discrimination and who is faithful to himself even unto the death of Jesus. I cannot, however, gloss over the part of Jesus' proclamation that paradoxically appears to promote the idea of a God in opposition to the God spoken of earlier "who makes the sun rise and the rain fall upon the good and the bad alike." To those who do not welcome the message of Jesus, this proclaimed God could appear as a menacing judge. Here we come across what might be described as the "expected behavior" of the God revealed in the Mosaic law (or at least one version of it)—namely, that He is good with the good and stern with the evil-doers. Certainly, the Christian tradition and the redactor of the Gospel (and I am thinking in particular of Matthew) have a tendency to augment the sentences of judgment. Nonetheless, certain words transmitted by the Q source are in all likelihood the words of Jesus himself. I refer specifically to the threats of judgment proffered against the impenitent cities of Chorazin, Bethsaida, and Capernaum (Lk 10:13–15; Mt 11:21–23). There is incontestably therefore an element of violence in the words of Jesus.

How are we to understand this genre of invective in the mouth of Jesus? Does he know two different countenances of God? Must one distinguish between a time of patience when God employs mercy and offers an unlimited love to everyone and a final time of judgment when God will pay each according to his works? There can be no doubt that the heart of the message of Jesus concerns the God of grace who extends his goodness to everyone and who does not hesitate to leave the ninety-nine sheep to look for the lost one. This God is precisely the God of the *eschaton* who already erupts into history. The fact that the Gospel tradition containing the words of Jesus on the coming of the kingdom of God places this coming both in the present and the future confirms this identification. One could not imagine a difference between, on the one hand, the God who is proclaimed to be near and already causes us to feel the effects of his presence, and, on the other, the God who is still to come in a future intervention and from whom one awaits the eschatological kingdom.

It is this eschatological dimension of Jesus' proclamation that confers all the gravity upon the situation. It is not God who changes. It is man who finds a choice placed before him upon which his future depends. The God who offers to everyone his love without limit demands a response equally radical on the part of man. One cannot play hide-and-seek with such a God and his offer of salvation. When confronted with refusal or intransigence before a situation where the eternal destiny of man is decided, the voice of Jesus becomes menacing and his tone becomes harsher. Jesus assumes the function of the prophet and employs the traditional images of the God-Judge who condemns the recalcitrant.

In reality, it is not God who changes and then contradicts himself. As noted earlier, it is man who before the God of Jesus finds a choice of life or death. In this regard, the parable of the Prodigal Son (Lk 15:11–32) is helpful. The welcome that the father in the parable reserves for the son who had taken flight changes everything in the relations lived up until then by the elder son. He had to enter into the logic of his father's gratuitous love if he wished to maintain his place in the family. But it is not his father who pushes him away. The faithful son has his destiny in his own hands. He becomes his own judge, depending on his acceptance or refusal to renew his relationship with his brother. From this point of view, I think that John's theological reflection is coherent and clear. Everything is staked not on a morally good or bad behavior, but on whether one loves with the *love* that leads to eternal life and not with a false love that can lead to nothing more than illusion and death. In short, there is no other *life* than that of God as revealed by Jesus. Therefore, the human decision before the Word Incarnate is already an eschatological judgment.

Jesus and Jewish Leaders

There is finally another category of violent words, which Jesus (or so it could seem from one reading of the Gospels) directed against the Jewish people and their leaders. These words are encountered in particular in the Gospel of Matthew, which I would like now to take into consideration. The harshness of these words is difficult to reconcile with the demand to love one's enemies proclaimed by the same Gospel. In this polemic, the Gospel writer makes use of preexistent traditions, above all the Q source, but no doubt in large part accentuates the confrontation of Jesus with the fellow Jews of his time. In effect, a number of anachronisms (such as the role of the Pharisees viewed as Jesus' adversaries par excellence, as well as the minimization of differences between the Pharisees and Sadducees [Mt 16:6, 11, 12; cf. Mk 8:15–21]) confirms that the Gospel reflects not the conditions of Jesus' own time but the latter conflict between the Matthean church and the synagogue around the year 80.[3]

The confrontation is particularly violent starting in chapter 21. A series of three parables—the Two Sons, the Wicked Vine-Growers, and the Wedding Banquet (Mt 21:28–32; 21:33–41; 22:1–14)—assumes the form of a prophetic indictment against Israel. The accusations are formulated as infidelity of the people and of their representatives who refuse to believe, and the persecution of those who have been sent to them. Matthew synthesizes the history of Israel as a series of obstinate refusals and violence that culminate in the death of the Son.

The invectives of Matthew's Jesus reach their zenith with the maledictions launched against the scribes and the Pharisees (chapter 23). Once again the Gospel writer utilizes the scheme of a trial—for example, the formulation of accusations (Mt 23:13–33), followed by foreseen consequences: the destruction of the Temple. In apparent reference to this indictment, the Gospel writer seems to say there will not remain any "stone upon a stone" (Mt 23:34–39; 24:2). Jesus places the weight of responsibility for his death squarely upon the leaders of the people of Israel: "Upon you may come all the righteous blood shed on earth" (Mt 23:35). The assembled crowd, however, later assumes the responsibility for the death of Jesus: "His blood be upon us and upon our children!" (Mt 27:25).

Yet this is the same Gospel that highlights the Sermon on the Mount, which begins with the proclamation of beatitudes, with its exhortation to go beyond the *lex talionis* and to love one's enemies, not to judge. Surprisingly, this sermon ends with a violent indictment of Israel and its leaders. One would be correct in critiquing this text for its lack of coherence: how are we to reconcile the severe verdict against the leaders with the commandment to love one's enemies and the exhortation to nonviolence? We can safely discard right away the accusation that Matthew might be anti-Jewish. The Gospel writer is himself a Christian of Jewish origin, and he lives within a Judeo-Christian community. It is precisely this violence that shows his proximity to the synagogue. It is, therefore, a question of a conflict between brothers who are quarreling over the question of who is the true inheritor of the history of Israel.

To that, let us add one other consideration: the author of the first Gospel is just as severe against the possible infidelity of the members of his own church. The condemnation of an unfaithful Israel, far from inciting revengeful reactions, becomes, on the contrary, a warning to the Christian community not to become subject to the same fate as a consequence of its own infidelity. In the context of the polemic against the leaders of Israel, their behavior acquires the role of a negative model to be used as a *parenesis* for the believers themselves. It is, above all, infidelity to the divine will that Matthew indicts, whether it be Jewish or Christian. From this vantage point, Matthew is nonsectarian. There are, therefore, attenuating circumstances that can allow us to understand, if not in part excuse, the seeming violence of Matthew.

We must refer ourselves to the historic situation of the Matthean community in order to grasp a little better the apparent severity of the Gospel writer against the Jews. We are in the years 80–90 CE. Judaism seems to be in the process of reconstituting itself and of affirming its own religious identity under the aegis of Pharisaic doctrine. Christians, henceforth, will be considered "heretics," expelled from the synagogue, and persecuted as described in Matthew 22:6 and 23:34. As heretics, Christians would be denied any right to the heritage of the chosen people. Consequently, the Matthean church imagines itself to be a minority with its very existence threatened. To affirm its legitimacy as the authentic inheritor of the law and the promises of the testament of Israel is a matter of survival. Cut off from the synagogue, this community must legitimize its own religious system, not in accord with rabbinic Judaism, but *against* it, since rabbinic Judaism disputes the church's legitimacy. The rupture is made, and each system thereafter must stake its claim to legitimacy in opposition to the other. As one exegete says, "The cloth has been torn. One fights for the heritage."[4] Daniel Marguerat has drawn attention to the crucial moment when the Judeo-Christian church of Matthew, expelled from the synagogue, turned toward the pagan world.[5] In these circumstances, the Matthean polemic against the synagogue is no longer a family quarrel. The church henceforth sees itself placed outside of the institution of the synagogue and reacts therefore from the outside:

> Received outside of the Jewish debate, the Matthean polemic thus changes status. It does not seek any longer to justify its own identity as a Jewish sect, but now must legitimize itself as a religious system cut off from the institution of the synagogue.[6]

For its own survival, Matthew's community strongly affirmed its own identity as the true Israel, without that affirmation, however, authorizing them to persecute the Jews.

In such a historical situation, could the church of Matthew have acted differently, let us say, in a more evangelical way? Need it, in order to correspond to the demand to love its enemies, renounce its roots and its own convictions of faith? I think not. It is only regrettable that throughout the long history of the church, the Gospel of Matthew has served as a support for anti-Jewish persecutions.

Notes

1. This text is an edited version of Robert Connolly's English translation of Gérard Rossé's original French paper, "Un Evangile qui prêche la non-violence et suscite la violence."

2. I refer the reader to the classical work of Gerd Theissen, *The Sociology of Early Palestinian Christianity* (Philadelphia: Fortress, 1978).

3. I refer the reader to the work of Daniel Marguerat, *Le Jugement dans l'Evangile de Mattieu* (Geneva: Labor et Fides, 1995). Also pertinent is the Pontifical Biblical Commission's publication of *The Jewish People and Their Sacred Scriptures in the Christian Bible* (Vatican City: Libreria Editrice Vaticana, 2002).

4. Hubert Frankemölle, *Matthäus* (Dusseldorf: Patmos, 1994), cited in Marguerat, *Le Jugement*, 389.

5. Marguerat, *Le Jugement*, 579.

6. Ibid.

EIGHTEEN

"Exilic" Identities, the Samaritans, and the "Satan" of John

ANN W. ASTELL

Gérard Rossé and William Martin Aiken (following N. T. Wright) remind us that the people of first-century Palestine, a land under Roman occupation, claimed diverse "exilic" identities that aspired to regain (albeit by different means) the homeland promised to members of the true Israel. Commenting on the Gospel according to Matthew, Rossé emphasizes the sectarian divisions within Judaism that resulted in Christian Jews being expelled as heretics from synagogues by their Jewish coreligionists.[1] Aiken associates the temptations of the Lukan Jesus in the desert with the impulse to choose for himself from among the theoretically possible identities of the Essenes, the Herodians, the Sadducees, the Pharisees, or the Zealots—all of these standing as rival groups within Judaism from which Jesus somehow distanced himself for the sake of his unique vocation as the Father's Son, thus exposing himself to the fate of an outcast.

As Rossé and Aiken show, too, coloring the two evangelists' portrayals of Jesus is the figure of Moses, whose own identity struggle (as an Egyptian prince, an exiled murderer, a shepherd of Midian, the husband of Jethro's daughter and of a Cushite woman, and, finally, the divinely appointed leader of the Israelites) is understood to prefigure Jesus' double potential as a second Moses both to unite God's people and to be rejected by them as an outsider and a scapegoat. Rossé sees the Matthean Jesus on the mount (Mt 5–7) as a Moses-like lawgiver and judge, who opposes the actions of the "scribes and Pharisees [who] sit on Moses' seat," while at the same time upholding and advancing their teaching: "Do whatever they teach you . . . but do not do as they do" (Mt 23:2–3).[2] Aiken shows that Jesus' temptations in the desert are versions of temptations previously suffered by Israel and, more particularly, by Moses himself.

In this brief response essay, I wish to complement and corroborate the essays of Rossé and Aiken by pointing to yet another Israelitic identity potentially available to Jesus, that of the Samaritans, who claimed descent from Jacob and revered Moses, as did the Jews, but who were despised by the latter as a heretical offshoot.[3] Among the four Gospels, the Gospel according to John is the only one to record that Jesus preached to Samaritans. The passage, John 4:1–43, marks an important transition in the Gospel, coming, as it does, shortly after Jesus' cleansing of the Temple from the money-changers at Passover (2:13–22); his nocturnal conversation with the noble Jewish leader, Nicodemus (3:1–21); and the testimony to Jesus given by John the Baptist (3:22–36). It falls, moreover, between the first and second of Jesus' signs in Galilee: the miracle at the wedding feast in Cana (2:1–11) and the healing of the royal official's son (4:46–54). Jesus' chosen route between Jerusalem and Galilee goes through Samaria.

Unlike the synoptic Gospels, the Gospel according to John does not tell the story of Jesus' temptations in the wilderness. The meeting with the Samaritan woman at the well arguably parallels in many ways, however, those synoptic accounts. Jesus is alone. He thirsts and hungers. He converses with an interlocutor who probes him about his identity. When his disciples return from their errand, bringing him food, Jesus declines to eat, saying, "My food is to do the will of him who sent me and to complete his work" (Jn 4:34). He thus sounds a theme that, as Raymond E. Brown notes, "is not far from that of Deuteronomy 8:3: 'Man does not live by bread alone but by every word of God'—a citation attributed to Jesus in Matthew 4:4" (as well as Lk 4:4).[4]

While the Samaritan woman of John 4 is decidedly not the "devil" of Luke 4 and Matthew 4 (or the "Satan" of Mark 1:13)—indeed, she is emphatically human and ultimately becomes Jesus' disciple—she does have a shadowy, apparently promiscuous past (her five husbands perhaps representing Samaritan idol-worship). She is, most importantly, a Samaritan and thus belongs to a people with a "diabolic" relationship to the Jews.

What is certain is that John uses the episode consciously to comment on the satanic nature of mimetic competition (the very theme to which Aiken has drawn attention in his masterful exposition of Luke 4). The framing of the episode in Samaria is important. In John's account, the Baptizer first tells his disciples that, far from being offended by Jesus' success, he rejoices in it, even as "the friend of the bridegroom" rejoices in the bridegroom's happiness (Jn 3:29). Jesus similarly leaves Judea and enters Samaria precisely in order to avoid being drawn into a perceived rivalry with his cousin, John the Baptist: "Now when Jesus learned that the Pharisees had heard, 'Jesus is making and baptizing more disciples than John'—although it was not Jesus himself but his disciples who baptized—he left Judea" (4:1). As preachers and baptizers close in age, attitude, and familial relation, John and Jesus are twin-like, but they eschew the satanic temptation to compete with one another, referring and submitting instead to the complementary mission each one has been given by the Father: "No one can receive anything except what has been given from heaven" (3:27).

Similarly to the twin-like relationship between John and Jesus, the relationship between Samaria and Judea, between Samaritans and Jews, poses the problem of mimetic desire within Israel in a conflictive, dyadic (and therefore markedly diabolic) way. As Steven Weitzman has noted, "The Samaritans' genesis as described by Josephus seems to exemplify the Girardian drama of mimetic rivalry—the Samaritans see what the Jews have; model themselves on them; and eventually becomes mimetic rivals."[5] Even as the Jews had their temple in Jerusalem, the Samaritans had had theirs on Mount Gerizim—a temple to which the woman and Jesus allude in John 4:20–21. Reinhard Pummer observes, "The belief that Mt. Gerizim is the place which God has chosen is [even today] the cardinal tenet that separates Samaritans from Jews."[6] Described by Josephus as "similar to that in Jerusalem" (*Antiquities* 11.310), the Samaritans' temple suggests (Weitzman writes) that the people of Samaria "had developed into full-fledged doubles" of the Jews.[7] The historical destruction of that Samaritan temple, which was burned by order of the Jewish high priest, John Hyrcanus, in 128 BCE, eerily portends in John's Gospel the destruction of the temple in Jerusalem in 70 CE by the Romans (a destruction that, Brown and others aver, preceded the writing of the fourth Gospel).

The much earlier rebuilding of the temple in Jerusalem after the Babylonian exile is, moreover, historically and biblically connected with a satanic characterization of Samaria. Neil Forsyth points to the part played by Satan in Zechariah 3:1–5, a text that scholars generally date to the early Persian period (contemporary perhaps with the composition of the book of Job), a time before the Zadokite priesthood and its supporters (a group that later evolved into the Sadducees) had fully established their control over the new temple cult, with its close ties to a new and powerful monarchy. According to Forsyth, the Satan in Zechariah 3:1, who stands before the Lord at the right hand of the high priest Joshua in order to accuse him of defilement, is "a cosmic projection of the groups hostile to the temple hierocracy"—groups that included the Samaritans and the "people of the land" (those who had remained behind in Judah during the Babylonian exile, a remnant associated with prophetic movements).[8] These two groups were regarded by the former Jewish refugees, who had returned from Persia to restore Judah, as rivals and stumbling blocks. Whereas "many Samaritans seem to have regarded the Babylonian exile of Judah as a divine judgment on the heretical direction of its monarchist theology," the priestly group asserted "that Yahweh himself had removed to Babylon with themselves during the exile."[9] The Zadokite party excluded "its rivals from any but the most perfunctory participation" in the temple cult—a move that encouraged the Samaritans eventually to build their own temple on Mount Gerizim and the "people of the land" to take an antitemple stance (represented in Jesus' time by the Essenes).[10]

Accusing each other and justifying themselves, the remnants of the northern and the southern kingdoms of Israel—Samaria and Judah—continued their "long and bitter rivalry" to the time of Jesus, when, we are told, "Jews [did] not share things in common with Samaritans" (Jn 4:9).[11] Jesus' observable Samaritan sympathies identified him in the minds of his Jewish enemies not only with the Samaritans but also with Satan. When Jesus questions whether his enemies are truly children of Abraham, they retort, "Are we not right in saying that you are a Samaritan and have a devil?" (8:48).

Jesus' encounter with the Samaritan woman at Jacob's well takes place at the foot of Mount Gerizim. The "descriptions of Chapter 4 show a good knowledge of the local Palestinian scene," according to Brown, who concurs with "a large group of scholars [who have come] to agree that the principal background for Johannine thought was the Palestinian Judaism of Jesus' own time."[12] Among these scholars is David Rensberger, who writes: "Once regarded as the most Hellenistic of the New Testament Gospels, breathing the same air as Gnosticism and the mystery religions, written for Gentile believers far removed from the issues of Christianity's Jewish origins, John has undergone a remarkable facelift. . . . Rather than being a Gospel for Gentile Christians . . . , John is now understood to have arisen out of a conflict between a group of Jewish Christians and their fellow Jews, and to be addressed primarily to those Jewish Christians."[13]

What was that conflict? The Johannine community, which almost certainly included Samaritan members, was struggling toward the realization of a more capacious, pluralistic understanding of Israel—an Israel composed of Jews and Samaritans united in Christ and welcoming to Gentile believers. For Christian Jews, to accept Samaritans as their brothers and sisters in the Lord was already to go a long way toward the acceptance of non-Jews. Only such a united and open "house of Israel" could be a light to the nations (cf. Is 60:3). Significantly, the successful preaching of Philip, Peter, and John in Samaria in Acts 8 precedes the accounts of the conversion of Paul (Acts 9) and of Peter's baptism of the centurion Cornelius (Acts 10), both of which serve to inaugurate the church's conscious, committed mission to the Gentiles.

Jesus' conversation with the Samaritan woman at Jacob's well powerfully counters the temptation of a destructively mimetic, Jewish-Samaritan rivalry by substituting for it an attractive Mosaic discipleship, one that proves to be also an *imitatio Christi*. Its very wordplay, its artful repartee, is mimetic. Jesus first asks the woman for a drink, in order to encourage her to ask the same of him: "If you knew . . . who it is that is saying to you, 'Give me a drink,' you would have asked him, and he would have given you living water" (Jn 4:10). Jesus asks for the water of a cistern so that she, in turn, might ask for and receive "living water," the water of an overflowing "spring" (4:14), which, in the vocabulary of John, signifies the cleansing, inner movement of the Holy Spirit.

The woman, at first resistant, tempts Jesus to play the adversarial part of a Jew against her part as a Samaritan, asking him, "How is it that you, a Jew, ask a drink of me, a woman of Samaria?" (4:9). Later she reminds him of the doctrinal differences between Jews and Samaritans: "Our ancestors worshipped on this mountain, but you say that the place where people must worship is in Jerusalem" (4:20). Acknowledging that he is Jewish ("We worship what we know, for salvation is from the Jews"), Jesus nonetheless refuses to let himself be bound by her too limited definitions of what being Jewish means. He refuses a diabolic definition of "the Jews" as those pitted against Samaritanism and Samaritans. As Jesus observes, she does not know "who it is who is [speaking] to [her]," nor does she know whom she worships (4:10, 22). When the woman attempts to mislead Jesus, telling him she has no husband, Jesus does not accuse her of deception, but seizes upon the element of truth in her lie: "You are right in saying, 'I have no husband,' for you have had five husbands, and the one you have now is not your husband. What you have said is true!" (4:17–18). Having spoken the truth, she is set free to hear Jesus speak the truth about truth: "God is spirit, and those who worship him must worship in spirit and truth" (4:24).

Although the woman in John uses the Jewish term "Messiah," instead of the Samaritan word *Taheb*, Jesus presents himself to her in accord with the Samaritan expectation of the *Taheb* — that is, not an anointed, Davidic king, but a Moses-like teacher and prophet who will (as the woman says) "proclaim all things to us" (4:25).[14] The woman calls Jesus a "prophet" (4:19), an identification that recalls the promise of Moses: "The Lord your God will raise up for you a prophet *like me* from among your own people; you shall heed such a prophet" (Dt 18:15, emphasis added). The woman's awakening faith in Jesus as Messiah is based on his ability to read her soul: "Come and see a man who told me everything I have ever done!" (Jn 4:29). Whereas Jesus works physical miracles in Galilee and Judea, in Samaria his sign is simply his "truth," his "word," on account of which "many . . . believed" (4:41). Indeed, the Samaritans acclaim Jesus as "the Savior of the world" (4:42), an unusual title, which portends the proclamation of the gospel of Jesus even to the Gentiles. Seeing the approach of the Samaritans from the city, Jesus likens that sight to the view of a ripening field. Jesus, who is about to preach to the Samaritans, prophesies for his disciples a rich harvest of souls, linking his "food" (of obedience to the Father) to the reward his disciples will receive when "sower and reaper may rejoice together" (4:36).

The well at which Jesus meets the Samaritan woman is believed to be the very well at which Jacob met Rachel (Gn 29:1–20), but the scene as a whole also evokes two other biblical encounters of a man with a prospective bride: that of Isaac's servant with Rebekah (Gn 24:10–61) and Moses' with Zipporah (Ex 2:15b–21). The memory of Jacob, who fled from his twin brother Esau, evokes the dangers of fraternal strife even as it recalls the familial relationship between Jews and Samaritans as Jacob's descendants. The memory of Moses at the well takes this marital and covenantal theme one step further. John's Jesus, occupying the metaphoric seat of Moses as he sits, conversing with the woman beside the well, joins the image of Moses as a prophet and teacher to that of the patriarch, a joining with messianic implications for Samaritans and Jews alike.

As scholars have noted (in the words of Brown), "The whole story of Moses and of the Exodus is a very dominant motif" in the Gospel according to John.[15] Moving beyond the citation of Old Testament allusions to a reading of rabbinic commentary on the story of Moses and Zipporah at the well, I argue that Christian Jews, familiar with this interpretive tradition, would have recognized in Jesus' words and actions in John 4 a prophetic *ressourcement,* a prophetic call for the full recognition not only of the Samaritans, but also of believing Gentiles, as fellow Israelites—a forward-looking imperative issued on the traditional basis of Moses' own example. It may be objected, of course, that the *Midrash Rabbah* was compiled long after the writing of John's Gospel. The compilation of rabbinic discussions concerning the first part of Exodus dates from the eighth or ninth century CE. It gives us nonetheless some insight into a long tradition of oral commentary traceable back to the Pharisiac Judaism of Jesus' own time. Brown notes "many parallels between Johannine and rabbinic thought" and observes, "Jesus is called a rabbi more frequently in John than in any other Gospel."[16]

Past scholarship has emphasized the difference between Jesus' tendency toward inclusion and the Jewish tendency toward closedness and exclusion. In evoking the Old Testament scene of Moses and Zipporah in Exodus 2, however, the Jesus of John's Gospel looks as much backward as forward, to highlight the Messianic reality already present within Judaism at its very roots.

> But Moses fled from Pharaoh. He settled in the land of Midian, and sat down by a well. The priest of Midian had seven daughters. They came to draw water and filled the troughs to water their father's flock. But some shepherds came and drove them away. Moses got up and came to their defence and watered their flock. When they returned to their father Reuel, he said, "How is it that you have come back so soon today?" They said, "An Egyptian helped us against the shepherds; he even drew water for us and watered the flock." He said to his daughters, "Where is he? Why did you leave the man? Invite him to break bread." Moses agreed to stay with the man, and he gave Moses his daughter Zipporah in marriage. (Ex 2:15–21).

Rabbinic commentary on this passage shows the meaning it may have had for Jesus, who imitated Moses, and for the readers of John's Gospel, who recognized the well scenes as parallel. The rabbis asked: "Does not God hate idolaters, yet He allowed Moses to find refuge with an idolater?"[17] The *Midrash Rabbah* explains that although Jethro had been a priest of Midian, he rejected idolatrous worship and, resigning his priesthood, he was excommunicated. Jethro's other name "Reu-el" indicates his status as a Gentile worshipper of the true God. An outcast among the Midians, who (the rabbis explain) refused to work for him or to associate with him, he was forced to employ his own daughters as shepherdesses. When the shepherds saw the maidens drawing water at the well, they "*drove away* his daughters as a woman divorced."[18] As the rabbis note, the Hebrew verb "to drive out" is the same verb used in divorcing a wife. Some commentators imagine that it was the intent of the shepherds to ravish them, and that they threw the maidens into the water,[19] from which Moses drew them, even as he had been drawn from the water. At any rate, Moses saved them, in anticipation of his saving role for Israel.[20]

The daughters told their father, "An Egyptian delivered us." The rabbis were intrigued by this apparent misidentification, which points to the problematic identity of Moses as a Hebrew adopted by Pharaoh's daughter, clothed as an Egyptian, and educated in the Egyptian court. The daughters were confused by Moses' appearance, the rabbis suggest. Alternatively, they find truth, not error, in the saying: "An Egyptian delivered us," since it was Moses' murder of an Egyptian that brought Moses providentially into the wilderness to be their deliverer.[21]

Drawing water for the daughters of Jethro/Reuel, Moses accomplishes a miracle, according to the midrash, watering the whole, combined flock (that of the Midianite shepherds and of the daughters) with a single bucketful, "for the water was blessed at his hands."[22] This action allows Reuel to recognize Moses as a descendant of Jacob, "who also stood near a well which was blessed for his sake."[23]

Asking his daughters, "Why is it that ye have left the man?" Reuel goes on to tell them: "Call him that he may eat bread." The rabbinic commentators find the "eating of bread" to be a circumlocution for "taking a wife," finding a parallel text in Genesis 39:6 where Potiphar leaves everything in Joseph's care, except the "food he ate," namely, his wife.[24] Zipporah, whose name means "bird" (*zippor*), flies back to Moses at the well and brings him to her father's house. Married to Moses, Zipporah is, the rabbis suggest, an offering, the equivalent of a bird-sacrifice that cleansed her father's household of every vestige of idolatry: "Because she cleansed the house like a bird," whose blood is offered in atonement.[25]

Like Zipporah, who first leaves the unfed Moses waiting at the well and then, at her father's word, flies back to him to bring him home, the Samaritan woman leaves a still fasting Jesus at the well, relates what has happened to the people in the nearby city, and then returns in haste to Jesus, bringing a throng with her. Like Jethro, who welcomes Jesus, the people "asked [Jesus] to stay with them" (Jn 4:40). The Samaritan woman, once an unclean outcast among her own people, as Zipporah had been among the Midianites, becomes the very means of drawing the Samaritan people to Jesus, whose Moses-like wisdom she proclaims to them.

An imitator of Moses, Jesus meets the Samaritan woman at the well. Jesus' idea of purity allows for the cleansing, the making clean, of sinners, outcasts, Samaritan heretics, and Gentile idolaters, but only at the cost of an outwardly defiling, contagious contact with the unclean. In atonement, some sort of sacrifice must be offered up, albeit in an anti-sacrificial, anti-idolatrous way. The body of Zipporah, offered in marriage, was bread for Moses, incorporating him into the community of the Midianites but also incorporating them into the Hebrew nation. Jesus' body, offered in the form of living bread in John 6:51, substitutes for all the "bodies" of "Zipporahs" and the related sacrifices of animals in order to accomplish their cleansing. The "living water" he offers her in John 4:14 has the power, John suggests, to nourish from a single source the combined "flock" of Samaritans, Jews, and Gentiles.

Jesus' testing at the well substitutes, in John, for Jesus' temptation in the desert, as related in the synoptic Gospels. Aiken has shown that the Lukan narrative offers a rhetorically sophisticated treatment of diabolic *skandalon*. In the Gospel according to John, Jesus himself risks becoming a scandal to his disciples by speaking to a Samaritan woman, someone who is herself a scandal not only to Jews but also to her fellow Samaritans. (Significantly, she comes to the well at noon and alone, rather than earlier in the day, as would be usual, in the company of other women.) Jesus overcomes her sexual and sectarian temptation in a manner that allows her also to overcome the obstacle that he represents to her as a man, a Jew, and a prophet.

Whereas the devil in Luke 4:13 leaves Jesus to await an opportune time for further testing, the human *diabolos* in John 4 is converted. Potentially "devils" to one another, Jesus and the woman become, albeit in different ways, angels of reconciliation, capable of uniting people not in the mimetic lie of a victim's guilt, of scapegoating, but rather in the revealed truth to which Jesus bears witness (cf. Jn 8:4), first to the woman, then to the disciples, and, finally, to the assembled Samaritans.

This transcendent moment, marking a unification by love instead of violence, is, of course, followed in John with the account of Jesus' rejection by the Jewish leaders and by Pilate, both of whom deny this very truth. Concerning the Gospel according to John, René Girard has written, "The Johannine Logos is foreign to any kind of violence; it is therefore forever expelled. . . . The Johannine Logos discloses the truth of violence by having itself expelled. . . . The Logos came into the world, yet the world knew him not, his own people received him not."[26] If, in John 4, the Samaritans do receive Jesus, and the "astonished" disciples allow Jesus to be so received (Jn 4:27), that very reception by outcasts only proves the point that the Jesus of John's Gospel is always already an outsider to a world of sectarian division that defines itself by excluding others. That world is forever a desert to Jesus, a place of exile, albeit a desert or exile in which a well, Jacob's well, the well of "Israel," can be found.

Notes

1. The resulting Christian trauma, evident in the language of the Gospel according to Matthew, tempted some Christians, in turn, to deny their Jewish roots and to embrace a heretical replacement theology that transferred God's original covenant with Israel to the church, the "true Israel." The orthodox Christian stance was more complex, insisting both on God's faithfulness to the Jews and on the church's own unbreakable relationship to Judaism. Throughout the early centuries, there was conflict between Jews and Christians, but also contact and assimilation. See Marcel Simon, *Verus Israel: A Study of the Relations between Christians and Jews in the Roman Empire AD 135–425,* trans. H. McKeating (London: The Littman Library of Jewish Civilization, 1996).

2. I use throughout the New Revised Standard Version of the Bible (Oxford: Oxford University Press, 1977), giving citations parenthetically.

3. Jews and Samaritans alike revere the Torah (the five books of Moses), but Samaritans do not include the prophets and the writings in their sacred scripture. Reinhard Pummer notes that the Israeli government does consider Samaritans to be Jews. See Pummer, *The Samaritans,* Iconography of Religions series, Section 23: Judaism, Fascicle 5 (Leiden: E. J. Brill, 1987), 3.

4. Raymond E. Brown, in *The Gospel According to John (i–xii), The Anchor Bible,* vol. 29, ed. Raymond E. Brown (Garden City, NY: Doubleday, 1966), 173.

5. Steven Weitzman, "Mimic Jews and Jewish Mimics in Antiquity: A Non-Girardian Approach to Mimetic Rivalry," *Journal of the American Academy of Religion* 77, no. 4 (2009): 922–40, at 924. Weitzman's article came to my attention after the present essay had been written. I am glad to be able to cite it.

6. Pummer, *The Samaritans,* 8.

7. Weitzman, "Mimic Jews," 924.

8. Neil Forsyth, *The Old Enemy: Satan and the Combat Myth* (Princeton, NJ: Princeton University Press, 1987), 117.

9. Ibid., 115–16.

10. Ibid., 116.

11. Ibid., 115.

12. Brown, *The Gospel According to John,* 169, lix.

13. David Rensberger, "Anti-Judaism and the Gospel of John," in *Anti-Judaism and the Gospels,* ed. William R. Farmer (Harrisburg: Trinity Press, 1999), 126. For a counterargument, see R. Alan Culpepper, "Anti-Judaism in the Fourth Gospel as a Theological Problem for Christian Interpreters," in *Anti-Judaism and the Fourth Gospel,* ed. Reimund Bieringer, Didier Pollefeyt, and Frederique Vandecasteele-Vanneuville, 61–82 (Louisville, KY: Westminster John Knox Press, 2001).

14. See Brown, *The Gospel According to John,* 172.

15. Ibid., lx. Brown cites, for example, J. J. Enz, "The Book of Exodus as Literary Type for the Gospel of John," *Journal of Biblical Literature* 76 (1957): 208–15; R. H. Smith, "Exodus Typology in the Fourth Gospel," *Journal of Biblical Literature* 81 (1962): 329–42.

16. Brown, *The Gospel According to John,* lx, lxiv.

17. *Midrash Rabbah: Exodus,* vol. 3, trans. S. M. Lehrman (London: Soncino Press, 1983), 40.

18. Ibid.

19. Ibid., 40–41.

20. Ibid., 42.

21. Ibid., 41.

22. Ibid., 41–42.

23. Ibid., 42.

24. Ibid.

25. Ibid., 42.

26. René Girard, *Things Hidden since the Foundations of the World,* trans. Stephen Bann and Michael Metteer (Stanford, CA: Stanford University Press, 1987), 271.

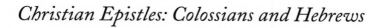

Christian Epistles: Colossians and Hebrews

.

NINETEEN

Aristotle's "Natural Slaves" and Colossae's Unnatural "Scythians"

A Generative Exegesis of Colossians 3:11

CHRISTOPHER S. MORRISSEY

The Epistle to the Colossians has presented two seemingly unrelated puzzles to its modern reader.[1] The first concerns the exact nature of the divisive false teaching (the so-called Colossian heresy) against which Saint Paul issues a warning in 2:4–23. The second concerns a textual matter, the odd reference in Colossians 3:11 to "barbarian and Scythian," a pairing that seems to violate the syntactic pattern of joined opposites in that verse. Focusing attention on the second of these puzzles, I find in its solution an interpretative key with which to unlock the first. As near synonyms, "barbarian" and "Scythian" reveal, I argue, a generative mimetic conflict among Greek Christians, some of whom have adopted Judaic practices. To argue this point, I will first outline the textual problem, then proceed to propose and reject two possible solutions. Finally, I will propose and settle upon a third solution.

The Problem: A Lack of Symmetry in an Apparent Double Chiasmus

Although surrounded by three other antithetical couplets, "Scythian" in Colossians 3:11 is not an obvious antonym in its apparent pairing with "barbarian": *Hellên kai Ioudaios, peritomê kai akrobustia, barbaros, Skuthês, doulos, eleutheros* (Greek and Jew, circumcised and uncircumcised, barbarian, Scythian, slave, free person).[2] In fact, Scythians are proverbially the most barbaric of barbarians. Exegetes have therefore had trouble explaining why this couplet is part of the sequence of the verse.[3]

Two ingenious theories, Troy W. Martin's "Scythian perspective" theory and Douglas A. Campbell's "elusive chiasmus" theory, both attempt to demonstrate why the opposition between "barbarian" and "Scythian" is real, although less than obvious, and hence to preserve a consistent sequence of antitheses in the passage.[4] Martin argues that "Scythian" is an antonym for "barbarian," because, from a Scythian Cynic's perspective (for example, the wise man Anacharsis),[5] everyone else is a barbarian. Campbell, however, observes that "barbarian" and "Scythian" were synonyms to be contrasted with "Greek," even among Cynics. Campbell argues instead that the Scythian antithesis is part of a pattern of double chiasmus in the passage, but he fits Scythians into the double pattern by arguing that Scythians were often thought of as slaves and barbarians as free men.

Neither theory is satisfactory. It is hard to see, on the one hand, *pace* Martin, why the author of Colossians would adopt the obscure perspective of a Cynic (instead of the obvious and customary opposition between Greek and barbarian).[6] It is hard to see, on the other hand, *pace* Campbell, why the elaborate formal construction of a double chiasmus would be deployed using such an elusive connection (between slaves and Scythians, and between free men and barbarians), since the first chiasmus' pattern is so obvious whereas no convincing evidence provides an obvious pattern for the apparent second chiasmus.

Another solution is required, to explain both the presence of "Scythian" in the passage as an apparent antonym and the apparent double chiasmus. I wish to discuss two possible solutions. One is a conjectural emendation of the passage. The other is a hypothesis about the passage's generative context that makes good sense of both the passage's chiastic form and content. While the former solution ought to be rejected, nevertheless a discussion of it will demonstrate how the latter solution is the most plausible. Rather than emend the text, the crux can instead be explained with the generative hypothesis that there were Gentile Christians in Colossae who adopted certain Jewish customs that put them at odds with other Gentile Christians. The epithet

"Scythian" is a clue to this debate, which can be reconstructed on the basis of a parallel with 2 Macabees 4:47. But before arguing for this I first turn to consider a compelling textual emendation.

A Rejected Solution: A Conjectural Emendation to "Greeks versus Barbarians"

One possible solution is a conjectural emendation of the passage to: *Hellên kai Ioudaios, peritomê kai akrobustia,* **Hellên**, *barbaros, Skuthês, doulos, eleutheros* (Greek and Jew, circumcised and uncircumcised, **Greek**, barbarian, Scythian, slave, free person).[7] This emendation adds *Hellên* (Greek) to the beginning of the second chiasmus, an emendation that places *Skuthês* (Scythians) in the center of the second chiasmus, in "the eye of the storm" of the second chiasmus, so to speak.

Observe that, even before the emendation, common "scapegoats" occupy the inner positions of each chiasmus.[8] In the first chiasmus, Jewish and circumcised individuals occupy the inner positions:

> *Hellên kai Ioudaios, peritomê kai akrobustia*
> [Greek and Jew, circumcised and uncircumcised]

In the second chiasmus, Scythian and slave occupy the inner positions:

> *barbaros, Skuthês, doulos, eleutheros*
> [barbarians, Scythian, slave, free person]

That is, the circumcised Jews are the proverbial scapegoats of the uncircumcised Gentiles (the Greeks); slaves are the proverbial scapegoats of free men; and the Scythians are proverbially the most barbaric, the worst barbarians.

With the emendation, observe that the Scythians would occupy a central scapegoat position in the second chiasmus (barbarian/Scythian/slave):

> *Hellên, barbaros, Skuthês, doulos, eleutheros*
> [**Greek**, barbarian, Scythian, slave, free person]

In this central position, no contorted explanation of how "Scythian" is an antonym to "barbarian" is required. With Campbell, we can affirm that the apparent second chiasmus in Colossians 3:11 is real; but with the emendation, we read "Greek/barbarian" as the third couplet that begins it. With Martin, we can affirm that an apparent antonym in the third couplet is real; but with the emendation, we replace his "Scythian Cynic perspective" with the common "Greek perspective" and read "barbarian," not as an antonym to "Scythian," but as the antonym to "Greek." "Scythian" in the center of this second chiasmus' "Greek perspective" serves then to emphasize how the Greek scapegoating of barbarians is overturned by the biblical perspective. In this new perspective that the Colossians author articulates, barbarians are embraced along with Greeks. Barbarians? Yes, and even Scythians.

This emendation can be seen as intrinsically suitable to the text. It would make sense of the formal structure of the passage by relating it to the content and meaning of the verse. On this basis, as well as on the basis of making sense of the corrupt readings in the transmitted text, the emendation could be said to recommend itself by its inevitability.[9] But before I argue the case against this emendation, let me review the strength of the case for it.

It may be argued that the difficulty in Colossians 3:11 with *Skuthês* stems from a primary corruption. To defend the emendation, one would argue that the primitive error in this passage, older than extant witnesses, is the intentional deletion in the second chiasmus of the second *Hellên*. The intentional deletion of the second *Hellên* was made by a scribe who thought it a repetition of *Hellên* from the first chiasmus.[10]

Subsequent corruptions to the text, then, would have been errors of the mind that brought in phrases from Galatians 3:28,[11] and these secondary corruptions are attested in the extant witnesses.[12] But these errors perhaps also testify to an inability of those scribes to cope with the apparent laundry list—*barbaros, Skuthês, doulos, eleutheros* (barbarian, Scythian, slave, free person)—that follows *Hellên kai Ioudaios, peritomê kai akrobustia* (Greek and Jew, circumcised and uncircumcised). Unable to discern a definite pattern (for example, an obvious chiasmus) in the laundry list, the mind of the wayward scribe could have felt free to introduce apposite items from Galatians into the Colossians list.

These secondary corruptions (which editors have rightly corrected on the basis of the extant witnesses) would thus have ultimately stemmed from the primitive error of the scribe who deleted the second *Hellên* of the passage from the second chiasmus. With a second *Hellên* restored by means of the conjectural emendation, however, one could argue that the passage is not only conceptually but also stylistically coherent.

At first glance, however, the primitive scribe would seem to be correct to delete the second *Hellên*. It would appear to be an inadvertent repetition of the first *Hellên*. Moreover, the words that follow it (*barbaros, Skuthês, doulos, eleutheros*) would appear to be a block of four words, a second chiasmus, roughly parallel to the first block of four in the first chiasmus. So then, on this basis, it may be objected: what need is there for a second *Hellên* in the passage?

If one answers, along with the primitive scribe, "No need," then one merely repeats his error, and we are stuck with a passage that has an *apparent* (and obscure) second chiasmus (with free men and barbarians as synonyms) or an *apparent* (and obscure) pairing of Scythian with barbarian (as its antonym). And then we may as well read our own items into the laundry list, whether from Galatians ("male and female") or from contorted exegeses (Martin's "Scythian Cynics" or Campbell's "free barbarians" and "Scythian slaves"). This, however, is the aporia at the crux to which Martin and Campbell, in their ingenuity, have drawn acute attention.

Another Rejected Solution: A Girardian Reading of Colossians 3:11

The way out of the difficulty, however, perhaps lies in reading the Scythian as a scapegoat placed in the center of an emended second chiasmus. Emended or not, the second chiasmus—*Hellên, barbaros, Skuthês, doulos, eleutheros* (**Greek,** barbarian, Scythian, slave, free person)— does not make use of *kai* as the first chiasmus does (*Hellên kai Ioudaios, peritomê kai akrobustia*) ("Greek and Jew, circumcised and uncircumcised"). But this is a formal indication that the pattern of the first chiasmus is being broken in the second one: perhaps deliberately, in order to place Scythians in the center of the second X.

Until now, commentators have not explained the stylistic feature of the *kai*s dropping out in the second chiasmus (other than as the degeneration of a laundry list). But, with the conjectural emendation, the formal structure of the second chiasmus could now have a reason for omitting the *kai*s: it could be an intensification of the first chiastic structure that removes *kai*s from the second chiasmus in order to focus attention on the word in the center of that second chiasmus: *Skuthês* (Scythian).

This variation in the formal structure would highlight the pivotal content of the passage: the Scythian at the center of the second chiasmus. To see Greeks paired in the chiasmus with free men, and to see barbarians paired in the chiasmus with slaves, makes perfect sense.[13] One may recall the chapter on natural slaves in Aristotle's *Politics* (I.2, 1252b7–9) where he quotes a famous line from Euripides on the Greeks as natural masters and the barbarians as natural slaves. As Iphigenia says in the play (*Iphigenia in Aulis* 1400–1401): "It is natural for Greeks to rule barbarians, and not, mother, for barbarians to rule Greeks. They are a slave race, Greeks are free."[14] But how can the meaning of Colossians 3:11 pivot on a Scythian inserted into the center of this Greek perspective, this second chiasmus voicing a Greek commonplace?

I once suggested to a group of scholars that the answer to this question could be that the Scythians are placed in the center because of the concern of the biblical revelation to highlight victims. In this case, the proverbial status of the Scythians in the Greek mind as being, among barbarians, "the worst of the worst," would make them the ultimate scapegoat, and eminently suitable to be highlighted formally "in the center" here. Even Girardian scholars, usually sympathetic to reading Scripture as an unparalleled text in defense of unjustly maligned victims, were not persuaded by this kind of special pleading. For the fact remains that this solution depends on a formal nicety that seems, not only far too subtle, but a hypothesis constructed a priori and not subject to verification by any possible evidence from the historical context that generated the letter. As a conjectural emendation, then, the solution hardly can be said to be inevitable.

Yet even if the proposed conjectural emendation is to be rejected, the unemended Scythian crux in Colossians 3:11 might still be read in a way amenable to the Girardian view. For even if the emendation is bracketed out, notice that, all the same, carrying over from the first chiasmus, "Greek" (*Hellên*) might still nonetheless be *implied* for the second chiasmus. In the writer's intent, it may be meant *to be held over in one's mind,* that is, held over from the first chiasmus—*Hellên kai Ioudaios, peritomê kai akrobustia* (Greek and Jew, circumcised and uncircumcised)—to the second chiasmus *Hellên, barbaros, Skuthês, doulos, eleutheros* (**Greek,** barbarian, Scythian, slave, free person). In other words, *akrobustia* (= *Hellên*) is part of both chiasmi. Whether this link is made on the page or in one's mind, it could be argued that this "conjectural emendation in the mind" (and not on the page) could be the key to seeing the verse's unity of structure and content.

Were one to accept this solution, one might conclude that, with its "Scythian" in the center, Colossians 3:11 mimics, in its formal structure, not simply how the last are to be made first, but also how the mysterious scapegoat is, by biblical revelation, placed in the center of our concern, even when at first glance he does not appear to be. For even if we should not want to emend the text to make him our central concern, the marginalized Scythian, the most barbaric barbarian, the barbarian scapegoat, still strangely confronts us as a problem, a crux. That is, until we discern the consistent and elaborate scapegoating pattern (as Girardian theory is wont to do):[15] a pattern hidden "since the foundation of the world" but there in view all along for those who know how to read it.[16]

But even as a Girardian reading of scripture to be made "in the mind only," and not a conjectural emendation proposed for the page, this still seems to be special pleading, and much too subtle a reading even for those inclined to the worst sort of "Gnostic" abuses of Girardian theory. Nevertheless, the exercise of entertaining these implausible solutions has still clarified the path we ought to take to reach a plausible solution. By entertaining the possibility of an emendation that restores a *Hellên* to be paired with *barbaros* in the second chiasmus, however, a second solution suggests itself. This second solution does not require a conjectural emendation. Nor does it involve special pleading for a "Girardian" reading of the passage.

The Proposed Solution: "Barbarian" Greeks Accusing Unnatural "Scythian" Greeks

The more plausible solution is to read the "*barbaros, Skuthês*" of the second chiasmus as a *substitution* in local discourse for the usual proverbial pair in the Greek mind: *Hellên kai Ioudaios*. This solution would have to be founded on a hypothesis about the historical reality of the generative context that occasioned the composition of the Letter to the Colossians.[17] In short, my hypothesis is that there was a generative context in which one group made an accusation against another, and the other made a reply that paralleled 2 Macabees 4:47.

Here is my reconstruction of the generative context. Both groups were Gentile Christians. The dispute was over the need for Jewish customs to be maintained in the practice of Christianity by Greek converts to Christianity. One faction rejected the Jewish customs of early Christianity, and the other did not.[18] The one faction asked of the other: "Are you Greeks or barbarians?" (*Hellên ê Ioudaios*). The implication was that the Jewish customs were barbaric, that is, slavish and unworthy of free Greeks. The other faction answered sarcastically in reply: "Yeah, we're Scythians!" (*Kai Skuthês!*). What is implied by this sarcastic reply is that it is the accusers who are in fact the barbarians: it is the accusing Greeks who are the real barbarians, whereas the Greeks who are defending themselves against the charge of practicing a "barbaric" Christianity are the Greeks who are, in contrast, the "Scythians" of the dispute.

But why would the defending Greeks invert the accusation this way? Calling the accusing Greeks the real "barbarians" would be a plausible *tu quoque* argument. But why would the defending Greeks not then likewise claim that they are the real "Greeks"? Why would they instead call themselves, not "Greeks," but the "Scythians" of the dispute?

The answer lies in 2 Macabees 4:47, where Greeks are compared unfavorably to Scythians.[19] In that passage, the customary derogatory Greek comparison between Greeks and barbarians, well attested in the ancient world (for example, by Aristotle and Euripides),[20] is inverted by the Jews to denigrate the Greeks. Greeks, say the Jews there, are even worse than Scythians, the worst of all barbarians.[21]

The import of the reply that is founded on 2 Macabees 4:47 can be reconstructed by placing the implied generative context of the accusation in brackets: "Are you Greeks [who are Christians], or barbarians [by virtue of the barbaric Jewish customs that you have adopted, wrongly thinking them to be demanded of Christians]?" The reply to this accusation turns the accusation on its head by calling the non-kosher Greeks "barbarians" and the kosher Greeks "Scythians," as we can see if the reply to the accusers is likewise glossed with the generative context placed in brackets: "Yeah, we're [(in your eyes)] Scythians [because of our Judaic practices, but (in our own eyes, and as 2 Macabees 4:47 illustrates) you are the real barbarians]!"

In other words, the "barbaric" Scythians can proverbially behave better than Greeks, as 2 Macabees 4:47 recounts. So it would be a good slogan for the defending faction to choose to call themselves the "Scythian" Greeks in the dispute: on the face of it, barbaric, but nevertheless in the right, for it is the accusing Greeks who ironically are acting like the real "barbarians."

The Greek commonplace about barbarians that was the backdrop for Aristotle's reflections on natural slavery ("They are a slave race, Greeks are free")[22] is thus inverted from *Hellên, barbaros* into the sarcastic factional slogan of the Colossians' heresy.[23] This slogan is preserved in the first antithesis of the second chiasmus: *"barbaros, Skuthês."* The story in 2 Macabees reminds Greeks that even the scapegoat barbarians, the Scythians, can behave more nobly than Greeks (especially in that story's notable historical circumstances). A Greek, of course, would number Jews among the barbarians, among the slave population.[24] Hence the allusion to 2 Macabees is the rejoinder to the accusing Greek perspective of the defending Greek Christians who have adopted Jewish customs. It is a shorthand way of saying: "Greeks free, and barbarians slaves? But there are even Scythians who are not as barbaric as you Greeks! So, in this sense, if you want to call me a barbarian, then call me a Scythian. For it is you, dear Greek, with your slogan of 'Greek versus Jew,' who is (in this dispute about proper Christian practices) the one who is the real barbarian."

This, therefore, is the sense in which the *Skuthês* after *barbaros* is to be read, on a parallel with 2 Macabees 4:47, in the second chiasmus.

That is, taken as a pair, "*barbaros, Skuthês*" is the rejoinder slogan of the defending Greek faction. It is a slogan precisely because it inverts the "*Hellên ê Ioudaios*" of the accusing Greek faction: in *tu quoque* fashion, the accusing "Greeks" (in the accusers' words) are called "barbarians" (in the defenders' words), and the defending "barbarians" (in the accusers' words) call themselves "Scythians" (implying that they are just as Greek as the accusing Greeks, but that the accusing Greeks are acting like the real "barbarians" of the dispute, on a parallel with 2 Macabees 4:47).

In other words, the defending Greeks are not natural Scythians, for they are born Greeks. But, in the generative context of this dispute, they call themselves unnatural "Scythians" as a witty and sarcastic rejoinder, thereby turning the tables on their accusers with a biblical inversion of the accusation that they are guilty of unnatural, barbarian, Jewish practices. It is precisely this kind of generative context that (short of a textual emendation) can plausibly account for the formal structure of a double chiasmus in Colossians 3:11. Given this context, we see that the first chiasmus records the viewpoint of the accusing Greeks, that is, of accusing Greeks being opposed to the Jewish customs of other, accused Greeks. The second chiasmus, in turn, records the viewpoint of the defending Greeks who have adopted the Jewish customs, that is, of unjustly maligned "Scythian" Greeks who find themselves accused by Greeks who are the real "barbarians" in the dispute, and who are proud to associate themselves with the "slavish" traditions of Judaism in contrast with the practices of "free" Greeks.

The lack of *kai*s in the second chiasmus indicates the uncustomary nature of the dichotomy voiced by the defending Greeks: it is an inversion of the usual *Hellên kai Ioudaios,* and the lack of *kai*s marks the fluidity of the reciprocal inversion and the dissolution of differences in the *tu quoque* exchange of ironic allusion to 2 Macabees 4:47. The intent of the author of the Letter to the Colossians, therefore, is to transcend the terms of the dispute used by both parties: all are to be reconciled in Christ. The sloganeering of the Colossians' (Jewish) heresy, preserved in the first antithesis of the second chiasmus of Colossians 3:11 (*barbaros, Skuthês*), a mimicry of the undifferentiation of quarreling factions, is rejected by the author, along with all the other antitheses that Christ has dissolved.

A Judaizing Faction as the "False Teaching" at Colossae

In the generative context of the first antithesis of the second chiasmus of Colossians 3:11, the defending Greeks were defending themselves against the accusation of unnatural Judaic practices. They were defending themselves against the accusation of barbaric practices, that is, of practices unnatural to, and unfit for, free Greeks. Their response was to craft a slogan in response to their accusers' "Greek/barbarian" hyperbole. That slogan found them (natural Greeks) calling themselves unnatural "Scythians" and calling their accusers (likewise natural Greeks) "barbarians." Since both are natural "masters" of barbarians, because both are natural Greeks, the slogan war that is characterized by a reciprocal exchange of "barbarian" as an insult for unnatural Greek behavior becomes a war over who is the better unnatural barbarian. The followers of the false teaching at Colossae ironically and sarcastically call themselves "Scythians" to trump the charge of their accusers. As defenders, they reassert their natural "mastery" in the dispute by verbally turning the tables on their accusers. Thus the conventional "Greek/barbarian" dichotomy that was the original generative context for Aristotle's reflection on natural slavery is transcended in this dispute of the Colossians. This exhaustion of the rhetoric of the Aristotelian master/slave distinction, originally made in a Greek/barbarian context, historically marks the transition from the classical world era to the common Christian era.[25]

The evidence for this generative context (the quarreling factions at Colossae) is the puzzling but carefully structured double chiasmus in Colossians 3:11. Until now, interpreters have been puzzled by both the asymmetry in the double chiasmus and by the nature of the "false teaching" at Colossae. As a solution, I propose a plausible hypothesis concerning the generative context that can account for both puzzles in the Letter to the Colossians. The dispute was between two Christian factions of the Greeks at Colossae: one a Judaizing Greek faction, the other a Hellenistic Greek faction. Just as Paul had sided against James' Judaizing in the past,[26] so too the author of Colossians aims to resolve the key dispute of nascent Christianity by advocating a universalism that would transcend both the practices of the Judaic faction and the intemperate accusations of the Hellenizing faction.[27] In effect, though, this would, of course, implicitly favor the so-called ongoing "Hellenization" of Christianity, but as Pope Benedict XVI has recently reminded us, this must not be understood as something deleterious but rather as providential.[28]

Notes

1. Portions of this essay were first delivered as part of a paper read at the Colloquium on Violence and Religion 2002, "The Scythian Crux: A Conjectural Emendation for the Scapegoats at Colossians 3:11." For conversations in which we debated various conjectural emendations of Colossians 3:11, I am indebted to Prof. Max Nelson, Department of Classical and Modern Languages, University of Windsor, an expert aficionado of all things Scythian, to whose attention I called the verse and with whom I began proposing to emend the text. Prof. Nelson alerted me to the Campbell/Martin debate and also educated me in the ways of the Scythians. This paper would have been impossible without his friendship.

2. Markus Barth and Helmut Blanke, *The Anchor Bible Colossians: A New Translation with Introduction and Commentary*, trans. Astrid B. Beck (New York: Doubleday, 1994). I have used this English translation throughout.

3. Barth and Blanke, *The Anchor Bible Colossians*, 416n80, quoting Josephus, *Against Apion* 2.269, "The Scythians enjoy killing people, and they hardly differentiate themselves from animals."

4. Troy W. Martin, "The Scythian Perspective in Col. 3:11," *Novum Testamentum* 37, no. 3 (1995): 249–61; Douglas A. Campbell, "Unravelling Colossians 3.11b," *New Testament Studies* 42 (1996): 120–32; Douglas A. Campbell, "The Scythian Perspective in Col. 3:11: A Response to Troy Martin," *Novum Testamentum* 39, no.1 (1997): 81–84; Troy W. Martin, "Scythian Perspective or Elusive Chiasmus: A Reply to Douglas A. Campbell," *Novum Testamentum* 41, no. 3 (1999): 256–64. One may note the amusingly appropriate temporal order of this controversy: Martin, Campbell, Campbell, Martin; that is, it is chiastic.

5. Cf. J. F. Kindstrand, *Anacharsis: The Legend and the Apophthegmata* (Uppsala: Uppsala University, 1981).

6. For this customary opposition in the New Testament, see Rm 1:14; cf. 1 Cor 14:11, Acts 28:2,4. Cf. also Gal 3:28 and its antitheses echoed in 1 Cor 12:13 and Rm 10:12.

7. I am indebted to Prof. Max Nelson of the Department of Classical and Modern Languages, University of Windsor, for this suggested emendation, and for the amicable conversations in which we debated it.

8. In this paper I use the term "scapegoat" in its loosest and most nontechnical sense, that is, in the tertiary, popular "psychosocial meaning" that René Girard discusses in "Generative Scapegoating," in *Violent Origins: Walter Burkert, René Girard, and Jonathan Z. Smith on Ritual Killing and Cultural Formation*, ed. Robert G. Hamerton-Kelly (Stanford, CA: Stanford University Press 1987), 74.

9. I refer to the criteria for conjectural emendation set forth in Bruce M. Metzger, *The Text of the New Testament: Its Transmission, Corruption, and Restoration*, 3rd ed. (New York: Oxford University Press, 1992), 182–85.

10. Cf. ibid., 196–98.

11. Cf. ibid., 192–93.

12. A *kai* between *doulos* and *eleutheros* is found in A D* F G 629 lat syp Hil and *arsen kai thēlu* in D* F G 629 it vgmss Hil Ambr (all variants taken from the apparatus in Nestle-Aland's *Novum Testamentum*).

13. Cf. Edith Hall, *Inventing the Barbarian: Greek Self-Definition Through Tragedy* (Oxford: Clarendon Press, 1989), 101, 110, 164–65, 193–94, 196–97. For the Greeks, the difference between slave and free was not absolute. It was obviously subject to contingencies (cf. Sophocles, *Trachiniae* 296–306).

14. I modify (substituting "Greek" for "Hellenes") the translation of Moses Hadas, *Ten Plays by Euripides* (New York: Bantam, 1981), 348. Hadas' translation is chiastic but the Euripidean Greek is not: *barbarōn d'Hellēnas arkhein eikos, all' ou barbarous, mēter, Hellēnōn. to men gar doulon, hoi d'eleutheroi*. For a judicious assessment of Aristotle's views on slavery and, in their philosophical context, how much integrity they possess, see W. W. Fortenbaugh, *Aristotle on Emotion: A Contribution to Philosophical Psychology, Rhetoric, Poetics, Politics and Ethics* (London: Barnes and Noble, 1975), 45–61, esp. 53–57. For a sympathetic and reliable exegesis of Aristotle's *Politics*, see Harry V. Jaffa, *The Conditions of Freedom: Essays in Political Philosophy* (Baltimore: Johns Hopkins University Press, 1975), 9–72.

15. Cf. René Girard, *Job, the Victim of His People*, trans. Yvonne Freccero (London: Athlone, 1987).

16. In this way, the conjectural emendation of the second chiasmus merely serves to indicate what has been implicit in the unemended second chiasmus of Col 3:11 all along: the biblical pattern of inverted perspectives.

17. Cf. Bruce Chilton, "A Generative Exegesis of Mark 7:1–23," *Journal of Higher Criticism* 3, no. 1 (1996): 18–37. For an excellent articulation of the principles of generative exegesis, see Bruce Chilton, *A Feast of Meanings: Eucharistic Theologies from Jesus through Johannine Circles*, Supplements to *Novum Testamentum* 72 (Leiden: Brill, 1994), 146–58.

18. I subscribe therefore to the opinion of Peter T. O'Brien that the Colossians' heresy "seems to have been Jewish, because of the references to food regulations, the Sabbath, and other prescriptions of the Jewish calendar," and that this "ascetic and mystical" Judaic piety "was one in which asceticism and mysticism were featured, and where angels, principalities, and powers played a prominent role in

creation and the giving of the Law"; quoted from O'Brien's entry on Colossians in Bruce M. Metzger and Michael D. Coogan, *The Oxford Companion to the Bible* (Oxford: Oxford University Press, 1993), 128. For other views of the false teaching at Colossae, cf. Raymond E. Brown, *An Introduction to the New Testament* (New York: Doubleday, 1997), 604–8 on Col 2:8–23.

19. See 2 Mc 4:39–50. "Menelaus, the cause of all the evil, he acquitted of the charges against him, while he sentenced to death those unfortunate men, who would have been freed uncondemned if they had pleaded even before Scythians [*kai epi Skuthôn*]" (47).

20. Cf. Helen H. Bacon, *Barbarians in Greek Tragedy* (New Haven, CT: Yale University Press, 1961), 1–14, and Timothy Long, *Barbarians in Greek Comedy* (Carbondale: Southern Illinois University Press, 1986), 129–57.

21. In this way, the Jews of 2 Mc 4:47 reaffirmed, in a moral context, the opposition of Jew/Greek as more fundamental than the Greek opposition of Greek/barbarian.

22. Euripides, *Iphigenia at Aulis* 1401, in Hadas, *Ten Plays*.

23. Cf. n. 18 above and also Barth and Blanke, *The Anchor Bible Colossians*, 26–27.

24. Cf. Nietzsche, *Beyond Good and Evil*, section 195.

25. Similarly, Eric Gans has observed how the exhaustion of victimary rhetoric (e.g., in the denunciations of Zionism as Nazism) is now one mark of the transition from the postmodern era to the postmillennial; cf. "Our Neo-Victimary Era," available at http://www.anthropoetics.ucla.edu/views/vw257.htm. But cf. David Pryce-Jones, "The New Fellow-Traveling," *National Review*, June 30, 2003, 37–39.

26. Bruce Chilton, "James in Relation to Peter, Paul, and the Remembrance of Jesus," in *The Brother of Jesus: James the Just and His Mission*, ed. Bruce Chilton and Jacob Neusner, 138–60 (Louisville, KY: Westminster John Knox Press, 2001).

27. For the generative anthropological significance of the Christian revelation emerging from the context of the Mosaic revelation, see Eric Gans, *Science and Faith: The Anthropology of Revelation* (Savage, MD: Rowman & Littlefield, 1990), 49–116. Cf. also Eric Gans, "Christian Morality and the Pauline Revelation," *Semeia* 33 (1985): 97–108.

28. Cf. James V. Schall, *The Regensburg Lecture* (South Bend, IN: St. Augustine's Press, 2007).

TWENTY

Is an Anti-sacrificial Reading of Hebrews Plausible?

POONG-IN LEE

René Girard's anti-sacrificial reading of the Bible reveals the anthropo-logical structures of cultic violence in the cultures from which it comes and also unveils the God who desires love and justice rather than sac-rifice and burnt offerings. According to Girard, a critical revelation of the truth of sacrificial violence is present in the Hebrew scriptures and reaches its climax in the Gospels, especially in the Passion narratives, where the murder of Jesus, an innocent victim, results from the collec-tive effort of human beings who unite against him. The Gospel of John presents the figure of the High Priest, Caiaphas, who states the logic of sacrificial violence straight out, when he explains to his fellows (who are anxious about Roman retaliation against the Jews), "You do not un-derstand that it is better for you to have one man die for the people than to have the whole nation destroyed" (Jn 11:50).[1]

Among New Testament texts, the Epistle to the Hebrews has proven most resistant to Girard's anti-sacrificial interpretation. Iden-tified by George Wesley Buchanan as "a homiletical midrash based on Psalm 110,"[2] the Letter to the Hebrews is, according to Fred B. Crad-dock, "not only the most extended treatment of the Old Testament in the New, but is also, alongside Luke, the most respectful of continuity."[3] The "extraordinary achievement at the heart of the letter" is establish-ing that Jesus was a priest, even though not a Levite."[4] At the center of its argument Christ is depicted as the one who is both priest and vic-tim. The author uses as a central focus and frame of reference for the community the categories of priesthood and sacrifice. By using these categories the author explains the significance of Christ.[5] Written for an unknown audience of Jewish (not Samaritan) Christians sometime between 60 and 95 CE, the letter may or may not have preceded the destruction of the Temple in Jerusalem in 70 CE, but it certainly addresses readers who knew and valued the Temple observances as expressions of piety and as a traditional, communal means for atonement for sin.[6] As Craddock insists, "To read Hebrews as an attack on Judaism is to misread Hebrews."[7]

An admirer of prophetic Judaism, Girard has been uncomfortable with the "sacrificial theology" in the Letter to the Hebrews, which he sees as "a form of regression . . . to [some of] the notions of the Old Testament."[8] In an early attempt to read Hebrews anti-sacrificially, Girard was confronted with difficult passages like those in chapters 9 and 10 where an anti-sacrificial reading seemed impossible: "[H]e has appeared once for all at the end of the age to remove sin by the sacrifice of himself" (9:26b) and "[W]e have been sanctified through the offering of the body of Jesus Christ once for all" (10:10). Rather than criticizing human sacrifice, with its "all against one" dynamic (and the related animal sacrifices that substitute for it), such passages appeared to Girard to affirm the value of Christ's bodily sacrifice *qua* sacrifice, albeit "once for all."

Girard sees the blood of Christ as salvific because Christ's Passion reveals the sacrificial violence against scapegoats that stands behind "every ritual on the entire planet."[9] Viewed from Girard's perspective, the Letter to the Hebrews cannot be considered "anti-sacrificial" unless it assists this same revelation. For the epistle's author to criticize the practice of ritualistic, animal sacrifice is not enough for his criticism to be "anti-sacrificial" in the Girardian sense. For it to be such, he must either base that criticism on the ritual's link (substitutive or expiative) to human sacrifice, or he must praise the "sacrifice" of Christ as anti-sacrificial (that is, revelatory of sacrificial violence), or both. Unable to find in the epistle a "mad chorus of victimage" in the death of Jesus (as he did in the Gospels), Girard could not at first read Hebrews anti-sacrificially. Hebrews does not compare Jesus to the passive lamb but primarily to the high priest.

There are, however, innocent victims in the Letter to the Hebrews, and their blood provides us with a key, I argue, for interpreting anti-sacrificially the sacrificial image of the blood of Christ. The epistle is an exhortation addressed to Jewish Christians who have suffered a great deal for their faith, having "endured a hard struggle with sufferings, sometimes being publicly exposed to abuse and persecution and sometimes being partner with those so treated" (Heb 10:32). They have lost property (10:34). Some of them have been imprisoned and tortured (13:3). In the "struggle against sin," however, they "have not resisted to the point of shedding blood" (12:4). This verse, with its reference to the shedding of blood in the "struggle against sin," provides the necessary connection between Christ's nonviolent sacrifice of obedience and his sacrifice of blood.

In this essay, I first examine Girard's own, successive understandings of Hebrews and then test the plausibility of applying Girard's theory to the study of Hebrews by investigating the tension between anti-sacrificial and sacrificial stances in the epistle. This tension is evident in the way the author portrays the death of Jesus as a sacrifice, and how he presents the old cultic system as inadequate—and, in fact, superseded. The author uses a distinctive strategy of comparison and contrast that includes opposed earthly and heavenly perspectives. New anti-sacrificial notions of sacrifice and of covenant result from this creative tension, I argue, when it is understood rhetorically, in the context of the author's exhortation to members of a persecuted group. Taking the audience more fully into account enables us to read Hebrews, in the end, as one of the New Testament books that is actually most supportive of Girard's evolutionary theory.[10]

Girard's Understanding(s) of Hebrews

In *Things Hidden since the Foundation of the World,* Girard concedes that Hebrews is one text in the New Testament that advocates a sacrificial interpretation of Christ's Passion. The author of Hebrews seems to interpret Christ's death "on the basis of sacrifices under the Old Law."[11] The new covenant is likewise inaugurated in Christ's blood. This is achieved not by the blood of "bulls and goats," which cannot "take away sins" (Heb 10:4), but through the blood of Christ, for "without the shedding of blood there is no forgiveness of sins" (9:22).

Because of Christ's perfection, his blood sufficiently accomplishes "once for all" what the sacrifices under the law could not, "for by a single offering he has perfected for all time those who are sanctified" (10:14). Although there is a difference between Christ's death and the old sacrifices, the difference is eventually effaced, Girard believes, because it is "still defined within the context of the sacrificial."[12] Girard laments "the Epistle's failure to see anything but irrational structural analogies among the whole range of sacrifices, including the one attributed to Christ."[13]

Girard examines the author's use of Psalm 40 in Hebrews 10:5–7 in order to show how blind the author is to the operation of "the scapegoat mechanism"[14] in the death of Jesus. He compares the extract from Psalm 40 in its original context within the psalm with the quoted passages of the same Psalm 40 in Hebrews and its function in the context of that letter. In its original setting, the psalm describes the unjust death of the righteous man,[15] according to Girard, but the author of Hebrews puts the passages into Jesus' own mouth to justify a sacrificial reading of Jesus' death: "Sacrifice and offerings you have not desired, but a body you have prepared for me; in burnt offerings and sin offerings you have taken no pleasure. Then I said, 'See, God, I have come to do your will, O God' (in the scroll of the book it is written of me)" (Heb 10:5–7).[16] The author of Hebrews interprets this text "as if it were a sacrificial dialogue between God and Christ, with mankind excluded," but in the psalmist's intention this passage (Ps 40:9–11) is addressed to "all the faithful," who refuse to listen to God's summons.[17] They refuse to obey God because of their deafness and instead conspire together against the Just Man. They treat him as a collective victim, even as he cries out against them: "Let all those be put to shame and confusion who seek to snatch away my life" (Ps 40:14). Girard concludes that the Epistle to the Hebrews silences these protests by excising "a number of the most important actors in a scene whose consequences are fully developed only in the Gospels, though it is sketched in the psalm: the scene of the collective murder of the Just Man."[18]

By the 1990s, Girard had changed his view on Jesus' death as a sacrifice to admit a broader understanding, inclusive of Jesus' self-offering. As is evident in a published interview with James G. Williams, Girard has come to be more positive about the words *sacrifice* and *sacrificial:* "I now accept calling this [Jesus' death] *sacrifice* in a special sense. Because one person did it, God the Father pardons all, in effect. I have avoided the word scapegoat for Jesus, but now I agree with Raymund Schwager that he is scapegoat for all—except now in reverse fashion, for theologically considered the initiative comes from God rather than simply from the human beings with their scapegoat mechanism."[19] In 2002, in answer to a pointed question by Ann Astell about his reading of Hebrews, Girard again attributed the change in his view to conversations with Raymund Schwager, S.J., who pointed out to him that Hebrews is not only "sacrificial" (in the positive meaning of that term) but also "anti-sacrificial" (in terms of Girard's own theoretical idiom). Christ's "sprinkled blood," after all, is said to speak "more graciously than the blood of Abel" (Heb 12:24).[20]

Girard's stated, current agreement with Schwager (whom he regards as his close collaborator) prompts us to examine the latter theologian's treatment of the Letter to the Hebrews. In his book *Jesus in the Drama of Salvation,* Schwager sees the Letter to the Hebrews bringing into conscious confrontation two contrastive traditions in the Old Testament: the "tradition critical of sacrifice" and that finding positive, "metaphorical and symbolic meaning" in it.[21] Its anti-sacrificial stance, continuing that of the Hebrew prophets, emphasizes obedience to God's will as what is essential, not burnt offerings (Heb 10:5–6). Its sacrificial stance "describes Christ as a high priest who offered a sacrifice," using, however, "numerous antitheses" that "totally alter . . . the concepts of both priest and sacrifice."[22] Most obviously, Schwager notes, Christ offers not the blood of others (human and animal victims), but his own blood, as a symbol of his very life, given to God on behalf of others.

Probing the matter more deeply, Schwager asks whether Christ may be understood to have redirected and internalized the violence of his murderers in a self-killing, using "violence against himself" (albeit passively) and thus, through complicity with his killers, making himself guilty and actually deserving of death.[23] Did God, in other words, lead "the crucified one through obedience to self-aggression and thereby judged him"?[24] Schwager rejects this understanding as untenable, given the goodness and justice of Jesus and God.

The question for Schwager is how that goodness can be reconciled with the stated necessity of a bloody, human sacrifice. Hebrews 10:10 makes the sanctification of all dependent not simply on Christ's obedience to God's will ("Lo, I have come to do thy will"), but also on the offering of his body: "And by that will we have been sanctified through the offering of the body of Jesus Christ once for all." Taken in context, the "offering of the body" clearly means the crucifixion of Jesus, not his incarnation.

Schwager argues that sanctification came about through a transformation of violence that only Christ, "God with us," could accomplish. Identifying with his enemies not as killers but as "victims in killing, insofar as they were under the spell of an external power," Jesus freely "underwent together with them the blows of a destructive power," thereby turning "the radical delivering of himself to his enemies, as he experienced this in being executed, into a radical surrender to the Father."[25] The "offering of the body" in Hebrews is understood to be the indispensable means for the surrender of Christ's Spirit—both his human spirit, as the dying Jesus breathed his last, and his "eternal Spirit" (Heb 9:14) as God's Son—to God.[26] This offering enables, in turn, the outpouring of Christ's Spirit upon humankind as the seal for the "new covenant," which had been announced to Israel and Judah in Jeremiah 31:31–34 (a prophecy quoted in Heb 8:8–12). With the gift of the Holy Spirit, human conscience and consciousness can be altered: "I will write my laws in their hearts" (Heb 10:16; Jer 31:33).[27] This spiritual offering—the gift of the "eternal Spirit" given by the Son on the cross to the Father—is the culmination of the whole process of Christ's living and dying. Taken together, this process is "the one event described by the letter to the Hebrews as the sacrifice of Christ," Schwager maintains.[28]

Schwager finds the key to an anti-sacrificial reading of Hebrews in Jesus' merciful understanding of his enemies, his identification as a victim with them as victims of the murderous, impersonal violence that infiltrates interpersonal relationships. Such a reading, I argue, is in keeping with the way the author of Hebrews emphasizes the compassion of Jesus, the Son of God, who is able "to sympathize with our weaknesses" because "in every respect [he has been] tempted as we are, yet without sinning" (Heb 4:15).

Addressing the Hebrews as Members of a Persecuted Group

Following Schwager, it would seem that such a reading — an anti-sacrificial reading of an epistle about Christ's sacrifice — is indeed plausible. Complementing Schwager's theological argument with a rhetorical analysis of the biblical text, I see an ethos of compassionate understanding in the pathetic and logical appeals the author of the letter uses in addressing his audience. The essential message of Hebrews is contained in its sections of exhortation: 10:19–25, 32–39; 12:1–29; 13:1–21. Hebrews is not a theological treatise but a sermon for a specific audience in a specific situation. The author calls his letter to the Hebrews his "word of exhortation" (13:22), which is a technical term for sermon in Acts 13:15. He assures his persecuted audience of Jewish Christian readers, who are attracted to ritual sacrifice as a possible solution for their problem of sin[29] (and probably traumatized by the Roman destruction of the Temple and the loss of divine-human mediation it represented), that the old sacrificial system has became obsolete and invalid. They already enjoy in full through Christ what was only partially available to their ancestors in the faith. Hans-Josef Klauck explains this well: "the paradox of this work is that it uses a thoroughly cultic language to make a deeply uncultic statement."[30] What has not been recognized is that this "uncultic statement" is also an anti-sacrificial statement in the Girardian sense of that word.

What one must remember is that the author of Hebrews is appealing to an audience of scapegoats who are tempted to believe the lie of their persecutors that they have been justly rejected by the community because they are guilty, unclean, indeed cut off from the very means of cleansing from sin. In his opening exhortation, the author counters this lie with the trustworthy word of God's Son, who has "spoken to us" (Heb 1:2), with quoted passages from the scriptures, and with the "valid" message of angels (2:2) — all of which affirm the value of human beings as God's children, beloved by him, and destined for glory. Sharing "flesh and blood" with the "children" of God, the Son has "suffered death," so that he might "free those who all their lives are held in slavery by the fear of death" (2:14, 9, 15). Addressing a persecuted people in fear of dying, the author of the letter emphasizes that Jesus too has suffered and therefore "is able to help those who are being tested" (2:18).

The third and fourth chapters of the epistle continue these themes, urging the people to consider the faithfulness of Jesus, who remained ever obedient to God during his time of testing. This positive example of obedience under trial is juxtaposed with the negative example of the Israelites who failed to hear God's voice, hardening their hearts during the day of testing in the wilderness.[31] Exhorted to faithfulness and obedience, the Hebrews are reminded that Jesus is "able to sympathize with our weaknesses" because "in every respect [he] has been tested as we are, yet without sin" (4:5). If they are suffering persecution, so has the Son of God, who is forever the God of scapegoats, of slaves, of outcasts. Jesus, however, has suffered "without sin" because he has remained faithful to God and obedient to God's word, which is "living and active" (4:12). Recognizing the "devil" to be "the one who has the power of death," Jesus has opposed him "through death," while regarding all people as "his brothers and sisters" (2:14, 17).

Chapters 5 and 6 include exhortations urging the people to advance in their faith and virtue, moving beyond "the basic teaching about Christ" that is the "milk, not solid food" of beginners in the faith (6:1, 5:12). If they do not advance, becoming mature disciples, they are in danger of relapsing. The author frames their choice as that between being victims with Christ or being a part of the mob that kills him. Fallen away from Christ and "on their own, they are crucifying again the Son of God and holding him up to contempt" (6:6). Similarly, Girard has written, "If we don't see that the choice is inevitable between the two supreme models, God and the devil, then we have already chosen the devil and his mimetic violence."[32] For those who are "adversaries," who live by the law of competition, revenge, and the exclusion of others, there is "a fury of fire" awaiting them (10:27). To refuse to be a victim with Christ, witnessing to him and with him to God's truth, is to "have spurned the Son of God" and profaned his blood by shedding it (10:29).

In chapter 10, the author of the letter renders allegiance to Christ concretely by translating it into the "good deeds" (10:24) that he recommends his readers practice: speaking words of encouragement to each other, meeting together for instruction and prayer, rejecting sin, enduring hardships cheerfully, showing compassion to those in prison, sharing the lot of the abused, and exercising patient endurance. These exhortations are followed in chapter 11 with an anaphoric listing of good examples, beginning with Abel, whose faith pleased God. The series concludes with a description of nameless saints, all of whom endured the lot of scapegoats: "Others were tortured. . . . Others suffered mocking and flogging, and even chains and imprisonment. They were stoned to death, they were sawed in two, they were killed by the sword; they went about in the skins of sheep and goats, destitute, persecuted, tormented—of whom the world was not worthy. They wandered in deserts and mountains, and in caves and holes in the ground" (11:35–38).

For the author of the letter to the Hebrews, Jesus Christ, the Son of God, is the eternal model for these saints, the "pioneer" (12:2) whose response to being rejected by others was completely untarnished by bitterness toward them, by competition with them, because he was so entirely surrendered to God.[33] Striking is the way in which the author's Christology develops out of a rhetorical engagement with his audience. Seeing them in their persecuted situation, the author sees Christ anew in them, even as he urges them to grow into a full conformity with Christ through mimesis.[34] Like them, Jesus has "endured . . . hostility against himself from sinners," so that they might "not grow weary or lose heart" (12:3). Because Jesus loved his enemies, they should "pursue peace with everyone" and resist being "defiled" by any "root of bitterness," especially the bitterness resulting from fraternal strife, such as that which divided Esau from his brother Jacob (12:14–16). Because the Son of God has been compassionate, suffering in the flesh, they too have had "compassion for those who were in prison" and been "partners" with the victims of persecution, sharing their lot (10:33–34). Only such "holiness" ensures that people "will see the Lord" in them (12:14).

Although it is obvious that the addressees of the epistle have mortal enemies and are being tempted to regard themselves negatively, as their enemies do, the author never names these enemies, nor does he name the human opponents of Jesus. For the author, as for Girard, the true antagonist is impersonal, is the "hostility" that is diabolic, is "sin" itself: "In your struggle *against sin* you have not yet resisted to the point of shedding your blood" (Heb 12:4, emphasis added).

If blood is shed in this resistance to sin (a passivity that is profoundly active), it is a martyr's offering that is continuous with, and a culmination of, a life of obedience. Therefore, in the final chapter of the letter, the author links Jesus' bloody sacrifice "outside the city gate" (13:12) to the life lived by "the Hebrews" as outcasts who willingly join Jesus "outside the camp and bear the abuse he endured" (13:13). This life of compassion with Jesus and one another realizes itself in the continual offering through Christ of "a sacrifice of praise to God" and the performance of charitable good works, "for such sacrifices are pleasing to God" (13:15–16). Here, sacrifice is a metaphor for moral self-dedication,[35] for the acceptance of responsibility before God and for obedience to him—an obedience that may cost blood.

The passages dealing with Temple sacrifice in the epistle must be interpreted within the context of these exhortations to a persecuted community of Jewish Christians. According to Girard's understanding, the sacrifice of animals has served historically as a substitute for human sacrifice and thus as a ritual means for preventing group violence against an innocent victim, arbitrarily chosen to bear the guilt of communal division. In that limited sense, the Temple sacrifices offered in Jesus' time were indeed "anti-sacrificial," according to Girard—all the more so because they were prescribed for the Israelites by the God of victims, who explicitly prohibited idol-worship and murder (Ex 20:4, 13). The violence of these rituals also dangerously preserved, however, "the vestiges of the sacrificial mentality."[36] By comparing and contrasting the self-offered sacrifice of Jesus to the animal sacrifices offered by the Levitical priests, the author of the Letter to the Hebrews powerfully extends the "anti-sacrificial" logic of the Temple cult, to make it bear critically upon itself.

In order to demonstrate the superiority of Jesus' priesthood and sacrifice,[37] the author includes many features in his depiction of Jesus' priesthood and sacrifice that correspond to those of the old covenant. Jesus' priesthood is comparable with that of other high priests in the following ways: Jesus is compassionate and able to sympathize with human weakness because he has become like his brothers and has been tempted in every respect (2:17–18; 4:15; 5:7–8; 13:12). His appointment comes from God (5:1, 4–6; 7:28), and he intercedes for human beings in the presence of God (7:25; 9:24). Jesus must have something to offer, like the priests of old (5:1; 8:3), and he enters the tent with a bloody sacrifice (9:11–14, 24–26). In both covenantal orders, blood provides some access to God (9:7, 12, 25; 10:19).[38] This depiction of Christ's high priesthood does not differ from that of other high priests. Through these corresponding features the author suggests that the important characteristics of the high priest are fully found in Christ, so that the addressees need neither go back to Judaism nor remain inconsolable over the destruction of the Temple.[39]

The author also points to differences between the old Temple cult and Jesus' "better" priesthood and sacrifice,[40] as shown in table 1.[41]

Taken together, these comparison and contrasts serve to qualify the priesthood of Jesus as belonging to an entirely different, nonviolent order, which the author names the order of Melchizedek.

TABLE I. Chart Comparing Old and New Covenants

	Old Covenant	*New Covenant*
Priesthood	Many mortal priests	One high priest forever
	Appointment by law	Appointment by word of oath
	Offering for their own sins	Sinless, blameless
	Daily earthly ministry	Superior heavenly ministry
Sanctuary	Copies of the heavenly things	The very heavenly things
	Holy places made with hands	Heaven itself
	Figures of the "real"	God's presence
Sacrifice	Many offerings	Once-for-all offering
	Many (annual) entries	One entry
	Limited access	Access to the "real"
	Sacrifice of animals	Sacrifice of himself
	Animal blood	Christ's own blood
Effect	No final purgation	Sins permanently removed
	Limited access to God	Access to God

The Greater Priesthood of Jesus: His High Priesthood according to the Order of Melchizedek

Hebrews is the only Christian writing before Justin Martyr that refers to Melchizedek,[42] a mysterious figure who appears and disappears abruptly in Genesis 14:18–20:

> And King Melchizedek of Salem brought out bread and wine; he was priest of God Most High. He blessed him and said,
>
>> "Blessed be Abram by God Most High,
>> Maker of heaven and earth;
>> And blessed be God Most High,
>> Who has delivered your enemies into your hand!"
>
> And Abram gave him one-tenth of everything.

Claiming that Jesus is a priest "resembling Melchizedek" (Heb 7:15),[43] the author of Hebrews uses that likeness to show the excellence of Jesus' priesthood and its superiority over the Levitical priesthood. The author provides three logical proofs. First, the lack of genealogy. Because the mysterious Melchizedek appears in the biblical narrative "without father, without mother, without genealogy, having neither beginning of days nor end of life," he resembles "the Son of God," Jesus (Heb 7:3). Second, the paying of tithes. Since the patriarch Abraham gave tithes to Melchizedek, the author of Hebrews argues that Abraham's descendants and, in particular, the Levitical priests, should acknowledge Jesus, as a priest "in the order of Melchizedek" (Ps 110:4; Heb 7:17), to be superior. Third, Melchizedek's blessing of Abram. Since "the inferior is blessed by the superior" (Heb 7:7),[44] when Abram is blessed by Melchizedek, Abram himself models an acceptance of Melchizedek's superiority. In conclusion, the author of Hebrews quotes Psalm 110 as a prophetic attestation to Jesus' priesthood "according to the order of Melchizedek" (Heb 7:17)—an ordination sealed by the Lord's own oath forever: "The Lord has sworn and will not change his mind, 'You are a priest forever'" (7:21).[45]

In this section, the connection between priesthood and divine Sonship is a decisive point, for the eternity of the priesthood in the order being described results from the divine Sonship: "He holds his priest-hood permanently, because he continues forever" (7:24). The divine Sonship occupies two key positions in the chapter, one at the beginning, where it is invoked to throw light on the figure of Melchizedek, who resembles "the Son of God" (7:3), and the other at the end to define Christ's priesthood: "The word of the [Lord's] oath . . . appoints a Son who has been made perfect forever" (7:28).[46]

The inauguration of Christ's priesthood results not simply in the amendment of the law but in its definite abrogation: "There is, on the one hand, the abrogation of an earlier commandment because it was weak and ineffectual (for the law made nothing perfect); there is, on the other hand, the introduction of a better hope, through which we approach God" (7:18–19).[47] Harold Attridge explains properly, "the problem was not in the personnel of the Levitical priesthood, but in the whole system or law that was based upon that priesthood."[48] The positive presentation of Jesus' "better," Melchizedekian priesthood, characterized by the peaceful, Eucharistic offering of "bread and wine" (Gn 14:18), is coupled rhetorically with a negative evaluation of the Levitical priesthood: "Now if perfection *were* attainable through the levitical priesthood—for the people received the law under this priesthood—what further need *would there be* to speak of another priest arising according to the order of Melchizedek, rather than one according to the order of Aaron?" (Heb 7:11).[49] The very existence in Jesus of a priest resembling Melchizedek suggests to the author the inadequacy of the old covenant and the "betterness" of the new.[50]

A Better Sacrifice of Jesus: His Sacrifice in the Heavenly Sanctuary

The main argument of Hebrews seems simple at first glance: Jesus as the high priest offered himself, atoning for sin "once for all" (9:26), so that there is no need of the ineffective sacrifices of the Temple cult. But on closer inspection we find a more complicated picture. Countering this horizontal thought pattern, its linear progression, and its earthly perspective is a vertical one that shows the influence of Jewish apocalyptic ideas.[51] Jesus does not simply end sacrifice on earth, but rather he offers his sacrifice eternally in heaven in the presence of God. In this sacrifice, moreover, his followers may participate, offering their own lives in spiritual union with him. As Aelred Cody notes, "The difficulties are compounded by a certain ambivalence in the Epistle's use of the same terminology, now in a horizontal, purely historical perspective measured by time, now in a vertical perspective of eternity touching upon time."[52]

Jesus' heavenly high priesthood is seen from these vertical and horizontal perspectives. The Letter to the Hebrews confronts its readers with references to heavenly things—a sanctuary, a throne, an altar: "We have such a high priest, one who is seated at the right hand of the throne of the Majesty in the heavens, a minister in the sanctuary and the true tent that the Lord, and not any mortal, has set up" (Heb 10:1–2). The author interprets Jesus' death in comparison to the sacrifice offered once a year on the Day of Atonement by the high priest (cf. Lv 16).[53] As a perfect heavenly high priest, Jesus can accomplish what the earthly high priest could not. The imperfect Levitical priesthood, exercised by men who are under the burden of moral imperfection, is not capable of carrying out a mediatory role between God and human beings. Sacrifice offered by the Levitical priests cannot cleanse the consciences of the people from sin (Heb 9:9; 10:1), and therefore it is impossible for the people to approach God by it (7:19). By contrast, Christ perfected the people for all times by a single offering (10:14) as he appeared in the last days as a heavenly high priest. The perfection of the people following Christ depends on the perfection of their leader and priest (5:9).[54] By his description of the heavenly sanctuary and sacrifice, and through his emphasis on the finality of Jesus' sacrifice, the author of Hebrews emphasizes that the earthly cult is inferior, indeed irrelevant, except (along the horizontal axis) as a preparation for Christ's perfect offering of himself ("old covenant" versus "new covenant") and (along the vertical axis) as a "sketch and shadow of the heavenly [sanctuary]" (8:5).

As I have noted, the epistle contains statements describing the Levitical system as faulty (8:7), imperfect (7:11), abrogated (7:18; 8:13), ineffectual in cleansing the conscience (9:9–10; 10:1), and displeasing to God (10:5–6)—statements that imply a discontinuity between the ministry of Jesus and the cult of Temple sacrifice. In these passages the author discloses the problem of the cultic system and also passes judgment on it. How, then, can he apply sacrificial principles to the death of Jesus in passages such as Hebrews 9:13 ("Christ entered once for all into the Holy Place, not with the blood of goats and calves, but with his own blood, thus obtaining eternal redemption"), 9:22 ("Without the shedding of blood there is no forgiveness of sins"), and 9:26 ("He has appeared once for all at the end of the age to remove sin by the sacrifice of himself")?

One answer, although not a sufficient one, would be to argue (in the words of Graham Hughes) that, "in his massive reinterpretation of the Old Testament cultus," the author of Hebrews "has actually replaced the sacrificial ritual with the infinitely more profound concept of the sacrifice of the will."[55] Certainly, as we have seen, the author emphasizes the act of conformity to God's will by quoting Psalm 40:6–8 in Hebrews 10:5–7: "Sacrifices and offerings you have not desired, but a body you have prepared for me; in burnt offerings and sin offerings you have taken no pleasure. Then I said, 'See, God, I have come to do your will, O God.'" The author immediately follows this quotation of the Psalm with an exegetical comment. Focusing on the opposition between external cultic acts and interior obedience,[56] he claims that the cultic system requiring external sacrifices and offerings is annulled, and that a new principle of obedience to God's will is established: "He abolishes the first to establish the second" (Heb 10:9). Attridge explains, "The actual abrogation of the old, ineffective way of atonement and of incomplete access to God is now seen to have occurred in Christ's act of obedience."[57]

To be sure, both Psalm 40 and the Letter to the Hebrews find the essence of worship not in external sacrifices but in obedience to God. Animal sacrifices without an offering of obedience have no value, whereas good deeds enacted through obedience are pleasing to God without any burnt offerings. The emphasis on the conscience is remarkable. The author describes it as the place where Christ's death takes effect, "purifying our conscience from dead works to worship the living God" (Heb 9:14). The new covenant, announced earlier in Jeremiah 31, is an interior covenant, imprinted not on tablets of stone but on the human heart (Heb 8:10–11; 10:16). It is also a covenant by which sins are efficiently forgiven (8:12; 10:17).[58] The letter, however, explicitly refers to "the offering of the body of Jesus Christ" and to "the blood of Christ," through which he obtained "eternal redemption" for all (Heb 10:10, 9:12, 9:14).

Reading Hebrews Anti-sacrificially

Have we reached a conclusion, then, regarding the questions with which we began? Can Hebrews be read anti-sacrificially? The answer becomes clear when the descriptions of Christ's sacrifice I have just enumerated are seen in the context of the rhetorical appeals of the author to a persecuted community whose obedience to God, nonviolent love of others, and resistance to sin are being tested. When the shedding of one's own blood is the indirect consequence of one's faithfulness, that blood becomes the symbolic means and expression of one's victory over the world, union with God, and redemption from sin. Christ offers his life of obedience—and therefore also his death—as the inaugural sacrifice for the new covenant, which unites God's children in love, not in sacrificial violence against victims. By joining in Christ's sacrifice through their own faithful witness as his disciples, the Hebrews to whom the author writes can offer in, with, and through Christ a "once for all" sacrifice, a sacrifice to end killing and the fear of death. Thus understood, Hebrews corresponds to Girard's anti-sacrificial reading of the Bible. It stands as one of the New Testament texts that matches well with his theory.

Notes

1. I use *The NRSV Bible with the Apocrypha* (Oxford: Oxford University Press, 1995) throughout this chapter. For Girard's commentary on this verse, see chapter 10, "That Only One Man Should Die," in René Girard, *The Scapegoat*, trans. Yvonne Freccero (Baltimore: Johns Hopkins University Press, 1989), 112–24.

2. George Wesley Buchanan, ed., *The Anchor Bible: To the Hebrews* (New York: Doubleday, 1972), xix.

3. Fred B. Craddock, *The Letter to the Hebrews: Introduction, Commentary, and Reflections,* in *The Interpreter's Bible* (Nashville: Abingdon Press, 1994), 12:18.

4. Ibid., 12:11.

5. See Andrew Chester, "Hebrews: The Final Sacrifice," in *Sacrifice and Redemption: Durham Essays in Theology,* ed. S. W. Sykes (Cambridge: Cambridge University Press, 1991), 59.

6. Jewish sacrificial ideology was still alive after the destruction of the Jerusalem Temple. See William Horbury, "The Aaronic Priesthood in the Epistle to the Hebrews," *Journal for the Study of the New Testament* 19 (1983): 43–71. For a general introduction of Hebrews' audience, see Marie E. Isaacs, *Sacred Space: An Approach to the Theology of the Epistle to the Hebrews,* Journal for the Study of the New Testament Supplement Series 73 (Sheffield: Sheffield University Press, 1992), 22–44; see also Harold Attridge, *The Epistle to the Hebrews* (Philadelphia: Fortress, 1989), 9–12.

7. Craddock, *Letter to the Hebrews,* 12:11.

8. René Girard, *Things Hidden since the Foundation of the World,* trans. Stephen Bann and Michael Metteer (Stanford, CA: Stanford University Press, 1987), 231, 226.

9. Ibid., 167.

10. Cf. Louis-Marie Chauvet, "Le sacrifice de la messe: Un statut Chrétien du sacrifice," *Lumière et Vie* 146 (1980): 85–106; see also Jean-Paul Michaud, "Le Passage de l'Ancien au Nouveau, selon l'Epître aux Hébreux," *Science et Esprit* 35, no. 1 (1983), 49–51.

11. Girard, *Things Hidden since the Foundation of the World,* 227.

12. Ibid., 228.

13. Ibid., 229.

14. By "the scapegoat mechanism," Girard means "the collective transfer of violence to a random victim." See his explanatory essay, "Generative Scapegoating," in *Violent Origins: Walter Burkert, René Girard, and Jonathan Z. Smith on Ritual Killing and Social Formation,* ed. Robert Hamerton-Kelly, 73–105 (Stanford, CA: Stanford University Press, 1987). In this essay he examines the pattern of scapegoating and collective persecution in the three myths — a myth of the Yahuna Indians, the myth of Oedipus, and a myth from the Ojibway Indians — in each of which there is an initial loss of social order due to an external circumstance (such as an epidemic), the subsequent transference of blame for that disorder and disease onto a victim, followed by violence directed towards that victim, and, finally, the restoration of order.

15. See Psalm 40:13–15: "Be pleased, O Lord, to deliver me; O Lord, make haste to help me. Let all those be put to shame and confusion who seek to snatch away my life; let those be turned back and brought to dishonor who desire my hurt. Let those be appalled because of their shame who say to me, 'Aha, Aha!'" These verses, Girard argues, show an "all against one" situation.

16. The reading "body you have prepared" follows the Septuagint. The Hebrew text is, "You have given me an open ear" or "ears you have dug for me."
17. Girard, *Things Hidden since the Foundation of the World,* 229.
18. Ibid., 230–31.
19. "Interview with René Girard," *Religion* 27 (1997): 253. See also René Girard, "Mimetische Theorie und Theologie," in *Vom Fluch und Segen der Sündenböcke,* ed. J. Niewiadomski and W. Palaver, 15–29 (Thaur: Kulturverlag, 1995), esp. 25, 28 ("Gott selber wendet das Schema des Sündenbocks wieder an, diesmal allerdings auf seine eigenen Kosten, um es umzustürzen. . . . Anstatt zu einem sakralisierten Sündenbock unter vielen zu werden, ist Christus zu *dem* Sündenbock geworden."); René Girard, "Tatsachten, nicht nur Interpretationen," in *Das Opfer– aktuelle Kontroversen,* ed. B. Dieckmann, 261–79 (Münster: LIT Verlag, 2001).
20. The exchange between Girard and Astell took place during a panel discussion at the Meeting of the Colloquium on Violence and Religion, held at Purdue University, June 5–8, 2002.
21. Raymund Schwager, S.J., *Jesus in the Drama of Salvation: Toward a Biblical Doctrine of Redemption,* trans. James G. Williams and Paul Haddon (New York: Crossroad, 1999), 183.
22. Ibid., 182.
23. Ibid., 184.
24. Ibid.
25. Ibid., 187, 189.
26. The phrase "eternal Spirit" in Hebrews 9:14 is unusual, appearing only once in the Christian Bible.
27. Hebrews 13:18 refers to the gift of a "clear conscience." On the importance of conscience in Hebrews, see Craddock, *The Letter to the Hebrews,* 12:108.
28. Schwager, *Jesus in the Drama of Salvation,* 188.
29. There have been many debates on the identity of the audience and their situation. I accept Barnabas Lindars' opinion that they were Jewish Christians who had a problem of consciousness of sins so that they were tempted to return to Judaism to solve their problem; see his *The Theology of the Letter to the Hebrews* (Cambridge: Cambridge University Press, 1991), 4–15.
30. Hans-Josef Klauck, "Sacrifice and Sacrificial Offerings (NT)," in *Anchor Bible Dictionary,* vol. 5, ed. D. N. Freedman (New York: Doubleday, 1992), 890.
31. In this section, the author quotes repeatedly from Psalm 95:7–11.
32. René Girard, *I See Satan Fall Like Lightning,* trans. James G. Williams (Maryknoll, NY: Orbis Books, 2001), 42.
33. Attridge, *The Epistle to the Hebrews,* 281. In several passages of Hebrews, the author implicitly reveals the notion that the addressees should imitate him. In 2:10 Jesus is described as the leader of salvation. In 2:18, 3:5–6, and 14, the fidelity of Jesus the high priest is suggested as a model to be followed. In 10:5–10 and clearly in 12:2, Christ emerges explicitly as the supreme model of faith. He is

surely superior to other models, so that he is called "the pioneer and perfector of the faith" in 12:2. In running their race, the addressees are to look towards a model because he is the specific source of their faith and more importantly he is the first person to have obtained faith's ultimate goal, which the Old Testament ancestors saw only from afar. For the believers who are wavering on a journey to the heavenly place, it is a safe mode of life to have fidelity, trust, and obedience towards the leader of their salvation.

34. In Hebrews, Jesus is depicted as a model of faith whom the believers should follow in their journey to the heavenly Jerusalem. It is interesting to see that the word *mimesis* occurs twice in relation to faith (6:12; 13:7; cf. 12:2).

35. Cf. Robert Hamerton-Kelly, *Sacred Violence: Paul's Hermeneutic of the Cross* (Minneapolis, MN: Augsburg Fortress, 1992), 150–51. For the influence of the "prophetic moralising" tradition, see Frances M. Young, *The Use of Sacrificial Ideas in Greek Christian Writers from the New Testament to John Chrysostom* (Cambridge, MA: Philadelphia Patristic Foundation, 1979), 103–7.

36. Girard, *Things Hidden since the Foundation of the World*, 205.

37. On the theme of a superior priesthood, see J. Schierse, *Verheissung und Heilsvollendung* (Munich: Karl Zink, 1955), 49; Susanne Lehne, *The New Covenant in Hebrews* (Sheffield: Sheffield Academic Press, 1990), 98–99.

38. Lehne, *The New Covenant in Hebrews*, 98.

39. Chester, "Hebrews: The Final Sacrifice," 62–63.

40. For the comparative, see Hebrews 1:4; 6:9; 7:7, 19, 22; 8:6; 9:23; 10:34; 11:16, 35, 40; 12:24.

41. See also Lehne, *The New Covenant in Hebrews*, 98–99.

42. David Hay, *Glory at the Right Hand: Psalm 110 in Early Christianity*, Society of Biblical Literature Monograph Series 18 (Nashville: Abingdon, 1973), 47–51, 140. Justin Martyr was the first person who quoted the entire psalm as a testimony about Jesus. Justin's main concern was to establish Jesus' glory as the Christ.

43. See Dale Leschert, *Hermeneutical Foundations of Hebrews: A Study in the Validity of the Epistle's Interpretation of Some Core Citations from the Psalms* (New York: Edwin Mellen Press, 1994), 199. Leschert summarizes the essence of the argument in syllogistic form: "Christ is a priest of Melchizedek's order / *Priests of Melchizedek's order are superior to priests of Levi's order* / Therefore, Christ is superior to priests of Levi's order."

44. Joseph Fitzmyer, "Now this Melchizedek . . . ," *Catholic Biblical Quarterly* 25 (1963): 314–21.

45. Cf. M. Delcor, "Melchizedek from Genesis to the Qumran Texts and the Epistle to the Hebrews," *Journal for the Study of Judaism in the Persian, Hellenistic, and Roman Period* 2 (1971): 125–26.

46. Albert Vanhoye, *Old Testament Priests and the New Priest According to the New Testament*, trans. J. Bernard Orchard (Petersham, MA: St. Bede's Publications, 1986), 155–58.

47. Attridge, *The Epistle to the Hebrews*, 203. The term occurs in the New Testament only in Hebrews. The uses of the term in the Septuagint do not reflect the technical sense operative in Hebrews 7:18. For examples of the technical legal use, see Mark 7:9 and Galatians 3:15. The noun was used for the deletion of a suspect passage.

48. Attridge, *The Epistle to the Hebrews*, 199. See also Heinrich Zimmermann, *Das Bekenntnis der Hoffnung* (Köln: Peter Hanstein Verlag, 1977), 103–7.

49. Westcott translated Hebrews 7:11 as a past contrary-to-fact condition: "If there had been perfection . . . what need would there have been . . ." (Brook Foss Westcott, *The Epistle to the Hebrews* [London: Macmillan, 1889; 3d ed., 1909], 180). I, however, think that the ordinary syntactical pattern of a present contrafactual condition is suitable: "If there were . . . what need would there be . . ." See Attridge, *The Epistle to the Hebrews*, 199n17.

50. Mary E. Isaacs, "Hebrews," in *Early Christian Thought in Its Jewish Context*, ed. John Barclay and John Sweet (Cambridge: Cambridge University Press, 1996), 153; Robert J. Daly, S.J., *Christian Sacrifice: The Judaeo-Christian Background before Origen*, The Catholic University of America Studies in Christian Antiquity 18 (Washington DC: Catholic University, 1978), 264–67.

51. C. K. Barrett, "The Eschatology of the Epistle to the Hebrews," in *The Background of the New Testament and Its Eschatology*, ed. D. Daube and W. D. Davis, 366–90 (Cambridge: Cambridge University Press, 1956); Ronald Williamson, *Philo and the Epistle to the Hebrews* (Leiden: Brill, 1970); Paul S. Minear, "The Cosmology of the Apocalypse," in *Current Issues in New Testament Interpretation*, ed. W. Klassen and G. F. Snyder, 23–37 (London: SCM Press, 1962). See also Christopher Rowland, "Apocalyptic, Mysticism, and the New Testament," in *Geschichte — Tradition — Reflexion: Festschrift für Martin Hengel zum 70. Geburtstag*, vol. 1, ed. Hubert Cancik, Hermann Lichtenberger, and Peter Schäfer, 405–30 (Tübingen: J. C. B. Mohr [Paul Siebeck], 1996). In his essay Rowland points out the necessity of the study of Hebrews from the perspective of Merkebah mysticism. For scholarship arguing for a Platonist explanation of the thought patterns, see James W. Thompson, "Hebrews 9 and Hellenistic Concepts of Sacrifice," *Journal of Biblical Literature* 98, no. 4 (1979): 567–78; James Moffatt, *A Critical and Exegetical Commentary on the Epistle to the Hebrews* (Edinburgh: T & T Clark, 1924), xxxi–xxxiv; George W. MacRae, "Heavenly Temple and Eschatology in the Letter to the Hebrews," *Semeia* 12 (1978): 190–91; L. D. Hurst, *The Epistle to the Hebrews: Its Background of Thought* (Cambridge: Cambridge University Press, 1990), 21–22.

52. Aelred Cody, O.S.B., *Heavenly Sanctuary and Liturgy in the Epistle to the Hebrews: The Achievement of Salvation in the Epistle's Perspectives* (St. Meinrad, IN: Grail, 1960), 1.

53. In Hebrews, the author does not make use of the characteristic scapegoat ritual. What interests him is the action of the high priest. But *The Epistle of Barnabas* explains that the scarlet wool used in the Red Heifer ritual is a type of

the blood of Christ (8:1–6). See Young, *The Use of Sacrificial Ideas,* 145–47. Young also explains that in Hebrews 9:19 various rituals are conflated: covenant sacrifice, the purificatory rite of the Red Heifer (Nm 19:1–10), and the cleansing of a leper (Lv 14:4–7). Throughout the chapter there are allusions to the annual purification of sin on the Day of Atonement, other sin offerings, and the covenant sacrifice. All these are brought into association. The author deals with each type separately (see Young, *The Use of Sacrificial Ideas,* 151). See also Daly, *Christian Sacrifice,* 272–73.

54. Cody, *Heavenly Sanctuary and Liturgy in the Epistle to the Hebrews,* 99–100.

55. Graham Hughes, *Hebrews and Hermeneutics: The Epistle to the Hebrews as a New Testament Example of Biblical Interpretation* (Cambridge: Cambridge University Press, 1979), 89.

56. On the body/soul dualism, see Jonathan Klawans, *Impurity and Sin in Ancient Judaism* (Oxford: Oxford University Press, 2000), 155. Schierse shows the parallelism of Hebrews 9:13 and 9:23. According to him, the purification of the conscience in 9:13 corresponds to the cleansing of the heavenly things in 9:23, whereas the purification of the flesh in 9:13 corresponds to the cleansing of the copies in 9:23. See Shierse, *Verheissung und Heilsvollendung,* 40.

57. Attridge, *The Epistle to the Hebrews,* 276.

58. Ibid., 226.

TWENTY-ONE

Hermeneutics, Exegesis, and René Girard
A Response to Christopher Morrissey and Poong-In Lee

ANTHONY W. BARTLETT

Girardian biblical criticism is practically a contradiction in terms. Critical method operates on objective criteria, without presuppositions, with external rules of inquiry and evidence. Girardian anthropology arrives at the text formidably armed with a hypothesis that covers every instance of meaning, such that if it is not disclosed by the text it is because in some way the text is masking it. There is no escaping the universal implications of violent origins.

This embarrassment of power—something like a Jedi knight moving in a stone-age world—leaves Girardian scholars prone to twin temptations that are really mirror images. On the one hand, the temptation is to abuse the force, to bend the text to the interpretation, shortcutting the disciplined tasks of criticism. On the other: to be excessively diffident or modest, to use the hypothesis so sparingly and in some way against itself that it loses its essential strength.

The crucial intellectual step vis-à-vis the Bible is to appreciate the hermeneutic quality of Girardian thought. The claim of a biblical hermeneutic is to allow the whole text to speak and in a way that is somehow organic to itself, arising from its authentic revelatory nature. This is expressly what Girard argues when he says that the Bible uniquely among cultural documents discloses the victim at the basis of human order and society. This is not banal reportage; it is intrinsic to the nature of the text as such, to its very life. In addition, the quality of revelation is a matter not of metaphysical doctrine, the nature of God or Christ, and so forth, but of the constitution of culture and indeed its very crisis. The text's power of disclosure, reaching its most intense focus in the person of Jesus, is "capable of undermining and overturning the whole cultural order of humanity and supplying the secret motive force of all subsequent history."[1] Within the Girardian hermeneutic, therefore, biblical criticism must always emerge as an apocalyptic criticism. The vital apocalyptic nature of the New Testament will always inform the exegesis of individual verses or pericope, supplying them with a tonality understood as their original character but with a vastly increased urgency. To be true to the dynamic of Girardian thought—neither overselling nor underselling it—the text is released in its authentic apocalyptic force, both in its first-century meaning and in its twenty-first-century reverberation.

To make Christopher Morrissey and Poong-In Lee fully successful in a Girardian sense, their research needs to be taken at this level. We need to read it and understand it in this frame. Christopher Morrissey gives us two possible accounts of Colossians 3:11, the first of which is slightly more "Girardian" than the second. This is because he emends the text to place the category of "Scythians" in a physically central role of archetypal scapegoat, "the eye of the storm" as he calls it. This is itself a dramatic retrieval/overwriting of the text in tune with the biblical hermeneutic of revealing the victim. But he rightly rejects this hypothesis as lacking historical-critical underpinning. (Where in fact is the literary evidence of any other chiasmus constructed with such an odd hanging crux?) However, his refinement of this hypothesis does contain, I think, the germ of a solution. He suggests that even if the term "Greek" was not present originally in the second string of names (just before "barbarian"), it may be implied in that position. He still sees this as antonym to barbarian, so reproposing the hanging-Scythian solution. Instead I would suggest that "Greek" is echoed in "barbarian" precisely in opposition to Scythian, because everybody, including barbarians, thought themselves "Greek" in comparison to Scythians. And this too would be a genuine product of the Girardian hermeneutic, for indeed every group has its scapegoat.

His second account suggests a complex inversion of significances in respect of the antithesis of barbarian and Scythian. This itself is controlled by a speculative historical reconstruction. Its Girardian nature is reflected in the intensified loss of differences in the second string of ethnic and social groups. Thus the named barbarians are (really) Greeks who have adopted the Pauline view of liberty from the law and claim (according to Morrissey) Greek Aristotelian freedom vis-à-vis slaves (of the law), that is, other Greeks who have adopted Jewish practices. The Scythians are these latter Greeks who have defended themselves against the accusation (from the first set of Greeks) of being in practice barbarian, by returning the accusation to the accusers, calling *them* barbarians via a sarcastic naming of themselves as hyper-barbarians, that is, Scythians, in line with a piece of rhetoric from a nationalist Jewish second-century deuterocanonical text that says Greeks are more barbarian than Scythians. This is a full-blown mimetic crisis and invests the text of Colossians with a fugue of meaning and loss of difference that certainly exceeds any possibility of historical control. It also includes a very modern exhaustion of victimary rhetoric where a group oppositionally takes the role of the most discriminated party. Had New Testament willingness to see things from the perspective of the victim so quickly distilled into Nietzschean *ressentiment* where the underdog counts it kudos to be on the bottom?

As I say, I prefer Morrissey's first simpler hint that "barbarian" may really parallel "Greek." This is reinforced by the historical evidence that the epithet Scythian is used also among non-Greeks (barbarians) as a byword for savagery. Thus the barbarians set themselves up in opposition to Scythians, dismissing the group that is the most barbarian of all. Here the Scythians are the bottom of the barrel, a barrel where in fact everyone has someone lower than themselves, and so the barrel really is bottomless. In the New Testament context the true exhaustion of the rhetoric is not a matter of the infinite regress of conflictive oppositions but is due to the new humanity experienced in Christ, the bringing to crisis of the schemes of this world by an entirely new reciprocity overcoming all victimary difference. "Above all clothe yourselves with love, which binds everything together in perfect harmony" (Col 3:14). It is at this point the text breaks open, as it always will, to the apocalyptic, the new heavens and new earth generated by Christ.

Poong-In Lee sticks closely both to the overall text of Hebrews and to the key Girardian hermeneutic. The question becomes whether Hebrews reinstitutes the grammar of sacrifice in Christian terms or is a genuine break from it by and through those terms. Does it establish a sublimated architecture of the Temple in a way parallel to that of the Rabbis in their writing post–70 CE? In which case the anthropology of the Temple is reconstituted, and certainly in a more brutal way by Christianity because it occurs with a visible metaphysical and heavenly realism. This is what Girard was reacting against, but Poong-In convincingly shows that Hebrews is a layered piece that contains the subversion or deconstruction of its master image or trope. But again the apocalyptic dimensions are underestimated.

Hebrews should be understood as apocalyptic Christian literature in the proximate aftermath of Jesus' death and resurrection but with a question arising from lapse of time and persecution that made imminent parousia less certain. It seems very difficult to see how it could be written post–70 CE; the author, who is so well acquainted with and respectful of Jewish Temple worship, gives no hint of spiritual trauma at the Temple's destruction. And even without this sensitivity the exhortation would surely be led to underline the value of Christ's definitive sacrifice, given the destruction of animal sacrifice to the God of Israel. Instead, the notion of a perfect remaking of the sanctuary by divine intervention is easily understood as part of the immediate first-century Judaic apocalyptic background (see especially 1 Enoch 90:28–29; also 11QTemple 29.8–10). Hebrews itself sees Jesus' sacrifice as an event of "the end of the ages" (Heb 9:26), and the perspective of the work is of the present approach of history to "the city of the living God, the heavenly Jerusalem" (12:22). It is true, as Poong-In shows, there is a Platonic dualism in the scheme of earthly copy and heavenly truth, but this is Greek language internally conditioned by the temporal dynamic, the already-now "once and for all" of Jesus' historical action.

What in fact is simultaneously the authentic apocalyptic element and the radical deconstruction of sacrifice is the quality of Jesus' surrender of will—the "massive reinterpretation of Old Testament cultus" as Poong-In's quotation from Graham Hughes states it. At 9:14, Hebrews says, "Through the eternal spirit [Jesus] offered himself unblemished to God." Here unblemished (*amômon*) carries the surface connotation of the sacrificial victim who has no defect, according to Old Testament legislation. This could be understood in Girardian terms as the absence in the ritual victim of any mimetic counter-violence to the programmed violence of the cult. This would occur if the visual blemish were able to awaken a sense of defiance in the worshipper and thus interrupt the flow of the sacrifice. But in the concrete existential event of the crucifixion, the absence of blemish means the bottomless, abyssal trust and compassion of Jesus, something that introduced the anthropological possibility of absolute forgiveness into the world. This in itself constitutes the endless futural spirit (*pneumatos aiôniou*) and then, in the experience of resurrection, it is confirmed as endless divine Spirit.

This anthropology of the cross breaks open human time and runs through Hebrews as the profound subversion of its apparent Temple ideology. The subversion of the Temple can also be rooted in the historical Jesus of the Gospels and in his concrete attitude toward the Temple, as E. P. Sanders has argued.[2] The overall anthropological hermeneutic derived from Girard enables a much more profound understanding of this New Testament criticism, even as it clarifies the direction of exegesis to be taken. Poong-In has made a significant step forward in this respect. But, as I say, to complete the picture it is necessary to refer consciously to apocalyptic criticism within the Girardian hermeneutic and continue to develop this reference with respect to the material. The project of Jesus has world-historical significance, and this significance has risen to a formal level of expression in mimetic anthropology. There is an essential convergence between the first-century apocalyptic prophet named Jesus, who enacted the destruction of the Temple, and the twenty-first-century crisis of human society and meaning that we are all living through and to which Girard gives such powerful articulation.

Notes

1. René Girard, *Things Hidden since the Foundation of the World*, trans. Stephen Bann and Michael Metteer (Stanford, CA: Stanford University Press, 1987), 209.

2. E. P. Sanders, *Jesus and Judaism* (Philadelphia: Fortress Press, 1985).

CONTRIBUTORS

William Martin Aiken, an alumnus of Yale University, is an independent scholar, currently resident in Racine, Wisconsin. A frequent presenter at the Colloquium on Violence and Religion, he has contributed articles to the on-line *Girardian Lectionary*, started, moderated, and edited by Paul Nuechterlein.

Ann W. Astell (Ph.D., University of Wisconsin–Madison, 1987) was professor of English at Purdue University, where she chaired the program in Medieval and Renaissance Studies. In 2007, she joined the department of theology at the University of Notre Dame. The recipient of a John Simon Guggenheim Memorial Fellowship, she is the author of six books, including *The Song of Songs in the Middle Ages* (1990), *Job, Boethius, and Epic Truth* (1994), and *Eating Beauty: The Eucharist and the Spiritual Arts of the Middle Ages* (2006).

Anthony W. Bartlett (Ph.D., Syracuse University, 1999) was ordained a Catholic priest in 1973. He studied philosophy at Jesuit Pontifical Athanaeum, Heythrop, Oxfordshire, and theology at London University and Lateran College, Rome. The author of *Cross Purposes: The Violent Grammar of Christian Atonement* (2001), he currently writes on contemporary culture, mimetic theory, and biblical anthropology. One of the founders of Wood Hath Hope, a Bible education project and community, he has presented often at the Colloquium on Violence and Religion.

Chris Allen Carter (Ph.D., University of Oklahoma, 1982) wrote his dissertation on the sociolinguistics of Kenneth Burke. An independent scholar, he is the author of *Kenneth Burke and the Scapegoat Process* (Oklahoma Project for Discourse and Theory, vol. 12, 1996).

Bruce Chilton (Ph.D., Cambridge University, 1976) is Bernard Iddings Bell Professor of Philosophy and Religion at Bard College, where he is also Chaplain of the College and executive director of the Institute of Advanced Theology. A former member of the Jesus Seminar, he has been a frequent collaborator with Jacob Neusner. Chilton's many books include *A Galilean Rabbi and His Bible: Jesus' Use of the Interpreted Scripture of His Time* (1984); *God in Strength* (1987); *The Temple of Jesus: His Sacrificial Program within a Cultural History of Sacrifice* (1992); *A Feast of Meanings: Eucharistic Theologies from Jesus through Johannine Circles* (1994); *Judaic Approaches to the Gospels* (1994); *Jesus' Prayer and Jesus' Eucharist* (1997); *Jesus' Baptism and Jesus' Healing* (1998); *Rabbi Jesus: An Intimate Biography* (2002); *Rabbi Paul: An Intellectual Biography* (2005); *Mary Magdalene* (2006); and *Abraham's Curse* (2008).

Robert Daly, S.J. (Dr. Theol., Julius Maximilans Universität, Würzburg, Germany, 1972) is emeritus professor of theology at Boston College. The author of *Christian Sacrifice: The Judeo-Christian Background before Origen* (1978) and many important articles on sacrifice, violence, and the Eucharist, he served as editor of *Theological Studies* from 1991 to 1995. He edited *Eucharist in the West: The History and Theology,* the magisterial study by the late Edward J. Kilmartin, S.J. (d. 1978), which was published posthumously in 1998.

Louis H. Feldman (Ph.D., Harvard University, 1951) is the Abraham Wouk Family Professor of Classics and Literature at Yeshiva University. The recipient of numerous academic honors and awards, including a John Simon Guggenheim Memorial Fellowship, and editor of the prestigious Loeb Library critical edition of Josephus (1965; 1981), he is the acknowledged world authority on Philo and Josephus. The author of 138 articles, he is also the author or editor of fifteen books. Among the more recent titles are *Jew and Gentile in the Ancient World: Attitudes and Interactions from Alexander to Justinian* (1993), *Josephus's Interpretation of the Bible* (1998), *Studies in Josephus's Rewritten Bible* (1998), and *Philo's Portrayal of Moses in the Context of Ancient Judaism* (2009).

Michael Fishbane (Ph.D., Brandeis University, 1971) is the Nathan Cummings Professor of Jewish Studies in the School of Divinity at the University of Chicago, and chair of the Jewish Studies Committee. An influential scholar and teacher, his life and work will be noted in the upcoming new edition of the *Encyclopedia Judaica.* Winner of the National Jewish Book Award (1985; 1994), he received the Lifetime Achievement in Textual Studies Award from the National Foundation of Jewish Culture. He is editor-in-chief of the Jewish Publication Society Bible Commentary (for the Prophets and Writings), and his commentary on the Haftorot appeared in the widely used

Torah commentary *Etz Hayyim*. His hundreds of articles and many books include *Biblical Interpretation in Ancient Israel* (1989); *The Garments of Torah: Essays in Biblical Hermeneutics* (1992); *The Kiss of God: Spiritual and Mystical Death in Judaism* (1994); *The Midrashic Imagination: Jewish Exegesis, Thought, and History* (1995); *The Exegetical Imagination: On Jewish Thought and Theology* (1998); *Text and Texture* (1998); and *Biblical Myth and Rabbinic Mythmaking* (2003).

René Girard (Ph.D., Indiana University, 1950) is a world-renowned French historian, literary critic, and philosopher of social science. Admitted in 2005 to the *Académie française,* he holds honorary doctorates from universities in Austria, the Netherlands, Belgium, and Italy. He is the retired Andrew B. Hammond Professsor of French Language, Literature, and Civilization at Stanford University. Twice the recipient of a John Simon Guggenheim Memorial Fellowship, he is honorary chair of the international Colloquium on Violence and Religion formed around his work on the "mimetic hypothesis." His hundreds of articles and many books include *Mensonge romantique et vérité romanesque* (1961; *Deceit, Desire, and the Novel,* 1966); *"To Double Business Bound": Essays on Literature, Mimesis, and Anthropology* (1978); *La violence et le sacré* (1972; *Violence and the Sacred,* 1977); *Des choses cachées depuis la fondation du monde* (1978; *Things Hidden since the Foundation of the World,* 1987); *Le bouc émissaire* (1982; *The Scapegoat,* 1986); *La route antique des hommes pervers* (1985; *Job, the Victim of His People,* 1987); and *Je vois Satan tomber comme l'éclair* (2000; *I See Satan Fall Like Lightning,* 2001).

Sandor Goodhart (Ph.D., State University of New York–Buffalo, 1977) is associate professor of English and Jewish studies at Purdue University, where he also directed the Jewish Studies Program. The author of *Sacrificing Commentary: Reading the End of Literature* (1996) and *Reading Stephen Sondheim* (2000), he is a former president of the Colloquium on Violence and Religion. He teaches, writes, and lectures widely on French theory, dramatic literature, and Jewish studies (especially Bible as literature and Emmanuel Levinas).

Erich S. Gruen (Ph.D., Harvard University, 1964) is the Gladys Rehard Wood Professor of History and Classics at the University of California–Berkeley. A notable American classicist, his first five books focused on the later Roman Republic, culminating in *The Last Generation of the Roman Republic* (1974). Turning to the Hellenistic-Roman period, he has authored many monographs, most recently *Heritage and Hellenism: The Reinvention of Jewish Tradition* (1998) and *Diaspora: Jews amidst Greeks and Romans* (2002).

Christopher S. Morrissey (Ph.D., Simon Fraser University, 2006) is currently a lecturer in classics in the department of humanities at Simon Fraser University. A specialist in Aristotelian-Thomistic philosophy, he is the author of articles in the online journal *Anthropoetics,* numerous reviews of books and films, and the editor of the *Bibliography of Generative Anthropology.*

William Morrow (Ph.D., University of Toronto, 1988) is associate professor in the department of religious studies at Queens University, Ontario, Canada. An expert in the Hebrew scriptures, he is the author of *Protest against God: The Eclipse of a Biblical Tradition* (2006).

Matthew Pattillo (M.Div., Princeton Theological Seminary, 2007) is a founding member of Munkhaus, a Christian anarchist collective, and the managing editor of the *Journal for the Suppression of Reality.* His article, "Violence, Anarchy, and Scripture: Jacques Ellul and René Girard," was published in *Contagion* 11 (2004).

Poong-In Lee (Ph.D., Oxford University, 2004) is dean of academic affairs at Westminster Graduate School of Theology in Seoul, Korea, and a Presbyterian pastor. He writes on mimetic theory and Christian studies.

Stuart D. Robertson earned his Ph.D. at the Annenberg Research Institute (formerly Dropsie College of Hebrew and Cognate Languages) after completing two M.A. degrees (one in History, from Sterling College, and one in philosophy of religion, from Trinity Evangelical Divinity School) and a Master of Divinity degree (Princeton Theological Seminary). His dissertation, "The Ancient Israelite Tabernacle and First Priesthood in the Jewish Antiquities of Flavius Josephus," written under the direction of Louis Feldman, is currently being revised for publication by Scholar's Press. A Presbyterian pastor, he teaches biblical Hebrew at Purdue University. He regularly reviews books related to Philo, Josephus, and Second Temple Judaism for *Shofar.*

Gérard Rossé teaches at the Mystici Corporis Institute near Florence, Italy, and in Switzerland. A member of the Abba School (the interdisciplinary study center of the Focolare Movement), he is the author of several books that have been translated into English, including *The Cry of Jesus on the Cross: A Biblical and Theological Study* (1987) and *Spirituality of Communion: A New Approach to the Johannine Writings* (1999), *An Introduction to the Abba School* (2002), and *A Community of Believers: A New Look at Christian Life in the Writings of Saint John* (2009).

Thomas Ryba (Ph.D., Northwestern University, 1988) is the Notre Dame theologian-in-residence at Purdue University, where he has taught since 1990. He is the author of *The Essence of Phenomenology and Its Meaning for the Scientific Study of Religion* (1991) and editor, with George D. Bond and Herman Tull, of *The Comity and Grace of Method: Essays in Honor of Edmund F. Perry* (2004). The author of numerous articles and an internationally known speaker, he recently served as the North American editor of the highly respected journal *Religion.*

Alan F. Segal (1945–February 13, 2011) (Ph.D., Yale University, 1975) was Ingeborg Rennert Professor of Jewish Studies at Barnard College, Columbia University. The recipient of many academic honors and grants, including a John Simon Guggenheim Memorial Fellowship, he authored numerous articles and books, including *Paul the Convert: The Apostasy and Apostolate of Saul of Tarsus* (1992), *Rebecca's Children: Judaism and Christianity in the Roman World* (1986), and *The Other Judaisms of Late Antiquity* (Brown Judaic Studies, no. 127, 1987). His posthumously published contribution to this volume reflects themes in his last book, *Life after Death: A History of the Afterlife in Western Religions* (2004).

Stephen Stern (Ph.D., University of Oregon, 2002) is assistant professor of Judaic studies and chair of the Judaic studies committee in the department of religion at Gettysburg College. He teaches and writes on Hebrew Bible, Talmudic commentary, modern Jewish thought, and Holocaust studies.

INDEX OF SCRIPTURAL CITATIONS

GENERAL INDEX